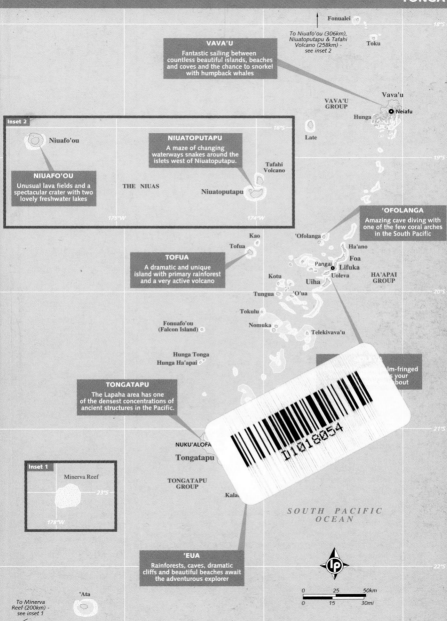

TONGA

Fonualei

To Niuafo'ou (306km),
Niuatoputapu & Tafahi
Volcano (258km) -
see inset 2

Toku

VAVA'U
Fantastic sailing between
countless beautiful islands, beaches
and coves and the chance to snorkel
with humpback whales

VAVA'U
GROUP

Vava'u

Neiafu

Hunga

Late

Inset 2

Niuafo'ou

NIUATOPUTAPU
A maze of changing
waterways snakes around the
islets west of Niuatoputapu.

Tafahi
Volcano

NIUAFO'OU
Unusual lava fields and a
spectacular crater with two
lovely freshwater lakes

THE NIUAS

Niuatoputapu

'OFOLANGA
Amazing cave diving with
one of the few coral arches
in the South Pacific

Kao

'Ofolanga

Ha'ano

Tofua

Foa

TOFUA
A dramatic and unique
island with primary rainforest
and a very active volcano

Pangai

Lifuka

Uoleva

Kotu

Uiha

HA'APAI
GROUP

Tungua

'O'ua

Tokulu

Fonuafo'ou
(Falcon Island)

Nomuka

Telekivava'u

Hunga Tonga
Hunga Ha'apai

lm-fringed
s your
bout

TONGATAPU
The Lapaha area has one
of the densest concentrations of
ancient structures in the Pacific.

D1018054

NUKU'ALOFA

Tongatapu

Inset 1

Minerva Reef

TONGATAPU
GROUP

Kala

SOUTH PACIFIC
OCEAN

'EUA
Rainforests, caves, dramatic
cliffs and beautiful beaches await
the adventurous explorer

0   25   50km
0   15   30mi

To Minerva
Reef (200km) -
see inset 1

'Ata

Vityaz Deep
(10,882m)

Tonga
4th edition – November 2001
First published – March 1990

Published by
Lonely Planet Publications Pty Ltd ABN 36 005 607 983
90 Maribyrnong St, Footscray, Victoria 3011, Australia

Lonely Planet Offices
Australia Locked Bag 1, Footscray, Victoria 3011
USA 150 Linden St, Oakland, CA 94607
UK 10a Spring Place, London NW5 3BH
France 1 rue du Dahomey, 75011 Paris

Photographs
Many of the images in this guide are available for licensing from
Lonely Planet Images.
email: lpi@lonelyplanet.com.au

Front cover photograph
Star fish (Michael Aw)

Photograph facing map
Clapboard house, Pangai (Matt Fletcher)

ISBN 1 74059061 9

Contents – Text

Contents – Maps

The Authors

Matt Fletcher

Matt's earliest travel experiences were family holidays to small, rain-soaked English beach resorts, usually in the off season. Trips to the wonderful northern coast of Spain in a VW van and a shoestring tour of the railway stations of Europe managed to cement an incurable wanderlust. Travels to eastern and southern Africa in 1996 inspired a career in travel writing and photography and Matt has been broke ever since. He is a contributor to Lonely Planet's *Walking in Spain* and *Walking in Australia*, as well as the *Morocco*, *Kenya* and *East Africa* guides, and has only just recovered from Polynesian paralysis.

Nancy Keller

Born and raised in northern California, Nancy worked in the alternative press for several years, doing every aspect of newspaper work from editorial and reporting to delivering the papers. She returned to university to earn a master's degree in journalism, graduating in 1986. She's been travelling and writing ever since. Nancy is author or co-author of several Lonely Planet books including *Rarotonga & the Cook Islands*, *New Zealand*, *California & Nevada*, *Mexico*, *Guatemala, Belize & Yucatán – La Ruta Maya* and *Central America on a Shoestring*.

FROM THE AUTHOR

Thanks firstly to Clare Irvin who once again helped tremendously. In Tonga a number of people went above and beyond the call of duty: thanks to Ceri (aka Cliff Barns) and Cleetus (I hope your rash clears up), Tony and Kesi (thanks for churches), Henk and Sandra (you were great), Janine and Jeff (I'll catch something next time), Trevor Gregory (thanks for the food and pertinent info), Masahiko and Hiroyuki (it was a great day out), Alan (keep trekking), Paul (when's the kegger?), the staff at the New Zealand high commission (thanks for the information and the beer) and Sione, Viliami, Falati, Puluno and Melinita at the TVB (thanks for everything). Also thanks to Pippa, Fran, Steve Burling, Robert Bates, Marina Strong, Mahe Tupouniua, the Honourable 'Akau'ola, Meleane, Rosamond, Heinz Betz, the Calkins, Connellys, Hibberds and all the American Peace Corps volunteers who contributed information. Also thanks to Errol Hunt and Leonie Mugavin at LP (for sorting out power adapters and great GTA information respectively). Cheers Zero for an insight into Nuku'alofa's nightlife (and low life), and thanks to Rick and Clara for good times at the Hula Hula and drunkenness in Auckland. Lastly, thanks to my old man, Debbie, Matt and Steve for beer and proofing, and to Bando, who helped in no way whatsoever but gave advice from his sofa.

This Book

The first two editions of *Tonga* were written by Deanna Swaney, with Nancy Keller responsible for the 3rd edition. This 4th edition was updated by Matt Fletcher.

FROM THE PUBLISHER

This book was produced in Lonely Planet's Melbourne office by Shelley Muir (editorial) and Pablo Gastar (mapping and design). Kusnandar and Corinne Waddell assisted with mapping, Carolyn Papworth was responsible for proofreading and Emma Koch compiled the Language chapter. Margie Jung designed the cover, the new illustrations were provided by Clint Curé, Mick Weldon, Martin Harris, Kate Nolan and Ann Jeffree, and the chapter end illustrations were drawn by Pablo. Photographs were supplied by Lonely Planet Images – thanks to Glenn Beanland and Brett Pascoe. Mark Germanchis provided Quark support.

ACKNOWLEDGEMENTS

Thanks to the National Library of Australia for permission to reproduce the following illustrations from the Rex Nan Kivell Collection: 'Cérémonie du Kava chez le Chef Palou, Tonga Tabou' (p. 72), PIC U1778, NK3340; 'Double Pirogue des Iles des Amis' (p. 87), PIC U8147/32, NK3030; 'Mr Mariner in the Costume of the Tonga Islands' (p. 134), PIC U6806, NK2775.

Thanks also to the National Library of New Zealand, Te Puna Matauranga o Aotearoa, for permission to use the following illustrations from the Alexander Turnbull Library: 'The Place Where our Boats are Lying to Take in the Casks of Water' (p. 13), PUBL-008-189; 'A View in Annamooka, one of the Friendly Isles' (p. 149), PUBL-008-189.

THANKS

Many thanks to the following travellers who used the last edition and wrote to us with helpful hints, useful advice and interesting anecdotes.

Hayley Anderson, Michael Begg, Ross Brown, Nancy & Andrew Carson, Angela Ceriani Contreas, Kerry Cummings, Ellen Daniell, J Daulton, Dave Duckett, Jennifer Duncan, Wayne Finucane, Margaret Grace, Trevor Gregory, Dr Goran Gustafsson, Shane Heaps, Anna Hodson, William Hood, Mike Houlding, Ken Johnson, Juergen Kretschmer, Micheala Lawerence, Diana Lea, Jordi Llorens Estape, Hamish MacGibbon, Uli Mathesius, Louise & Mike Nash, Paul Neville, Barbara Patterson, Glenda Pepper, Jim Peters, Lynda Shepherd, Michelle Skarpisek, Clive Smith, Dr Graham Smith, Siegfried Stapf, Andrea Louise Walker, Hine Ward-Holmes, Christina Willesen, Catherine Wood

Foreword

ABOUT LONELY PLANET GUIDEBOOKS

The story begins with a classic travel adventure: Tony and Maureen Wheeler's 1972 journey across Europe and Asia to Australia. Useful information about the overland trail did not exist at that time, so Tony and Maureen published the first Lonely Planet guidebook to meet a growing need.

From a kitchen table, then from a tiny office in Melbourne (Australia), Lonely Planet has become the largest independent travel publisher in the world, an international company with offices in Melbourne, Oakland (USA), London (UK) and Paris (France).

Today Lonely Planet guidebooks cover the globe. There is an ever-growing list of books and there's information in a variety of forms and media. Some things haven't changed. The main aim is still to help make it possible for adventurous travellers to get out there – to explore and better understand the world.

At Lonely Planet we believe travellers can make a positive contribution to the countries they visit – if they respect their host communities and spend their money wisely. Since 1986 a percentage of the income from each book has been donated to aid projects and human rights campaigns.

Updates Lonely Planet thoroughly updates each guidebook as often as possible. This usually means there are around two years between editions, although for more unusual or more stable destinations the gap can be longer. Check the imprint page (following the colour map at the beginning of the book) for publication dates.

Between editions up-to-date information is available in two free newsletters – the paper *Planet Talk* and email *Comet* (to subscribe, contact any Lonely Planet office) – and on our Web site at www.lonelyplanet.com. The *Upgrades* section of the Web site covers a number of important and volatile destinations and is regularly updated by Lonely Planet authors. *Scoop* covers news and current affairs relevant to travellers. And, lastly, the *Thorn Tree* bulletin board and *Postcards* section of the site carry unverified, but fascinating, reports from travellers.

Correspondence The process of creating new editions begins with the letters, postcards and emails received from travellers. This correspondence often includes suggestions, criticisms and comments about the current editions. Interesting excerpts are immediately passed on via newsletters and the Web site, and everything goes to our authors to be verified when they're researching on the road. We're keen to get more feedback from organisations or individuals who represent communities visited by travellers.

> Lonely Planet gathers information for everyone who's curious about the planet – and especially for those who explore it first-hand. Through guidebooks, phrasebooks, activity guides, maps, literature, newsletters, image library, TV series and Web site we act as an information exchange for a worldwide community of travellers.

Research Authors aim to gather sufficient practical information to enable travellers to make informed choices and to make the mechanics of a journey run smoothly. They also research historical and cultural background to help enrich the travel experience and allow travellers to understand and respond appropriately to cultural and environmental issues.

Authors don't stay in every hotel because that would mean spending a couple of months in each medium-sized city and, no, they don't eat at every restaurant because that would mean stretching belts beyond capacity. They do visit hotels and restaurants to check standards and prices, but feedback based on readers' direct experiences can be very helpful.

Many of our authors work undercover, others aren't so secretive. None of them accept freebies in exchange for positive write-ups. And none of our guidebooks contain any advertising.

Production Authors submit their raw manuscripts and maps to offices in Australia, USA, UK or France. Editors and cartographers – all experienced travellers themselves – then begin the process of assembling the pieces. When the book finally hits the shops, some things are already out of date, we start getting feedback from readers and the process begins again ...

WARNING & REQUEST

Things change – prices go up, schedules change, good places go bad and bad places go bankrupt – nothing stays the same. So, if you find things better or worse, recently opened or long since closed, please tell us and help make the next edition even more accurate and useful. We genuinely value all the feedback we receive. A well-travelled team reads and acknowledges every letter, postcard and email and ensures that every morsel of information finds its way to the appropriate authors, editors and cartographers for verification.

Everyone who writes to us will find their name listed in the next edition of the appropriate guidebook. They will also receive the latest issue of *Planet Talk*, our quarterly printed newsletter, or *Comet*, our monthly email newsletter. Subscriptions to both newsletters are free. The very best contributions will be rewarded with a free guidebook.

We may edit, reproduce and incorporate your comments in all Lonely Planet products, such as guidebooks, Web sites and digital products, so let us know if you don't want your comments reproduced or your name acknowledged.

Send all correspondence to the Lonely Planet office closest to you:

Australia: Locked Bag 1, Footscray, Victoria 3011
USA: 150 Linden St, Oakland, CA 94607
UK: 10a Spring Place, London NW5 3BH
France: 1 rue du Dahomey, 75011 Paris

Or email us at: talk2us@lonelyplanet.com.au

For news, views and updates see our Web site: www.lonelyplanet.com

HOW TO USE A LONELY PLANET GUIDEBOOK

The best way to use a Lonely Planet guidebook is any way you choose. At Lonely Planet we believe the most memorable travel experiences are often those that are unexpected, and the finest discoveries are those you make yourself. Guidebooks are not intended to be used as if they provide a detailed set of infallible instructions!

Contents All Lonely Planet guidebooks follow roughly the same format. The Facts about the Destination chapters or sections give background information ranging from history to weather. Facts for the Visitor gives practical information on issues like visas and health. Getting There & Away gives a brief starting point for researching travel to and from the destination. Getting Around gives an overview of the transport options when you arrive.

The peculiar demands of each destination determine how subsequent chapters are broken up, but some things remain constant. We always start with background, then proceed to sights, places to stay, places to eat, entertainment, getting there and away, and getting around information – in that order.

Heading Hierarchy Lonely Planet headings are used in a strict hierarchical structure that can be visualised as a set of Russian dolls. Each heading (and its following text) is encompassed by any preceding heading that is higher on the hierarchical ladder.

Entry Points We do not assume guidebooks will be read from beginning to end, but that people will dip into them. The traditional entry points are the list of contents and the index. In addition, however, some books have a complete list of maps and an index map illustrating map coverage.

There may also be a colour map that shows highlights. These highlights are dealt with in greater detail in the Facts for the Visitor chapter, along with planning questions and suggested itineraries. Each chapter covering a geographical region usually begins with a locator map and another list of highlights. Once you find something of interest in a list of highlights, turn to the index.

Maps Maps play a crucial role in Lonely Planet guidebooks and include a huge amount of information. A legend is printed on the back page. We seek to have complete consistency between maps and text, and to have every important place in the text captured on a map. Map key numbers usually start in the top left corner.

Although inclusion in a guidebook usually implies a recommendation we cannot list every good place. Exclusion does not necessarily imply criticism. In fact there are a number of reasons why we might exclude a place – sometimes it is simply inappropriate to encourage an influx of travellers.

Introduction

Spread across 700,000 sq km of ocean, the Kingdom of Tonga comprises 171 islands (fewer than 40 of them inhabited) and has just about everything you could desire in a South Pacific paradise. You'll discover coral atolls, dramatic volcanoes, idyllic palm-fringed beaches, warm turquoise lagoons and incredibly vibrant coral reefs teeming with tropical fish. The Tongans are among the most laid-back people you'll ever meet. They form a homogeneous society united by their native language (70% of Tongans also speak English) and a fascinating traditional culture.

The country consists of four main island groups, each with its own character. Starting in the south, there is Tongatapu, the main island and the centre of government and culture. Nuku'alofa, the capital of Tonga, gets the greatest exposure to foreign influence and it shows, but dotted around the rest of the Tongatapu Group are archaeological and geological wonders that you'll see nowhere else. Bushwalkers will be surprised to find rugged and pristine wilderness on the island of 'Eua, a short ferry ride away.

About 100km north, Ha'apai's low-lying, beach-fringed islands are paradise on a budget – just the places to sit and do nothing, far from the madding crowd. Anyone wanting a little more luxury and plenty of organised activities will love Vava'u, which lies another 100km or so north of Ha'apai. There's so much more to the place than magnificent sailing. The Niuas, which are just about as far off the beaten track as it's possible to get these days, offer a unique travel experience. Lying 400km north of Vava'u, this is the

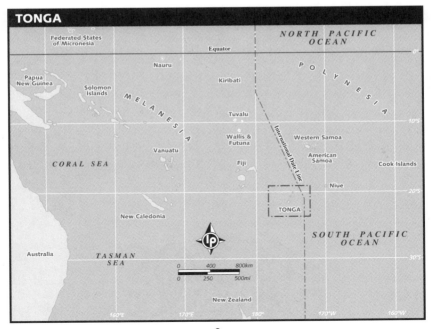

9

kind of place where you could get stranded for weeks – and not care.

Tonga is not a place to which you should bring too many preconceived ideas. It may be beautiful in places, but it's shabby in others. Fascinating in so many respects, it can also be frustrating, and although Tongans are renowned for their friendliness they do not excel in gushing hospitality of the kind travellers sometimes experience in the region. Tonga does not offer a stereotypical South Pacific tourist experience. In fact, the Kingdom of Tonga is best imagined not so much as a tourist destination but as a traditional monarchy with a rich cultural heritage that still shapes much of day-to-day life. With the Christian church forming its cornerstone, this society can seem conservative to many travellers. Indeed, the sight of a woman wearing a bikini on the beach is still considered offensive in many parts of Tonga. But it's largely thanks to the country's traditions and conservatism that Tonga remains a unique and rewarding place to visit, one of the last great travellers' destinations in the South Pacific.

Facts about Tonga

HISTORY
Mythology

One legend tells that the islands of Tonga were fished from the sea by the mighty Polynesian god Tangaloa. His tortoiseshell and whalebone fish-hook snagged on an opening in the island of Nuapapu in the Vava'u Group. The islands emerged as a single landmass, but the fishing line broke and bits of land sank back into the sea, leaving the islands that break the surface today.

In another story the demigod Maui (a temperamental and heroic figure in Polynesian mythology) was fishing using a hook borrowed from an old man named Tonga. Maui yanked up the islands one by one and graciously named the largest after the man who had made the marvellous hook.

Maui fishes up Tonga

Human Settlement

The Tongan people are Polynesians whose ancestors entered the Pacific from the west – the East Indies or the Philippines. Lapita pottery similar to that found in the Bismarck Archipelago and New Caledonia has been found in Tonga and Samoa, supporting the theory that Tonga was among the first Polynesian settlements. Archaeologists and anthropologists estimate the date of the initial colonisation to have occurred around 3000 BC, but the earliest date confirmed by radiocarbon testing is around 1100 BC.

It is believed the Lapita people, who arrived in Tonga between 3300 and 3500 years ago, had their first capital at Toloa, near present-day Fua'amotu International Airport on Tongatapu. The only remaining evidence of the capital is several mounds which are believed to have supported significant buildings. The capital was later shifted to Heketa, near the north-eastern tip of Tongatapu, where King Tu'itatui constructed the famous Ha'amonga 'a Maui Trilithon.

With their rugged coastlines offering no adequate shelter or landing sites for canoes, however, neither Toloa nor Heketa was a suitable location for a capital. Shifting the capital to Mu'a was a pragmatic move by Tu'itatui's son, Talatama, to increase access to the centre of government from the sea, especially for larger double-hulled canoes. The capital also required better protection and Mu'a was indeed a well-fortified settlement.

The theory put forward by the unconventional Norwegian scientist Thor Heyerdahl, that the Polynesians migrated not from Asia but from the Americas, is based primarily on the historical presence of the *kumala* or *kumara* (sweet potato) in the Pacific and South America but not in Asia. Mormons throughout the Pacific tell their own interesting tale in which South American mainlanders colonise the islands, but this theory has little support within the greater part of the scientific community.

Early Royalty

According to Tongan legend, the first *Tu'i Tonga* (the royal title of a Tongan ruler) was the product of a union between the sun god Tangaloa and a beautiful young earthling named 'Ilaheva. The girl was caught shellfishing one day by the amorous god on a small island near Tongatapu. Nine months later she gave birth to 'Aho'eitu, who was to become the first in a long line of Tu'is. Thanks to the wealth of oral history surrounding the period of European contact, the date of this event has been placed at AD 950.

The Tu'i Tonga commanded a great deal of respect from the people of Tonga. Distinctive ceremonies emerged to legitimise and symbolise a Tu'i Tonga's marriage, burial and mourning. Addressed in a manner previously reserved for the gods, he was also exempt from such Tongan rituals as tattooing and circumcision. His responsibilities encompassed both governmental and religious matters and he presided over the festival of *'inasi*, an agricultural fair in which the biggest and best produce was presented to the gods in order to appease their wrath.

Over the following 400 years or so, the Tongans subscribed to the Fijian attitude that war and strife were activities pursued by noble and worthy men and that peace-loving fellows could only be considered cowardly and effeminate.

Accordingly, Tongan warriors in huge canoes called *kalia* wreaked all sorts of mayhem and were able to extend the Tu'i Tonga's empire so that it included territory from parts of Fiji and stretched eastward to Niue and northward as far as the Samoas and Tokelau.

The Tu'i Tonga title was passed from father to son, or to the title-bearer's brother if there was no direct heir. The 24th Tu'i Tonga, however, created a position which would take over the temporal responsibilities of his office. It carried the title *Tu'i Ha'atakalaua* and its first bearer was the Tu'i Tonga's brother.

Some time during the mid-17th century another title – *Tu'i Kanokupolu* – emerged and the power associated with it quickly sur-

Cannibalism

Cannibalism was practised in Tonga until not long after the arrival of the missionaries. A few missionaries ended up in the *'umu* (underground oven) while trying to get their point across but it's well over 100 years since the last Tongan guest of honour became the main course. Cannibalism was associated with absorbing the power of one's adversaries, and was not a remedy for a lack of protein!

passed the other two. At the time of European contact, the newly installed Tu'i Kanokupolu was the most powerful figure in Tonga.

European Contact

The first known contact between Europeans and Tongans was in 1616 when a couple of bumbling Dutchmen (an entrepreneur named Jacob Lemaire and his navigator, Willem Cornelius Schouten) visited the Niuas en route to the East Indies in their ships *Eendracht* and *Hoorn*. Although they never landed, they had a brief encounter with a Tongan sailing canoe, resulting in at least one Tongan killed and several taken captive.

The next visitor happened to be another Dutchman, Abel Janszoon Tasman, who passed through the southernmost Tongan islands in 1643 with his ships *Heemskerck* and *Zeehan*. Tasman traded with the people of 'Ata, 'Eua and Tongatapu (which he named Pylstaart, Middleburgh and Amsterdam), and he took on board water from the freshwater springs on the island of Nomuka (this one he named Rotterdam!) in the Ha'apai Group.

Over a century later came two English explorers. First, in 1767, was Captain Samuel Wallis, then just seven years later Captain James Cook (on his second Pacific expedition). Cook was the most peripatetic of all European explorers of the day; and said of himself '...ambition leads me not only farther than any other man has been before me, but as far as I think it possible for man to go'. He had instructions from King George III to 'observe the genius, temper, disposition and number of the natives or inhabitants, if there be any, and endeavour by all proper means to cultivate a friendship and alliance with them...'.

During the course of his trip he stopped twice, both times briefly, in Tonga. In October 1773 he spent two days visiting 'Eua and five days on Tongatapu. Upon his arrival in the former, Tongans swarmed over his ship. Smiling, friendly and ready to trade (they undoubtedly had heard legends about Tasman's visit), they offered Cook and his men *tapa* (mulberry bark cloth) and women in exchange for iron. Cook's men performed

Tongatapu in 1643 as depicted by Abel Tasman's artist, showing Tasman's boats, at bottom right, taking on water supplies, and a welcoming ceremony on the beach

musical numbers on the bagpipes, Tongan women sang and danced for the visitors, and food and *kava* (a drink made from the root of the pepper shrub) were served (see the boxed text 'Kava Culture' under Drinks in the Facts for the Visitor chapter). Among the Europeans only Cook himself had the nerve to partake of kava.

Eight months later, on his return voyage, Cook spent four days trading and taking on water at Nomuka. On his third Pacific voyage, however, he stayed from April to July 1777 on the islands of Tonga. On Nomuka, his first landfall, chief Finau of Ha'apai told Cook of a wealthier island, Lifuka, where supplies would be available. On Lifuka Cook and his men had such a good time being feted that he bestowed the name 'Friendly Islands' on the Ha'apai Group, without ever knowing that the locals' friendliness was part of a plot to kill him and his men, which went awry. See the Ha'apai Group chapter for more on this fateful event.

Although Cook had been aware of the existence of the Vava'u Group, he'd never visited it and its European 'discovery' was

left to the Spaniard Don Francisco Antonio Mourelle of the ship *Princesa*, en route to Spanish America in 1781. He stopped only briefly, landing first at the island of Fonualei and then Vava'u Island, where he named Puerto de Refugio (Port of Refuge) and claimed the entire group for Spain. See the Vava'u Group chapter for more information.

In 1787, en route from Siberia to Australia, the French explorer Jean de la Pérouse spent a short time in Tonga while recovering from the infamous attack his expedition had suffered on Tutuila, in Samoa. La Pérouse landed in Australia's Botany Bay just few days after the arrival of the First Fleet, but after leaving the colony he was never seen again. (Both his ships were subsequently discovered wrecked off Vanikolo Island, in the Solomons.) Antoine d'Entrecasteaux, in search of La Pérouse, arrived in Tongatapu in 1793. His ship's botanist wrote an account of the visit, but little else came from the French connection in Tonga.

Meanwhile, Mourelle's raving accounts of the Vava'u Group and his claim to the islands created some excitement back in Spain.

In 1793 Captain Alessandro Malaspina was sent all over the Pacific – to Peru, Alaska, the Philippines, New Zealand and Vava'u – to make observations and surveys and to investigate the feasibility of occupying Vava'u. He placed a decree of Spanish ownership in a bottle and buried it somewhere on the main island. It was never found but that wasn't much of an issue – with numerous concerns in the Americas, Spain lost interest in the project.

The first Europeans to settle permanently in Tonga were six deserters from the American ship *Otter*, landing at 'Eua and Ha'apai in 1796. The following year, 10 lay missionaries from the London Missionary Society arrived at Tongatapu on the ship *Duff*. Three were murdered in a local scuffle, six escaped to Australia and one missionary, George Vason, renounced Christianity, married a Tongan woman and remained among the islanders until 1804. During this time, the chief of Ha'apai, Finau 'Ulukalala, forcefully gained control of all the major island groups and the three royal titles began to fall into disuse.

Mutiny on the *Bounty*

In April 1789 Tonga became the setting for a tale which would be told and retold around the world for centuries to come. Off the volcanic island of Tofua in the Ha'apai Group, a mutiny occurred on the England-bound HMS *Bounty* as it was returning from Tahiti. Deteriorating relations on board between captain and crew saw Captain William Bligh and 18 crewmen involuntarily relieved of their duties and set adrift in an open boat with minimal supplies.

They landed at Tofua briefly, hoping to secure provisions, but local unrest forced them to cast off after loading only the most meagre of rations. Quartermaster John Norton was attacked and killed by islanders and the other English sailors only narrowly escaped. They reached Timor in the Dutch East Indies on 14 June, having survived the longest ever ocean voyage in an open boat.

On 29 November 1806 the *Port-au-Prince* privateer landed on Lifuka, in the Ha'apai Group. Locals ransacked the ship and most of the crew were killed, but William Charles Mariner, a boy working on the ship, was spared and taken under the wing of chief Finau. Mariner ended up telling the story of his four-year adventure in *An Account of the Natives of the Tonga Islands*, a masterpiece of Pacific literature. See the Ha'apai Group chapter for more information on Mariner.

Christianity

After the London Missionary Society fled Tonga in 1799, the kingdom was more or less free of salvationists, until 1822 brought a Wesleyan minister, Reverend Walter Lawry, to Tongatapu. Resistance to his ideas sent him back to Australia after only a year. After he left, a Tongan chief became interested in Christianity and when the Wesleyans returned to the islands several years later, they enjoyed much more success. By the time the French Catholic missionaries arrived the Wesleyans had succeeded in converting the nephew of the Tu'i Kanokupolu and the course of Tongan history was suddenly careening in a new direction.

This particular young man, Taufa'ahau, had become the ruler of his native Ha'apai in 1826, having forcefully attained the title of Tu'i Tonga from its heir apparent, Laufilitonga. Upon his baptism in 1831, Taufa'ahau took the Christian name Siaosi, or George, after the king of England, and adopted the surname Tupou. His wife, who had previously been the wife of poor Laufilitonga, was baptised Salote, after Queen Charlotte.

Under George's influence all of Ha'apai converted to Christianity and shortly thereafter, upon the conversion of George's cousin, King 'Ulukalala III of Vava'u, the Vava'u Group followed suit. Upon the death of 'Ulukalala, George assumed his title.

On Tongatapu the Wesleyans were already having considerable success, including the conversion of George's great-uncle, the Tu'i Kanokupolu. Upon the death of that influential man in 1845, George Tupou assumed his title, thus becoming the most powerful man in a united Tonga under the name King George Tupou I.

The House of Tupou

After uniting Tonga and ascending to its throne, King George found that his troubles were only just beginning. On one side he had the Wesleyan missionaries battling the encroachment of the Catholics, who had succeeded in converting several influential chiefs. On the other side he had traditional chiefs and nobles, who were accustomed to wielding the power of life and death over their subjects.

As early as 1838, quite a while before consolidating his power over all Tonga, King George saw a need for uniform laws to govern the islands. His first effort was the Vava'u Code, which forbade worship of the old gods and prevented those in power from forcefully acquiring property or goods belonging to Tongan people. In 1853 the king paid a visit to Australia and, concluding that not all foreigners are as ignorant as Wesleyan missionaries, he decided to seek the help of Australia in drafting a revision of the code.

The rift between the king and the Wesleyans grew until Reverend Shirley Baker appeared on the scene as a member of the Tongan Mission from Britain. George immediately took a liking to Baker and together they began working on government revisions. As a result serfdom was prohibited and it was stipulated that no land in the kingdom could be sold to a foreigner. Lastly, the revised code mandated the distribution of land to male subjects over 16 years of age. Every man was to receive a village lot and an 'api (a plantation of 3.34 hectares) for an annual fee of T$3.20.

Jealous of Baker's preferential treatment, the missionaries launched an unsuccessful effort to have him expelled from the church and Tonga on charges of adultery. Undaunted, Baker continued on his course of statesmanship. Together, he and the king created a national flag, a state seal and a national anthem, and then embarked on the drafting of a constitution. The constitution included a bill of rights, a format for legislative and judicial procedure and a section on land tenure. It also contained laws of succession to the throne. The new constitution was passed on 4 November 1875.

In 1879 the church dissociated Shirley Baker from its mission. The king responded by cancelling Wesleyan leases and appointing Shirley Baker prime minister of Tonga, much to the dismay of nearly everyone. In 1885 Baker created the Free Church of Tonga and the king urged all his subjects to abandon the Wesleyans and join the new church. A small-scale 'holy war' ensued. An attempted assassination of the prime minister resulted in the execution of six Wesleyans and exile for four others. Subsequently most of the remaining Wesleyans in Tonga emigrated to Fiji.

The strife caught the attention of Britain, which saw Tonga's moment of weakness as an opportunity to gain influence in the country. Assuming that the 89-year-old king had gone a bit senile and that Baker had turned the situation to his own advantage, Britain sent an investigatory committee to Tonga to ascertain the political situation. While the committee found the king's mental health to be sound, it forcefully convinced him that religious freedom was necessary in Tonga and eventually had Baker deported.

In 1893, upon King George's death at the age of 96, his great-grandson assumed the throne and took the name George Tupou II. By no means a statesman, he lacked the flair and character of his great-grandfather and predecessor. The British, fearing loss of control under such an administration, coerced him into signing a treaty which placed Tonga under British protection in the field of foreign affairs. King George Tupou II died at the age of 45 in 1918, and his 18-year-old daughter Salote became queen.

Queen Salote's primary concerns for her country were health and education, not squabbling churches and greedy chiefs. With her intelligence, compassion and naturally regal bearing, she made friends for Tonga throughout the world and was loved by her subjects and foreigners alike. Her attendance at Queen Elizabeth II's coronation in 1953 is legendary. Tongan tradition does not allow imitation of those whom one holds in great respect, so while Elizabeth rode in a covered carriage through pouring rain to Westminster Abbey, the Tongan queen refused to allow her own carriage to be covered. When she died in 1965 she was mourned by the world and Tonga seemed like a child that had lost its mother.

King Taufa'ahau Tupou IV

Queen Salote's son, King Taufa'ahau Tupou IV, is the current ruler of Tonga. Although he is known worldwide primarily for his ample girth – and now for having lost a great deal of weight through a diet that created great interest in Tonga (see the boxed text) – his numerous accomplishments include the re-establishment of full sovereignty for Tonga on 4 June 1970 and admission to the Commonwealth of Nations shortly thereafter. In 1976, realising that his nation was being largely ignored by the Western powers, the king established diplomatic relations with the Soviet Union. As a result, New Zealand, the USA and Australia immediately began taking notice of his awakening kingdom in the South Pacific.

King Taufa'ahau's reign has emphasised economic development and modernisation for Tonga, not an easy task for this small island nation. It seems Tonga would like to plunge wholeheartedly into the modern economic world – with new cars, television, videos, international travel and other trappings of capitalism – while at the same time preserving the traditional customs and values which come from a different time and economic situation. It's a very fine tightrope to walk.

The Pro-Democracy Movement

Corruption and increasing foreign influence both led in the early 1990s to a measure of popular dissatisfaction with Tonga's traditional government.

In February 1990 a parliamentary election resulted in an unexpected success for the dissident Tongan Pro-Democracy Movement (TPDM), against established (and often noble) candidates. The TPDM had campaigned for a constitutional monarchy based on the British model rather than one in which government ministers must also be nobles and enjoy lifetime appointments. In elections throughout the '90s the democratic movement remained strong, but in Tonga the nobles have an automatic majority making any constitutional change impossible. The monarchy's strong grip on power verges on the autocratic at times – a number of reporters were jailed in 1996 for making critical comments about a minister. This was not the first time that the government had been heavy-handed – in 1992 it banned public broadcasts of news or information concerning a TPDM conference.

The Reducing Royal

King Taufa'ahau Tupou IV was once the world's heaviest monarch – in the 1976 *Guinness Book of World Records*, he weighed in at 201kg (444lb). He was by no means the only person in Tonga to be on the hefty side – it has been estimated that as many as 60% of all Tongans may be clinically obese. Traditionally, the people of Tonga's royal and noble families are much larger than the commoners.

In recent years the king has been on a diet and fitness program which initially lost him around 75kg. Although well into his 80s, the king still does regular exercise, working out with weights at the gym. He continues to urge his subjects to take care of their health, not only by telling them to do so but by setting a good example himself.

PATRICK HORTON

King Taufa'ahau

The TPDM became the Human Rights and Democracy Movement (HRDM) in 1998.

Recent Developments

In November 1998 Tonga broke diplomatic relations with the Republic of China (Taiwan) and established relations with the People's Republic of China. Taiwanese in Tonga were given 48 hours to leave. After a suitable period the Chinese moved into the now empty Taiwanese embassy, a building the crown prince had only recently had built for Taiwan.

Tonga's reasons for this move are complex but in the end are based on self-interest. The Chinese economy looks set to have a huge influence over the Pacific in coming years. Most noticeably China has been moving against Taiwanese interests in the Pacific and as a friend of Taiwan, Tonga would have found its application to join the United Nations (UN) blocked by China. Chinese aid, trade and influence have increased steadily since 1998 and Tonga provides a number of satellite 'slots' to China (see Economy later in this chapter).

Tonga was granted membership of the UN in September 1999.

Despite the king's stated aim that economic development would be a priority, the economy is currently in very poor shape. Not even the millennium celebrations (see the boxed text) could boost an economy that is bouncing along the bottom. Reform and modernisation are required, as is an end to the habit that some in the Legislative Chamber have of putting private interests above the good of the state.

In January 2000 Prince 'Ulukalala Ata, younger brother of the crown prince, was appointed prime minister, a move welcomed in many quarters. The king is in good health but is well into his 80s, and it's widely believed that in coming years the prime minister and crown prince (who is popularly perceived to be self-interested) will gradually assume more responsibility. The crown prince isn't afraid to rock the boat (the king is a placid character in contrast) and, helped by his younger brother, is likely to usher in considerable change upon becoming king.

Millennium Fever

'The land where time begins'

Tonga had long thought it would be the first country to welcome the new millennium, but in 1995 Kiribati moved the International Date Line within its own borders, giving its easternmost islands an hour's head start on Tonga. King Taufa'ahau Tupou IV reacted quickly and put Tonga's clocks forward an hour (a ploy also made by Fiji, among others), putting the kingdom 14 hours ahead of GMT. It was close, but in the end (though technically Kiribati was the first to see the dawn of the new millennium), Tonga's physical proximity to the date line gave it the credibility that attracted many tourists and considerable media interest; hotels were told to prepare for total capacity.

On New Year's Eve there was a tremendous party on Vuna Rd in Nuku'alofa, with fireworks, traditional Tongan dancing, feasting and a choir of 10,000. At dawn the king sailed off on a magnificent *kalia* (Tongan seagoing canoe) built for the occasion. Unfortunately for the economy, tourist numbers were not as high as was hoped, but few people cared in the excitement of the party.

However, while a change of kings may mean economic and bureaucratic change, it will not mean a change to full democracy. The Tongan people love their king and are traditionally conservative; the vast majority is not in favour of major democratic change.

The pro-democracy HRDM recently appointed Lopeti Senituli, a political heavy hitter with international connections, as its head and began to gather funds from church organisations overseas. The HRDM enjoys the backing of the Wesleyan and Roman Catholic churches, two of Tonga's largest and most powerful religious bodies, and may well be repositioning for influence once there's a change in Tongan politics.

GEOGRAPHY

The Kingdom of Tonga comprises four major island groups. From south to north these are Tongatapu, Ha'apai, Vava'u and the Niuas. Altogether the four groups include 171 islands and a total land area of 688 sq km.

The Tongatapu Group is the largest in both area and population. It includes the main island of Tongatapu as well as 'Eua, 'Ata, 'Eue'iki, Kalau and numerous small islands within the barrier reef north of the main island. Minerva Reef, 350km southwest of Tongatapu, is Tonga's southernmost extremity (although its ownership is currently disputed with New Zealand).

The Ha'apai Group, 150km north of Tongatapu, is a cluster of 36 major islands and numerous submerged reefs. The main inhabited islands include Lifuka, Ha'ano, Foa, 'Uiha, Ha'afeva and Nomuka. Tonga's highest point is the summit of Kao, whose perfect volcanic cone rises sharply to 1046m above sea level. Kao's sister island, Tofua, is an active volcano. The 'up and down' island of Fonuafo'ou, which builds up and erodes completely away with some frequency, occupies the westernmost extremity of the Ha'apai Group.

Another 100km to the north are the 34 major islands of the Vava'u Group, the largest of which is Vava'u Island. The smaller islands are mere peaks rising out of drowned valleys of the same landmass – Hunga, Nuapapu, 'Ovaka, Pangaimotu, 'Utungake, Koloa, Kapa, 'Ofu and Vaka'eitu. Volcanic outliers include Toku, Fonualei, Late and Late'iki.

The three islands of the Niuas Group, nearly 400km north of Vava'u, comprise the farthest reaches of the kingdom. Niuatoputapu is a reef-encircled, eroded volcano, while its near neighbour Tafahi is a perfect cone reaching 656m above sea level. The doughnut-shaped island of Niuafo'ou is the remnant of an enormous cone which collapsed violently and was destructively active as recently as 1946.

PATRICK HORTON

Typical Tongan vista of tiny, low-lying islands surrounded by lagoons and coral reefs

GEOLOGY

At the Tonga Trench, which reaches a depth of 10,882m at Vityaz Deep, the Pacific tectonic plate is being subducted – or is sliding – underneath the Indo-Australian plate. The four island groups of Tonga lie in two parallel lines which trend north-south along the Tonga Ridge, on the Indo-Australian plate just west of the trench. To the west of this ridge is the Lau Basin, where the sea floor is opening and spreading.

At the subduction zone, where the plates are interacting, the materials which constitute the Pacific plate are being melted and recombined deep in the earth's mantle. This process is accompanied by a great deal of seismic activity; earthquakes and vulcanism are the results apparent on the surface. According to geologists, the nation of Niue, to the east of Tonga, is approaching Vava'u at a rate of about 20cm per year. The maximum subduction rate occurs near Niuatoputapu, where the Pacific plate enters the trench at a rate of about 24cm annually.

Most of Tonga's high islands were created by geologically recent activity. As mentioned previously, Tafahi, Late and Kao form nearly perfect cones, and Niuafo'ou and Tofua remain active. Fonualei and 'Ata are well eroded but their fiery origins remain obvious. The two very recently formed islands of Fonuafo'ou and Late'iki evidence a most bizarre geological phenomenon of repeated eruption and erosion. (For more information on this see the Fonuafo'ou section in the Ha'apai Group chapter and the Late'iki section in the Vava'u Group chapter.)

The eastern line of islands is the result of the sagging weight of the new crust along the zone of vulcanism to the west, centred on Kao and Tofua. This line of islands has been pushed up mainly by displacement. The islands of 'Eua, Tongatapu and Vava'u are the best examples of tilted blocks of crust – all are leaning towards the great weight of Ha'apai's Kao and Tofua volcanoes on the earth's crust. Their east ('Eua), south (Tongatapu) and north (Vava'u) coastlines consist of abrupt cliffs, while their respective west, north and south coastlines

are submerging. In the case of Vava'u and Tongatapu, this is evidenced by mazes of islets, reefs and mangrove-choked lagoons on the Ha'apai side.

The main body of the Ha'apai Group consists of two large and eroding coral atolls, the Nomuka and Lulunga Groups, and a raised barrier reef (the Lifuka Group). The Ha'apai Group contains several *motu* (coral islets) and countless shoals and barrier reefs, all sustained by coral polyps.

CLIMATE

Despite its great latitudinal range, Tonga does not experience dramatically diverse climatic conditions, although Vava'u and the Niuas are noticeably warmer than Tongatapu, and 'Eua is noticeably cooler (for different reasons). The Vava'u and Niua Groups receive

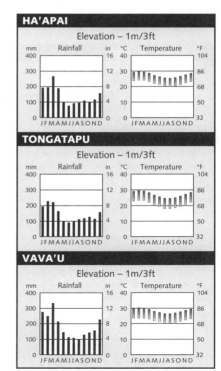

both more precipitation and higher average temperatures than the more southerly islands.

Tonga is far enough from the equator to enjoy a milder and more comfortable climate than that of the Samoas and the Solomons. Winter (July to September) temperatures range from a pleasant 18°C to a much warmer 27°C or so but southerly winds and strong south-east trades can create less-than-idyllic conditions, with rainstorms and extremely chilly weather.

Summer (December to April) temperatures vary from 22°C to 35°C, but cooler nights are not unusual. Extreme humidity is normally tempered by a light breeze. During early summer, Tonga experiences one of the world's ideal climates, but later in the season the islands receive most of their annual rainfall.

Tonga lies squarely within the South Pacific's notorious cyclone/typhoon belt and has experienced quite a few devastating blows over the years. Cyclone season is from the start of November to the end of April, with January to March having the greatest likelihood of cyclones.

Yachties should head for New Zealand or the Solomons by at least the end of November. The only cyclone shelter for yachts is Vava'u's Port of Refuge, but winds of over 50 knots render it potentially hazardous. A severe cyclone may occur about every 20 years, while milder ones occur on average every three or four years.

About 60% of the time the prevailing winds are south-easterly or easterly. North-easterly and southerly winds occur about 10% of the time. Westerly and north-westerly winds bring the worst weather, mostly in summer. The average annual precipitation at Nuku'alofa is 1700mm and measurable rainfall occurs on 35% of days. Vava'u is the wettest of the island groups with around 2200mm of rain falling annually.

Global Warming

The predicted increase in average temperature may seem small – about 4°C (7°F) in the next 100 years – but this rate of increase is vastly faster than any change in the last 10,000 years.

One of the most obvious effects of global warming will be a rise in sea level from thermal expansion of the oceans and the melting of polar icecaps – a 0.5m to 1m (1½ to 3 feet) increase in the next 100 years is a conservative estimate. Other important effects are an increase in the severity of storms in some regions, an increase in the frequency of droughts in other areas, and coral bleaching.

While it's accepted that the temperature of the earth is increasing, claims of increasing storm severity and the exact cause of coral bleaching are hotly debated. Some claim the earth's warming is a natural event. However, the dire predictions mentioned above are all sourced from the United Nations Environment Program, the Intergovernmental Panel on Climate Change, and the South Pacific Regional Environment Program, and have been accepted by the international insurance community and even British Petroleum (BP) – hardly the lunatic left!

Tonga will not be affected by rising sea levels as much as low-lying islands such as Kiribati. But sea flooding and coastal erosion will occur and force the translocation of coastal communities. Higher seas will increase the severity of storms and cyclones, and the rising seawater table will poison crops and reduce available fresh groundwater. Ha'apai will be the most affected island group.

Even small increases in sea temperatures destroy coral reefs, as coral cannot survive in water warmer than 28°C. Called 'coral bleaching', its most visible symptom is the annihilation of the colourful symbiotic algae that live within coral. Colourless, dead coral is left behind.

Cyclones regularly batter Tonga's coral reefs and if the bleached coral can't regenerate, Tonga's protection against storms, already worsened by rising sea levels, will decrease.

However, waves of coral bleaching have occurred in the past and reefs have the ability to regenerate over a decade or so – that is if the seas don't continue to warm.

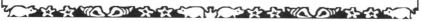

The Tonga Meteorological Service (☎/fax 23401, W www.kalianet.to/weather/weather .htm) provides local weather information, but for long-term forecasts and storm-tracking you should contact the Fiji Meteorological Service (☎/fax 679 720 190, W www.met .gov.fj).

ECOLOGY & ENVIRONMENT

Although most of the land in Tonga has been converted into either 'api (plantations) or town tracts, there are large areas of primary rainforest and bushland on the Niuas, 'Eua and on the volcanic islands of Kao, Tofua and Late.

FLORA & FAUNA

Tonga's national flower is the *heilala*, a small, sweet-smelling, reddish flower that blooms in winter, coinciding with Tongatapu's Heilala Festival in early July. Many other flowers are seen in Tonga, including several varieties of hibiscus. Many of the plants entwined with Tongan culture are not indigenous but were introduced by the first settlers; these include *tuitui* (candlenut), taro, yams, kava and breadfruit.

The most common plant you will see in Tonga is the drought-resistant coconut palm, which represents the 'tree of life' for all South Pacific peoples. Its nuts are used for food and drink all year round and its leaves are used to make houses.

Over 150 species of colourful tropical fish, including the tiny and brilliant blue damselfish, brightly coloured clownfish and parrotfish and a host of others, are readily observed by snorkellers and divers. The reefs form beautiful gardens of shapes and colours of hard and soft corals. Black coral – which is in fact not black when living underwater – is common around Tonga and is (unfortunately) carved into jewellery.

If you're flying around the islands at certain calmer periods of the year, you'll observe vast fields of coloured streaks on the surface of the ocean, some stretching for many kilometres. These are caused by a species of orange or brown algae measuring just 2mm in length. It collects in masses until it's broken up by rough wave action.

What's in a Name?

You may notice that Tongans have a rather ethnocentric way of referring to their flora and fauna. For example, fleas and body crabs are called *kuto fisi* (or Fijian bugs) and *kuto ha'amoa* (Samoan bugs) respectively. Likewise, poisonous kava plants are called *kava fisi* while good drinking kava is *kava tonga*. Large tuna are called *valu tonga* while the smaller variety are *valu ha'amoa*.

Migrating humpback whales bear their young and breed in Tongan waters from June to November (see the boxed text 'Singing Whales' in the Activities special section). Porpoises are here year-round and can often be seen offshore from the major islands. Flying fish and sailfish are sometimes spotted from sailboats in deep water. Sharks are not abundant, with the nonaggressive reef and leopard sharks being the most commonly seen.

The only land mammals native to Tonga are small insectivorous bats, and flying foxes *(peka)*. The latter – an extremely large fruit bat with a wingspan of up to 1m – is a common sight at dusk even on inhabited islands.

Tonga is home to only one species of snake, the (nonaggressive) banded sea snake, but reptiles, in the form of several species of skink and gecko, are found in abundance. The banded iguana *(fokai)* lives in bushland throughout Tonga, but its green colouring makes it extremely difficult to spot in the bush. It is believed that iguanas arrived in the Pacific from Central America on drifting vegetation some one million years ago.

Tonga is home to surprisingly few species of birds, but of interest are the blue-crowned lorikeet *(henga)* found on some islands of the Vava'u and Ha'apai Groups, the red shining parrot *(koki)* of 'Eua, and the Niuafo'ou megapode *(malau)*, found only on the island of Niuafo'ou.

Protected Areas

Tonga has eight officially protected areas. These include five national marine parks and reserves which were established to protect vulnerable coral reefs and beaches and their rich underwater ecosystems. A national historic park surrounds the Ha'amonga 'a Maui Trilithon, and national parks protect tracts of rainforest on 'Eua and Vava'u's Mt Talau.

The forest plantation on 'Eua covers much of the island's water catchment area and the recently established Ha'apai Conservation Area incorporates a code of practice to protect both land and sea in the Ha'apai Group. It's hoped that national parks will be established on Ha'apai's isolated volcanic islands of Kao and Tofua.

Unfortunately, conservation isn't a particularly high priority when it comes to scarce government funding in Tonga and protection of the areas mentioned above is rarely enforced. According to one cynical conservationist, some Tongans take the words 'marine reserve' to mean 'fishing reserve'.

Various NGOs fund community conservation education projects which in the long term may prove the most effective way to protect the environment.

Visitors should note that the collecting of plants, shells, coral or fish is prohibited within any of the protected areas. The collecting of live shells is officially discouraged, and the disturbance of giant clams (*Tridacna derasa*, or *tokonoa* in Tongan) and Triton's trumpet shells is prohibited throughout the kingdom.

Tonga's eight officially protected areas are:

'Eua National Park (449 hectares) – on 'Eua's east coast

Ha'amonga 'a Maui Trilithon National Historic Park (23 hectares) – on north-eastern Tongatapu Island

Ha'atafu Beach Reserve (8.4 hectares) – 20km west of Nuku'alofa, on the western tip of Tongatapu Island

Hakaumama'o Reef Reserve (126 hectares) – 14km north of Nuku'alofa

Malinoa Island & Reef Reserve (73 hectares) – 7km north of Nuku'alofa

Monu'afe Island & Reef Reserve (33 hectares) – 6.5km north-east of Nuku'alofa

Mt Talau National Park – 2km west of Neiafu, Vava'u Island

Pangaimotu Reef Reserve (49 hectares) – northeast of Queen Salote Wharf in Nuku'alofa

GOVERNMENT & POLITICS

Technically, Tonga is a constitutional monarchy based on the British parliamentary system. However, the current king, Taufa'ahau Tupou IV, is almost unique in the world in that he has absolute power. Since it was first drafted in the 1870s, the constitution has undergone relatively little amendment.

The Tongan system provides for a sovereign and a privy council. The king or queen is the head of both the nation and its government. The monarch's cabinet consists of the prime minister and ministers of the crown. All of these positions are appointed by the monarch and the occupants remain in office until voluntary retirement or death. The governors of Ha'apai and Vava'u are also members of cabinet. When presided over by the monarch, the cabinet is called the privy council.

The legislature is unicameral and is composed of an appointed speaker, the cabinet, nine nobles elected by Tonga's 33 hereditary nobles and nine representatives elected by literate taxpayers over the age of 21. Elections are held every three years, and the political scene is driven by personalities, rather than parties.

Tonga's highest judicial assembly is the court of appeal, composed of the privy council and the chief justice. Below it is the supreme court, the land court (also presided over by the chief justice) and the magistrates' court. In criminal law, the accused may opt for trial by jury or by a judge alone.

Local governments consist of town and district officers, who respectively preside over villages and groups of villages. The Tonga Defence Services include the Royal Tongan Marines, Tongan Royal Guards, the Maritime Force and the police.

ECONOMY

On the face of it, Tonga's economy is at a low ebb, with a huge trade deficit holding it down. In 1999 exports amounted to about T$11.5 million, while imports ran to almost T$105 million. GDP was US$1,543 per capita and inflation was around 7.1% in 2000 (largely due to high oil prices) when the pa'anga began falling against foreign currencies. At the time of writing, federal cash reserves were down to about T$25 million, enough for only 2½ months of imports.

So why does everyone look so happy? New cars (or at least second-hand imports) and consumer goods continue to flood into the country and consumer banks maintain that there's plenty of cash around. Standards of living have risen dramatically over the last 15 years, thanks mainly to remittances from Tongans living and working overseas. Remittances totalled a massive T$78.6 million in 1999, and continue to increase year on year. Many Tongans may live at an almost subsistence level, but family members in Australia, New Zealand and North America are running in the rat race for serious cash. If all of these expats start to put down deep roots and stop supporting the folks back home, Tonga will be in big trouble.

Agriculture

Agriculture in Tonga is largely subsistence-based (ie, crops are produced for home use rather than for sale); staple products include squash, pineapples, papayas, kava, taro, watermelons, bananas, manioc, yams, sweet potatoes and, of course, coconuts. Subsistence crops are traditionally rotated, to preserve soil fertility, but land shortages have meant that decreasing amounts of farmland are left fallow at any given time. In addition, most households have breadfruit and mango trees and keep horses, pigs and chickens. Many families supplement their diet with seafood.

Leading agricultural exports are squash, coconut products and vanilla beans. Tonga also produces export quantities of peppers, tomatoes, watermelons, limes and kava. For a while Tonga filled a seasonal niche in the supply of squash to Japan. Land was cleared and large quantities of pesticides and fertilizers were used to maximise production. Many farmers made good money, but the good times didn't last and as more and more middle-men became involved profits fell.

At the time of writing, the most lucrative crop was kava for export to North America. Unlike squash kava requires very little maintenance, but takes three to five years to be productive.

Fishing & Forestry

Small, privately owned fishing boats provide a modest income for many Tongans, but overfishing has severely depleted coastal fish stocks and longline tuna fishing is becoming big business. With a catch zone of over 700,000 sq km including some of the world's richest tuna areas, tuna fishing is an underdeveloped resource of great potential for Tonga. In 2000 the 16 registered longline vessels caught tuna with an estimated export value of T$8 to T$10 million.

There is a small forestry industry on 'Eua. Prudent planting in past years means that non-native species such as pine, eucalyptus and red cedar and even mahogany are found in the 'Eua Plantation Forest. Most timber goes for local use, but some is exported. The island's large tract of primary rainforest is protected.

Industry

In order to encourage overseas investments and new business in Tonga, the government offers five-year tax holidays and other tax breaks. Businesses in Tonga, however, may not be more than 49% foreign-controlled. Furthermore, land may not be purchased by foreigners and leasing of land requires parliamentary approval.

The Princess & the Satellite

In a move of much cunning, Tonga grabbed six satellite orbit 'slots' in 1989. TongaSat was formed as the government's agent to exploit these new assets, with the king's daughter, Princess Pilolevu, at the helm. Although there have been mutterings about nepotism and royal exploitation of the country's assets, the princess took a huge financial risk which is only just starting to pay off, as the company has been able to secure lucrative leasing agreements with some major players (including the Chinese). It's speculated that the scheme has made Princess Pilolevu a multimillionaire.

Manufacturing in Tonga is in a poor state. A Small Industries Centre in the Maufanga suburb of Nuku'alofa has been successful in producing knitwear, paper products, paint, furniture and sporting goods, but production is very small-scale and mostly for local consumption.

Tongan exports receive duty-free access to Australasian markets and favoured trading status in North America and the European Union.

Tourism

Receipts from tourism were worth T$10 million in 1999 and, while the industry is not embraced with tremendous enthusiasm by the government, visitor numbers are increasing. With increasing tourism in the South Pacific, Tongan tourism businesses are hoping to cash in on their share of Australian, North American and European tourists. Aid programs aimed at developing Tonga's tourist infrastructure are in place, but Royal Tongan Airlines needs to improve before the double-edged sword of mass tourism has a hope in Tonga.

Emigration

Many Tongans who have migrated in search of greener pastures discover that they cannot cope with the hectic pace of life there and ultimately return to Tonga. Tongans invariably find that thriving abroad requires a rigid schedule dominated by work (except for a very privileged few). However, the money sent home by those Tongans who stick it out in Australia, New Zealand and the USA keeps the Tongan economy going.

This system allows Tongan life to continue at a suitably Polynesian pace, while much of the cash economy and its associated headaches are contained elsewhere. Families in Tonga are justifiably concerned that the second overseas generation, reared in a foreign culture, won't be so generous toward the folks back in the 'old country', relatives they may never have met.

But a series of clouds lurk on the horizon. Tighter immigration rules instigated by New Zealand, Australia and the USA (bonds are now required in some cases before visas are issued) mean that a young male workforce that once worked overseas now remains unemployed at home. Deportation from the USA of Tongans found guilty of the smallest criminal act is also having an impact on the situation, while Tonga's birth rate is still as high as ever and will lead to increased population pressure.

POPULATION & PEOPLE

Tongans are a fairly homogeneous Polynesian group and they make up the vast majority of people who live in Tonga. There are a few expats, mainly from Europe, New Zealand and Australia, and a small population of Chinese immigrants. Life expectancy is 70 years for males and 71 for females.

The average annual population growth rate is 0.4% and in 2000 Tonga's total population was estimated to be 99,005. The population density of the country as a whole is about 150 per square kilometre, but varies widely throughout the kingdom.

Tongatapu has over 65% of the total population and Nuku'alofa (the capital) over

Passports for Sale

From 1984 to 1998, Tongan passports and citizenship were on the open market for US$20,000. Imelda Marcos bought one, as did many thousands from China, Taiwan and Hong Kong; they saw the purchase as a stepping stone to Australia, New Zealand and the USA. These countries, however, refused to recognise the validity of the mail-order passports.

The sale of passports accounts, at least in part, for the increase in the number of Chinese-owned businesses in Tonga (many *fale koloa* – small grocery kiosks – are now Chinese-owned). The growth of the Chinese population is the cause of much local resentment, with fear at the prospect of being economically and politically sidelined by dynamic Chinese businesses as they become more established.

20%. Vava'u has 16% of the population, Ha'apai 8%, 'Eua 5% and the far-flung Niuas just 2%. On many islands the population is growing, but on parts of Ha'apai and the Niuas numbers continue to fall as people head to Tongatapu or overseas.

Widespread emigration relieves a bit of the pressure on the limited space and resources of the archipelago. You'd be hard-pressed to find a Tongan without relatives in New Zealand, Australia or the USA. Estimates state there are 50% to 100% more Tongans living abroad than there are in Tonga.

EDUCATION

Education is compulsory for children between the ages of six and 14. All students contribute something financially and official figures put attendance at nearly 100%. There are 117 primary schools in Tonga and roughly 90% are state-run. Christian institutions make up the remaining percentage.

Of Tonga's 39 secondary schools, 19.5% are state-run and these schools take the top students in an exam-based selection process. The rest attend church and nongovernment schools, with Mormon schools the most heavily subsidised and best equipped. Teaching in church schools is one of the most common forms of work available to foreigners in Tonga (see Work in the Facts for the Visitor chapter).

About 53% of secondary school students go on to further education. Tonga has 10 technical and vocational colleges and one teacher training college. Tertiary education is available at the University of the South Pacific extension and the private 'Atenisi Institute, both on Tongatapu. The government and other Commonwealth countries also offer scholarship programs enabling Tongan students to go overseas for higher education.

ARTS
Dance

Unlike the vibrant *tamure* of Tahiti and the Cook Islands or the erotic *hula* of Hawaii, Tongan dances for females are subtle, artistic and require the dancer to convey meaning with an economy of motion.

The most frequently performed traditional dance in Tonga is called the *lakalaka*. The dancers, most often women but occasionally including men, stand in rows, dressed in similar costumes decorated with leaves, shells, flowers and pandanus. They sway, sing, smile broadly and tell stories with their hand movements. One person of high rank, called the *vahenga*, performs apart from the other dancers and is dressed differently.

The *ma'ulu'ulu* is a dance performed at feasts, on public holidays and at special state functions. The movements, known as *haka*, are choreographed by the *punake*, who is always a man of high rank. He also writes the song that the dance is meant to illustrate. The dancers are always women; they seat themselves in rows and use only hand movements to convey the story.

The female solo dance, the most beautiful and graceful of all Tongan dances, is called the *tau'olunga*. The dancer performs wearing a flowing knee-length dress with bare shoulders and with flowers in her hair and on her wrists and ankles. Her body is covered with coconut oil in order to draw attention to her skin. The dancer must always smile genuinely and keep her knees together. The tau'olunga is performed at government and village functions, on the birthdays of influential people and for visits by dignitaries. A bride will also perform it at her wedding, a suitable occasion to display her charms.

While the female dances are gentle and accompanied by music, the male dances are meant to convey the fierce warrior spirit of Tongan tradition. The most popular is the *kailao*, the war dance, reminiscent of the days when canoes full of Tongan men set out on raiding missions to neighbouring islands. The rapid movements re-enact violent attacks and are accompanied by loud, ominous drumming, fierce cries, beating feet and the pounding of *pate*, or spear-like pales, which represent war clubs.

The fire dance, perhaps the most dramatic Tongan dance, is also the favourite of most visitors. One or two dancers gyrate, leap and spin while juggling flaming knives to the rhythm of a rapid, primeval drumbeat.

The *fakapale* is a curious custom associated with Tongan dancing. The word means 'to award a prize'. Originally, the prizes consisted of fine mats and tapa heaped before a dancer in recognition of ability. Nowadays, notes are plastered onto the oiled bodies of the dancers or tucked into costumes during the performance by admiring spectators. Tongan dances are excellent for fundraising.

Music

Outside of a church setting, the most typical form of musical expression that visitors to Tonga are likely to experience is the string band accompanied by harmonious singing, usually by the musicians themselves. This is archetypal Polynesian stuff, involving instruments such as the guitar, banjo, bass and ukulele. Sometimes these musicians accompany dancers (drums are often added in this case), but often perform solo at feasts, private parties and the like.

Wonderful choirs can be heard singing hymns in churches all across Tonga. Congregational singing can be excellent, with the larger, more established churches often being your best bet. There are practice sessions on Sunday evening. Most hymns are Western numbers translated into Tongan, though *hiva usu* – which are more like traditional chants than imported hymns – can sometimes be heard in the Free Church of Tonga and Free Wesleyan Church.

Traditional Tongan instruments are an uncommon sight these days. They include the *fangufangu* (a bamboo nose-flute), *mimiha* (pan pipes), *nafa* (a skin drum) and *kele'a* (a conch shell blown as a horn).

Literature

Tales of the Tikongs and *Kisses in the Nederends* by 'Epeli Hau'ofa are books not to be missed by anyone travelling to Tonga. They are tales of the coming of age of a small Pacific island kingdom called Tiko (a thinly disguised Tonga), by Tonga's most respected and renowned author; humorous and thought-provoking reading.

Po Fananga: Folk Tales of Tonga by Tupou Posesi Fanua is a highly enjoyable

book of traditional Tongan tales, told in Tongan and English. *Tales from the Friendly Islands* by Vaka Pole'o is another book of Tongan tales, written in English.

Tales and Poems of Tonga by EEV Collocott, a classic 1928 work, is now back in print.

Konai Helu Thaman, a Tongan woman with an illustrious personal history, has published several excellent books of poetry including *YOU, The Choice of my Parents; Langakali; Hingano; Kakala* (all in English) and *Inselfeuer* (in German).

Malo Tupou: An Oral History by Tupou Posesi Fanua with Lois Wimberg Webster tells the story of the author's first 21 years, from 1913 to 1934, recounted when she was 81 years old. An oral history of early-20th-century Tonga told from a woman's perspective, it's a very good read.

Tapa

Tapa, a mulberry bark cloth, is considered part of the *koloa*, or wealth, of Tongan families, along with pandanus weavings. On important occasions such as weddings, funerals, graduations or royal events, large amounts of tapa in lengths of 25m to 150m are made and exchanged.

In the Tongan language, this product is only referred to as tapa in its undecorated stage; the elaborately decorated finished product is known as *ngatu*. Tapa is made from *hiapo*, the inner bark of the paper mulberry tree *(Broussonetia papyrifera)*, which grows primarily on 'Eua and Tongatapu.

When the trees are still young the bark is removed in thin strips. After a day or two of drying, the rough outer bark is peeled away leaving the soft, fibrous inner bark. It is then beaten with a *toa* (ironwood) mallet called an *'ike* on a long wooden anvil, or *tutua*, to separate and spread the fibres. When it is about 45cm in width, it is folded with another piece and pounded further. A single length of cloth is known as a *feta'aki*; once it has been pasted into long strips it is known as *langanga*. These strips placed side by side are also pasted together using sticky, half-cooked tubers of manioc.

To decorate it, first a *kupesi*, or relief of the pattern, is made by sewing a design of coconut fronds onto a woven pandanus base. The strips of tapa are then placed over the kupesi tablet and rubbed with feta'aki and coconut husk dipped in a ruddy vegetable dye to bring out the design.

After the tapa has dried, the designs are hand-painted in black and rich earthy reds and browns, usually derived from candlenuts and mangrove bark. The cloths have a purely decorative purpose – displayed on walls, covering beds – but traditionally were also used to line the walls and ceilings of huts.

Pandanus Weaving

Like tapa, woven pandanus mats are traditionally considered a form of wealth by Tongan families and are therefore exchanged as tokens of esteem on special occasions. Tongan weaving, however, is not limited to mats – hats, clothing, toys, baskets, belts and trays are also woven of pandanus and put to everyday use. Historically, the long-distance sailing canoes carried sails of woven pandanus.

The preparation of the pandanus leaf is quite involved. First, it is cut and stripped of thorns and rough spots. Once this initial process is completed, different methods are used to bring out the unique qualities and colours of each type.

Four types of pandanus are used in Tonga, each with its own texture and colour. They are *tofua*, which is nearly white, *paongo*, which is brown, *tapahina*, off-white or light brown, and *kie*, the finest of all, which is creamy white.

Tofua is the simplest to prepare. The leaves are boiled in water for an hour or two and laid in the sun to dry. To prepare paongo and tapahina, leaves are covered with a mat and turned daily to prevent rot. After a few days they turn a chocolate-brown colour and are braided into plaits called *fakate'ete'epuaka* and then hung in a dark place to dry.

The soft fibres of the kie leaves are peeled away from the coarser undersides, tied into bunches and blanched by placing them in the sea for up to a fortnight. The leaves are then carefully washed to remove the salt, and dried in the sun. When dry, each leaf is curled and made softer by pulling it between the fingers and the lip of a sharp shell or piece of metal.

The kie fibres, once cut into threadlike strips, are woven into extremely valuable, fine, silk-like mats called *fihu*, unmatched anywhere in the world. A good *fala fihu* will require thousands of hours of weaving, and mothers often begin work on one at the birth of a daughter in the hope of finishing in time to present it as part of her dowry.

Other types of mats include the *fala tui*, *fala paongo* and *fala tofua*. The fala tui is a complex mat of double thickness, one layer woven of coarse tofua and the other of finer paongo. The fala paongo is dark in colour and is normally presented to those of high status in the society. The fala tofua is of a lighter colour.

The black colour seen in many pandanus baskets is produced by dyeing the leaves with the juice of *loa 'ano* or *manaui* before weaving. Baskets are stiffened by weaving around ribs of coconut frond, and fibres of *fau* or hibiscus bark are often used along with the pandanus when making baskets or dancing costumes.

Carving

Although most Tongan wood carvings are skilfully made and quite beautiful, they are on the whole untraditional. The style is copied from Tahitian and Hawaiian culture and made to appeal to the tourist market. The most common subjects are turtles, pigs and whales (some are superbly carved to incorporate the natural shape of the wood), *tikis* (wooden statues representing an old Polynesian god), miniature war clubs and masks. Some kitsch items like salad bowls, floor lamps, ashtrays and soap dishes are also produced.

Specialist wood carvers, known as *tufunga*, were always men and this remains the case today. Traditionally carvers made neck rests, war clubs, fly whisks, kava bowls and small figurative sculptures. Among the most ornate of these items are the war clubs. These fearsome objects were often beautifully inlaid with shell and ivory images of birds, the sun, the moon and stars and incised with figures and intricate geometric patterns.

All the known figurative sculpture depicts shapely female ancestors and goddesses

PATRICK HORTON

Craftsman carving wooden mask

with bent knees and simple, mask-like faces. Carved from wood or ivory, these small, finely worked figures were often hung in religious buildings or buried in tombs.

Ahi (sandalwood), with its distinctly beautiful fragrance, is a very popular wood used in tourist sculpture, but it's becoming increasingly rare due to overharvesting and illicit export to Asian markets. Please take this into consideration before purchasing such items.

SOCIETY & CONDUCT

Although on the whole Tongans are open and extremely hospitable, Western visitors are frequently bewildered by local behaviour and sense that they are not being let in on some vital details about the Tongan way.

Few outsiders, if any, will ever come to understand all the underlying nuances of any Polynesian culture. Ritual and custom may be easily observed, but to grasp the meaning of it all is another issue indeed. A couple of examples: Christianity is professed loudly but some old Polynesian superstitions quietly remain. Warm and generous adults invite foreigners into their homes and lavish gifts and food on them yet seem to regard their own children coldly and without affection.

Social Hierarchy

With the advent of Christianity as the state religion, all Tongans became theoretically equal 'under God' and social ranking lost a great deal of its importance. The constitution of 1875 abolished the traditional feudal system of subservience and serfdom for commoners, and chiefs and nobles were denied the privilege of indiscriminate pillage to which they'd been previously accustomed. Old habits die hard, however, and remnants of the traditional system may still be seen today.

Although caste is not as rigid and elaborate as it was before European contact, there remains a two-tier system which determines privilege among individuals and in which no upward mobility is possible. The royal family and the 33 hereditary nobles and their families enjoy the highest rank in Tongan society. All other Tongans are commoners. Nobles may not marry commoners without risk of losing their titles. A commoner who marries a noble can never attain noble status.

Non-Tongans, especially expatriates of European descent, receive deferential treatment by virtue of their relative wealth (in most cases) and education. Asian immigrants, on the other hand, are often treated in an openly racist manner and their businesses are preferred targets for criminals.

The Family

In Tonga, the basic social unit is the extended family, which in a sense serves as a mini social welfare system. Within families, all wealth, belongings, work, problems and even shame are shared and the excessive accumulation of wealth and personal belongings is considered to be out of line.

So fundamental is the concept of the communal extended family that in Tongan there are no separate words for 'brother/sister' and 'cousin'. Aunts and uncles may also be referred to as 'parents' and all older people may be considered 'grandparents' by the younger generations.

The notions of childless families and orphaned children are unknown. Parents have no real sense of 'possession' of their children and children are frequently shifted from one household to another. In the end, they are effectively reared by the entire extended family and they may have several places to call home.

Social Protocol

Respect for those considered superior to oneself is a principal motivation in Tongan behaviour. When in the presence of royalty, nobles, high commissioners, politicians or religious leaders, Tongans become more guarded and deliberate. As a foreigner, you may be regarded in a similar fashion, hence the 'arm's length' feeling many visitors get when dealing with hospitable locals.

Tongan commoners physically lower themselves before a royal who is standing, in order to demonstrate willing subservience, and in no way imitate their actions. At any gathering at which royalty is to be present, everyone else must be seated before the guests of honour arrive. Once royalty is seated, no other commoners may be admitted or seated (in this one case, Western-style punctuality is absolutely necessary). For those who are privileged enough to address royalty, there is a special level of the Tongan language which must be used.

One practice which is in no way unique to Tonga but is ubiquitous here is gift-giving. Gifts most often come in the form of agricultural produce. Foreigners are often presented with food and handicrafts. Family members abroad get tinned corned beef and kava. New parents, newly married couples and royalty receive the finest agricultural produce, pigs, intricately designed fine mats and immense rolls of tapa.

Gifts are given ceremoniously and accepted graciously. A gift will most often be prefaced by verbal self-abasement, such as 'We are a poor family and our gift is very humble but please accept it as it represents the best that we are capable of producing'. This speech will often refer to a fine mat which represents hundreds or thousands (yes, thousands!) of hours of work. Although the giver of the gift downplays its worth, the recipient praises the gift and shows how delighted they are to receive it.

Shame and loss of face are not taken lightly by Tongans and in extreme cases people are driven to suicide. Foreigners should be especially sensitive to this. If a travel agent botches a reservation, a waiter delivers the wrong plate, or a person on the street admits they don't know where a particular point of interest is (it requires some

Amazing Graves

Tongan cemeteries provide the ultimate examples of post-mortem kitsch. Non-Catholic burial sites (Catholics use monuments) consist of sandy mounds topped with artificial flowers beneath inverted goldfish bowls, plastic images or photos of Jesus Christ, teddy bears, ribbons, banners, shells, volcanic rocks and beer bottles, often backed up with a handmade quilt.

Memorable remembrances

SIMON ROWE

Church on Sunday

Sunday is protected by Tongan law, and set aside as a day for eating, sleeping and going to church. Even the Seventh Day Adventists, who normally celebrate their Sabbath on Saturday, conceded to worship on a Sunday (apparently because of the kink in the International Date Line that bends around Tonga – so it's *really* only Saturday).

A Sunday stroll in Tonga will give a visitor the eerie feeling that someone has dropped the bomb. Buses don't operate, businesses are closed, sports events are prohibited and planes may not land. Contracts signed on Sunday are considered null and void and any Tongan caught fishing or guilty of any other breach of the Sabbath is subject to a T$10 fine or three months' hard labour. Even swimming at the beach is a no-no on Sunday for Tongans.

Bakeries are the only shops allowed to open on Sunday afternoon thanks to an emergency law that was enacted after a devastating cyclone in the 1980s and never repealed. A few restaurants and tourist facilities open and the odd taxi is available, but that's about it. What most people do on Sunday is go to church.

Tongans normally attend at least two worship services; the main service begins at 10am with other services at dawn and late afternoon. Going to a Tongan church is a real cultural experience for visitors. The musical ability displayed can be astonishing and the rendition of traditional hymns is often magnificent.

There are some rules of etiquette to be followed when attending church in Tonga. First and foremost, dress to avoid offence. Your appearance should be neat and respectable. Women should dress modestly, wearing a loose dress or skirt with a hemline below the knee and keep their chests and upper arms covered; trousers are inappropriate. Men should wear a shirt preferably with a collar and tie, long trousers and proper shoes. Punctuality is important, especially if you're attending the service in Centenary Chapel where the king worships. Tradition demands that everyone is seated when royalty arrives so get there half an hour early. No-one can come in once the king is seated and no-one is permitted to leave before he does.

Picking your Church

Tonga has some beautiful and fascinating churches. While in many countries, deep-rooted tradition has governed the way churches are built, in Tonga church architects seem to have been given a free reign. Some churches are made from space materials and others look like glorified chocolate boxes.

Listed here are some of the highlights, all of which are shown on the relevant maps (for more details on many of them, see the regional chapters). When checking these places out bear in mind that only Catholic churches are always open.

St Joseph's Cathedral, Neiafu

Church on Sunday

Hallelujah! Hymn singing at a Lifuka church service

Tongatapu
Basilica of St Anthony of Padua, Nuku'alofa – the town's distinctive Catholic worship house resembling the hat of a Chinese peasant.

St Mary's Cathedral, Nuku'alofa – another Catholic place, with an impressive altar and lofted ceiling.

Centenary Chapel, Nuku'alofa – where the king goes to worship; a bit of a barn but the singing is beautiful.

Mormon temple, Liahona – set among beautifully tended gardens and crowned with a golden messenger (Mormons only).

Catholic Church, Mu'a – looks as if it was teleported straight from England; climb the tower and check out the stained glass.

Free Wesleyan Church, Fua'amotu – Tonga's answer to the Millennium Dome, built in 1986 and structured like an open-air concert stage; its translucent skin provides a weird sort of light.

Free Church of Tonga, Lavengatonga – a beautiful red and white clapboard church in the classic missionary style.

Free Wesleyan Church, Pelehake – part Tongan *fale*, part rocket ship, showing some fantastically eclectic influences; one of the first churches you'll see driving in from the airport.

Free Church of Tonga, Ha'ateiho – looks like something from Disneyland; much coloured glass has been used and the interior, bathed in yellow and red light, is simple and beautiful.

Ha'apai
Free Church of Tonga, Lifuka – the influence of Islamic architecture on the architect of this place can clearly be seen.

Free Wesleyan Church, Lifuka – a huge, box-like, angular monster quite unlike anything you'll see elsewhere.

Free Wesleyan Church, 'Uiha – a fairy-tale church with cannons taken from the *Margarita* after it sank.

Vava'u
St Joseph's Cathedral, Neiafu – with a facade that's a masterpiece of Catholic colonial architecture.

Free Wesleyan Church, Neiafu – a modern construction containing fine stained glass.

fortitude to do this), a foreigner who becomes outwardly upset in most cases inspires feelings of shame that go deeper than is immediately visible. A *laissez-faire* attitude will also go a long way towards preserving a traveller's mental health.

In traditional Tongan culture, women are not permitted to freely associate with men on their own – they must be chaperoned. Foreign women should bear this in mind when socialising with Tongan men and be careful not to send out the wrong signals. This different cultural assumption also applies to foreign men relating to Tongan women – for example, a local woman may refuse to go somewhere alone with a man, even for a simple thing like lunch or a coffee, because in her culture she cannot do this.

Tongan Dress

Although their attire is growing increasingly Western, Tongans are by law required to dress modestly in keeping with fundamentalist Christian ideals.

Tongan men experience fewer restrictions than women but they are required to wear a shirt at all times in public. This rule doesn't apply to the beaches, where men are permitted to go shirtless. Tongan women, however, may not go topless at any time and usually cover their shoulders and chests completely and cover their legs at least to the knees.

You'll often see Tongans wearing distinctive pandanus mats called *ta'ovala*, secured around the waist with a cord of coconut sennit called a *kafa*. Ta'ovala are worn frequently for going to work or to church, on formal occasions or whenever meeting someone of noble status. The ta'ovala serves roughly the same social purpose as a tie (for men) or a special dress (for women) in Western culture: it signifies that the wearer is 'dressed up'. Ta'ovala are handed down through several generations as valued heirlooms and the older they are the more precious they become.

In place of a ta'ovala, women often wear a *kiekie*, a decorative waist band from which dangle woven strips of pandanus, strands of seeds or strips of cloth. Men often wear a wraparound cloth skirt known as a *tupenu* extending below the knees and women an ankle-length *vala* (skirt) and *kofu* (tunic).

When mourning a relative or friend, Tongans dress in black and wear particularly prominent ta'ovala. The death of a monarch sets off a six-month period of mourning during which all Tongans are required to don ta'ovala and wear black. If a prominent royal dies then the civil service and most commercial activity ceases for an indefinite period.

Dos & Don'ts

In most cases, visitors will not be expected to participate in or even be aware of Tongan codes of behaviour, but those who do are likely to be more accepted by the people.

It seems that the smaller the island, the more warmly visitors are welcomed. Having said that, life on the outer islands is often at subsistence level and hospitality must not be abused. Prospective visitors will be least disruptive if they have a contact on the island and announce their intention to visit in advance. They should also bring enough supplies for themselves as well as gifts for their hosts (tinned corned beef will be heartily welcomed).

Tonga is not the place for nude or topless sunbathing and Western-style swimwear is only worn at tourist resorts and usually only by foreigners. Very few Tongans possess bathing costumes and Tongan women usually swim in shorts and a T-shirt (at the very least) or in their normal clothes.

As a traveller, a clean and presentable appearance will signify to Tongans your respect for both yourself and others, and respect is extremely important in Tongan culture. Men should wear a shirt at all times in public. Short shorts will cause offence and should not be worn by either men or women. Women will be most accepted if they wear loose skirts or dresses, with hemlines below the knee. Sleeves are probably best, but modest sleeveless shirts or dresses are all right in casual situations. Don't walk around in a halter top or with a low-cut neckline, and don't wear sheer, see-through clothing. Long, baggy shorts are acceptable for casual wear – eg, for going to the beach.

Coconuts galore, 'Utukalonga Market, Neiafu

A shy *'Malo e lelei'* – Welcome to Tonga!

It's all yours; deserted beach on Lifuka's eastern coast

Silver Saviour & friends, Pangai

Checking in at Kaufana Airport, 'Eua

Local skipper, Uoleva

Bus stop with a message, Vava'u

Preparing a spit-roast for a church feast, Ha'apai

Shirley Baker monument, Pangai

RELIGION

Tongans take their religion seriously, or at least that's what they'd have you believe. Since the constitution of the nation was outlined by a missionary, Shirley Baker, it's not surprising that national adherence to Christian principles was written into it.

The Free Wesleyan Church, where the Royal Family worships, claims the largest number of adherents (about 41% of the population), followed by Roman Catholics (16%), Mormons (14%), Free Church of Tonga (12%) and then Seventh Day Adventists, Anglicans and a host of other small, mostly evangelical churches imported from the USA. The most entertaining of these religions is Jump for Jesus, whose adherents advertise the 'word of the Lord' by jumping through flaming hoops on motorbikes (though unfortunately this cannot be seen in Tonga).

Christianity is very strong in Tonga and church ministers hold a strong influence over their congregations. The church has the power to influence politics and to raise large amounts of money through the pulpit. Few Tongans can afford to donate much, though peer pressure is such that some people will even take out loans in order to donate a suitably impressive sum.

Of all the denominations in Tonga, Roman Catholics are the most liberal and least shy in tackling social issues, while the Mormons (The Church of Jesus Christ of the Latter Day Saints) have the most money and are growing rapidly. In 2000 they spent over T$20 million on church and school building and maintenance. Their schools are well equipped, though cynics often quip that many Tongans become Mormons shortly before their kids reach school age. It is the Mormons' stated intention to transform Tonga into the first Mormon state.

However, the king is said to be ill at ease with these newly imported religions that are often intolerant of local traditions and promise a reward in the next life as opposed to practical solutions for the present.

With all the hoopla over Christianity, one would assume that the pre-European religious beliefs had been totally abandoned. But many Tongans still believe in the spirits, taboos, superstitions, medical charms and Polynesian gods that characterised the well-defined religious traditions before the arrival of the missionaries.

LANGUAGE

Tongan is a West Polynesian language and belongs to the Oceanic branch of Austronesian languages. It is the official language of Tonga and is spoken throughout the country, although on the island of Niuafo'ou, a dialect closer to Samoan is spoken.

Both Tongan and English languages are used in the schools throughout Tonga, so you won't have any problem using English to communicate. On major islands (Tongatapu, Vava'u), almost everyone speaks English as a second language. On smaller, more remote islands people may speak less English, but communication can always somehow be achieved.

For a list of useful Tongan words and phrases, see the Language chapter at the back of the book.

Facts for the Visitor

SUGGESTED ITINERARIES

Depending on the time you have available, you might want to consider some of the following options:

A Few Days Take a trip around Tongatapu Island (don't miss the dramatic Mapu'a 'a Vaca blowholes and the Ha'amonga 'a Maui Trilithon) then soak up the essence of paradise at 'Atata, Fafá or Pangaimotu, north of Tongatapu.

Two Weeks Explore Tongatapu and discover its hidden treasures and northern islands, then hop over to 'Eua to experience its natural wonders. Alternatively, head up to Vava'u and indulge in water sports and good food, or just relax and do nothing on Ha'apai's stunning beaches.

One Month Take time to fully explore a single island group. Boat to remote islands in Ha'apai, island-hop through Vava'u, even visit the isolated Niuas.

Two Months There's time to do some real exploring. Buy a Royal Tongan Airlines Kingdom Pass and visit all the island groups, including the Niuas. Try your hand at some activities or take an extended tour.

PLANNING
When to Go

The ideal time to visit Tonga is between May and July, when there are a number of festivals, the climate is pleasant, the sea is still warm and humpback whales arrive. July to October is also a good time to visit, but it's cooler in July. Summer, from November to April, is hot, humid and wet. It's also cyclone season and, although serious cyclones are rare, yachties will want to avoid summer. March tends to be the wettest month, especially in Vava'u. See Climate in the Facts about Tonga chapter for more information.

If you plan to come during the December-January holiday period, when huge numbers of Tongans return for the holidays (mostly from New Zealand, Australia and the USA), it's wise to book flights well in advance. It's also worth noting that some activity companies close between December and April.

Highlights

- **Snorkelling and diving** – these are world-class here, especially in Ha'apai and Vava'u.
- **Humpback whales** – the 'singing whales' visit Tonga annually between June and November. Whale-watching trips in which you can snorkel with these huge creatures are an unforgettable experience.
- **Tongan feast** – pig-out Tongan-style and enjoy beautiful traditional music and dance.
- **Mapu'a 'a Vaca blowholes, Tongatapu** – Mapu'a 'a Vaca is a spectacular section of coastline where dozens of blowholes spout dramatically.
- **Ha'amonga 'a Maui Trilithon, Tongatapu** – one of Polynesia's most impressive ancient monuments, this is believed to have been used for astronomical observations.
- **Ha'apai's beaches** – fringed with coconut palms, the white-sand beaches of Ha'apai are among the South Pacific's best.
- **Lapaha tombs, Mu'a, Tongatapu** – this ancient site of tombs and ruins marks the location of Lapaha, early capital of Tongatapu.
- **Bushwalking on 'Eua** – the quiet rural island of 'Eua offers forests, caves, sea cliffs, beaches and a large network of tracks, trails and camping possibilities.
- **Tofua, the Ha'apai Group** – the mutiny on the *Bounty* took place near here and it's a fantastic place for bushwalking. There's a beautiful blue crater lake, stands of primary rainforest and a very active volcano.
- **Sailing in the Vava'u Group** – these islands are heaven on earth for yachties, and the sea kayaking is excellent too.
- **Hiking around Niuafo'ou, the Niuas** – the island of Niuafo'ou is the home of unusual lava fields and a spectacular crater containing two lovely lakes.
- **Waterways of western Niuatoputapu, the Niuas** – wade through the maze of waterways separating the islets west of Niuatoputapu and soak up the pervading sense of mystery.

What Kind of Trip?

Tonga may be visited alone, as part of an island-hopping jaunt through the South Pacific, or as a stopover when crossing the Pacific between the USA and Australia or New Zealand. Most travellers arrive by plane, but some come by yacht – Vava'u's Port of Refuge is a major stopover on the Pacific yachting route.

Travellers should bear in mind that flying directly from Europe or North America to Tonga and back again doesn't represent good value for money. It's worth considering a stop elsewhere in the Pacific. See the Getting There & Away chapter for more information.

Maps

Offices of the Tongan Visitors' Bureau dispense a very simple map of Tonga's major islands and island groups, plus street maps of Nuku'alofa (Tongatapu), Neiafu (Vava'u) and Lifuka (Ha'apai). A sketchy map of the island groups is sometimes available at the Friendly Islands Bookshop. Good 1:50,000 maps of 'Eua are also available at this bookshop as well as at the Ministry of Agriculture and Forestry office.

In Nuku'alofa, Tonga's Ministry of Lands, Survey & Natural Resources (☎ 23611, fax 23216, PO Box 5) on Vuna Rd sells large-scale topographic, black-and-white dyeline prints of individual island groups (T$14 each). Unfortunately these dark prints do not give much detail, though most are scaled 1:50,000. Colour topographic maps are no longer available.

Navigational sea charts (T$14) are available from the Hydrographic Unit (☎ 24696, fax 23150, PO Box 72) at Touliki Naval Base in Nuku'alofa. Island groups are covered individually, as are Tonga's major harbours. But stocks may be running low and, at 1:72,600, these charts aren't accurate enough for GPS navigation.

A reduced-size sea chart of the Vava'u Group (T$15) is available from a number of places in Neiafu.

What to Bring

Given Tonga's comfortable and relatively consistent climate, clothing can be kept to a minimum. It can sometimes get chilly in winter, so take a light jacket or fleece, and bring wet-weather gear for any time of year. Bear in mind Tonga's dress etiquette (see Society & Conduct in the Facts about Tonga chapter for details).

Items like sunblock, tampons, contraceptives, mosquito repellent and contact lens solution should all be brought from home, as availability and price are unpredictable in Tonga. Film and camera equipment is also best brought from home. A few paperbacks to read on the beach, a torch (flashlight) for exploring caves, Swiss army knife, universal-type sink plug, mosquito net and your own snorkelling gear are also worth bringing.

If you'll be bushwalking or travelling by overnight ferry, a sleeping bag and ground cover will make life more comfortable in winter. A tent affords the freedom to stay overnight on a particularly appealing beach, forest or mountain (with prior permission of course), but will be unbearably stuffy from November to April.

RESPONSIBLE TOURISM

Dress code is important throughout Tonga, especially away from the larger towns. An effort to respect tradition will bring greater rewards for the traveller. See Society & Conduct in the Facts about Tonga chapter.

Do not buy souvenirs made from endangered animals or plants and don't collect or buy coral or shells, especially triton shells which protect reefs from the ravages of the crown-of-thorns starfish.

Tonga is not a signatory to the UN Convention on International Trade in Endangered Species (CITES) so even if you do splash the cash on something endangered it will most likely be confiscated on arrival in another country.

While Tonga has some fabulous reefs, many have been damaged by storms and by the overharvesting of subsistence foods such as shellfish and octopus. Be careful not to further damage this fragile environment and avoid walking on and destroying live coral (see both Diving and Snorkelling in the Activities special section for more information on reef preservation).

Non-biodegradable rubbish is taking its toll on Tonga's beauty spots and beaches. Litter disposal is a growing and largely unmanaged problem, with plastic bags and soft-drink bottles (smart move, Coca-Cola) the largest culprits. Tonga has no recycling facilities, so save the shopkeepers some money and use your own bags, not their plastic ones, and purify or boil water for drinking rather than buying soft drinks or bottled water.

See the Activities special section for information on responsible bushwalking.

TOURIST OFFICES
Local Tourist Offices
The Tonga Visitors Bureau (TVB) has its headquarters in Nuku'alofa (☎ 25334, fax 22120, **e** tvb@kalianet.to, **w** www.vacations.tvb.gov.to, PO Box 37), on Vuna Rd, and offices in Ha'apai and Vava'u.

Tourist Offices Abroad
For advance information, contact the TVB in Nuku'alofa or at one of the following offices:

Australia (☎ 02-9519 9700, fax 9519 9419) 642 King St, Newtown, Sydney, NSW 2042
New Zealand (☎ 09-634 1519, fax 636 8973) PO Box 24-054, Royal Oak, Auckland
USA (☎ 510-233 1381, **e** tonga@value.net) 4805 Driftwood Court, El Sobrante CA 94803-1805

VISAS & DOCUMENTS
Passport
Your passport must be valid for at least six months from the date of entry to Tonga.

Visas
A visa is not required to visit Tonga, but you will need to present a valid passport and an onward ticket on arrival to be granted a stay of 30 days (sometimes a stay of only three weeks is granted).

For information on arriving by yacht, see the Getting There & Away chapter.

Visa Extensions Your stay may be extended for up to six months at any immigration office; each island group has one, usually located next to the police station in the main town. The immigration office (☎ 24763) in Nuku'alofa is down the long corridor on the market side of the police station – head to the second window from the north end. It's open 9am to noon weekdays and 2pm to 4pm on Monday, Tuesday and Thursday. You'll need to surrender your passport overnight, pay T$26, present your onward ticket and provide evidence of sufficient funds for your stay in Tonga.

For details on long-term residency, see Work later in this chapter.

Travel Insurance
Always take out travel insurance. You should be covered for the worst-case scenario – eg, an accident that requires medical evacuation and repatriation. There's a wide variety of policies available, so check the small print. Some policies specifically exclude 'dangerous activities', which may include diving, motorcycling and even trekking.

If you are planning long-term travel, insurance may seem very expensive – but if you can't afford it, you certainly won't be able to afford a serious medical emergency overseas.

Driving Licence
International and home country driving licences are not valid in Tonga. You need a Tongan driving licence from the police station in Nuku'alofa or Neiafu. The cost depends on what you want to drive. There's a standard T$15 administration charge, then an additional T$5 for a scooter, T$10 for a private car or T$45 to drive a rental car. There are no tests; just produce your home driving licence, your passport and cash.

Some travellers have reported that licences are cheaper in Vava'u; check current prices with the TVB in Nuku'alofa.

Copies
Important documents (passport data page and visa page, credit cards, travel insurance policy, air tickets, driving licence etc) should be photocopied before you leave home. Leave a copy with someone at home and keep another copy with you, separate from the originals.

EMBASSIES & CONSULATES
Tongan Representatives Abroad

Tonga has diplomatic representatives in the following countries:

Australia (☎ 02-9929 8794) 158 Pacific Hwy, North Sydney, NSW 2059
Germany (☎ 040-2783 9350) Alster City, Osterbekstr 90a-22083, Hamburg
UK (☎ 020-7724 5828) 36 Molyneux St, London W1H 6AB
USA (☎ 808-521 5149) 220 South King St, Suite 1603, Honolulu, Hawaii
  (☎ 415-781 0365, e tania@sfconsulate.gov.to) 360 Post St, Suite 604, San Francisco, CA 94108

Foreign Representatives in Tonga

The following foreign diplomatic representatives are found in Nuku'alofa:

Australia *High Commission* (☎ 23244, fax 23243) Salote Rd
Canada (limited consular services available at the Australian High Commission)
China *Embassy* (☎ 24554, fax 24596) Vuna Rd
European Union *European Commission* (☎ 23820, fax 23869) Taufa'ahau Rd
Germany *Consulate* (☎ 23477, fax 23154) Taufa'ahau Rd
New Zealand *High Commission* (☎ 23122, fax 23487, e nzhcnuk@kalianet.to) Taufa'ahau Rd
Spain *Consulate* (☎ 25034) Hala'o Vave Rd
Sweden *Consulate* (☎ 22855, fax 22882) Salote Rd
UK *High Commission* (☎ 24395, fax 24109) Vuna Rd

It's important to understand just what the diplomatic representative of the country of which you are a citizen can and can't do to help if you get into trouble. Generally it won't be much help if the trouble you're in is remotely your own fault. Remember that you are bound by the laws of the country you are in and you'll get little sympathy if you end up in jail after committing a crime, even if such an action is perfectly legal in your own country.

In genuine emergencies you might get some assistance, but only if other channels have been exhausted. For example, if you must get home urgently, a free ticket is exceedingly unlikely – you are expected to have insurance for such an event. If your money and documents have been stolen, you may be assisted in getting a new passport, but a monetary loan is out of the question.

CUSTOMS

Travellers aged 18 and older may import up to 500 cigarettes and 2L of spirits duty-free. Animals, fruit and other plant products require a quarantine certificate. Firearms, ammunition, drugs and pornographic material may not be imported into Tonga under any circumstances.

MONEY
Currency

Tongan banknotes come in denominations of one, two, five, 10, 20 and 50 *pa'anga* (written T$1, T$2 etc). T$1 is divided into 100 *seniti* and these coins come in denominations of one, five, 10, 20 and 50 seniti. Older T$1 and T$2 coins sometimes turn up in change, but are now collectors' items. For further information on numismatics in Tonga, contact the National Reserve Bank of Tonga (☎ 24057, fax 24201) on Salote Rd, Nuku'alofa.

Exchange Rates

At the time of writing, exchange rates were:

country	unit		pa'anga
Australia	A$1	=	T$1.10
Canada	C$1	=	T$1.42
Euro zone	€1	=	T$1.83
Fiji	F$1	=	T$0.94
Japan	¥100	=	T$1.72
New Zealand	NZ$1	=	T$0.88
United Kingdom	UK£1	=	T$3.05
United States	US$1	=	T$2.16

Exchanging Money

A currency exchange window at the airport on Tongatapu is open for all international arrivals and departures. In Nuku'alofa and Neiafu you can change cash and travellers cheques at the Bank of Tonga, ANZ and MBF. The ANZ has automated teller machines. The Bank of Tonga also has offices in 'Ohonua ('Eua) and Pangai (Ha'apai) and at the time of writing offered the best exchange rates.

Banks are open 9am to 3.30pm or 4pm weekdays; in Nuku'alofa and Neiafu they're open 8.30am to 11.30am or noon Saturday as well. Money can be changed at the Treasury offices on the more remote islands of Niuatoputapu and Niuafo'ou.

Visitors must produce their passport to change currency at a bank or hotel. Several middle- and upper-range hotels will change cash, travellers cheques and even give advances on credit cards.

The International Dateline Hotel in Nuku-'alofa (24-hour currency exchange) and the Paradise International Hotel in Vava'u will exchange currency, but at a lower rate than the banks.

Cash Currency exchange is fairly straightforward. US, New Zealand and Australian dollars and British sterling are the most easily exchanged currencies (both cash and travellers cheques), but euros and yen are also acceptable, as are Fijian dollars.

Travellers Cheques All brands of travellers cheques are acceptable and fetch 4% to 5% more than cash. There is a nominal transaction charge of 10 seniti per cheque.

ATMs The ANZ is the only bank with automated teller machines (ATMs). There is a 24-hour machine at the Nuku'alofa branch (another available inside during business hours) and one inside the Neiafu branch. These machines accept credit and debit cards from Visa, MasterCard and Cirrus.

Credit & Debit Cards Visa and Master-Card are the most frequently accepted cards in Tonga; an increasing number of tourist facilities, shops and restaurants (especially on Tongatapu) accept them.

The ANZ has also introduced an Eftpos credit/debit card payment system so you can, in theory, also get a cash advance when you shop (though most businesses add a 5% service fee).

Cash advances on Visa and MasterCard can be made at the Bank of Tonga in Nuku-'alofa, 'Eua, Pangai and Neiafu. In Neiafu and Nuku'alofa you can get cash advances

also at the ANZ (Visa and MasterCard) should you not be able to use the ATM. The MBF is not as user-friendly and only gives advances on MasterCard.

Some of the bigger hotels and resorts that exchange money (see earlier) will give cash advances on credit cards (including a commission of up to 10%).

International Transfers Given the amount of money sent home by Tongans overseas, it's no surprise that two multinational money-transfer companies are heavily represented in Tonga. Western Union (W www.western union.com) has dozens of offices, while MoneyGram (W www.moneygram.com) is represented by the Bank of Tonga. Check out their Web sites for contact details in your home country.

Both companies charge similarly (for example, the sender of US$800 pays roughly US$50 in charges) for transferring money around the globe and their services are quick (a matter of minutes) and straightforward.

Security

Travellers cheques are one of the safest ways to carry money (be sure to keep the receipts separate) and insure against credit/debit card theft or fraud. Keep a handful of small denomination notes handy for day-to-day transactions but put the rest in a money-belt or another safe place.

Theft from the person is very rare in Tonga. On the other hand, things left lying around in hotels or on the beach can wander. See Security under Dangers & Annoyances later in this chapter.

Costs

For imported goods such as electronic equipment, film and packaged foods, prices in Tonga are considerably higher than in the USA or Europe, and a bit higher than in Australia or New Zealand. Import duty on cars and motor spares is very high.

Food and accommodation are generally more reasonably priced than in other South Pacific countries – considerably lower than in French Polynesia but slightly higher than in Samoa and Fiji. You can get by quite

Money in Tonga

In the early 1800s, when the young William Mariner explained the monetary system used by Europeans to the Tongan chief Finau, the chief immediately grasped its advantages over Tonga's traditional barter system. He also perceived a potential drawback of such a system and deemed it unsuitable for Tonga. From Mariner's book:

'If money were made of iron and could be converted into knives, axes and chisels there would be some sense in placing a value on it; but as it is, I see none. If a man has more yams than he wants, let him exchange some of them away for pork... Certainly money is much handier and more convenient but then, as it will not spoil by being kept, people will store it up instead of sharing it out as a chief ought to do, and thus become selfish... I understand now very well what it is that makes the *papalangis* so selfish – it is this money!'

Chief Finau had been disappointed to find so little of value to him on the *Port-au-Prince*. Unlike Captain Cook's ships, which had carried all sorts of valuables, the ship Mariner had travelled in contained only whale oil, bits of iron and 10,000 pieces of metal resembling *pa'anga* (bean-shaped playing pieces used in the game called *lafo*).

Finau had taken the pieces of metal to be worthless and assumed that the ship belonged to a very poor man indeed (King George's cook, perhaps – a cook being the lowest rank in Tongan society at the time). Having ordered the ship to be burned, the chief later realised with regret that he had burned the ship of an extremely rich man without first securing its pa'anga. Not surprisingly, the Tongan unit of currency is now called the pa'anga.

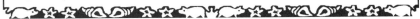

comfortably in Tonga on T$50 a day and can survive on T$30 a day.

Tipping & Bargaining
Tipping and bargaining are not the usual custom in Tonga, though in some tourist facilities they do occur. Dances (see Arts in the Facts about Tonga chapter) are among the few social occasions at which tipping is considered acceptable.

Taxes & Refunds
All prices in Tonga include 5% VAT. Hotel prices are subject to an additional 2.5% room tax which is usually, but not always, included in the quoted room price. No tax refunds are available to foreigners.

POST & COMMUNICATIONS
Post
Postal services are slow but usually reliable; service to Europe, North America and Australasia is quite good. There's a post office on every major island, generally open 8.30am or 9am to 4pm weekdays, except holidays, with special opening hours and reduced services around the Christmas and New Year period.

If possible, avoid posting anything from the Niuas, particularly Niuafo'ou, since communications are limited and weeks can go by without mail service.

Postage rates for letters under 15g are 60 seniti to the South Pacific region (including Australia and New Zealand) and 80 seniti to the rest of the world. Postcard stamps cost 45 seniti to anywhere in the world.

Parcels mailed to you in Tonga may, upon collection, incur import duty to the value of the goods enclosed.

Tongan postage stamps are very collectible. They depict colourful shells and birds or commemorate such events as royal birthdays, exhibitions and visits by foreign heads of state; the island of Niuafo'ou has its own unique and colourful stamps. Old and unusual stamps may be purchased at the Philatelic Bureau (☎ 22455) upstairs at the GPO in Nuku'alofa.

Telephone & Fax
Tonga Communications Corporation (TCC) has offices in Nuku'alofa (Tongatapu), 'Ohonua ('Eua), Pangai (Ha'apai), Neiafu (Vava'u), Hihifo (Niuatoputapu) and also Niuafo'ou. International telephone and fax

services are available. Some offices are open 24 hours a day, seven days a week.

Reverse charge (collect) calls can be made only to Australia, New Zealand, USA, UK and South Pacific island nations.

Telephone calling cards from some international systems, (including AT&T and NZ Telecom) are accepted. Check the compatibility of your card before leaving home. Visa and MasterCard are accepted at all TCC offices.

There's a T$1 connection charge for international calls. From Nuku'alofa calls to Australia, New Zealand and Pacific islands are T$1.20 a minute, while calls to the rest of the world are T$2.40 a minute. Calls on prepaid cards are more expensive, at T$1.35 and T$2.70 respectively. From Vava'u and Ha'apai calls from the phone office are more expensive still, at around T$5 for three minutes to Pacific Rim countries (not including the USA) ãnd around T$9.50 to the rest of the world.

'Station to Station' calls (where you speak to whoever answers) are slightly cheaper than 'Person to Person' calls, but with a Person to Person call an operator ensures that the person you want is on the phone before connecting you. If they can't be reached you don't pay.

Local calls are 10 seniti per minute within the same island, and T$1.40 for three minutes (and 46 seniti per minute thereafter) to other islands in Tonga.

The telecommunications industry in Tonga was undergoing a restructure at the time of writing and, if the papers are to be believed, prices are set to fall. A GSM mobile phone system is also planned.

The emergency phone number throughout Tonga is ☎ 911, the international operator is ☎ 913 and directory assistance is ☎ 910.

Tonga's country code is ☎ 676; there are no local area codes.

Coconut Wireless

A rather less orthodox means of communication is used throughout the islands: the 'coconut wireless'. All over Tonga, especially in Tongatapu, people somehow know what's going on in government, what each foreigner is up to (they're watching you), who is sleeping with whom, what the king is doing at the moment and so on – while it's happening or immediately thereafter.

Email & Internet Access

The state telecommunications monopoly TCC runs Kalianet, Tonga's only Internet Service Provider. Internet access is expensive (expect to pay between T$8 and T$15 per hour) and only available on Tongatapu where the cheapest access is at TCC's international call centre in Nuku'alofa. However, a few cybercafes are springing up around town and some guesthouses now offer Internet access.

Vava'u has an email-only server and Ha'apai has no server at all. In the few places it's available on these island groups, sending/receiving email cost T$5/1.

Remember that if you want to check your email account back home via a Web-based email account (like Yahoo), you'll need your incoming (POP or IMAP) mail server name, your account name and your password.

See Post & Communications in the relevant chapters for more information.

INTERNET RESOURCES

The World Wide Web is a rich resource for travellers. You can research your trip, hunt down bargain air fares, book hotels, check on weather conditions or chat with locals and other travellers about the best places to visit (or avoid!).

There's no better place to start your Web explorations than the Lonely Planet Web site ([W] www.lonelyplanet.com). Here you will find succinct summaries on travelling to most places on earth, postcards from other travellers and the Thorn Tree bulletin board, where you can ask questions before you go or dispense advice when you get back. You can also find travel news and updates to many of our most popular guidebooks, and the subWWWay section links you to the most useful travel resources elsewhere on the Web.

An increasing number of Tongan businesses have Web pages, though some are not updated regularly. A good place to start looking for information is the Web site of the Tonga Visitors Bureau (W www.vacat ions.tvb.gov.to). Other general sites are Tonga on the Net (W www.tongatapu.net .to) and Tonga Online (W www.tongaon line.com). A site with good links to activity operators is the Tonga Tourism Project's 'Tonga Holidays' site (W www.tongaholid ay.com). The Royal Tongan Airlines site (W www.flyroyaltongan.com) gives sched ule information, but should be treated as a rough guide only.

BOOKS

Given the brief history of its written lan guage and relatively obscure geographical position, a surprising number of books have been written about Tonga.

Many books are published in different editions by different publishers in different countries. As a result, a book might be a hardcover rarity in one country while it's readily available in paperback in another. Fortunately, bookshops and libraries search by title or author, so your local bookshop or library is best placed to advise you on the availability of the following recommenda tions. The Internet has revolutionised the search for out of print books. The Amazon site (W www.amazon.com) is a good start ing point.

Some of these books, though, are avail able only in Tonga and can be ordered from the main branch of the Friendly Islands Bookshop (☎ 23787, fax 23631, e fibs@ kalianet.to, Box 124) in Nuku'alofa.

Lonely Planet

If you're travelling farther afield in the Pa cific, check out Lonely Planet's *South Pacific* guide, and for languages of the re gion, including Tonga, *South Pacific phrase book*. The Health section later in this chapter offers further suggestions for Lonely Planet titles and there's a complete list of Lonely Planet publications at the back of this book.

Guidebooks

If you're travelling by yacht in Tonga or else where in the Pacific, the hard-to-find *Land falls of Paradise: The Guide to the Pacific Islands* by Earl R Hinz is highly recom mended. The author, who has been a Pacific yachtie for much of his life, provides all the nitty-gritty on anchorages, navigation, mar inas, fees and officialdom throughout the South and central Pacific region.

The Cruising Yachtsman's Guide to the Kingdom of Tonga by Colin Bailey, a more recent yachting book, and *A Yachtsman's Guide to Ha'apai* by Phil Cregeen, are avail able at the Friendly Islands Bookshop in Nuku'alofa.

Travel

An entertaining account of travel through the South Seas is *Slow Boats Home* by Gavin Young, the sequel to his earlier book *Slow Boats to China*. Combined, they recount the author's 1979 around-the-world voyage aboard a wide range of maritime transport. Although there are only a few pages dealing with Tonga, a good part of his journey is aboard a Tongan boat. It's a worthwhile read for any South Pacific traveller. It is out of print now but you might turn up a copy at second-hand shops.

The Pacific by Simon Winchester is an entertaining but rather hastily assembled ac count of his journalistic journeys around the great ocean. *Transit of Venus: Travels in the Pacific* by Julian Evans chronicles the au thor's shoestring travels around the Pacific by boat and ship. It includes a very enter taining chapter on Tonga and is probably the best modern travelogue about the Pa cific. Unfortunately it's now out of print, and might take some hunting down.

Then there's the book travellers love to hate, *The Happy Isles of Oceania: Paddling the Pacific* by Paul Theroux. This time, the perpetually miserable Theroux finds him self kayaking around in the South Pacific islands. Cynics will love the amusingly downbeat prose; his observations all seem to have been made through grey-coloured glasses and he is particularly hard on Tonga in general and Nuku'alofa in particular.

History

Tonga Islands: William Mariner's Account by Dr John Martin was originally published as *An Account of the Natives of the Tonga Islands* in 1817, and is the best work available on the nature of pre-Christian Tonga. It tells the story of the capture of the *Port-au-Prince* and Mariner's enforced stay on Tonga from 1805 to 1809. The religion, language, customs and the lifestyle of the Tongan people are discussed. It makes very interesting and entertaining reading. *The Tonga Book* by Paul W Dale is a contemporary reworking of Mariner's story.

Island Kingdom: Tonga Ancient and Modern by Ian Campbell is an up-to-date, very readable history of Tonga.

Pathways to the Tongan Present by Kurt Düring is an introduction to the ancient history and archaeology of Tonga, with interesting maps and photos. *Archaeology of Tonga* by WE McKern is an academic work describing a detailed archaeological study made here in 1920–21.

The Journals of Captain Cook, edited by JC Beaglehole, is a straight-from-the-horse's-mouth account of early exploration in the Pacific and elsewhere. *The Mutiny on Board the HMS Bounty* by William Bligh is taken from his journals during and after his command of the *Bounty*.

Slavers in Paradise by HE Maude is a tragic and enlightening account of the kidnapping of Pacific Islanders by the Peruvian slave traders in the early 1860s.

A Dream of Islands by Gavan Dawes deals with the lives and perspectives of island-inspired authors and artists such as Gauguin, Melville and Stevenson.

Shirley Baker and the King of Tonga by Noel Rutherford tells the story of Revd Shirley Baker and King Tupou I.

The Fire Has Jumped, edited by Garth Rogers, gives a rather disorganised but interesting account of the volcanic eruptions on Niuafo'ou in the mid-1940s and the subsequent resettlement of the people who lived on the island.

The King of Tonga: King Taufa'ahau Tupou IV by Nelson Eustis is a biography not only of Tonga's current king but also of the royal lineage that preceded him. It concentrates particularly on his mother, the beloved Queen Salote.

Salote: Queen of Paradise by Margaret Hixon and *Queen Salote of Tonga: The Story of an Era 1900–1965* by Elizabeth Wood-Ellem both give an insight into the popular monarch's reign. The book by Ellem, who lived in Tonga for many years, is warm, incisive and highly recommended.

Missionaries & Churches

Church & State in Tonga by the Tongan historian Sione Lalukefu gives an account of the political influence of Wesleyan Methodist Missionaries between 1822 and 1875. It's now out of print, though.

In Some Sense the Work of an Individual: Alfred Willis and the Tongan Anglican Mission, 1902–1920 by Stephen L Donald tells the story of the introduction and development of the Anglican Church in the Kingdom of Tonga.

Sociology & Anthropology

Tongan Society by Edward Gifford, the definitive 1929 study, was reprinted in New York in 1985 and was being reprinted again at the time of writing.

The New Friendly Islanders by Kenneth Bain deals with the recent social changes and how they relate to Tongan tradition and world trends. It's an interesting and entertaining read.

Becoming Tongan: An Ethnography of Childhood by Helen Morton is a study of the raising of children in Tongan society.

Kinship to Kingship: Gender Hierarchy and State Formation in the Tongan Islands by Christine Gailey is an ethnohistorical anthropology book presenting a feminist view of women's loss of power over a 300-year period as the state of Tonga evolved.

Language

Introduction to the Tongan Language by Edgar Tu'inukuafe is a simple introduction to Tongan grammar, phrases and vocabulary. *Tongan Grammar* by C Maxwell Churchward is a complete study of the Tongan language, but you need to be familiar with the principles of linguistics.

For serious students, Eric Shumway has put together *An Intensive Course in Tongan*, with 200 lessons accompanied by 23 cassette tapes. It costs around US$100. Contact the Institute for Polynesian Studies, BYU, PO Box 1979, Laie, HI 96762, USA. The book, and a limited number of tapes, are available through the Friendly Islands Bookshop in Nuku'alofa.

The Student's English-Tongan and Tongan-English Dictionary by Rev Richard & 'Ofa Thompson and *A Simplified Dictionary of Modern Tongan* by Edgar Tu'inukuafe are good, simple paperback Tongan-English dictionaries. CM Churchward's *Tongan-English Dictionary* is a more complete (though somewhat dated) English-Tongan and Tongan-English tome.

Art, Music & Dance

The Art of Tonga by Keith St Cartmail is a high-quality coffee-table book on Tongan art and artefacts.

Sounds of Change in Tonga: Dance, Music and Cultural Dynamics in a Polynesian Kingdom by Ad Linkels is a study of changes taking place in traditional music and dance in Tonga.

Otuhaka by Kik Velt is a detailed diagrammatic explanation of movements in this ancient sit-down dance. *Poetry in Motion* by Adrienne Kaeppler is a detailed description and explanation of Tongan dancing, for the specialist. Also by Kaeppler is *From the Stone Age to the Space Age in 200 Years*, a fine book detailing the evolution of Tongan art and society up to the present day.

Tapa in Tonga by Wendy Arbeit presents photos and text showing and explaining the manufacture, uses and significance of tapa in Tonga. *Making Mats and Barkcloth in the Kingdom of Tonga* by KE James gives more information about Tongan mats and tapa.

Cookbooks

The Niu Idea Cookbook (The Peace Corps), available only at the Friendly Islands Bookshop, is a good collection of recipes for delicious Tongan dishes.

The Tastes of Tonga by the Vaiola Hospital Board of Visitors is another fine book containing a selection of Tongan and international recipes.

Nature

Birds of Fiji, Tonga & Samoa by Dick Watling is the definitive book on the birds of the South Pacific region. It includes lovely colour illustrations of all the region's endemic and migratory birds.

Field Guide to Landbirds of Tonga by Claudia Matavalea is available at the Tongan Wildlife Park and at the Friendly Islands Bookshop in Nuku'alofa.

Tongan Herbal Medicine by W Arthur Whistler is a good book relating how Tongans use the vegetation around them to heal illnesses and wounds.

Waterproof copies of *Reef Fish In-A-Pocket – Indo-Pacific* by Paul Humann & Ned Deloach includes many photos of fish found in Tongan waters, while *The Snorkeller's Guide to the Coral Reef* by Paddy Ryan is a practical manual and guide to marine life.

Residents' Accounts

The most famous account by a resident of Tonga is of course the account of William Mariner's sojourn in pre-Christian times; see the preceding History section.

Friendly Isles: A Tale of Tonga; *'Utulei, My Tongan Home*; and *The Tongan Past* by Patricia Ledyard all relate anecdotes of Tongan life. They make easy, interesting reading and give an insight into Tonga's recent past. (See the boxed text on the author in the Vava'u Group chapter.)

South Sea Reminiscences: Mrs Emma Schober in the Kingdom of Tonga 1902–1921 is the autobiography of the postal bride of a German trader who lived in Tonga.

Tales of the South Pacific; *Rascals in Paradise*; and *Return to Paradise*, by James Michener, are collections of short stories dealing with life in, and observations of, the South Pacific from WWII onwards.

Miscellaneous

Tonga the Friendly Islands by Fred Eckert is a fine, glossy book of photographs of people and places.

Pacific Tourism: As Islanders See It, published by the University of the South Pacific in Fiji, contains essays by islanders on the increase of tourism and, consequently, outside influences on their cultures and lifestyles – a pertinent moral dilemma.

Tongan Place Names by Edward Gifford gives 4776 place names, their meanings and explanations.

A fun book for yachties and mariners is *Stars Over Tonga* by Kik Velt. It has lots of information about Tongan tradition and language, and astronomical descriptions and 'star charts' for Tonga.

NEWSPAPERS & MAGAZINES

The Tonga Chronicle, a bilingual paper published in Tongan and English, is the official paper of the Tongan government and tells only what the government wants foreigners in Tonga to know about – crime and other news considered unpleasant goes unreported. Most news is local, with little information about the outside world. It comes out on Thursday and costs T$1.

Taimi Tonga (Tonga Times), published in Tongan, is an independent newspaper representing the views of the middle class both inside Tonga and abroad. It's a very middle-of-the-road paper, but since it is independently published and doesn't only give the official government line, it's considered pretty challenging for Tonga. It comes out every Tuesday and Thursday and costs T$1.

The most radical newspaper is the *Ko e Kele'a* (The Conch Shell), published in Tongan by the Human Rights and Democracy Movement. Suffice to say that you'll read things here that don't appear in the *Chronicle*! This paper comes out as the need arises, usually monthly or bimonthly, and costs 80 seniti.

For the best read and the best coverage of Tongan issues at home and abroad, try the bimonthly news magazine, *Matangi Tonga* (Wind of Tonga). It's published in English and has been known to address quite sensitive issues. It costs T$3.35.

Pacific Magazine, a wide-ranging business/news magazine, covers current affairs in the Pacific. The focus is often on Fiji, but it's a well-researched and interesting read.

The Friendly Islands Bookshop in Nuku'alofa carries all the Tongan newspapers and a range of international newspapers and magazines. English-language newspapers for sale include the *New Zealand Herald* and *Fiji Times*, both dailies arriving in Tonga on a weekly basis, *The Guardian Weekly* and the American *Weekend Herald*. Among the magazines you'll find *The Economist* (a weekly international business magazine) and the international edition of *Time*.

RADIO & TV

The government-owned Radio Tonga, A3Z and Four FM, broadcasts a mix of traditional Tongan music, international rock music and worldwide news between 88.6 and 97 FM. Radio Nuku'alofa is found on 88.8 FM and is not bad really. Vava'u also has its own radio station, FM1, at 89.3 FM.

Radio New Zealand International (W www .rnzi.com) broadcasts to the region on 11725kHz, 15120kHz, 15175kHz and 17675kHz. Radio Australia (W www.abc .net.au/ra) can be found on 12080kHz and 17715kHz pretty much all day, while the BBC World Service (W www.bbc.co.uk/worldservice) is broadcast at 9580kHz, 9740kHz, 11955kHz and 15360kHz.

Only Tongatapu and Vava'u have television. Tongatapu has two TV stations, Channel 7 – a private Christian broadcasting station – and TV Tonga, the government channel. In Vava'u there's just Channel 9 which broadcasts religious programs and 1970s reruns. In the Niuas, you can pick up American Samoan broadcasting on very clear days.

BBC News 24 is aired on TV Tonga at 8pm weekdays.

VIDEO SYSTEMS

Tonga has both the PAL system used in Australasia and most of Western Europe and the NTSC system used in North America and Japan. So if you want to record or buy video tapes to play back home be sure to check the compatibility.

PHOTOGRAPHY & VIDEO
Film & Equipment

Film is expensive in Tonga, so stock up before you leave home. In the shops of

Nuku'alofa the average cost of 100ASA 35mm colour print film is T$7/8 for a roll of 24/36 exposures (200ASA and 400ASA film is available but more expensive). APS film is T$13/15 for 25/40 exposures (100ASA). Colour slide film is harder to find and a roll of 24/36 200ASA costs around T$16/19. Film in Vava'u and Ha'apai is more expensive and the range smaller.

Colour print processing can be done in Nuku'alofa (T$14.70/21 for 24/36 prints). There's nowhere in Tonga to process slides or black-and-white prints.

Passport photos (T$2.10 per photo on average) are available from a few places around Tonga.

Good quality camera equipment is very difficult to get in Tonga and impossible to fix so bring everything from home. Useful accessories include a small flash, a cable release, a polarising filter (for photography in the middle of the day) and a lens cleaning kit. Silica-gel packs and resealable plastic bags are essential protection against Tonga's high humidity. A flexible, insulated and light-proof cool bag will help protect sensitive film.

If you're shooting video you'll need to buy all your tapes before you arrive and may wish to bring a 'surge breaker' or 'spike buster' to protect your AC adaptor from Tonga's erratic power supply.

Technical Tips

Points worth remembering about photography in Tonga include the heat, humidity, very fine sand, tropical sunlight, equatorial shadows and the wonderful opportunities for underwater photography. Don't leave your camera for long in direct sunlight and don't store used film for long in the humid conditions, as it will fade.

The best times to take photographs on sunny days are the first two hours after sunrise and the last two before sunset. This brings out the best colours and takes advantage of the colour-enhancing, long, red rays cast by a low sun. At other times, colours will be washed out by harsh sunlight and glare, although it's possible to counter this by using a polarising (UV) filter. If you're shooting on

beaches, it's important to adjust for glare from water or sand (and keep your photographic equipment well away from them!).

When photographing outdoors, take light readings on the subject and not the brilliant background or your shots will all turn out underexposed. Likewise for people shots: dark faces will appear featureless if you set the exposure for background light.

Photographing People

If you think the quest for the perfect 'people shot' is a photographer's greatest challenge, go to Tonga. It would be safe to say that nowhere else in the world will you find so many willing and photogenic subjects for your camera as in Tonga. In fact, if you're not quick about it, your perfect 'people shot' could easily turn into a crowd scene!

Having said that, some Tongans may be suspicious of your motives or want money to be photographed. Others may simply be self-conscious about their appearance.

Always ask permission to photograph and always respect the wishes of anyone who declines. Never try to snap a picture anyway.

Though kids often just want to appear in your photographs for a laugh, sometimes your subjects will want a copy of the photo. Many tourists agree enthusiastically to do this when on the spot but never get around to sending the pictures, which doesn't help the path of future travellers. Don't make this mistake.

TIME

Tonga promotes itself as the 'land where time begins'; along with the Chukotka Peninsula in far eastern Russia, Tonga is the first place to see a new day.

Due to an odd kink in the International Date Line, Tonga is actually 20 minutes east of the 180th meridian, placing it 13 hours ahead of Greenwich Mean Time. Noon in Tonga is 3pm the previous day in Los Angeles, 11pm the previous day in London and 9am the same day in Sydney. In the Samoas, which are directly north of Tonga, the time would be noon the previous day! When New Zealand is on summer daylight saving time, Tonga and New Zealand share the same time; the rest of the year New Zealand is one hour behind.

ELECTRICITY

Power in Tonga is 240V AC, 50Hz. Three-pronged plugs used in New Zealand and Australia are OK here. European appliances require a plug adaptor. US appliances require a plug adaptor plus a voltage converter. Bring a 'surge breaker' or 'spike buster' to protect sensitive appliances from Tonga's erratic power supply.

WEIGHTS & MEASURES

Tonga uses the standard metric system for everything except land area, which is measured in acres (though this is slowly changing). For help converting between metric and imperial units, see the table inside the back cover of this book.

LAUNDRY

All places to stay in Tonga make some provision for guests' laundry needs, offering a laundry service, a place to wash your own clothes, or both. Unfortunately, because most places just use cold water really dirty clothes are difficult to get clean. Nuku'alofa (Tongatapu) and Neiafu (Vava'u) have commercial laundries. Their average price is T$2 to T$3 for a whole load.

TOILETS

Tonga has flush toilets. There are a few public toilets and you can usually duck into a restaurant in an emergency. In remote areas pit toilets are used.

HEALTH

Travel health depends on your predeparture preparations, your daily health care while travelling and how you handle any medical problem that does develop. While the potential dangers can seem quite frightening, in reality few travellers experience anything more than upset stomachs or 'Polynesian paralysis' (laziness).

Predeparture Planning

Immunisations Plan ahead for getting your vaccinations – some of them require

more than one injection, while some vaccinations should not be given together. Note that some vaccinations should not be given during pregnancy or to people with allergies, so discuss this with your doctor.

It is recommended you seek medical advice at least six weeks before travel. Be aware

Medical Kit Check List

Following is a list of items you should consider including in your medical kit – consult your pharmacist for brands available in your country.

- ☐ **Aspirin or paracetamol (acetaminophen in the USA)** – for pain or fever
- ☐ **Antihistamine** – for allergies, eg, hay fever; to ease the itch from insect bites or stings; and to prevent motion sickness
- ☐ **Cold and flu tablets, throat lozenges and nasal decongestant**
- ☐ **Multivitamins** – consider for long trips, when dietary vitamin intake may be inadequate
- ☐ **Antibiotics** – consider including these if you're travelling well off the beaten track; see your doctor, as they must be prescribed, and carry the prescription with you
- ☐ **Loperamide or diphenoxylate** –'blockers' for diarrhoea
- ☐ **Prochlorperazine or metaclopramide** – for nausea and vomiting
- ☐ **Rehydration mixture** – to prevent dehydration, which may occur, for example, during bouts of diarrhoea; particularly important when travelling with children
- ☐ **Insect repellent, sunscreen, lip balm and eye drops**
- ☐ **Calamine lotion, sting relief spray or aloe vera** – to ease irritation from sunburn and insect bites or stings
- ☐ **Antifungal cream or powder** – for fungal skin infections and thrush
- ☐ **Antiseptic (such as povidone-iodine)** – for cuts and grazes
- ☐ **Bandages, Band-Aids (plasters) and other wound dressings**
- ☐ **Water purification tablets or iodine**
- ☐ **Scissors, tweezers and a thermometer** – note that mercury thermometers are prohibited by airlines

that children and pregnant women are often at a greater risk of disease.

Discuss your requirements with your doctor, but vaccinations you should consider for this trip include the following (for more details about the diseases themselves, see the individual disease entries later in this section).

Diphtheria & Tetanus Vaccinations for these two diseases are usually combined and are recommended for everyone. After an initial course of three injections (usually given in childhood), boosters are necessary every 10 years.

Hepatitis A Hepatitis A vaccine (eg, Avaxim, Havrix 1440 or Vaqta) provides long-term immunity (possibly more than 10 years) after an initial injection and a booster at six to 12 months. Alternatively, an injection of gamma globulin can provide short-term protection against hepatitis A – two to six months, depending on the dose given. It is not a vaccine, but a ready-made antibody collected from blood donations. It is reasonably effective and, unlike the vaccine, it is protective immediately, but because it is a blood product, there are current concerns about its long-term safety. Hepatitis A vaccine is also available in a combined form, Twinrix, with hepatitis B vaccine. Three injections over a six-month period are required, the first two providing substantial protection against hepatitis A.

Hepatitis B Travellers who should consider vaccination against hepatitis B include those on a long trip, as well as those visiting countries where there are high levels of hepatitis B infection, where blood transfusions may not be adequately screened or where sexual contact or needle sharing is a possibility. Vaccination involves three injections, with a booster at 12 months. More rapid courses are available if necessary.

Polio Everyone should keep up to date with this vaccination, which is normally given in childhood. A booster every 10 years will maintain immunity.

Typhoid Vaccination against typhoid is recommended for travel in Tonga, though the risk is small. It is now available either as an injection or as capsules taken orally.

Carry proof of your vaccinations – you'll need a yellow fever vaccination certificate if you're entering Tonga from an infected area, such as sub-Saharan Africa or Latin America.

Health Insurance Make sure that you have adequate health insurance. See Travel

Insurance under Visas & Documents earlier in this chapter for details.

Travel Health Guides If you are planning to be away or travelling in remote areas for a long period of time, consider taking a more detailed health guide.

For all-round health advice try Lonely Planet's *Healthy Travel – Australia, New Zealand & the Pacific.* Dr Richard Dawood's *Travellers' Health* (Oxford University Press, 1995) is comprehensive, easy to read, authoritative and highly recommended, although rather large to lug around.

Lonely Planet's *Travel with Children* is a helpful book for travelling with younger children anywhere in the world.

There are also a number of excellent travel health sites on the Internet. From the Lonely Planet home page there are links (**W** www.lonelyplanet.com/weblinks/wlheal.htm) to both the World Health Organization and the US Centers for Disease Control & Prevention.

Other Preparations Make sure you're healthy before you start travelling. If you are going on a long trip make sure your teeth are OK. If you wear glasses take a spare pair and your lens prescription.

If you require a particular medication take an adequate supply, as you may find it's not

---

Everyday Health

Normal body temperature is up to 37°C (98.6°F); more than 2°C (4°F) higher indicates a high fever. The normal adult pulse rate is 60 to 100 per minute (children 80 to 100, babies 100 to 140). As a general rule the pulse increases about 20 beats per minute for each 1°C (2°F) rise in fever.

Respiration (breathing) rate is also an indicator of illness. Count the number of breaths per minute: Between 12 and 20 is normal for adults and older children (up to 30 for younger children, 40 for babies). People with a high fever or serious respiratory illness breathe more quickly than normal. More than 40 shallow breaths a minute may indicate pneumonia.

available locally. Take part of the packaging showing the generic name, rather than the brand, which will make getting replacements easier. It's a good idea to have a legible prescription or letter from your doctor to show that you legally use the medication, to avoid any problems.

Basic Rules

Food There is an old colonial adage which says: 'If you can cook it, boil it or peel it you can eat it...otherwise forget it'. Vegetables and fruit should be washed with purified water or peeled where possible. Beware of ice cream which is sold in the street or anywhere it might have been melted and refrozen; if there's any doubt (eg, a power cut in the last day or two), steer well clear. Shellfish such as mussels, oysters and clams should be avoided as well as undercooked meat, particularly in the form of mince. Note also that steaming does not make shellfish safe for eating.

Don't be paranoid about sampling local foods, though – it's all part of the travel experience and Tongan feasts shouldn't be missed. If a place looks clean and well run and the vendor also looks clean and healthy, then the food is probably safe. In general, places that are packed with travellers or locals will be fine, while empty restaurants are questionable. The food in busy restaurants is cooked and eaten quite quickly with little standing around and is probably not reheated.

Water The number one rule is *be careful of the water* and especially ice. If you don't know for certain that the water is safe, assume the worst and either purify or boil it.

Tap water in the larger towns of Nuku-'alofa (Tongatapu) and Neiafu (Vava'u) is usually safe to drink, but it doesn't taste too good – it has such a high natural mineral (limestone) content that you can see a white film floating on top of the water after you boil it.

Tap water is more suspect out in the villages or in the bush, and most people in Tonga drink rainwater, which is collected in concrete rainwater tanks *(vaisima)*. Remember that rainwater is only as clean as whatever it's kept in – while most rainwater is fine to drink, there's the possibility of contamination if it's not properly stored. Take special care immediately after a cyclone or bad storm.

Plastic bottles are fast becoming a litter problem in Tonga, so try and avoid buying imported bottled water – rainwater often tastes just as good. Reputable brands of bottled water are generally safe, although in some places bottles may be refilled with tap water so only use water from containers with a serrated seal.

Take care with fruit juice, particularly if water may have been added. Almost all milk available in Tonga is UHT which is fine if it is kept hygienically. Tea or coffee should be OK, since the water should have been boiled.

Water Purification The simplest way of purifying water is to boil it thoroughly and vigorously.

Consider purchasing a water filter for a long trip. There are two main kinds of filter. Total filters take out all parasites, bacteria and viruses and make water safe to drink. They are often expensive, but can be more cost-effective (and environmentally friendly) than buying bottled water. Simple filters (which can even be a nylon mesh bag) take out dirt and larger foreign bodies from the water so that chemical solutions work much more effectively; if water is dirty, chemical solutions may not work at all. It's very important when buying a filter to read the specifications, so that you know exactly what it removes from the water and what it doesn't. Simple filtering will not remove all dangerous organisms, so if you cannot boil water it should be treated chemically.

Chlorine tablets will kill many pathogens, but not some parasites like giardia and amoebic cysts. Iodine is more effective in purifying water and is available in tablet form. Follow the directions carefully and remember that too much iodine can be harmful.

Medical Care in Tonga

Medical care is limited in Tonga, especially away from Tongatapu and Vava'u, and all serious medical problems should be taken to New Zealand.

Vaiola hospital (Tongatapu) is the best in the country. Staff are well trained, but the facilities and equipment are not great. There are several private physicians in Tongatapu and Vava'u (see those chapters for details). The hospitals in Neiafu (Vava'u) and Hihifo (Ha'apai) are competent with minor ailments and will dispense medicines but are poorly equipped to deal with serious medical problems. An entire day should be set aside for a visit to hospital clinics. Nonresidents' consultations cost T$20 between 8.30am and 4.30pm weekdays (T$30 after hours). Medicines are charged at the market rate plus T$5 dispensary fee.

Medical Problems & Treatment

Self-diagnosis and treatment can be risky, so you should always seek medical help. An embassy, consulate, guesthouse or top-end hotel can usually recommend a local doctor or clinic.

Although we do give drug dosages in this section, they are for emergency use only. Correct diagnosis is vital. In this section we have used the generic names for medications – check with a pharmacist for brands available locally.

Note that antibiotics should ideally be administered only under medical supervision. Take only the recommended dose at the prescribed intervals and use the whole course, even if the illness seems to be cured earlier. Stop immediately if there are any serious reactions and don't use the antibiotic at all if you are unsure that you have the correct one. Some people are allergic to commonly prescribed antibiotics such as penicillin; carry this information (eg, on a bracelet) when travelling.

Environmental Hazards

Heat Exhaustion Dehydration and salt deficiency can cause heat exhaustion. Take time to acclimatise to high temperatures, drink sufficient liquids and do not do anything too physically demanding. Salt deficiency is characterised by fatigue, lethargy, headaches, giddiness and muscle cramps; salt tablets may help, but adding extra salt to your food or taking a rehydration mixture is better.

Anhidrotic heat exhaustion is a rare form of heat exhaustion that is caused by an inability to sweat. It tends to affect people who have been in a hot climate for some time, rather than newcomers. It can progress to heatstroke. Treatment involves removal to a cooler climate.

Heatstroke This serious, occasionally fatal, condition can occur if the body's heat-regulating mechanism breaks down and the body temperature rises to dangerous levels. Long, continuous periods of exposure to high temperatures and insufficient fluids can leave you vulnerable to heatstroke.

The symptoms are feeling unwell, not sweating very much (or at all) and a high body temperature (39°C to 41°C or 102°F to 106°F). Where sweating has ceased the skin becomes flushed and red. Severe, throbbing headaches and lack of coordination will also occur, and the sufferer may be confused or aggressive. Eventually the victim will become delirious or convulse. Hospitalisation is essential, but in the interim get victims out of the sun, remove their clothing, cover them with a wet sheet or towel and then fan continually. Give fluids if they are conscious.

Jet Lag Jet lag is experienced when a person travels by air across more than three time zones (each time zone usually represents a one-hour time difference). It occurs because many of the functions of the human body (such as temperature, pulse rate and emptying of the bladder and bowels) are regulated by internal 24-hour cycles. When we travel long distances rapidly, our bodies take time to adjust to the 'new time' of our destination, and we may experience fatigue, disorientation, insomnia, anxiety, impaired concentration and loss of appetite. These effects will usually be gone within three days of arrival, but to minimise the impact of jet lag:

• Try to select flight schedules that minimise sleep deprivation; arriving late in the day means you can go to sleep soon after you arrive. For very long flights, try to organise a stopover.

- Rest for a couple of days prior to departure.
- Avoid excessive eating (which bloats the stomach) and alcohol (which causes dehydration) during the flight. Instead, drink plenty of non-carbonated, nonalcoholic drinks such as fruit juice or water.
- Avoid smoking.
- Make yourself comfortable by wearing loose-fitting clothes and perhaps bringing an eye mask and ear plugs to help you sleep.
- Try to sleep at the appropriate time for the time zone you are travelling to.

Motion Sickness Even the saltiest of sea dogs have been known to get motion sickness on Tongan ferries. Eating lightly before and during a trip will reduce the chances of motion sickness. If you are prone to motion sickness try to find a place that minimises movement – near the wing on aircraft, close to midships on boats, near the centre on buses. Fresh air and looking at the horizon usually help; reading and cigarette smoke don't.

Commercial motion-sickness preparations, which can cause drowsiness, have to be taken before the trip commences. Ginger (available in capsule form) and peppermint (including mint-flavoured sweets) are natural preventatives.

Prickly Heat Prickly heat is an itchy rash caused by excessive perspiration trapped under the skin. It usually strikes people who have just arrived in a hot climate. Keeping cool, bathing often, drying the skin and using a mild talcum or prickly heat powder or resorting to air-conditioning may help.

Sunburn In the tropics you can get sunburnt surprisingly quickly, even through cloud. Use a sunscreen, hat, and barrier cream for your nose and lips. Take particular care when snorkelling (see Snorkelling in the Activities special section). Calamine lotion and commercial after-sun preparations are good for mild sunburn. Always protect your eyes with good quality sunglasses, particularly if you will be near water or sand.

Infectious Diseases

Diarrhoea Simple things like a change of water, food or climate can all cause a mild bout of diarrhoea, but a few rushed toilet trips with no other symptoms is not indicative of a major problem.

Dehydration is the main danger with any diarrhoea, particularly in children or the elderly as dehydration can occur quite quickly. Under all circumstances *fluid replacement* is the most important thing to remember. Weak black tea with a little sugar, soda water, or soft drinks allowed to go flat and diluted 50% with clean water are all good. With severe diarrhoea a rehydrating solution is preferable to replace minerals and salts lost. Commercially available oral rehydration salts (ORS) are very useful; add them to boiled or bottled water. In an emergency you can make up a solution of six teaspoons of sugar and a half teaspoon of salt to a litre of boiled or bottled water. You need to drink at least the same volume of fluid that you are losing in bowel movements and vomiting. Urine is the best guide to the adequacy of replacement – if you have small amounts of concentrated urine, you need to drink more. Keep drinking small amounts often. Stick to a bland diet as you recover.

Lomotil or Imodium can be used to bring relief from the symptoms, although they do not actually cure the problem. Only use these drugs if you do not have access to toilets, eg, if you *must* travel. For children under 12 years Lomotil and Imodium are not recommended.

In certain situations antibiotics may be required: diarrhoea with blood or mucus (dysentery), any diarrhoea with fever, profuse watery diarrhoea, persistent diarrhoea not improving after 48 hours and severe diarrhoea. These suggest a more serious cause of diarrhoea so gut paralysing drugs like Imodium or Lomotil should be avoided.

In these situations, a stool test may be necessary to diagnose what bug is causing your diarrhoea, so you should seek medical help urgently. Where this is not possible the recommended drugs for bacterial diarrhoea (the most likely cause of severe diarrhoea in travellers) are norfloxacin 400mg twice daily for three days or ciprofloxacin 500mg twice daily for five days. These are not recommended for children or pregnant women. The drug of choice for children would be co-trimoxazole with dosage dependent on weight. A five-day course is given. Ampicillin or amoxycillin may be given in pregnancy, but medical care is necessary.

Two other causes of persistent diarrhoea in travellers are giardiasis and amoebic dysentery.

Giardiasis is caused by a common parasite, *Giardia lamblia*. Symptoms include stomach cramps, nausea, a bloated stomach, watery, foul-smelling diarrhoea and frequent gas. Giardiasis can appear several weeks after you have been exposed to the parasite. Symptoms may disappear for a few days and then return; this can go on for several weeks.

Amoebic dysentery, caused by the protozoan *Entamoeba histolytica*, is characterised by a gradual onset of low-grade diarrhoea, often with blood and mucus. Cramping abdominal pain and vomiting are less likely than in other types of diarrhoea, and fever may not be present. It will persist until treated and can recur and cause other health problems.

You should seek medical advice urgently if you think you have giardiasis or amoebic dysentery, but where this is not possible, tinidazole or metronidazole are the recommended drugs. Treatment for giardiasis is a 2g single dose of tinidazole, or 2g of metronidazole once daily for three days. Treatment for amoebic dysentery is 2g of tinidazole once daily for three days, or 600mg of metronidazole eight-hourly for six to 10 days. Even if you treat yourself, do get yourself checked out by a professional at the earliest possible opportunity, as additional medication is needed for cases of acute amoebic dysentery.

Fungal Infections Fungal infections occur more commonly in hot weather and are usually found on the scalp, between the toes (athlete's foot) or fingers, in the groin and on the body (ringworm). You get ringworm (which is a fungal infection, not a worm) from infected animals or other people. Moisture encourages these infections.

To prevent fungal infections wear loose, comfortable clothes, avoid artificial fibres, wash frequently and dry yourself carefully. If you do get an infection, wash the infected area at least daily with a disinfectant or medicated soap and water, and rinse and dry well. Apply an antifungal cream or powder like tolnaftate. Try to expose the infected area to air or sunlight as much as possible and wash all towels and underwear in hot water, change them often and let them dry in the sun.

Hepatitis Hepatitis is a general term for inflammation of the liver. It is a common disease worldwide. There are several different viruses that cause hepatitis, and they differ in the way that they are transmitted. The symptoms are similar in all forms of the illness, and include fever, chills, headache, fatigue, feelings of weakness and aches and pains, followed by loss of appetite, nausea, vomiting, abdominal pain, dark urine, light-coloured faeces, jaundiced (yellow) skin and yellowing of the whites of the eyes. People who have had hepatitis should avoid alcohol for some time after the illness, as the liver needs time to recover.

Hepatitis A is transmitted by contaminated food and drinking water. You should seek medical advice, but there is not much you can do apart from resting, drinking lots of fluids, eating lightly and avoiding fatty foods. Hepatitis E is transmitted in the same way as hepatitis A; it can be particularly serious in pregnant women.

There are almost 300 million chronic carriers of **hepatitis B** in the world. It is spread through contact with infected blood, blood products or body fluids, for example through sexual contact, unsterilised needles and blood transfusions, or contact with blood via small breaks in the skin. Other risk situations include having a shave, tattoo or body piercing with contaminated equipment. The symptoms of hepatitis B may be more severe than type A and the disease can lead to long-term problems such as chronic liver damage, liver cancer or a long-term carrier state. Hepatitis C and D are spread in the same way as hepatitis B and can also lead to long-term complications.

There are vaccines against hepatitis A and B, but there are currently no vaccines against C, D and E. Following the basic rules about food and water (hepatitis A and E) and avoiding risk situations (hepatitis B, C and D) are important preventative measures.

HIV & AIDS Infection with the human immunodeficiency virus (HIV) may lead to acquired immune deficiency syndrome (AIDS), which is a fatal disease. Any exposure to blood, blood products or body fluids may put the individual at risk. The disease is often transmitted through sexual contact or dirty needles – vaccinations, acupuncture, tattooing and body piercing can be potentially as dangerous as intravenous drug use. HIV/AIDS can also be spread through infected blood transfusions, but Tonga's blood is all screened for this. AIDS is not yet a big problem in Tonga. But play safe – if you do need an injection, ask to see the syringe unwrapped in front of you, or take a needle and syringe pack with you.

Fear of HIV infection should never preclude you from seeking treatment for serious medical conditions.

Intestinal Worms These parasites are most common in rural tropical areas. The different worms have different ways of infecting people. Some may be ingested on food such as undercooked meat (eg, tapeworms) and some enter through your skin (eg, hookworms). Infestations may not show up for some time and, although they are generally not serious, if left untreated some can cause severe health problems later. Consider having a stool test when you return home to check for these and determine the appropriate treatment.

Sexually Transmitted Infections HIV/AIDS and hepatitis B can be transmitted through sexual contact – see the relevant sections earlier for more details. Other STIs include gonorrhoea, herpes and syphilis; sores, blisters or rashes around the genitals and discharges or pain when urinating are common symptoms. In some STIs, such as wart virus or chlamydia, symptoms may be less marked or not observed at all, especially in women. Chlamydia infection can cause infertility in men and women before any symptoms have been noticed. Syphilis symptoms eventually disappear completely but the disease continues and can cause severe problems in later years. While abstinence from sexual contact is the only 100% effective prevention, using condoms is also effective (bring them from home). The treatment of gonorrhoea and syphilis is with antibiotics.

Typhoid Typhoid fever is a dangerous gut infection caused by contaminated water and food. Medical help must be sought.

In its early stages sufferers may feel that a bad cold or flu is on the way, as early symptoms are a headache, body aches and a fever which rises a little each day until it is around 40°C (104°F) or more. The victim's pulse is often slow relative to the degree of fever present – unlike a normal fever where the pulse increases. There may also be vomiting, abdominal pain, diarrhoea or constipation.

In the second week the high fever and slow pulse continue and a few pink spots may appear on the body; trembling, delirium, weakness, weight loss and dehydration may occur. Complications such as pneumonia, perforated bowel or meningitis may occur.

Insect-Borne Diseases
Dengue Fever This viral disease is transmitted by mosquitoes and is present in Tonga. Unlike the malaria mosquito, the *Aedes aegypti* mosquito, which transmits the dengue virus, is most active during the day, and is found mainly in urban areas, in and around human dwellings.

Signs and symptoms of dengue fever include a sudden onset of high fever, headache, joint and muscle pains (hence its old name, 'breakbone fever'), and nausea and vomiting. A rash of small red spots sometimes appears three to four days after the onset of fever. In the early phase of illness, dengue may be mistaken for other infectious diseases, including influenza. Minor bleeding such as nose bleeds may occur in the course of the illness, but this does not necessarily mean that you have progressed to the potentially fatal dengue haemorrhagic fever (DHF). This is a severe illness, characterised by heavy bleeding, which is thought to be a result of second infection due to a different strain (there are four major strains) and usually affects residents of the country rather than travellers. Recovery even from simple dengue fever may be prolonged, with tiredness lasting for several weeks.

Seek medical attention and take a blood test as soon as possible if you think you may be infected. There is no specific treatment for dengue, though aspirin should be avoided, as it increases the risk of haemorrhaging. There is no vaccine against dengue fever. The best prevention is to avoid mosquito bites at all times (see the boxed text).

Cuts, Bites & Stings
Cuts & Scratches Wash well and treat any cut with an antiseptic such as povidone-iodine. Where possible avoid bandages and Band-Aids, which can keep wounds wet. Coral cuts are notoriously slow to heal and if they are not adequately cleaned and treated with antiseptic, small pieces of coral can become embedded in the wound.

Since the waters around populated areas of Tonga can harbour staphylococcus bacteria, it is best not to swim in these areas with an open wound. Staph infections are miserable and very difficult to treat. Sadly, Tongan villagers occasionally die of such infections that have ulcerated and spread to vital organs.

Bedbugs & Lice Bedbugs live in various places, but particularly in dirty mattresses and bedding, evidenced by spots of blood on bedclothes or on the wall. Bedbugs leave itchy bites in neat rows. Calamine lotion or a sting relief spray may help.

All lice cause itching and discomfort. They make themselves at home in your hair (head lice), your clothing (body lice) or in your pubic hair (crabs). You catch lice through direct contact with infected people or by sharing combs, clothing and the like. Powder or shampoo treatment will kill the lice and infected clothing should then be washed in very hot, soapy water and left in the sun to dry.

Bites & Stings There is no rabies in Tonga, but if you are bitten by a dog, clean the wound immediately. Scrub the bite thoroughly with soap and running water, apply alcohol or iodine and have a tetanus vaccination within a few hours if you haven't had one during the past three years.

There are centipedes called *molokau* in Tonga which are rarely seen but can grow up to 20cm in length, and can give a painful, irritating bite that may cause swelling – though it's not normally lethal to adults. Avoid walking outside barefoot.

Bee and wasp stings are usually painful rather than dangerous. However, in people

---

Mosquito Avoidance Techniques

Although outbreaks of dengue fever are uncommon in Tonga (and there's no malaria), it's better – and a lot more comfortable – to avoid being bitten by mosquitoes in the first place.

- Wear trousers and long-sleeved shirts; light-coloured clothing is the most effective.
- Use mosquito repellents containing the compound DEET on exposed skin (prolonged overuse of DEET may be harmful, especially to children, but its use is considered preferable to being bitten by disease-transmitting mosquitoes).
- Avoid perfumes or aftershave.
- Sleep under a mosquito net impregnated with mosquito repellent (permethrin). Sleeping in screened or air-conditioned rooms or under fans also lowers the risk of being bitten.
- Impregnating clothes with permethrin effectively deters mosquitoes and other insects.
- Fumigate your room with either a permethrin-based mosquito coil or insect spray.

Venomous Marine Life

Various fish and other sea creatures can sting or bite dangerously, or are dangerous to eat. Listen to local advice on how to avoid them.

Certain cone shells found in Tonga (and elsewhere in the Pacific) can sting dangerously or even fatally. Do not touch any cone-shaped shell.

Cone shell

Several species of jellyfish are found in Tongan waters (blue-bottle jellyfish are the most common) and can deliver a painful sting. Dousing in vinegar will deactivate any stingers which have not 'fired', while calamine lotion, antihistamines and analgesics may reduce the reaction and relieve the pain.

Stonefish have poisonous dorsal spines which deliver a very painful sting requiring medical treat-

ment. As the name suggests, they are very well camouflaged and inhabit coral or rocky areas. You'll also need medical treatment if you get stung by lionfish or stingrays.

As a rule don't touch anything unfamiliar while snorkelling or diving and wear reef sandals, wet-boots or old trainers when paddling or exploring rock pools.

More commonly encountered is stinging coral – it's the bright, sulphur-yellow-coloured coral with a smooth surface.

Stonefish

The sting is only bothersome, not dangerous, and can be neutralised by applying vinegar or fresh urine.

The sharks here tend to live in the open sea and though they do come across the reef they are not the human-eating variety and pose no danger to swimmers.

Tonga has one species of sea snake, the banded sea snake, which is extremely poisonous but rarely seen and nonaggressive. It's up to 1.5m in length, and easily recognised by its black bands. If you gently push it aside, it will usually swim away. It's extremely rare for anyone to be bitten.

Lionfish

who are allergic to them severe breathing difficulties may occur and require urgent medical care. Calamine lotion or a sting relief spray will give relief and ice packs will reduce the pain and swelling.

Women's Health

Gynaecological Problems Antibiotic use, synthetic underwear, sweating and contraceptive pills can lead to fungal vaginal infections, especially when travelling in hot climates. Fungal infections are characterised by a rash, itch and discharge; while they can be treated with a vinegar or lemon-juice douche, or with yogurt, Nystatin, miconazole or clotrimazole pessaries or vaginal cream are the usual treatment. Maintaining good personal hygiene and wearing loose-

fitting clothes and cotton underwear may help prevent these infections.

Sexually transmitted infections are a major cause of vaginal problems. Symptoms include a smelly discharge, painful intercourse and sometimes a burning sensation when urinating. Medical attention should be sought and male sexual partners must also be treated. For more details see the section on Sexually Transmitted Infections earlier. Besides abstinence, the best thing is to use condoms.

Pregnancy It is not advisable to travel to some countries while pregnant as some vaccinations normally used to prevent serious diseases are not advisable during pregnancy (eg, yellow fever). In addition, some diseases (eg, malaria) are much more serious for the mother (and may increase the risk of a still-born child) in pregnancy.

Most miscarriages occur during the first three months of pregnancy. Miscarriage is not uncommon and can occasionally lead to severe bleeding. The last three months should also be spent within reasonable distance of good medical care. A baby born as early as 24 weeks stands a chance of survival, but only in a good modern hospital. Pregnant women should avoid all unnecessary medication, although vaccinations and malarial prophylactics should still be taken where needed. Additional care should be taken to prevent illness and particular attention should be paid to diet and nutrition.

Less Common Diseases

Tetanus This disease is caused by a germ which lives in soil and in the faeces of horses and other animals. It enters the body via breaks in the skin. The first symptom may be discomfort in swallowing, or stiffening of the jaw and neck; this is followed by painful convulsions of the jaw and whole body. Seek medical attention, as the disease can be fatal. It can be prevented by vaccination.

WOMEN TRAVELLERS

Most of the time women travellers have no special problems in Tonga, but the closer you are to the culture and people, the more aware you'll need to be of Tongan traditional values.

The way you dress will have a lot to do with how people perceive and treat you in Tonga. This is a deeply Christian culture and Tongans expect women to dress modestly. (See Society & Conduct in the Facts about Tonga chapter).

An unaccompanied foreign woman is sometimes seen as a ticket to a better life and you may become the focus of unwanted attention. Comments are often best ignored and politeness on your part will be much more effective than abuse.

In traditional Tongan culture, it is not customary for a woman to be alone at any time. When women go outside their homes they are normally accompanied. In Nuku'alofa

and the other large towns, being a solo woman traveller will scarcely be an issue. Elsewhere you may feel more comfortable going places with other travellers or even a child of the family you're staying with.

There's no need to be paranoid about relating to people of the opposite sex but keep in mind that in traditional Tongan culture, women are not permitted to freely associate with men on their own – they must be chaperoned. If, for example, you go to an isolated place alone with a man, or go for a drink with him, you are giving him the signal that you are available for sex.

Alcohol is another important issue and if you drink with Tongan men, you could be putting yourself at risk. Although Tongans have no problem with a woman traveller going out for a drink with her male partner or with other foreign men, a respectable Tongan woman does not drink with men.

Women visiting nightclubs should not expect much peace, even when accompanied by partners/husbands – Tongan men can be incredibly persistent in their requests that you dance with them.

Safety Precautions

It's a good idea for women to take a few sensible precautions:

• Use common sense when going out at night and consider arranging a taxi rather than walking.
• Avoid walking alone on a deserted beach, bush track or back road.
• If you need a drink head for a larger hotel or tourist place rather than a small male-dominated bar.
• Don't hitchhike.

GAY & LESBIAN TRAVELLERS

Homosexuality is an accepted fact of life in Tonga, as in most of Polynesia, and you'll see plenty of gay men around. There are *fakaleiti* (like a lady) – men who dress and behave as women (see the following boxed text) – and there are other gay men around too. Whatever lesbian population exists is much more under cover and not at all vocal.

There's no need for gay or lesbian travellers to hide their sexuality in Tonga, but public displays of sexual affection are frowned upon, whether gay or straight.

Fakaleiti

Fakaleiti, men who dress and behave as women, are Tonga's most obvious example of creative sexuality.

While most fakaleiti are probably gay, not all of them are; while many consider themselves ladies and wouldn't think of relating sexually to anyone but a masculine man, this is not true of all fakaleiti – some are married to women! Fakaleiti get away with promiscuity with men on a scale forbidden to biological females, however.

Seeing the fakaleiti's open flaunting of sexuality and transvestitism, and their acceptance as part of Tongan society, it might seem there is no social stigma attached to being a fakaleiti. This is partly true, partly not. Although adult fakaleiti are accepted, growing up as a fakaleiti is not easy. Many are tormented by other children and teenagers and to most Tongan fathers it's not a great source of pride if their sons turn out to be effeminate.

On Tongatapu, the Tonga Leitis' Association is an active group – note that members prefer to call themselves simply *leiti* (ladies). The association sponsors several popular, well-attended annual events, including the international Miss Galaxy competition each June which attracts fakaleiti and transvestites from several countries. Contact the TVB for details.

DISABLED TRAVELLERS

Tonga has very few facilities suitable for the disabled. However, this does not make it out of bounds for those with a physical disability and a sense of adventure. Tongans are friendly and helpful people who will do their best to accommodate you.

Get in touch with your national support organisation before leaving home. It often has travel literature to help with holiday planning and can put you in touch with specialist travel agents.

SENIOR TRAVELLERS

Older people are respected and venerated in Tonga. Combine this with the very low crime rate, warm climate, relaxed pace of life and the easy-going friendliness of the Tongan people and you've got an excellent destination for older travellers.

TRAVEL WITH CHILDREN

Tonga is a great place to travel with children and there's plenty to keep them happy – swimming, snorkelling, beachcombing, bicycling, kayaking, short boat trips, visits to interesting places and cultural events (especially the Tongan feasts).

Some hotels in Tonga allow children to stay free of charge, others have a reduced children's rate, and a few do not accept children at all.

If you look hard enough you can buy just about anything you need for young children, though at a price. The larger supermarkets in Nuku'alofa and Neiafu are the best hunting grounds. However, bring as much as possible from home, including any special foods required, high-factor sunscreen and insect repellent. Disposable nappies (diapers) are unfortunately a practical solution when travelling, despite the environmental drawbacks. International brands are readily available.

To avoid stomach upsets, stick to purified or bottled water. Cartons of fruit juice, UHT and powdered milk are widely available. Be extra careful when choosing restaurants, steer clear of salads and stick to piping-hot dishes. Tongan markets have delicious fruit and vegies, but be sure to wash and peel them.

Always be careful to prevent dehydration and sunburn, even on cloudy days, and protect your child from mosquitoes.

Hire cars rarely have child seats, so you should bring your own, and check that it clips into seatbelts.

DANGERS & ANNOYANCES
Security

Tonga is one of the safest destinations in the South Pacific and theft from the person is not a problem, whether by robbery or pick-pocketing, so you don't need to be paranoid about carrying belongings around with you.

'Borrowing' is rife, though. By Tongan reckoning, all property is effectively communal. If one person has something another needs, the latter either asks for it or surreptitiously 'borrows' it. Of course, it can be 'borrowed' back if needed, but it will otherwise never again see its rightful owner. Unattended items are considered ripe for 'borrowing', so watch your possessions.

The threat of rape does exist, but you can easily protect yourself by using common sense and avoiding drinking alcohol alone with Tongan men (see the section on Women Travellers earlier in this chapter).

The police and government officials in Tonga seem friendly, helpful and straightforward, but don't overstay your visa, get caught with illegal substances or offend a member of the nobility.

Animals

There are a lot of dogs roaming around Tonga. Most are either friendly or will keep their distance, but a few (especially when they're in packs) are aggressive. Pretending to throw a stone often discourages them.

Sea Creatures

A number of creatures encountered underwater can sting or bite, including jellyfish, cone shells and stinging coral – see the earlier 'Venomous Marine Life' boxed text.

BUSINESS HOURS

Business hours are flexible, but usually run from 9am until 4.30pm. Shops are usually open 8.30am to 5pm weekdays (some close for an hour at lunch), and from around 9am to noon Saturdays. *Fale koloa* (small grocery kiosks) open the longest hours, from around 6am to 10pm Monday to Saturday.

Restaurants usually operate from 8am to 10am for breakfast, noon to 2pm for lunch, and 6pm to 10pm if they serve evening meals. Larger hotels and a few Chinese restaurants open to the public on Sunday, but most restaurants are closed. Produce markets normally get under way by about 6am and close around 4pm weekdays and are busiest from 6am to noon Saturdays.

On Sunday afternoons bakeries are permitted to sell bread and cakes. They open between about 4pm (6pm on smaller islands) and 8pm.

PUBLIC HOLIDAYS & SPECIAL EVENTS

Primary and secondary school holidays include two weeks beginning the second week of May, two weeks beginning the third week of August and six weeks beginning the first week of December. Public holidays include:

1 January New Year's Day
March/April Good Friday, Easter Sunday & Easter Monday
25 April Anzac Day
4 May HRH Crown Prince Tupouto'a's Birthday
4 June Emancipation Day
4 July King Taufa'ahau Tupou IV's Birthday
4 November Constitution Day
4 December King George I Day
25 December Christmas Day
26 December Boxing Day

You may get the feeling that '4' is the royal lucky number!

The king's birthday is celebrated on Tongatapu with the Heilala Festival, named after the country's national flower. It's a week-long bash featuring parades and processions, music festivals and competitions, cultural events and dance, art, craft, beauty and sports competitions. Coinciding with this festival is the torch-lighting ceremony Tupakapakanava in which people line the northern coastline of Tongatapu carrying flaming torches of dry reeds.

In Vava'u, the Crown Prince's birthday in early May sets the stage for the Vava'u Festival, a popular week of partying.

The most prominent annual event in the Ha'apai Group is the week-long Ha'apai Festival, which precedes Emancipation Day festivities in early June. 'Eua's recently established festival also takes place around this time, beginning on 28 May and continuing for two weeks, and is based around the national park.

The week-long Easter Festival features youth choirs, passion plays, band concerts and cultural performances. Another major event in Tonga is the Red Cross Festival, which is capped off with the Red Cross Grand Ball in Nuku'alofa. It takes place every year in May.

Agricultural fairs, which are derived from the ancient *'inasi* festivals, take place in all the major island groups from late August to October and are presided over by the king. The first is normally on Vava'u, followed by fairs on Ha'apai, Tongatapu and 'Eua.

In late September the Tonga International Billfish Tournament attracts both local and international anglers to Vava'u, while there is sometimes a sailing regatta in Nuku'alofa at the end of April. Another international competition, the Miss Galaxy pageant, is held in Nuku'alofa in late June – for men! Actually they are transvestites, or fakaleiti (see the earlier boxed text 'Fakaleiti'). Contestants from several countries participate. It's great fun, and a very popular event.

Tongan families need little excuse for a feast: a birthday, a visitor, an academic accomplishment, a birth, a marriage or just a sunny Sunday are all good reasons. University graduations, religious holidays, children's first birthdays and royal birthdays invite celebration on an even larger scale, often with several days of feasting, dancing and organised entertainment. Instead of fireworks, youngsters detonate home-made bamboo and kerosene bazookas that explode with the same impact as heavy artillery.

COURSES

Beginners and advanced diving courses are offered on Tongatapu, Vava'u and Ha'apai; see the Activities special section. Visitors spending some time on Tongatapu might want to check out the courses at the 'Atenisi Institute or the University of the South Pacific (USP) on Tongatapu.

WORK

Being in Tonga on a tourist permit means you're specifically prohibited from working. Like everywhere else in the world, the idea is to save jobs for locals, who need the work. Nevertheless, you'll see plenty of foreigners working in Tonga. Many have set up small businesses considered beneficial for Tonga, such as tourist resorts.

Foreigners also work here on various aid programs (eg, US Peace Corps, Australian Young Ambassadors and Japanese Overseas Cooperation Volunteers all get two-year stints in Tonga).

Church- and charity-run schools often require English-speaking teachers. St Andrew's High School (☎/fax 26050, [e] standr ew@tongatapu.net.to, PO Box 118) on the outskirts of Nuku'alofa is one such school. University graduates interested in one- to two-year appointments should approach Revd Tony Gerritsen. No specific teaching qualifications are required and accommodation plus T$100 per week is offered.

Officially, you must get a work permit from the immigration office in order to be employed in Tonga. You must have a specific offer of employment, file an application with the immigration office, pay a fee of T$76 and then wait quite a while for the processing. The immigration office at the police station in Nuku'alofa (☎ 24763, fax 23226, PO Box 8) can fill you in on all the current requirements.

Long-Term Residency

Unless you marry a Tongan citizen, non-business immigration is extremely difficult. Business immigrants are normally permitted to remain, but only as long as they retain their jobs. Those intent upon setting up a business will normally be required to place controlling interest in the hands of a Tongan partner.

For more information on business investments in Tonga, contact the Ministry of Labour, Commerce & Industries (☎ 23688, fax 23887, [e] tonga-trade@kalianet.to, [w] www .tongatrade.to, PO Box 110).

People with highly transferable and beneficial skills like medical professionals or secondary school teachers, or those willing to work voluntarily on long-term projects, will also normally have a chance of immigration.

ACCOMMODATION

Unless you're on a package holiday, don't trust accommodation bookings made by airlines or travel agents, since there are often weak or missing links in the system. Many hotels and guesthouses now have email.

[Continued on page 69]

ACTIVITIES

Numerous well-organised activities are possible in Tonga, with Vava'u currently reigning supreme as activity king of the island groups. The island supports plenty of activity companies offering everything from sea kayaking to whale watching. But Tongatapu has a host of companies offering many of the same activities as Vava'u, without the added expense of the flight to get there.

Tonga's best surf is off Tongatapu Island, which also has some great (and easily accessible) snorkelling. Good rock climbing, bird-watching and bushwalking are to be had on 'Eua. Ha'apai has some incredible diving and the volcanic island of Tofua offers real scope for adventurous exploring.

More information on all the operators mentioned in this chapter, and details of their tours, are given in the island group chapters. The Web site w www.tongaholiday.com has links to lots of activity operators in the fields of diving, surfing, sailing, kayaking, cruising, fishing and whale watching.

Bird-Watching

Although Tonga is not renowned for its birdlife, there are sea-bird colonies of noddies, terns, great frigate birds and tropic birds (white-tailed and the rare red-tailed variety) on all the main islands. Hufangalupe on Tongatapu, Lakufa'anga on 'Eua, Maninita in Vava'u and Luahoko in Ha'apai are just a few of the possible twitching spots.

The purple-crowned and many-coloured fruit doves are the most exotic species found on Tongatapu. The red shining parrot can be seen in the 'Eua Plantation Forest and National Park. Mt Talau on Vava'u Island is home to a number of bird species, and Whale Watch Vava'u (☎ 70747, e mounu@kalianet.to, PO Box 7, Neiafu) plans to offer specialist bird-watching trips all over Vava'u in the future.

Most twitchers will be more interested in seeing the Niuafo'ou megapode around Niuafo'ou's central lakes, though the logistics of this are problematic (see the Niuas chapter for further details).

The only book specifically about Tonga's birds is the *Field Guide to Landbirds of Tonga* by Claudia Matavalea. Contact the Tongan Wildlife Centre (☎/fax 29449, e birdpark@kalianet.to, PO Box 52, Nuku'alofa) for more information on this title and Tongan birds in general.

Bushwalking

'Eua offers the best, most accessible areas for bushwalking (mostly over forested terrain), while the Niuas and Tofua in Ha'apai have a combination of volcanic landscapes, ash fields and dense forest. Kao (1046m), Tonga's highest peak, can also be climbed. Vava'u Island is a maze of trails and 4WD tracks, and some beautiful sea-shore walking is afforded by hundreds of kilometres of sandy beaches (especially in

Title Page & Above: Game-fishing boat off Neiafu, Vava'u (Photograph by Matt Fletcher)

Responsible Bushwalking

- If you've carried packaging in, you can carry it out. Minimise rubbish by taking minimal packaging and by re-packaging your leftover food-stuffs. Make an effort to carry out rubbish left by others.
- Don't use bought water in plastic bottles. Disposal of these bottles is becoming a major problem in Tonga. Use iodine drops or purification tablets instead.
- Where there is no toilet, bury your waste. Dig a small hole 15cm (6 inches) deep and at least 100m (320 feet) from any watercourse or trail. Burn toilet paper and then bury it with the waste.
- If the area is inhabited, ask locals if they have any concerns about your chosen toilet site.
- Wash with biodegradable soap and water in a container. Cooking utensils should be washed in a container using a scourer and sand instead of detergent. Disperse the waste water over a wide area at least 50m (160 feet) from a watercourse.
- Stick to existing trails – by not doing so you'll create another potential watercourse after heavy rain that will eventually cause soil erosion and deep scarring.
- Don't depend on open fires for cooking – deforestation is already a problem.
- Seek permission before camping anywhere. Landowners are usually happy if asked but may be confrontational if not.
- Rural areas in Tonga tend to be very traditional and you must respect social and cultural values, especially with regard to dress (see Society & Conduct in the Facts for the Visitor chapter).

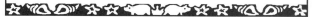

Ha'apai and on Niuatoputapu). However, it's important to remember that there is little history of bushwalking in Tonga and trails quickly become overgrown, meaning that in many areas it's not so much bushwalking as bushwhacking. See Maps in the Facts for the Visitor chapter for more information.

Depending on who you speak to, camping in Tonga is either problematic or not problematic. In Vava'u and Ha'apai camping is illegal unless you are in an organised group, but in practice as long as you have permission from the property owner you should have no problems. Camping next to a village, though, may be seen as an impolite rejection of Tongan hospitality.

To get the most out of bushwalking in Tonga bring a tent, good strong boots, tough trousers, mosquito repellent, cooking equipment (camping gas is not available), a compass and plenty of water containers – finding fresh water can be a problem and sometimes supplies for several days must be carried.

Caving

With dozens of limestone caves, caverns and tunnels, 'Eua is the best place for caving in Tonga. There's tremendous choice here for avid spelunkers and many caves are doubtless unexplored. Anecdotal evidence suggests that some cave systems are very large indeed.

Unfortunately, no operators offer caving in 'Eua. Caving here is for those already experienced underground and totally self-sufficient in terms of equipment and emergency support.

Happily on other islands smaller caves can be explored; 'Anahulu Cave on Tongatapu has a freshwater pool good for swimming, and on Vava'u, Swallows' Cave and Mariner's Cave can both be entered easily from the sea.

Sea caves are more accessible. Experienced divers can explore marvellous caves and caverns off 'Eua, Vava'u and Ha'apai.

Cycling

Cycling is a great way to travel in Tonga. Distances aren't great, the islands are reasonably flat (though Vava'u and 'Eua are hilly in places) and you can explore without spewing hydrocarbons into the beautiful Tongan sky.

Rental bicycles are available on all major islands (T$5 to T$15 per day) and mountain bike tours are possible on Vava'u with the Friendly Islands Kayak Company (☎ 70173).

Transporting your own bike into Tonga should be no problem (check all carriage details with the airline before purchasing your ticket), but internal flights can be tricky – baggage allowances are 10kg and cargo capacity small. You'll need to dismantle your machine completely and still your bike may not fit into Royal Tongan Airlines' Twin Otter. This rules out flying to 'Eua, Ha'apai and the Niuas – you'll have to take the ferry. Call Royal Tongan Cargo (☎ 24714) for further details and see the Air section in the Getting Around chapter for details of excess baggage charges.

A few notes of caution: before you leave home, go over your bike with a fine-tooth comb and fill your repair kit with every imaginable spare. Care should be taken around towns (Nuku'alofa especially) where vehicle numbers are high and driving skills poor. And watch out for crazed canines and wandering pigs.

Diving

Tonga has a great variety of scuba dive sites. Soft and hard coral teeming with tropical fish, vertigo-inducing drop-offs, huge caverns, tunnels, channels, magnificent geological formations (some volcanic) and wrecks are all found in Tonga's waters.

Between June and November you may also see, and often hear, humpback whales. Dolphins, sea turtles and rays are present year-round. The dive sites (for all abilities) are world-class, largely uncrowded, and often untouched.

Visibility is outstanding and averages 30m to 50m on the barrier reefs around Tongatapu and Vava'u, reaching up to 70m in winter. Visibility is slightly lower in Ha'apai during summer (25m to 30m) as the island group is more exposed; this means getting out to exciting,

Considerations for Diving

- Don't use anchors on live reef and don't condone the actions of dive operators who do.
- Be sure you feel healthy and comfortable before diving and you don't have any sinus congestion or cold symptoms.
- Avoid touching living marine organisms with your body or dragging equipment across the reef. Polyps can be damaged by even the gentlest contact. Never stand on corals, even if they look solid and robust. If you must hold on to the reef, only touch exposed rock or dead coral.
- Be conscious of your fins. Even without contact, the surge from heavy fin strokes near the reef can damage delicate organisms.
- Resist the temptation to feed fish (you may disturb their normal eating habits, encourage aggressive behaviour or just give them indigestion) and don't ride on the back of turtles and the like.

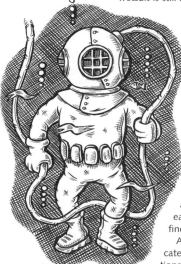

remote dive sites is more weather-dependent than elsewhere. Water temperatures range between 23°C and 29°C, with Vava'u's sheltered waters seeming to stay warmer longer. Nevertheless, a 3mm wetsuit is still a good idea.

There are at least two dive operators on every island group and all are affiliated either with PADI, NAUI, SSI or CMAS. Expect to pay between US$40 and US$60 for a two-tank dive (that's two separate dives on a single trip) inclusive of equipment. Booking a series of dives will get you a discount.

Tonga is an ideal place to learn to dive or to obtain further dive qualifications. The entry-level PADI Open-Water Diver course (lasting three or four days) costs between US$150 and US$200. Vava'u is probably the ideal location to learn as a huge variety of dive sites are easily accessible and Neiafu boasts two fine dive operators.

As long as you can produce a certificate from one of the associations mentioned earlier you can dive in Tonga. Make sure you explain your level of experience before planning any dive and don't be tempted to dive beyond your ability. It's worth remembering that there is no decompression chamber in Tonga – Suva (Fiji) has one, but patients are usually transferred to Auckland (New Zealand).

Fishing

Game fishing is increasingly popular in Tonga and attracts anglers from around the world. The main game fish are yellowfin tuna, bluefin tuna, skipjack, albacore, wahoo, barracuda, sailfish, mahi mahi and blue, black and striped marlin. Most marlin are caught between June and November (August and September are the peak months), though these fish can be caught year-round.

Trawling (towing a number of lures on long lines behind a boat) is the most common fishing method, but bottom fishing and salt-water fly fishing can be catered for and equipment is usually provided. Quality is variable. Salt-water fly fishermen should bring their own tackle.

Trawling takes place in the very deep waters that surround Tonga (the Tonga Trench is over 10,000m deep), some of it – in Vava'u and Tongatapu – focused around Fish Attracting Devices (FADs), long buoyed-up chains attached to the bottom, which over time, as algae and crustacea grow on them, develop into floating ecosystems with game fish as top predators.

Vava'u is the base of much game fishing in Tonga, but there are a number of fine boats available for charter in Tongatapu. In September the Tonga International Game Fishing Association (Tigfa) holds an international competition in Vava'u – temporary membership allows you to enter competitions – and tag and release is becoming popular.

For Tongan-style fishing trips (with hand lines) ask around at the various wharfs in Tonga or at the place you're staying.

Rock Climbing

The sheer, 150m-high limestone cliffs on 'Eua's east coast offer Tonga's best climbing. There are some great, largely unclimbed routes, though there's always a strong easterly wind off the ocean. The rock is pretty sharp, but there are plenty of holds. The best places to anchor off are around or on Lokupo and Lauua lookouts. Bring all your own gear.

Many of the islands in Vava'u have squat but promising 40m sea cliffs. These are untried and untested. You'd certainly need a boat or a knowledgeable local guide.

Sailing

Most of Tonga's yacht charter companies are based in Vava'u, which offers excellent, easy-going and relatively stress-free sailing. Easterly trade winds blow at a steady 15 to 18 knots across this group of idyllic, sheltered islands between May and November (the most popular sailing time), and there are many excellent anchorages and island resorts that welcome yachties into their restaurants. During the cyclone season – you'll be warned in plenty of time – cheap charters are sometimes available.

Ha'apai is just as picturesque as Vava'u, but Vava'u's charter companies don't allow their boats out of Vava'u. Ha'apai's anchorages offer protection from rough seas, but not from unexpected gales. Tongatapu is more limited for cruising yachts, but 'Eua, 'Ata, Minerva Reef

Resting inside 'Ana Kuma (Rats' Cave), 'Eua Plantation Forest

Take the plunge on Uoleva.

Hiking through the lush 'Eua Plantation Forest

Off to explore the depths, Vava'u

Vava'u offers some of the world's best diving.

Humpback whale family cruising off Vava'u

A garden of corals, sponges and fish to explore

Crystal-clear warm waters – who can resist?

and the beautiful coral islands north of Tongatapu can be explored. Royal Sunset Island Resort offers full-crewed yacht charters that can explore all of Tonga.

Sailors should be aware that Tongan sea charts are not 100% accurate and are thus inappropriate for GPS navigation. However, due to the great visibility, navigating around Tonga's reef systems is not difficult – though a moderate level of experience is required. See the Getting There & Away chapter for more information on sailing to and from Tonga.

Sea Kayaking

With its myriad islands, lagoons and beaches, Tonga offers great scope for sea kayakers. The clear, sheltered waters of the Vava'u Group are ideal for sea kayaking and you can rent kayaks from Beluga Diving (☎ 70087) and the Friendly Islands Kayak Company (FIKC; ☎ 70173) in Neiafu. FIKC concentrates on escorted trips around Vava'u. These excellent trips involve camping on deserted islands, snorkelling and occasionally paddling among humpback whales!

FIKC also runs trips in Ha'apai, which involve a bit more open sea (depending on your route), but there's also plenty of sheltered waters. Watersports Ha'apai (☎/fax 60097) has sea kayaks for hire.

No-one on Tongatapu offers sea kayaking, but the islands and reefs north and north-east of Nuku'alofa have good potential.

A 3mm wet suit is a good idea, and if you bring your own kayak to Tonga you'll have to transport it around the islands by ferry.

Snorkelling

Tonga's reefs are among the richest and most diverse ecosystems in the world. Many can be accessed straight from the shore, but reef quality generally improves the farther you are from a population centre, and you may need a boat to see the best reefs. Tagging along with a dive group can be a good way to discover coral gardens off the beaten track.

Marine Adventures (☎ 24563) in Tongatapu is unique in providing guidance for snorkellers. North of Tongatapu a collection of marine reserves and beautiful reefs (not least Makaha'a Reef) provide great and accessible snorkelling.

In Ha'apai you're never too far from a reef. The Community Clam Circle off Uoleva is great and there are a number of excellent coral gardens along the Lifuka Group.

Up in Vava'u most boat/snorkelling trips visit the coral gardens off Vaka'eitu, which are world-class.

Considerations for Snorkelling

- Never snorkel alone and always have someone spotting for you when diving down (free diving).
- Dress for protection from coral and the sun (wear reef boots, sandals or fins, T-shirts or UV-protective lycra tops, sunscreen and long shorts).
- Inquire locally about prevailing sea conditions (eg, currents) before entering the water.
- Bring all snorkelling equipment from home (gear available in Tonga is poor quality).
- Don't collect shells or coral or touch anything (many corals, fish and shells are poisonous).
- Thoroughly clean and apply antiseptic to all coral cuts.
- After snorkelling rinse out your ears with fresh water.

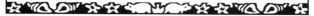

Surfing

Tonga's winter south swell season runs from April to October when surfing is reliant on storm activity around Australia and New Zealand. The summer north swell season runs from November to March, with prevailing swells originating both in the North Pacific (the same swells that hit Hawaii) and from cyclones in the South Pacific.

There are no beach breaks in Tonga. All surf is over shallow coral reefs, demanding an intermediate to advanced skill level. Carry a basic first-aid kit to deal with the inevitable cuts and grazes.

Great surf can be found throughout Tonga, but it's most accessible on Tongatapu, namely at Ha'atafu Beach. A number of surf spots here are only a short paddle (100m) across the lagoon. The Oceania Surfing Championship was held here in 2001.

Surf information on Ha'apai and Vava'u is hard to get. No doubt good waves await, but they take some finding.

For more information about surfing in Tonga, contact Steve Burling at the Tonga Surfriders Association (☎ 41088, fax 22970, e steve@surfingtonga.com, PO Box 490, Nuku'alofa). Steve runs Ha'atafu Beach Resort and has been surfing in Tonga for 20 years.

Natural Mystic Adventures (☎ 70599, e nmystic@kalianet.to, PO Box 30, Neiafu) may be able to help with surf spots in Vava'u.

Whale Watching

Tonga is an important breeding ground for humpback whales, and one of the best places in the world to see these magnificent creatures. They can be seen bearing young, caring for new calves, and engaging in elaborate mating rituals. It is thought that they come to bear their young in warm waters (conceived there 11 months earlier) because the newborn calves cannot cope with the freezing polar waters; the calmness of the reef-protected ocean is important too.

The whale-watching season is from June to November in Tongatapu and Ha'apai, and July to November in Vava'u, which is the centre for

'Singing Whales'

The whales seen around Tonga are humpback whales, dubbed 'singing whales', as the males sing during courtship routines. The low notes of their 'songs' can reach a shattering 185 decibels and carry 100km through the open ocean.

Humpbacks are also known for their dramatic antics in the water. They breach (throw themselves completely up out of the water, landing with a terrific splash), spyhop (stand vertically upright in the sea, gazing around at the world above water), barrel roll (splashing the water with their long pectoral fins as they do so), slap the water repeatedly with their tail flukes or pectoral fins (flippers), and perform other remarkable acrobatic feats.

A mature male adult is about 16m (52 feet) long and weighs around 40 to 45 tonnes. The whale's pectoral fins are the longest in the animal kingdom, measuring about 4m to 6m (13 to 20 feet). The calves are around 4m long at birth and weigh up to 2.5 tonnes. They gain approximately 25kg (55 pounds) each day – about a kilogram per hour – on their mothers' milk, which contains twice as much protein and 10 times as much fat as cows' milk. When the calves have put on around 10cm (4 inches) of blubber, the whales return to their Antarctic summer feeding grounds and calves stay with their mothers for two years.

Humpbacks feed by straining small fish and crustaceans through hundreds of keratin plates – keratin being the stuff that hair and fingernails are made of. The whales do not feed in their Tongan playground, surviving instead on their blubber store.

Interestingly, though humpbacks live in several parts of the world their populations do not mix. Tongan whales do not mix with the populations which breed in New Caledonia or eastern or western Australia, and northern and southern hemisphere humpbacks never see each other either. Southern hemisphere humpbacks are distinguished from those in the northern hemisphere by their undersides: southern hemisphere whales have white undersides, while the undersides of those in the northern hemisphere are dark.

whale watching in Tonga. Vava'u's sheltered waters are easily accessible by boat from Neiafu. Over 160 individual whales have been identified here and many return year after year.

While whale watching in Ha'apai is possible (there *are* whales to see), it is mostly concentrated on the western side of the group, which affords less protection from Pacific swells.

Whales can also be spotted in the deep-water channel between Tongatapu and 'Eua. Often they are so close to 'Eua they can be seen from the shore.

On the best whale-watching trips you will be given underwater microphones to hear the whales singing, and snorkelling gear so you can swim with the whales – Tonga is one of the few places in the world where this is possible.

Humpback populations in Tonga, as around the world, have declined rapidly since commercial whaling began in the early 20th century. In 1963 the International Whaling Commission established full protection for humpback whales in the southern hemisphere, but illegal poaching of humpbacks by Soviet whalers continued into the 1990s. Subsistence whaling in Tonga (where perhaps 10 whales were taken per year by primitive methods) continued until 1979 when the king banned all whaling.

Since the beginning of the 1990s, when the Soviets stopped whaling, there has been a noticeable increase in the number of humpback whales visiting Tongan waters and Tonga's whale-watching industry has grown proportionately. Consequently, pressure from Japan for permission to begin whaling 'for scientific purposes' has been resisted.

[Continued from page 58]

Making bookings yourself *should* guarantee a reservation. It's often worth making advance bookings between May and September and (especially) over Christmas.

There's a 7.5% government tax on all accommodation (5% VAT plus 2.5% room tax), which is usually, but not always, included in the quoted room price.

Camping
Camping is often discouraged in Tonga and is illegal in both the Ha'apai and Vava'u Groups unless it's part of a guided trip (eg, sea kayaking). In practice, seeking permission from the landowner will suffice.

It's possible to 'bush camp' on 'Eua, and a few accommodation places on 'Eua and Tongatapu will allow you to pitch a tent. See the Tongatapu chapter for more information.

If you do plan to camp somewhere first request permission from the landowner or local community or check in with the main police station for the island. Be sure to practise minimum-impact camping (see Bushwalking in the Activities special section).

Guesthouses
Budget accommodation is found throughout the islands and prices are quite low compared to those in neighbouring countries, with the possible exception of Samoa and Fiji. In every island group there are comfortable and homy guesthouses where you can settle in and spend some time savouring local culture without going broke in the process.

Most guesthouses are clean and several have cooking facilities. The average price per night will be between T$10 and T$25 per person for a bed, more if meals are included. Ordinarily, bath and toilet facilities are communal and often only cold showers are available outside Tongatapu.

Hotels & Resorts
Hotels are more upmarket, but don't expect to find anything like the choice available in Hawaii or French Polynesia. This is a three-star destination at best and some of the 'luxury' hotels just wouldn't cut it internationally.

Tonga also has a number of upmarket resorts, mostly on beautiful, uninhabited coral islands and these can represent good value. There are even a few low-budget resorts in such idyllic locations.

Homestays
Frequently, foreigners will be invited by friendly Tongans to stay in their homes. There could be no better way to learn about the culture and lifestyle of the country, and the hospitality of the Tongan people is abundant and genuine. Keep in mind, though, that their means are limited and although they might proudly refuse any monetary compensation, simple gifts such as kava or tinned corned beef will be greatly appreciated.

One word of warning: there have been occasional reports of local 'hospitality' resulting in robbery of gullible foreigners. Although many cases seem to involve prostitutes and their drunken or unwitting clients, a couple of travellers have reported that valuable items have gone missing while they were staying in local homes.

Bear in mind that in Tonga, Westerners' concepts of ownership apply more in law than in tradition or practice. Keep your valuables in a safe place and don't leave anything of obvious value lying around within view. (See Security in the Dangers & Annoyances section, earlier in this chapter.)

FOOD
The Tongan diet consists mostly of carbohydrate sources (cassava, yams, taro root, plantains and breadfruit), coconut products, taro leaves, fresh fruit, pork, chicken, corned beef and fish. The delicious and imaginative recipes derived from these items make good Tongan cuisine a favourite of anyone fortunate enough to try it.

Unfortunately, the health of the people is suffering as fried fast foods and expensive supermarket items become popular and replace the traditional healthy diet. Tinned vegetables, meat, fish and fruit, white bleached bread and greasy *sipi* (mutton) are often eaten in preference to fresh produce.

Fale koloa (kiosks which open all hours and stock milk, bread and tinned products)

Tuck into a Tongan Feast

A Tongan feast is an event not to be missed. Feasts are staged to commemorate notable events like a royal visit, a school graduation, an agricultural fair, a state holiday or the arrival of a friend or relative from overseas. For events like coronations or royal birthdays, whole villages spend days preparing enough food to feed entire islands! A pig is slaughtered and roasted for each invited guest and, after the VIPs have eaten their fill, the villagers feast on the ample remains.

A feast normally requires an *'umu*, an underground oven used to bake the food. Dishes traditionally served include roasted suckling pig, chicken, *'ika* (fish), *fingota* (shellfish), *'ota 'ika* (a raw fish dish similar to Mexican or Chilean *ceviche*), *lu pulu* (corned beef and boiled taro in coconut cream), *feke* (octopus), *manioke* (cassava), *kumala* (sweet potato), *lu* and *talo* (taro leaves and roots), *'ufi* (yams), curries and delicious *faikakai* (breadfruit pudding). An array of fresh

Preparing the 'umu

fruits and juices will also be served. Women spend hours preparing food, weaving *polas* (stretchers of coconut frond on which food is carried and served) and building palm-leaf pavilions to shelter the guests.

Making & Using an 'Umu

An 'umu is a very effective underground oven used throughout Polynesia and Melanesia. Those who attend a Tongan feast are likely to see the smoke wafting from a small sandy mound.

The Tongan 'umu is quite easy to make. First, a hole is dug in the ground 25cm or so deep and 1m in diameter. Enough coral or volcanic rocks (each 7cm or so in diameter) are collected to fill the bottom of the pit, before a large wood-fuelled bonfire is lit in the pit. Once the fire is alight, the rocks are thrown on top and, when they're glowing hot, the remnants of wood are removed and the rocks are covered with split banana tree trunks, banana leaves or bark.

Now for the food. The root vegetables (talo, 'ufi, manioke and kumala) together with the breadfruit are spread out evenly on top of the rocks. They are covered with a layer of sticks for ventila-

and markets sell the best fresh produce, and can be found in Nuku'alofa, Neiafu (Vava'u) and Pangai (Ha'apai). Private supermarkets and the Tonga Cooperative Federation (TCF) also exist in major towns.

Restaurants

Most Tongans are too poor to eat out in the evening, but a few cheap restaurants serving fried and raw fish dishes open at lunch time to feed office workers. The more expensive restaurants feature foreign cuisine –

Chinese, German and Italian in particular – aimed at tourists. Good Tongan cuisine is available at feasts, 'island nights', and some restaurants. Cheaper eating establishments often serve greasy and gristly variations of American fast food, barbecue dishes and large portions of staple Tongan dishes.

DRINKS
Nonalcoholic Drinks

One of the most refreshing and delicious drinks available is immature coconut milk,

tion and then the meat is placed on the sticks. If an entire animal is being baked it helps, also, if several of the heated rocks are put inside the animal in order to cook it throughout. More sticks, banana leaves and burlap (hessian) or flour sacks are placed over the meat. The pit is filled in with earth and packed tightly.

The less steam that escapes, the more effective the oven. Baking time depends on the nature of the meat. Whole pigs should bake for up to six hours, while small slices will be ready in two. Once everything's been dug out, you're ready to eat.

DIY Tongan Feasts

Try cooking Tonga-style with the following traditional recipes:

Lu Pulu

Lu Pulu is one of the few ways to turn tinned corned beef into a delightful ingredient. First, make coconut cream by grating the meat of three to four mature coconuts. Add one cup of hot water for each two cups of coconut meat, let it stand for a quarter of an hour or so, then pass through cheese-cloth or coconut sennit to extract the cream. Next, cut 20 young taro leaves (lu) into small pieces and boil with 340g of corned beef, one cup of coconut cream, one chopped onion and one teaspoon of salt for 10 to 15 minutes. For a more traditional version, wrap the mixture in a banana leaf, tie with a banana leaf rib and bake in an 'umu for an hour or so.

'Ota 'Ika

Clean and debone 1kg of raw fish (snapper, tuna etc), and cut it into 2cm chunks. Extract juice from four lemons, stir in one teaspoon of salt and allow fish to marinate in this for 1½ hours. Chop an onion, a carrot, a cucumber and a tomato into fine pieces. Drain the fish mixture and add coconut cream made from six mature coconuts (see the Lu Pulu recipe) and the juice from another lemon. When ready to serve, add the vegetables and half a teaspoon of pepper.

Faikakai Topai

Bake one breadfruit (in skin) for one hour. Pound the flesh into a paste and cut into small chunks. Melt two cups of sugar until brown. Add two cups of coconut cream and boil for about 10 minutes or until mixture thickens into a gooey mass. Pour over breadfruit chunks. At this point it may be served, or you can wrap the whole mixture in a banana leaf, tie it with a banana leaf rib and bake in an 'umu for up to an hour. It is also possible to use yam or taro in place of the breadfruit, or to add papaya to the sugar mixture. Be creative with this one – it's delicious!

which is slightly carbonated and renowned for its isotonic properties. If you hope to drink coconuts while bushwalking, always ask permission from landowners before collecting nuts and carry a bush knife to hack away the tough green husk. Mature nuts can be opened (with some difficulty) with a pointed stick and a bit of elbow grease. The meat of the green coconut is soft and pliable and many people prefer it to the crunchy meat of the brown nut. Fruit juices are available to those willing to extract them but un-fortunately most restaurants serve imported juice from cartons. Foreign soft drinks are available virtually everywhere. In addition to the ubiquitous Coca-Cola, Fanta, 7-Up and Lift, you can buy GLO, imported from New Zealand.

The locally grown Royal Coffee is excellent and is sold at the larger supermarkets and served in many of the top-end hotels and restaurants.

Kava, of course, is Tonga's most famous drink – see the boxed text 'Kava Culture'.

Kava Culture

Kava is a drink derived from the ground root of the kava plant (*Piper methysticum*), a pepper species, and is ubiquitous in Tonga. It's a murky liquid, with a slight peppery taste, that leaves your tongue feeling slightly numb and your mind very vague and hazy. The description, however, belies its popularity and Tongans can drink bucketfuls of it in one sitting. Kava circles are basic social units and on Friday nights Tongan men gather and drink kava from late afternoon to the wee hours of the morning.

The active ingredients in kava include 12 to 14 chemicals of an alkaloid nature. Kava is both anaesthetic and analgesic, high in fibre content, low in calories, and serves as a mild tranquilliser, an antibacterial and antifungal agent, a diuretic, an appetite sup-

Traditional kava bowl

pressant and a soporific. Kava is legal in North America, Europe and Australia, and Tongans habitually send packages of it to family members overseas who can't seem to do without it.

Kava is found in a number of Pacific nations, and some of the best kava in Tonga is grown on the island of Tafahi, in the Niuas.

The ground-up root of the kava plant is mixed with water in a carved four-legged bowl. The men (and on rare occasions women) seat themselves in a circle with the bowl at the head. Each man in turn claps and receives a coconut shell full of kava from the server (who is not permitted to drink), who is often a young woman but is occasionally a young man. He'll down it, reserving a bit to sprinkle over his shoulder or dump in an ash tray. Then he'll hurl the shell across the floor back to the server. This procedure continues for hours on end and the drinking rounds are often interspersed with music. Kava is not a narcotic, but it does make one feel lethargic or even nauseous when consumed in large quantities (which it usually is).

Most nights of the week and especially Friday night a *kava kalapu* (club) can be found anywhere in Tonga. Some are simply social events and others are used as fund-raisers and include entertainment and music. Visitors are always welcome and any taxi driver will be able to tell you the location of the nearest one, but bear in mind that kava circles are predominantly male affairs.

Kava also has a more serious side; it's an essential part of traditional Tongan culture. Marriages are not considered sealed until the bride consumes a half-coconut-shell of kava, offered to her by the groom. When a title of nobility is to be conferred, a kava ceremony is held and the new titleholder's drinking of a half-shell of kava confirms the acceptance and investiture of the new title. Contracts and agreements of all kinds are traditionally sealed not with a handshake, but a kava ceremony. Kava ceremonies are also held to commemorate important occasions – including the arrival of visitors. Don't be surprised if you're invited to a kava ceremony while you're in Tonga.

A kava ceremony taking place at the chief's house, Tongatapu, 1833

Alcoholic Drinks

Alcohol is very popular in Tonga, particularly on Tongatapu and Vava'u, where you're never far from a cold beer (except on Sunday, of course). The locally produced Royal is quite good. It comes in three varieties (Premium, Draught and Ikale) and is made in Tonga in cooperation with Pripps brewery of Stockholm, Sweden. Imported beers are also available.

The relatively high price of alcoholic beverages means that many Tongans resort to a yeasty home brew (also called bush beer) made from things found around the house. This is illegal and can also be dangerous. Get a complete rundown of the ingredients and preparation before you drink!

Wines imported from New Zealand, Australia, France, California and elsewhere are available in shops in Nuku'alofa and Neiafu. Some convenience stores sell beer and spirits.

ENTERTAINMENT

Don't miss attending a traditional feast while you're in Tonga. Feasts usually include welcoming kava ceremonies, string band music and performances of traditional Tongan singing and dancing. These events are put on for tourists to give them a taste of Tongan tradition, but you're likely to see just as many locals out for a good time as tourists. Bring along plenty of T$1 notes to stick onto the oiled skin of the dancers to show your appreciation should you feel so inclined – that's what the Tongans will be doing.

Feasts are held regularly on Tongatapu and Vava'u – see those chapters for details.

Friday is the big night for partying in Tonga and the party can last long into Saturday. Tongatapu has several nightclubs to choose from, Neiafu (Vava'u) has two, 'Eua has one and so does Ha'apai.

On Tongatapu there are several bars where you can hear live music, and in Vava'u, musicians play at the Mermaid Restaurant and Tapana Resort. Even 'Eua has a dance hall which occasionally hosts a live band.

Nuku'alofa has one cinema, Loni's, a cultural experience in itself. Several guesthouses and hotels have videos. Television is available in Tongatapu (two channels) and Vava'u (one channel).

SPECTATOR SPORTS

Tongans love sport. Rugby is the national favourite – rugby union and rugby league are played with all-out passion during rugby season, roughly from March to August, when important matches can be seen at Teufaiva Stadium on Tongatapu. The game is also played for fun all year round throughout the country, just about anywhere there's a field or vacant lot. Tonga's national rugby union team, 'Ikale Tahi, represents Tonga in international competitions. Alas many good players of Tongan origin choose to play for other nations – including the great Jonah Lomu – but members of 'Ikale Tahi play for club sides around the world.

Basketball, squash and athletics events are also held at Teufaiva and the stadium's gym is used by the king and crown prince to work out (at their own private times); you can work out here too.

The cricket season lasts roughly from March to July. This is a popular game in Tonga and many villages have a grassy area used for this purpose.

Soccer (football) has had a tremendous boost in recent years with the injection of large amounts of FIFA money. Most schools now have soccer posts and balls and the sport attracts both men and women. The season runs from March to November, but the local standard is not high. At the time of writing, the Tongan team had been beaten 25-0 by Australia.

Cricket and soccer matches are held at Tonga College (near the golf course) and at Mala'e Pangai, on the lawn beside the Royal Palace in Nuku'alofa.

Tennis is another popular sport played by both men and women. An international tennis tournament is held at the 'Atele Indoor Stadium on Tongatapu during the Heilala Week festivities in early July each year. Other sports played at 'Atele include volleyball, badminton, table tennis, boxing, basketball and netball.

Netball is probably the most popular women's sport. Nine-a-side netball is played from November to January. Golf is played on the golf course opposite the 'Atele Indoor Stadium.

SHOPPING

Tongan handicrafts are beautiful and, despite the skill, care and time required to create the expert carvings, weavings, basketry, jewellery and tapa, they are quite reasonably priced. With the exception of the carvings, Tongans themselves use the products they design and make.

The methods used in producing handicrafts are the same today as they were in ancient times and only natural materials are used, including bone, *ahi* (sandalwood), *pueki* (shells), mulberry bark, pandanus fronds and coral. *Taku misi* (sea urchin) are small salmon, peach or orange-coloured shafts which make lovely necklaces when polished. Even more commonly they are used to make wind chimes.

Locally grown vanilla pods and coffee are certainly worth buying, as is the coconut oil scented with ahi and *tuitui* (candlenut) which is great for the skin and hair. In Tongatapu especially, but also in Vava'u, you'll find some funky hand-designed, surfer-style Tongan T-shirts. Other easily transportable souvenirs are the beautiful woven baskets and mats and the tapa cloth which you see throughout the island groups (see the Arts section of the Facts about Tonga chapter for more details).

All Tongan handicrafts are made from natural products but many of these products are protected or restricted overseas, so be careful not to buy souvenirs made from en-

NANCY KELLER

Selection of Tongan handicrafts

dangered animals or plants such as sandalwood, whalebone and tortoiseshell. It is claimed that whalebone carved in Tonga is collected by divers who take it from whales that have died naturally. Black coral is becoming a popular medium but readers are encouraged not to buy products made from it, as this could potentially lead to stocks being wiped out (and, in any case, most Western countries prohibit its importation).

Getting There & Away

The South Pacific is a relatively expensive region to get to, and heading direct to Tonga often doesn't represent good value for money. So if you don't have unlimited funds allowing the luxury of whim-to-whim travel, some careful route planning that may enable further exploration of the South Pacific and Australasia is in order.

Remember that all passengers arriving in Tonga need either an air ticket out (or evidence they've enough money to buy one), an onward ticket on a cruise ship or, in the case of yacht owners, a guarantee that they'll be departing on the same boat on which they arrived.

AIR

The majority of visitors arrive on scheduled flights at Fua'amotu International Airport on Tongatapu, Tonga's main island. A smaller number enter the country at Lupepau'u International Airport on Vava'u, a popular tourist destination in the north of Tonga.

While Tonga isn't as remote or obscure a destination as Tuvalu or Kiribati, neither is it as popular as Fiji or Tahiti and pricey airfares are often a reflection of this. That said, Tonga is becoming increasingly popular as a stopover or cheap 'optional extra' on some tickets and round-the-world fares between Europe or North America and New Zealand. If this applies to you be sure to allow enough time and money to do the country justice.

From New Zealand, Australia, Fiji, Samoa and Hawaii, access to Tonga is fairly direct. From Europe, Asia or North America you will almost certainly need to travel via one of the regional air transport 'hubs' of Auckland (New Zealand) or Nadi (Fiji), 2½ and 1¼ hours from Tonga respectively.

Travellers from North America and Europe should be aware that flights direct to Fiji are more likely to be discounted than those to Tonga. There are direct flights from Nadi to Tongatapu, and at the time of writing, Air Fiji was planning a Nadi to Vava'u service. A return ticket between Nadi and Tonga

costs about US$200, so if you can turn up a great deal to Fiji you may save money.

Another option is to link up with the Air New Zealand flight from Los Angeles to Apia (Western Samoa). From Western Samoa you have the option of flying either to Tongatapu or Vava'u in Tonga.

Many flights from Europe, Asia and North America entail a change of carrier, though code-sharing and through-ticketing agreements make the change straightforward enough. The three major carriers in the region are Air New Zealand, Air Pacific (code-sharing with Qantas) and Polynesian Airlines.

Flight prices fluctuate throughout the year. Generally, the high season falls over the Christmas holiday period (December and January) when flights from New Zealand, Australia and the USA can be full with Tongan expats returning for the holidays. Fares from Europe and North America rise between June and August. Book well in advance if you want to travel at these times.

Buying Tickets

Airlines have never been more competitive, making international travel better value than ever, but you have to research the options carefully to get the best deal. The Internet is an increasingly useful resource for checking air fares.

Full-time students and anyone aged under 26 years (30 in some countries) have access to better deals than other travellers. You have to show a document proving your date of birth or a valid International Student Identity Card (ISIC) when buying your ticket and boarding the plane.

There is generally nothing to be gained by buying a ticket direct from the airline. Airlines release discounted tickets to selected travel agents and specialist discount agencies, and these are usually the cheapest deals going.

Booking on the Internet is one exception. Some airlines offer excellent fares to Web surfers; they may sell seats by auction or simply cut prices to reflect the reduced cost of electronic selling.

Many travel agencies around the world have Web sites, which can make the Internet a quick and easy way to compare prices. There's also an increasing number of online agents which operate only on the Internet.

Online ticket sales work well if you are making a simple one-way or return trip on specified dates. However, online fare generators are no substitute for a travel agent who knows all about special deals, has strategies for avoiding layovers and can offer advice on everything from which airline has the best vegetarian food to the most appropriate travel insurance to bundle with your ticket.

You may find the cheapest flights are advertised by obscure agencies. Most such firms are honest and solvent, but there are some rogue fly-by-night outfits around. Paying by credit card generally offers protection (though you may incur a surcharge), as most card issuers provide refunds if you can prove you didn't get what you paid for. Similar protection can be obtained by buying a ticket from a bonded agent, such as one covered by the Air Travel Organiser's Licence (ATOL) scheme in the UK. Agents who accept only cash should hand over the tickets straight away and not tell you to 'come back tomorrow'. After you've made a booking or paid your deposit, call the airline and confirm that the booking was made. It's generally not advisable to send money (even cheques) through the post unless the agent is very well established – some travellers have reported being ripped off by fly-by-night mail-order ticket agents.

If you purchase a ticket and later want to make changes to your route or get a refund, you need to contact the original travel agent. Airlines issue refunds only to the purchaser of a ticket – usually the travel agent who bought the ticket on your behalf. Many travellers change routes halfway through trips, so think carefully before buying a ticket which is not easily refunded.

Courier Flights

Getting to Tonga by courier flight is not easy. Courier flights between North America or Europe and Australia are possible, but probably only worth considering if they're *really* cheap (say US$450) and if they permit a long stay. From Australia and New Zealand courier flights to Nadi (Fiji), not Tonga, are possible.

For further information contact the airfreight companies in your home country, or the International Association of Air Travel Couriers (IAATC). It has US offices (☎ 561-582 8320, e iaat@courier.org, w www.courier.org) and UK offices (☎ 0800-0746 481, e info@aircourier.co.uk, w www.aircourier.co.uk). Membership is US$45 for US residents and US$50 for everybody else (£35 in the UK), but membership is no guarantee of courier work.

International Air Passes

International air passes are great for island-hopping around the Pacific. Polynesian Airlines' Polypass is good for 45 days (excluding the Christmas holiday period) and includes travel in Tonga, Samoa, American Samoa, Fiji, Australia and New Zealand.

Air Travel Glossary

Alliances Many of the world's leading airlines are now intimately involved with each other, sharing everything from reservations systems and check-in to aircraft and frequent-flyer schemes. Opponents say that alliances restrict competition. Whatever the arguments, there is no doubt that big alliances are the way of the future.

Courier Fares Businesses often need to send urgent documents or freight securely and quickly. Courier companies hire people to accompany the package through customs and, in return, offer a discount ticket which is sometimes a bargain. However, you may have to surrender all your baggage allowance and take only carry-on luggage.

Fares Airlines traditionally offer 1st class (coded F), business class (coded J) and economy class (coded Y) tickets. These days there are so many promotional and discounted fares available that few passengers pay full fare.

Lost Tickets If you lose your airline ticket, an airline will usually treat it like a travellers cheque and, after inquiries, issue you with another one. Legally, however, an airline is entitled to treat a ticket like cash and if you lose it then it's gone forever. Take very good care of your tickets.

Onward Tickets An entry requirement for many countries is that you have a ticket out of the country. If you're unsure of your next move, the easiest solution is to buy the cheapest onward ticket to a neighbouring country or a ticket from a reliable airline which can later be refunded if you do not use it.

Open-Jaw Tickets These are return tickets where you fly out to one place but return from another. If available, this can save you backtracking to your arrival point.

Overbooking Since every flight has some passengers who fail to show up, airlines often book more passengers than they have seats. Usually excess passengers make up for the no-shows, but occasionally somebody gets 'bumped' onto the next available flight. Guess who it is most likely to be? The passengers who check in late. If you do get 'bumped', you are normally offered some form of compensation.

Reconfirmation Some airlines require you to reconfirm your flight at least 72 hours prior to departure. Check your travel documents to see if this is the case

Restrictions Discounted tickets often have various restrictions on them – such as needing to be paid for in advance and incurring a penalty to be altered or cancelled. Others are restrictions on the minimum and maximum period you must be away.

Round-the-World Tickets RTW tickets give you a limited period (usually a year) in which to circumnavigate the globe. You can go anywhere the carrying airlines go, as long as you don't backtrack. The number of stopovers or total number of separate flights is decided before you set off and they usually cost a bit more than a basic return flight.

Ticketless Travel Airlines are gradually waking up to the realisation that paper tickets are unnecessary encumbrances. On simple one-way or return trips, reservations details can be held on computer and the passenger merely shows ID to claim their seat.

Transferred Tickets Airline tickets cannot be transferred from one person to another. Travellers sometimes try to sell the return half of their ticket, but officials can ask you to prove that you are the person named on the ticket. On an international flight, tickets are compared with passports.

The basic cost is US$999 (children under the age of 12 pay US$699). There's also an option to include Honolulu (US$1198), or Honolulu and Los Angeles (US$1449). Adding Tahiti costs an extra US$199. The USA/Australia/New Zealand sectors are limited to one round-trip each, but you are allowed unlimited travel between the Pacific islands.

The Pacific Explorer Air Pass is similar to the Polypass, but allows for more options for travel from the USA. The 45-day pass costs US$999 and allows for travel between Australia, New Zealand, Samoa, Tonga and Fiji. For US$1798 you can include travel to and from Honolulu, Los Angeles, San Francisco or Seattle.

The Triangle Pass, also from Polynesian Airlines, enables travel between Tonga, Fiji and Samoa for US$462.

The Visit South Pacific Pass offers discounted airfares on a wide variety of South Pacific routes. The options are many and varied – altogether the pass covers 45 possible routes. Airlines which participate in the scheme include Aircalin, Air Nauru, Air Niugini (Air New Guinea), Air Pacific, Air Vanuatu, Polynesian Airlines, Qantas, Royal Tongan Airlines and Solomon Airlines. The pass must be purchased in conjunction with an international air ticket from outside the Pacific region, but can offer fare savings of up to 50%. All passes are basically tailor-made; discuss your options with your travel agent.

Round-the-World & Circle Pacific Tickets

Round-the-World (RTW) tickets offered by various airline alliances give travellers an almost endless variety of possible airline and destination combinations. They can be excellent value – you'll pay around US$2100, A$2650 or UK£1250 for a RTW that takes in Tonga. Star Alliance (a code-sharing group of airlines that includes Air New Zealand) offers what is probably the best RTW for Tonga. Fifteen stops are allowed and the ticket is valid for up to 12 months.

Circle Pacific tickets use a combination of airlines to circle the countries and continents of the Pacific – including Australia, New Zealand, North America and Asia and allowing stops at a number of South Pacific islands. Circle Pacific fares are good value if you are travelling to Australia and the Pacific from destinations around the USA (from US$2199, at the time of writing), but are not such good value from Australasia. From North America, Air New Zealand offers some good Circle Pacific fares that include Tonga.

Travellers with Special Needs

If they're warned early enough, airlines can often make special arrangements for travellers such as wheelchair assistance at airports, visual notification of airport announcements for deaf travellers or special meals on the flight. Children aged under two travel for 10% of the standard fare (or free on some airlines) as long as they don't occupy a seat. They don't get a baggage allowance. 'Skycots', baby food and nappies should be provided by the airline if requested in advance. Children aged between two and 12 can usually occupy a seat for half to two-thirds of the full fare and do get a baggage allowance.

The disability-friendly Allgohere Web site (W www.everybody.co.uk) has an airline directory that provides information on the facilities offered by various airlines.

Departure Tax

Departure tax is T$20, payable at the airport in cash.

The USA

Los Angeles and Honolulu are the two major gateway cities for travel between North America and the South Pacific. Although a huge amount of Pacific traffic passes through Los Angeles, there are also direct flights to Honolulu from nearly every major city in the USA. In Honolulu you can connect with the weekly Air New Zealand flight going direct to Tonga.

A code-share agreement between Air New Zealand and United Airlines probably offers the quickest routing from Los Angeles to Tonga via Honolulu, but at the time of writing the cheapest return fare from LA to

Tonga was with Air Pacific via Nadi (Fiji) – US$1285 in the low season. A return fare on the same route from New York was US$2136. Flying via Nadi instead of Honolulu often makes little difference time-wise.

If you are coming from the USA, Air New Zealand's Coral Fare – a three-month Los Angeles to Auckland or Australia return – is a good-value fare option. Costing US$1178 in the low season, the fare allows for one free stopover in the Pacific – Tonga, Honolulu, Tahiti, Samoa, Rarotonga or Fiji – plus an extra three stopovers at US$150 per stopover.

Discount travel agents in the USA are known as consolidators (although you won't see a sign on the door saying 'Consolidator'). San Francisco is the ticket consolidator capital of America, although some good deals can be found in Los Angeles, New York and other big cities.

Council Travel, America's largest student travel organisation, has around 60 offices in the USA; its head office (☎ 800-226 8624) is at 205 E 42 St, New York, NY 10017. Call to find out the office nearest you or visit its Web site (W www.counciltravel.com). STA Travel (☎ 800-777 0112, W www.statravel.com) has offices in Boston, Chicago, Miami, New York, Philadelphia, San Francisco and other major cities. Telephone for office locations or visit its Web site.

Travel agents with more background knowledge and who specialise in the South Pacific region include Island Adventures (☎ 805-685 9230, toll-free ☎ 800-289 4957, e motuman@aol.com) and Discover Wholesale Travel (☎ 800-576 7770 in California, 800-759 7330 elsewhere, e disc_tvlix.netcom.com).

Ticket Planet is a leading ticket consolidator in the USA and is recommended. Visit its Web site (W www.ticketplanet.com).

The Sunday travel sections of papers like the *Los Angeles Times*, *San Francisco Examiner*, *Chicago Tribune* and *New York Times* always have plenty of ads for cheap airline tickets. The west-coast papers are especially useful for South Pacific flights. The magazine *Travel Unlimited* (PO Box 1058, Allston, Mass 02134) publishes details of the cheapest airfares and courier possibilities for destinations all over the world from the USA.

Canada

Canadians will probably find the best South Pacific deals are via Honolulu. Like travellers from the USA, you'll probably fly with at least two different code-sharing carriers. At the time of writing, the cheapest low-season return fares all went via Honolulu and Nadi (Fiji) – Toronto to Tonga was C$2946 with American Airlines; Vancouver to Tonga C$2550 with Air Pacific; and Calgary to Tonga C$1840 on Qantas/Air Pacific.

Air Canada flies between Vancouver and Honolulu, where you can connect with Air New Zealand's weekly flight from Honolulu to Tonga.

See the USA and International Air Passes sections for more details on air travel in the Pacific region from North America. Canadian consolidators' air fares tend to be about 10% higher than those in the USA.

Travel Cuts (☎ 800-667 2887, W www.travelcuts.com) is Canada's national student travel agency (though nonstudents can use it too) and has offices in all major cities.

The Toronto *Globe & Mail* and *Vancouver Sun* carry travel agents' ads. The magazine *Great Expeditions* (PO Box 8000-411, Abbotsford, BC V2S 6H1) is also useful.

South America

Lan Chile has three flights a week between Papeete (Tahiti) and Santiago (Chile), with a stop at Easter Island on the way. In Papeete you can connect with the Air New Zealand network for onward flights to Australasia and the South Pacific.

Australia & New Zealand

Travelling to Tonga from Australia or New Zealand is straightforward, but not necessarily inexpensive. There are a number of regular scheduled flights available, but bear in mind that the Christmas holiday season (December to January) is the busiest and most expensive time to fly. Standard fares increase by up to 25% though 'holiday specials' are occasionally offered.

Travellers should also be aware that ever-increasing code-share agreements mean that it should be easy to arrange through-ticketing from destinations across Australia and New Zealand.

From Australia, flights to Tonga are with Air New Zealand, Royal Tongan Airlines and Polynesian Airlines. Polynesian Airlines offers direct flights from Sydney and flights from Melbourne via Wellington in New Zealand. Royal Tongan Airlines flies direct to Tonga from Sydney once a week. Air New Zealand flights from Australia to Tonga are all via Auckland and low-season return fares start at A$1094 (from Sydney) rising to A$1262 (from Melbourne).

Air Pacific's flights via Fiji are another option. From Sydney, low-season returns start at A$1055.

Air New Zealand (twice weekly), Royal Tongan Airlines (Monday to Saturday) and Polynesian Airlines (once weekly) all operate direct flights between Auckland and Tonga. It's a 2½- to three-hour flight. Polynesian Airlines also offers a weekly service between Wellington and Tonga. Return low-season fares start at NZ$1002 (from Auckland) rising to NZ$1059 (from Wellington). Coming from Tonga flights start at around T$850 return, T$650 one-way.

Two well-known agents for cheap fares from Australia are STA Travel and Flight Centre. STA Travel (☎ 131 776 Australia-wide, W www.statravel.com.au) has its main office in Melbourne at 224 Faraday St, Carlton, and has offices in all major cities and on many university campuses. Call for the location of your nearest branch or visit the Web site. Flight Centre (☎ 131 600 Australia-wide, W www.flightcentre.com .au) has a central office at 82 Elizabeth St, Sydney, and there are dozens of offices throughout Australia.

Hideaway Holidays (☎ 02-9743 0253, W www.hideawayholidays.com.au) is a highly recommended South Pacific specialist.

In New Zealand, Flight Centre (☎ 09-309 6171, W flightcentre.co.nz) has a central office in Auckland at National Bank Towers (corner Queen and Darby Sts) and many branches throughout the country. STA Travel (☎ 09-309 0458, W www.statravel.com.au) has its main office at 10 High St, Auckland, and other offices in Auckland, Hamilton, Palmerston North, Wellington, Christchurch and Dunedin.

Numerous companies advertise cheap flights in the travel sections of many weekend newspapers.

The UK & Continental Europe

Europeans intending to travel direct to Tonga will most likely be routed through Los Angeles, Nadi (Fiji) or Auckland. Tonga is about as far away from Europe as you can get, so many travellers take the opportunity to explore the rest of the South Pacific and Australasia on the same trip (see the International Air Passes and Round-the-World & Circle Pacific Tickets sections earlier in this chapter).

The best fares from Europe to Tonga are currently with Air New Zealand from London via Los Angeles then Auckland or Nadi.

However, various code-sharing agreements with Air New Zealand's Star Alliance partners mean that other stopovers and routings through the South Pacific are possible.

At the time of writing, Air New Zealand's cheapest return fares to Tonga, via Los Angeles and Auckland, were UK£960/670 (high/low season). You are allowed one free stopover in each direction. Air New Zealand's flights via Fiji are at least 10% more expensive.

Discount air travel is big business in London. Advertisements for many travel agencies appear in the travel pages of the weekend broadsheet newspapers (probably the best places to look) and in *Time Out*, the *Evening Standard* and in the free magazine *TNT*.

For students or travellers aged under 26 years, popular travel agencies in the UK include STA Travel (☎ 08701-600 599, W www .statravel.co.uk), which has an office at 86 Old Brompton Rd, London SW7, and Usit Campus (☎ 0870-240 1010, W www.usitca mpus.co.uk), which has an office at 52 Grosvenor Gardens, London SW1. Both agencies have branches throughout the UK and will sell tickets to all travellers but cater especially to young people and students.

Other recommended travel agents for cheap deals include Trailfinders (☎ 020-7938 3939), Travelbag (☎ 0870-730 3201) and Bridge the World (☎ 0870-444 7474). All are helpful and highly recommended.

From Germany, Lufthansa flies from Frankfurt to Los Angeles where passengers connect with Air New Zealand flights to the South Pacific. Other cheap fares go via Sydney. Recommended German agencies include STA Travel (☎ 030-311 0950, Ⓦ www.statravel.de), Goethestrasse 73, 10625 Berlin plus branches in major cities across the country, and Usit Campus (call centre ☎ 01805 788336 or Cologne ☎ 0221 923990, Ⓦ www.usitcampus.de), which also has several offices throughout the country.

Travellers from Italy will probably have to fly via LA or Vancouver. Cheap flights from Rome/Milan via London are sometimes available. Recommended Italian travel agents include CTS Viaggi (06-462 0431), 16 Via Genova, Rome, a student and youth specialist with branches in major cities, and Passagi (☎ 06-474 0923), Stazione Termini FS, Galleria Di Tesla, Rome.

In the Netherlands, recommended agencies include NBBS Reizen (☎ 020-620 5071, Ⓦ www.nbbs.nl), 66 Rokin, Amsterdam, plus branches in most cities, and Budget Air (☎ 020-627 1251, Ⓦ www.nbbs.nl), 34 Rokin, Amsterdam.

In France, recommended agencies include Usit Connect Voyages (☎ 01 42 44 14 00), 14 rue de Vaugirard, 75006 Paris, and OTU Voyages (☎ 01 40 29 12 12, Ⓦ www.otu.fr), 39 ave Georges-Bernanos, 75005 Paris. Others include Voyageurs du Monde (☎ 01 42 86 16 00), 55 rue Ste-Anne, 75002 Paris, and Nouvelles Frontières (☎ 01 45 68 70 00, Ⓦ www.nouvelles-frontieres.fr), 87 blvd de Grenelle, 75015 Paris. These all have branches across the country.

Asia & Japan

Several convenient air routes exist between Tonga, Asia and Japan. Air Pacific operates direct flights connecting Tokyo and Osaka with Nadi (Fiji), while Air New Zealand operates direct flights between Nagoya and Nadi. In Nadi you can connect to a direct flight to Tonga with Air Pacific, Royal Tongan Airlines or Air Fiji. Coming from other parts of Asia, most flights are routed through Auckland (New Zealand) and Nadi.

Ticket discounting is widespread in Asia, particularly in Hong Kong, Singapore and Bangkok. Hong Kong is probably the discount capital of the region. There are a lot of fly-by-night operators in the Asian market so a little care is required. STA, which is reliable, has branches in Hong Kong (☎ 2390 0421), Tokyo (☎ 03-5391 2922), Singapore (☎ 737 7188) and Bangkok (☎ 02-236 0262).

Other Pacific Islands

If you want to see a host of other Pacific islands you'll be better off financially if you purchase an air pass (see the International Air Passes and Round-the-World & Circle Pacific Tickets sections earlier in this chapter), although return flights (usually valid for one month) between Tonga and its neighbours can occasionally be good value.

Air Fiji flies between Suva (Fiji) and Tongatapu twice a week, while Air Pacific and Royal Tongan Airlines (RTA) both fly between Tongatapu and Nadi (Fiji) three times a week. RTA's flights are cheapest: T$161 one way, T$203 for a 28-day return to both destinations. A return ticket open for a year costs around T$600. At the time of writing, Air Fiji was planning flights into Vava'u from Nadi.

From Tongatapu, Polynesian Airlines flies to Apia (Western Samoa) three times a week (T$334 one way, T$352 28-day return). Direct weekly flights between Vava'u and Pago Pago (American Samoa) are offered by Air Samoa (T$356/646 one way/return valid for 12 months) and onward connections from here to Apia are straightforward (T$425/850 one way/return).

Air New Zealand has a weekly flight from Tonga to Rarotonga via Auckland (T$1700 90-day return) and a weekly direct flight from Tonga to Honolulu (T$895/1268 one way/90-day return).

RTA also puts on a weekly Tongatapu to Niue flight via Vava'u (a two-hour trip). From Vava'u fares are T$214 one way and T$428 28-day return. Oddly, from Tongatapu the return fare is cheaper (T$380). RTA is the only international airline serving Niue.

SEA
Cargo Ship
Many travellers arrive in the South Pacific with grand dreams of island-hopping aboard cargo ships, but few actually manage it. All sorts of insurance and freight company restrictions have made such travel difficult and often very expensive (at least equal to the cost of a flight).

The only ship officially offering passages to and from Tonga is the MV *Southern Cross*. Once a month it leaves from Auckland bound for Tongatapu and Vava'u, and from there to Apia (Western Samoa) and Pago Pago (American Samoa) before returning to Auckland. The round trip costs US$1380 to US$1520 and the ship takes seven people. The hop between Nuku'alofa and Apia costs T$320 one way. Contact McKay Shipping (☎ 09-309 0229) in Auckland or Transam Shipping (☎ 23211, e transam@kalianet.to) in Nuku'alofa.

Western and American Samoa can also be reached by cargo ship from North America. The Internet is a great source of information on travel by freighter. Try Freighterman (w www.geocities.com/freighterman.geo/mainmenu.html), the Cruise & Freighter Travel Association (☎ 800-872 8584, w www.travltips.com) and Freighterworld (☎ 800-531 7774, w www.freighterworld.com).

If you fail to get a berth on the *Southern Cross* inquire with all the local shipping companies and at the docks in Nuku'alofa. Should you find a passage you may have to be signed on as crew for insurance purposes.

Travelling by yacht to and from Tonga is a more realistic possibility.

Yacht
Between May and October the harbours of the South Pacific swarm with cruising yachts from around the world, many following the favourable winds west from the Americas, while others come north from New Zealand.

The season's first flotilla from New Zealand to Tonga is organised by Island Cruising South Pacific (☎ 025-957 977, e hepburn@islandcruising.co.nz, w www.islandcruising.co.nz), PO Box 90255, Auckland.

Access to Tonga from the north is almost always via the Samoas. Often yachts anchor for a few days in Niuatoputapu where they check into Tonga before crowding into Vava'u's Port of Refuge, anchoring in front of the Paradise International Hotel and proceeding to set up the annual yachting social colony that is really going strong by October. Most yachties take day trips around the Vava'u Group before heading on to Nuku'alofa, with a possible intermediate visit to the Ha'apai Group.

The yachting community is quite friendly, especially toward those who display an interest in yachts and other things nautical. Sometimes they are looking for crew, and for those who'd like a bit of low-key adventure, this is the way to go. Most of the time, crew members will only be asked to take a turn on watch – that is, scan the horizon for cargo ships, hazardous objects and the odd reef – and possibly to cook or clean. In port, crew may be required to dive and scrape the bottom, paint or make repairs. Sailing experience is usually not necessary; 'green' crew members learn as they go. Most yachties charge crew US$10 to US$15 per day for food and supplies.

The best places for securing a passage on a cruising yacht include the west coast of the USA (San Francisco, Newport Beach, San Diego), Honolulu, Papeete (Tahiti), Pago Pago (American Samoa), Apia (Western Samoa) and Auckland (New Zealand). The best way to advertise your availability is to post a notice on the bulletin board of the yacht club in the port. It's also helpful to visit the docks and ask around for anyone needing crew. Be as flexible as possible – when an opportunity comes you should grab it.

It's a fact of life that the most successful passage-seekers tend to be young women who are willing to crew-on with male 'single-handers' (those sailing solo). Some male skippers will shamelessly advertise for young women; it shouldn't take a rocket scientist to work out the subtext of such advertisements.

Yachting Regulations

- Never anchor in coral beds or allow your anchor to drag through live coral.
- Always anchor in sand or deeper water.
- Loud parties, noise and making repairs/operating power tools are prohibited on Sunday.
- Nude (or, for women, topless) sunbathing on deck is not permitted in harbours or when anchored within view of shore.
- Export by yacht of any marine product, such as shells, carved black coral or commercial quantities of fish or shellfish, requires a permit from customs (this permit may also prevent hassles in subsequent ports of call). Uncarved black coral may not be exported under any circumstances.
- All commercial activities are officially discouraged.

For sanity's sake, bear in mind that the conditions of a long ocean voyage greatly magnify rivalries and petty concerns. Only set out on a long passage with someone with whom you feel relatively compatible and remember that, on board, skipper's rule is law.

To enjoy some freedom of movement on a yacht, it's a good idea to find one that has wind-vane steering. Nobody likes to spend all day and night at the wheel staring at a compass, and more often than not such a job goes to the crew member of the lowest status. Comfort is also greater on yachts with a furling jib, a dodger to protect against the elements, a toilet and shower.

Yachts rigged for racing are generally more manageable than simple live-aboards. As a general rule, about 3m yacht length per person aboard affords relatively uncrowded conditions.

Even if you aren't interested in cruising, yachties represent a good source of information with their mind-boggling knowledge of world weather patterns, navigation and maritime geography.

Despite the wealthy aura, most yachties are as impecunious as the average backpacker and are always looking for ways to pick up some extra cash. If you're looking for a babysitter or a day charter, just ask

around the harbours, particularly in Neiafu and Nuku'alofa. Many yachties will teach celestial navigation and sailing for a reasonable fee.

Arriving by Yacht Ports of entry for cruising yachts are Nuku'alofa (Tongatapu), Neiafu (Vava'u), Pangai on Lifuka (Ha-'apai), Falehau (Niuatoputapu) and Futu (Niuafo'ou).

In Nuku'alofa, in order to check in and clear immigration, raise your yellow quarantine flag and anchor in the restricted anchorage area, or pull up alongside Queen Salote Wharf or the yacht harbour (2.6m deep at the entrance and dredged to 3m inside). Summon customs and immigration officials by radioing VHF channel 69. Instruction will be given on VHF channel 12.

Customs and immigration officials will board, ask routine questions about food and health, and then request passports and a passenger list. Firearms and ammunition must be surrendered to customs, to be returned on departure. The boarding officers at Nuku'alofa are based in the One Stop Shop on Queen Salote Wharf (☎ 23967), open 8.30am to 4.30pm weekdays. Check-in is not possible on weekends. If you wish to leave on a weekend you must clear customs on Friday.

In Vava'u, pull up at the southern end of Neiafu Wharf and contact the boarding officers (☎ 70053) who work from 8.30am to 4.30pm weekdays.

At Niuafo'ou, it will be impossible to pull up alongside so you'll have to anchor offshore and wait for a calm moment to battle your way through the waves to the shore in a dinghy.

According to one report, caution should be used when approaching the port at Niuatoputapu; there is only one marker and two range sites, which are inaccurate by about 5m. If you get the range sites to line up you'll run aground!

There's a charge for anchoring anywhere in Tongan waters. This is payable upon departure at the Ports Authority (☎ 23168, fax 24267) at Queen Salote Wharf or whichever port you're using. The initial charge in

Tongan dollars for between one day and one month is calculated by multiplying 0.77 by the gross tonnage of the yacht.

Day cruising within island groups is unrestricted but for cruising between island groups (Tongatapu, Ha'apai, Vava'u and the Niuas), you'll have to pay all harbour dues and pick up a Coastal Clearance Permit from a customs officer. A permit to cruise between Nuku'alofa and Vava'u may be amended to include Ha'apai, allowing you to stop in Ha'apai without picking up a separate permit.

You must always check in with customs when visiting a new port, even if you've already been admitted to the country.

Emergencies To summon the harbour master and for emergencies use VHF channel 16. However, there's only a slight chance that any Tongan government or navy vessel will come to your assistance (they rarely have fuel); your best bet is the local sailing and fishing community. If you're in VHF range of Vava'u, contact the charter yacht companies Sunsail (VHF channel 68) and The Moorings (VHF channel 72) who can coordinate rescue efforts.

Any response to a triggered EPERB (a emergency beacon that sends SOS messages via satellite) will come from, or be coordinated by, the New Zealand navy. It may take days before help arrives.

Getting Around

AIR

Flying is the easiest and fastest way to get around Tonga, but travellers have only one choice; Royal Tongan Airlines (RTA), the national flag carrier. It operates three planes: an 18-seat Twin Otter and 36-seat Shorts 360 for domestic flights and a Boeing 737 for international flights.

Under-capacity and unreliability are a problem and flights are cancelled or re-scheduled at short notice, making delays and missed connections common. Reconfirm your flight 72 hours before departure (leaving a contact phone number) and then reconfirm again 24 hours before flying. If you have an international connection you *must* catch, return to Tongatapu two days beforehand, to be safe.

There are no flights in Tonga on Sunday. The busiest time of year for both domestic and international flights is between December and January, the Christmas holidays. Mid-June to mid-July is another busy time, as is Easter. Special events (church conferences, mostly) in the kingdom also put a strain on the network. RTA's Web site W www.flyroyaltongan.com gives a rough guide to schedules and prices.

Domestic Air Services

Only the small Twin Otter 18-seater plane can land at Ha'apai, 'Eua, Niuatoputapu and Niuafo'ou, while the larger 36-seater Shorts services Vava'u (and the weekly international flight to Niue, which goes via Vava'u). On some occasions the Twin Otter will continue on from Ha'apai to Vava'u before returning to Tongatapu, so when flying to Vava'u you'll sometimes have the choice between the smaller or larger aircraft.

Weekly flights between Tongatapu and the Niuas go via Vava'u, but this service is especially prone to cancellation. In addition, the islands of Niuatoputapu and Niuafo'ou are serviced on different days of the week and there's no connecting flight between them.

The baggage allowance on all domestic flights is 10kg unless you're connecting to or from an international flight, in which case you're allowed 20kg. You and your hand luggage (5kg is allowed) are weighed at check-in. There's often some discretion with excess baggage, which is charged at T$6 for the first kilogram and then T$1.35/T$0.70 (to Vava'u/Ha'apai) for every extra kilogram.

Fares, weekly frequencies and flight durations are given in the following table. Children aged between two and 12 years pay 67% of adult fare; children under two pay 10%.

Air Passes

RTA's Kingdom Pass allows for travel between Tongatapu, Ha'apai, Vava'u and 'Eua, all for T$250, and is sold in combination

Domestic Flights & Fares

flight	one way	return	No/week	duration
Tongatapu-'Eua	T$20	T$38	4	10 mins
Tongatapu-Ha'apai	T$71	T$131	6 *	50 mins
Tongatapu-Vava'u	T$136	T$261	6	1¼ hrs
Tongatapu-Niuatoputapu	T$239	T$455	1	2¾ hrs
Tongatapu-Niuafo'ou	T$293	T$563	1	3¼ hrs
Ha'apai-Vava'u	T$74	T$131	3	40 mins
Vava'u-Niuatoputapu	T$120	T$228	1	1¼ hrs
Vava'u-Niuafo'ou	T$179	T$347	1	1½ hrs

* Twice on Monday and Saturday

with international travel commencing in the northern hemisphere (Europe, USA, Japan etc). The pass may be purchased alongside an international ticket or from the main RTA office in Tongatapu (see the Tongatapu Group chapter). Domestic reservations may be made or changed after arrival in Tonga.

The pass is good for as long as your international ticket is valid. There's no charge to alter reservation dates, but there is a T$10 charge for route changes.

BUS

Local buses run on Tongatapu Island and Vava'u Island, and on Lifuka and Foa in the Ha'apai Group. Tongatapu has a fairly decent bus network, but on other islands transport is limited. In the urban areas of Tongatapu, bus stops are marked with a sign reading 'Pasi'. Elsewhere, flag down buses by waving your outstretched arm.

The biggest problem with bus travel on the outer islands is that the buses operate infrequently or only if enough passengers accumulate for a trip. Buses may quit running early in the day and remaining passengers counting on bus service may be stranded. Also, some buses in outlying districts often exist only to ferry students and villagers to and from town in the morning and afternoon. Don't rely on catching a bus after about 3pm.

Fares

Fares range from 40 seniti to T$1.20 depending upon the island and the distance travelled. On most buses, passengers pay the fare on exiting the bus.

CAR & MOTORCYCLE

Drinking and driving is strictly forbidden in Tonga, even though it's apparent that the practice is widespread. If there's an accident and you have alcohol on your breath, you're sent to prison whether or not you were at fault.

Drivers should keep their speed down to 40km/h in villages and towns and 65km/h elsewhere, especially now that the police have radar guns. If you're caught speeding, you'll have to pay a fine (T$1 for each kilometre per hour you're over the limit).

Tongan driving skills are not the sharpest in the world (you only need to pass a simple theory test to get a licence); many people drive everywhere at under 40km/h and some vehicles are only held together by the sheer will of the occupants. Expect the unexpected.

On Tongatapu – where a huge increase in vehicle numbers means you'll now see traffic jams in Nuku'alofa! – if you see a motorcade flanked by police motorcyclists and containing a large Dodge van with blacked-out windows, pull off the road and wait for it to pass. It's the king. Smaller motorcades containing the queen, the princess or one of the princes occasionally crawl through town and demand similar respect.

Rental

Rental cars are available on Tongatapu, Ha'apai and Vava'u (see those chapters for details) but away from Tongatapu it may often be easier, and cheaper, to hire a taxi for the day (at least the driver will know where they're going). Scooters are a cheaper alternative to hiring a car and are available on Tongatapu and Vava'u. Those choosing to drive or ride will need to buy a Visitor's Driving Licence (see Visas & Documents in the Facts for the Visitor chapter).

BICYCLE

Cycling is a great way to get around the kingdom and allows you to see the islands at island pace. You can probably transport your bike by plane to Vava'u, but you'll need to take it by ferry to Ha'apai and the Niuas.

See the Activities chapter for general information, and the island group chapters for specific information on bicycle hire.

HORSE

Horses can be hired on all inhabited islands: just ask anyone who owns a horse and you're likely to be able to strike up an informal deal. Expect to pay between T$10 and T$15 per day. Horses are usually only available without saddle, reins etc, so unless you're a good bareback rider, you could have problems. Tongan horses also seem adept at shedding unwanted objects from their backs, especially if they don't like you!

HITCHING

Hitching is never entirely safe in any country and we don't recommend it. Travellers who decide to hitch should understand that they are taking a small but potentially serious risk. People who do choose to hitch will be safer if they travel in pairs and let someone know where they are planning to go.

However, hitching is fairly common in Tonga, especially where public transport is rare. You will have better luck if you flag down a vehicle rather than sticking out your thumb. Only occasionally will you be asked to pay.

BOAT
Inter-Island Ferry

Several passenger ferries operate between the main island groups.

A trip by ferry in Tonga is a cultural experience on a major scale. Most passengers travel deck class (a cabin costs the same as an airfare) and indoor spaces are stuffy, cramped and claustrophobic, with nowhere to lie down, while outdoor spaces can be wet and/or cold. The toilets are truly awful, overflowing and sloshing around early into the journey, and vomiting fellow passengers

don't enhance the experience either – Tongans, though a seafaring people, tend to all get seasick as soon as the boat leaves the harbour if the sea is rough. Also, the boats are always running late. That said, if the weather is good and the sea calm it's easy going but finding somewhere to sleep can be hard.

The MV 'Olovaha, a squat, German-built boat, is owned by the Shipping Corporation of Polynesia (☎ 23853, fax 22617, e shipcorp@kalianet.to), which has an office on Queen Salote Wharf in Nuku'alofa and others near the wharves in Vava'u (☎ 70128) and Ha'apai (☎ 60699). The 'Olovaha is a flat-bottomed boat (which doesn't help in rough seas) and runs weekly between Tongatapu (Nuku'alofa), Ha'apai (Ha'afeva and Lifuka Islands) and Vava'u (Neiafu). Every month or so it continues to the Niuas, but is rarely able to land at Niuafo'ou.

The 'Olovaha offers three classes of fare: economy (grab a seat if you can), business class (complete with table, meals, chair and videos, but no bed) and first class (a berth in a two-bed cabin, meals included). On particularly crowded runs, the business-class section ends up filling with deck-class passengers, for lack of space elsewhere.

JACQUES LOUIS COPIA, 1764-99/NATIONAL LIBRARY OF AUSTRALIA

Inter-island travel circa 1800: traditional double canoe with islanders ferrying European man to Tongan island

Economy/business/first-class fares one way are (children aged under 12 pay 50%):

Tongatapu to Ha'apai (Lifuka)	T$31/56/126
Tongatapu to Vava'u	T$45/79/175
Tongatapu to the Niuas	T$89/131/365
Ha'apai to Vava'u	T$24/46/125
Vava'u to the Niuas	T$48/75/205
Niuatoputapu to Niuafo'ou	T$34/55/125

When the 'Olovaha goes to the Niuas, it often leaves on a Monday. From Vava'u to Niuatoputapu it takes about 24 hours. From there to Niuafo'ou it's another 12 to 15 hours.

'Uliti 'Uata Shipping or Walter Line (☎ 23855, fax 23860) has an office on Queen Salote Wharf in Nuku'alofa and operates the MV Tautahi, which does the inter-island run, and the MV Ikale, which runs the Nuku'alofa/'Eua route.

The Tautahi carries around 380 passengers, plus cargo, and offers only deck class, but it has a keel, which some travellers maintain gives a smoother journey. The fare from Tongatapu to Ha'apai is T$28, from Ha'apai to Vava'u it's T$24, and between Tongatapu and Vava'u it's T$43. Children aged under 12 pay about 45% less.

Both inter-island ferries leave from Queen Salote Wharf in Nuku'alofa. Their schedules are very prone to delay and alteration.

The MV Ikale is now the quickest ferry between Tongatapu (Nuku'alofa) and 'Eua. The journey takes 1½ hours on a good day. The ferry leaves from Tuimatamoana Harbour in Nuku'alofa at 12.30pm and the one-way fare is T$8 (buy your ticket on the boat). Returning from 'Eua, the ferry departs Nafanua Wharf at 5.30am the next morning. There's a service every day except Sunday.

Tofa Shipping (☎ 21326, fax 25970), Unga Rd, Nuku'alofa, operates the MV Alaimoana which also sails between Nuku'alofa and 'Eua. It's a smaller, slower vessel, but no less seaworthy. The trip can take 2½ hours and costs T$8/15 one way/return. Schedules and departure points are the same as for the Ikale.

The trip across to 'Eua is usually choppy, especially when the ferries pass out into the open sea. However, most of the time it's a simple crossing. The return leg from 'Eua to Nuku'alofa is usually a little quicker and smoother as the boat travels with the prevailing swell, not against it. The locals travelling to/from 'Eua are generally more used to sea travel and there's less seasickness. When the weather is good, catching the ferry to 'Eua is probably quicker (as well as cheaper) than flying, given that you'll need to take a taxi to the airport, check in, get delayed etc.

Yacht

October and November are the best months for yacht hitchhiking around Tonga, though once yachties have arrived here they're usually content to cruise around the islands leisurely and don't need extra crew. Details of yachting, crewing, permits and charges are in the Getting There & Away chapter. Yacht and sailing charters are available in Tongatapu and Vava'u (see those chapters).

Inter-Island Ferry Timetable

	port	MV 'Olovaha	MV Tautahi
Dep	Nuku'alofa	5pm Tues	5pm Mon
Arr	Ha'afeva (Ha'apai)	2am Wed	-
Dep	Ha'afeva	4am Wed	-
Arr	Lifuka (Ha'apai)	7am Wed	3am Tues
Dep	Lifuka	8am Wed	4am Tues
Arr	Neiafu (Vava'u)	2pm Wed	1pm Tues
Dep	Neiafu	3pm Thur	2pm Tues
Arr	Lifuka	11pm Thur	9pm Wed
Dep	Lifuka	1am Fri	10pm Wed
Arr	Ha'afeva	4am Fri	-
Dep	Ha'afeva	5am Fri	-
Arr	Nuku'alofa	11am Fri	8am Thur

A Slow Boat to Fiji

Take care when taking small boats between smaller islands. There's a local joke that fishermen heading out in unreliable boats take along a 14-day supply of coconuts. This will allow them to survive if the engine fails and their craft drifts off to Fiji (two weeks away) on the prevailing winds. So if you see a large number of coconuts in a boat, think twice before getting in.

Other Vessels

Smaller islands off the main ferry routes can be reached by smaller boats. The Tongatapu, Vava'u and Ha'apai Groups all have boats providing transport to islands within their groups; see the respective chapters for details. Or you can try your luck hitchhiking on fishing boats, freighters and launches. Ask around port and landing areas and contact the shipping companies.

But if it's luxury you're after, Coral Island Cruises (☎ 70975, fax 70976, e cicruise@ kalianet.to) runs a seven-day cruise between Tongatapu and Vava'u every second month. The MV *Oleanda* is an 18-cabin ship that cruises between the highlights of the three main island groups. There's a strong environmental and ecological emphasis to these trips, and prices range between T$1050 per person in a four-berth cabin to T$3600 for single occupancy of the Royal Suite.

LOCAL TRANSPORT
To/From the Airport

Taxis provide transport on every island with an airport. Airport shuttle buses meet incoming flights on Tongatapu and Vava'u. Hotels and guesthouses often provide air-port transfers for their guests, sometimes for free, sometimes not. Details are covered in the island group chapters.

Most travellers arrive at Fua'amotu International Airport on Tongatapu. A taxi ride from there to the kingdom's capital, Nuku-'alofa, will cost you T$15.

If your airport taxi driver insists that your selected hotel is closed, fully booked or no good, don't take it too seriously. Chances are you've chosen an establishment that doesn't pay commission to taxi drivers.

Taxi

Taxis throughout Tonga can be recognised by a 'T' at the beginning of the vehicle's licence plate (if it has a licence plate). There are plenty of taxis on Tongatapu and Vava'u, and a few on Lifuka (Ha'apai) and 'Eua. Although the taxis are not metered, government maximum rates are vaguely followed. Unwary foreigners have been taken for T$60 taxi rides, though, so always agree on the fare before you climb in. If you're overcharged, take down the number plate and report the driver to the Tonga Visitors Bureau.

A favourite scam in Tonga (and the world over) is for drivers to be out of change, so either have a fistful of dollars or be prepared to change larger notes at your destination.

ORGANISED TOURS

Organised tours can be a good introduction to an island and a quick, easy way to visit major sights. There are commercial tour operators on Tongatapu and Vava'u; less formal arrangements can be made on 'Eua and Ha'apai. Diving companies (and some of the tour companies) run tours to reefs and outlying islands. See the individual chapters for details.

The Tongatapu Group

area 260 sq km • pop 68,710 (est)

The Tongatapu Group is the largest of the Tongan island groups. In addition to Tongatapu Island and its offshore *motu* (coral islets), the group contains several other islands including 'Eua, Kalau, 'Eue'iki, 'Ata and, at the kingdom's southernmost extreme, Minerva Reef.

Many of the Tongatapu Group's highlights are not immediately obvious, but once off the beaten track you'll discover myriad beaches, caves and quiet villages. On the main island's south coast are the famous Mapu'a 'a Vaca blowholes and Hufangalupe, a dramatic natural limestone arch. Reefs and motu are abundant in the seas north of the main island where there's some fine diving and snorkelling. These outer islands are great either for staying over or for day trips from the capital.

'Eua, just east of Tongatapu, is a completely different place, slow-paced and hilly. It has the largest slice of tropical rainforest in Tonga and those choosing to explore will be rewarded with great bushwalking and some geological marvels.

Activities

A wealth of activities is available in the Tongatapu Group, including snorkelling, diving, surfing and fishing.

Diving & Snorkelling The diving and snorkelling around the Tongatapu Group is pretty good and ranges from snorkelling around the wreck off Pangaimotu and the excellent Makaha'a Reef to diving the sea caves on 'Eua.

Royal Sunset Island Resort (☎/fax 21254, e royalsun@kalianet.to, PO Box 960) on 'Atata is close to a host of dive sites. You have to pay to get out there, but it still represents good value. Two-tank dives cost T$70 to T$80 plus T$24 for full equipment hire.

Deep Blue Diving Centre (☎/fax 23576, e deepblue@kalianet.to, PO Box 913), Vuna Rd, Nuku'alofa, offers two-tank dives for

Highlights

- Tucking into a sumptuous Tongan feast while watching a traditional dance
- Exploring the trails and natural wonders of 'Eua National Park
- Watching the great natural spectacle of the Mapu'a 'a Vaca blowholes
- Visiting the ancient tombs at Lapaha and the Ha'amonga 'a Maui Trilithon
- Watching for whales, sharks, turtles and sea birds at Hufangalupe
- Spending a Sunday snorkelling among Tongatapu's outlying coral islands

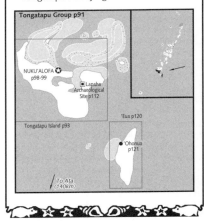

Tongatapu Group p91

NUKU'ALOFA
p98-99

Lapaha
Archaeological
Site p112

'Eua p120

Tongatapu Island p93

'Ohonua
p121

To 'Ata
(140km)

T$120 including lunch, snacks and all gear. Five/10-day dive packages cost T$540/1060 and a basic diving course is T$380. Snorkelling trips cost T$35 and three people are required for most trips/dives. Deep Blue's major drawcards are dive trips to 'Eua's enormous sea caves (minimum of four people) and a trips to Tau, a beautiful uninhabited island north of Tongatapu (T$100 with one dive, T$65 for nondivers, beach barbecue included). Extended dive charters are available, as well as accommodation (see the

Divers Lodge listing in Nuku'alofa's Places to Stay section).

Coralhead Diving (☎ 22176, e ulionlin@ kalianet.to, PO Box 211) caters for groups doing multiple dives. PADI Open Water Diver courses cost T$350 to T$400. Dive costs are calculated according to the size of groups and number of dives required.

Marine Adventures (☎ 24563, ☎/fax 25026 after office hours, e marine.adventures@ka lianet.to, PO Box 1351) charges T$40 per person (including lunch and pick-up) for a guided day or night snorkelling and cave swimming trip (other boat trips are offered). Soane is a knowledgeable guide and can improve your snorkelling technique. His trips to the north-west coast of Tongatapu have been recommended by locals and travellers alike.

Fishing Game fishing is best in the Tonga Trench or the deep water west of Tongatapu Island. A number of Fish Attracting Devices (see the Activities special section for a description) are located around the island.

'Atata sits only 15 minutes from some good fishing grounds, and the 7m (24-foot) sport-fishing boat belonging to the Royal Sunset Island Resort (see Diving & Snorkelling) can provide half/full-day charters for T$240/480 including gear (three people maximum).

MV *Topaz* (☎ 23722) is skippered by Carl Fisher. The boat can take up to three people and the emphasis is on tagging fish rather than bringing them home dead. Half/full-day charters cost T$400/600.

Flying Scotsman (☎ 23348, fax 24538, PO Box 869) is a well-respected operation offering half/full-day charters for T$285/395 (three people maximum). Cheaper charters for bottom fishing and island trips (T$50 per person) in its 5.7m (19-foot) sport-fishing boat are available.

Striker 2 (☎ 26019, fax 24365, PO Box 54) is an 8.4m (28-foot) sport-fishing boat with a

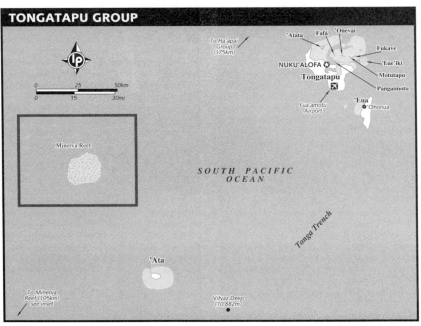

TONGATAPU GROUP

To Ha'apai Group (175km)

'Atata   Fafá 'Onevai

Fukave

NUKU'ALOFA

'Eue'iki

Tongatapu

Motutapu

Fua'amotu Airport

Pangaimotu

'Eua

Ohonua

0   25   50km
0   15   30mi

Minerva Reef

SOUTH PACIFIC OCEAN

Tonga Trench

'Ata

To Minerva Reef (105km) see inset

Vityaz Deep (10,882m)

good reputation and accommodating five people. Six/12-hour charters cost T$300/550.

Sailing Royal Sunset Island Resort (see Diving & Snorkelling) offers the beautiful 15m (51-foot) luxury yacht *Impetuous* for fully crewed charters visiting all of Tonga's island groups. This is the only Tongan yacht-charter operation offering this. Scuba-diving equipment is available and the daily rate is T$208 to T$503 per person for two to six people (seven days minimum). Add T$250 for yacht relocation.

Whale Watching Many of the game-fishing boats run whale-watching trips between June and December. Whale watching is also possible with Deep Blue Diving Centre, and available for guests at the Royal Sunset Island Resort (see Diving & Snorkelling for contact details of both). Operators charge T$50 to T$60.

Tongatapu Island

Tongatapu (meaning 'Sacred South'), along with its capital, Nuku'alofa (Abode of Love), is the hub of all activity within the Kingdom of Tonga. For most visitors Tongatapu is their first port of call. It's a place where old and new Tonga collide and, while Nuku'alofa is no advert for South Pacific tourism, hidden around Tongatapu are a few treasures of the South Pacific. There's certainly no need to move on quickly to other parts of the country.

Tongatapu is very flat, tilting slightly down toward the sagging weight of Ha'apai's volcanoes in the north. Cliffs on the southern shore rise to 30m while the northern coast is a drowned maze of islands and reefs.

The island constitutes one third of the kingdom's land mass and a third of the island's population live in Nuku'alofa. The island has been Tonga's capital for at least 600 years, and the Lapaha area in the east of the island contains most of the country's archaeological sites, and one of the densest concentrations of ancient structures in the Pacific. The Lapaha area is riddled with

langi (tiered tombs), and crisscrossed with a network of moats.

History

Thanks to oral tradition, the known history of Tongatapu reads like a long series of Old Testament 'begats' with a bit of editorialising thrown in when one Tu'i Tonga or another did something notable. The first Tu'i was the son of the sun god, Tangaloa, and a lovely Tongan maiden. He came to power sometime in the middle of the 10th century. Between that time and the ascent of King George Tupou I, 38 men held the title.

Around the year 1200, the Tu'i Tonga Tu'itatui set about building the only trilithic gate in Oceania, the Ha'amonga 'a Maui (Maui's Burden), near the village of Niutoua. Legend maintains that the Tu'i Tonga constructed it to remind two quarrelling sons that unity was better than division. After creating a wonderful future tourist attraction for Tonga, he moved his capital to Lapaha, on the calm lagoon near present-day Mu'a.

During the following 100 years or so, war canoes full of Tongan raiding parties set off for neighbouring islands. They created an empire ranging from the Lau Group in Fiji to the west, across to Niue in the east and northward to Futuna and Samoa, all of it ruled by the Tu'i Tonga from his capital on Tongatapu.

Sometime in the 1400s, the Tu'i Tonga Kau'ulufonua delegated some of his power and authority to his brother, creating the title Tu'i Ha'atakalaua. About 200 years later, the title of Tu'i Kanokupolu was created by the reigning Tu'i Ha'atakalaua, Mo'ungatonga.

All these title-holders struggled for power. The Tu'i Tonga gradually lost influence, and with the death of the last one, Laufilitonga, in 1865, the Tu'i Kanokupolu became the supreme power in the islands, and remains so.

Tongatapu's first European visitor was Dutchman Abel Tasman, who spent a few days trading with islanders and named the island Amsterdam. The next European contact came with Captain James Cook, who became close friends with the 30th Tu'i Tonga, Fatafehi Paulaho, and presented him with Tu'i Malila, the tortoise that was treated as a

TONGATAPU ISLAND

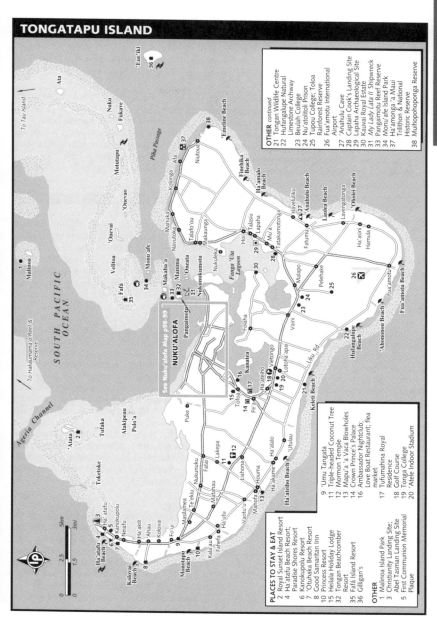

See Nuku'alofa Map p98-99

OTHER continued
21 Tongan Wildlife Centre
22 Hufangalupe Natural Limestone Archway
23 Beulah College
24 Nu'atolitoli Prison
25 Tupou College; Toloa Rainforest Reserve
26 Fua'amotu International Airport
27 'Anahulu Cave
28 Captain Cook's Landing Site
29 Lapaha Archaeological Site
30 Kauvai Royal Estate
31 My Lady Lata II Shipwreck
32 Pangaimotu Reef Reserve
33 Monu'afe Island Park
34 Ha'amonga 'a Maui Trilithon & National Historic Reserve
37 Muhopohoponga Reserve

PLACES TO STAY & EAT
2 Royal Sunset Island Resort
4 Ha'atafu Beach Resort; Paradise Shores Resort
6 Kanokupolu Resort
7 'Otuhaka Beach Resort
8 Good Samaritan Inn
10 Princess Resort
15 Heilala Holiday Lodge
32 Tongan Beachcomber Resort
35 Fafá Island Resort
36 Gilligan's

OTHER
1 Malinoa Island Park
3 Christianity Landing Site; Abel Tasman Landing Site
5 First Communion Memorial Plaque
9 'Umu Tangata
11 Triple-headed Coconut Tree
12 Mormon Temple
13 Mapu'a 'a Vaca Blowholes
14 Crown Prince's Palace
16 Ambassador Nightclub; Love Boat Restaurant; flea market
17 Tufumahina Royal Residence
18 Golf Course
19 Tonga College
20 'Atele Indoor Stadium

Tu'i Malila

While visiting Tongatapu on his third Pacific voyage in 1777, Captain James Cook befriended Fatafehi Paulaho, the 30th Tu'i Tonga. Cook was amazed at the reverence and ceremony that surrounded this person: 'I was quite charmed at the decorum...had nowhere seen the like...not even amongst more civilised nations.'

Out of respect and affection, Cook presented the Tu'i Tonga with a fully grown tortoise. Later given the noble title Tu'i Malila, the creature lived nearly another 200 years. At the time of its death in 1966, Tu'i Malila enjoyed a seat at the royal kava circle and the run of the palace gardens.

When the beloved tortoise died – no-one knows at what age – its remains were sent to Auckland Museum to be studied and possibly preserved. It was determined that the noble tortoise was of a species originally found in the Seychelles, an island group in the Indian Ocean.

Tu'i Malila was so sorely missed at the palace that another tortoise was brought over from Madagascar and named Tu'i Malila II.

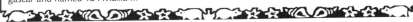

chief and given the run of the palace for nearly 200 years (see the boxed text).

NUKU'ALOFA
area 9.25 sq km • pop 22,162 (est)

Nuku'alofa is Tonga's big smoke and, while it may not be a vision of Pacific paradise, it does have all the trappings of a small-scale city, be it a rather drowsy one with the odd roaming pig. It's a good place to get organised and all points of interest are easily reached on foot.

Besides being the seat of government and home of the royal family, Nuku'alofa is also Tonga's industrial centre, transport hub and distribution point for many imported goods entering the country. As a result, prices and availability of imported goods are more favourable in Nuku'alofa than on the outer islands. Although locally produced items such as agricultural goods and handicrafts tend to be a little more expensive, the selection is greater than elsewhere.

These days, the city is expanding and swallowing up surrounding agricultural land and wetlands. Shantytowns are springing up around the outskirts. As long as the population continues to grow, migration from outer islands puts pressure on the capital to absorb the population, and some Tongans are growing concerned that their tranquil lifestyle is slipping away. There are now traffic jams at rush hour, the once-beautiful, mangrove-edged lagoon is suffering from pollution and the influence of American culture (especially on the young people) is increasing at the expense of Tongan traditions.

But the town is not a bad place to be. There's usually something going on, a few good restaurants to visit and out across the bay are a string of beautiful (and accessible) coral islands.

History

Nuku'alofa began life as a fortress for the western district of Tongatapu. It seems that attacks on this fort were a sort of annual jolly for raiders from Ha'apai, who had been faithfully returning for at least 11 years. Indeed, Will Mariner recounted the sacking of the fort of 'Nioocalofa' in about 1807 by Finau, the chief of Ha'apai. Finau and his men fired on the fort with cannons they took

Domestic pigs are at home everywhere in Tonga

from the *Port-au-Prince* (the British privateer which had brought Mariner to Tonga and had been subsequently destroyed), set fire to it and burned it to the ground.

After the destruction, the priests advised Finau that it would be necessary to reconstruct the fort in order to appease the gods. The fortress was rebuilt and provided the Ha'apai warriors the opportunity to embark on their annual holiday of destruction the following year! This time Tarki, a rival chief, set the fortress on fire shortly afterwards; Finau was watching from Pangaimotu, unable to stop the devastation. Finau later learned that Tarki had destroyed the building just to irritate him.

Orientation

Maps The Tonga Visitors Bureau, Vuna Rd, sells the Discover 2000 map and guide *Nuku'alofa & Tongatapu* (T$1) – which contains a reasonable street map of Nuku'alofa – and hands out simple hand-drawn maps of Tonga's major islands and island groups.

Black-and-white dyeline prints of Tonga's island groups (T$14) are available from the Ministry of Lands, Survey & Natural Resources (☎ 23611) on Vuna Rd. Head to the small, single-storey office behind the main building. No colour topographic maps are available.

Navigational sea charts (T$14) are available from the Hydrographic Unit (☎ 24696) at Touliki Naval Base, just past Queen Salote Wharf. See the Facts for the Visitor chapter for further information.

Information

Tourist Offices The Tonga Visitors Bureau (TVB; ☎ 25334, fax 22120, ⓔ tvb@kalianet.to, ⓦ www.vacations.tvb.to) is on Vuna Rd, just west of the International Dateline Hotel. It's open 8.30am to 4.30pm weekdays and 9am to 12.30pm Saturday.

Staff are helpful and produce a daily list of what's happening on Tongatapu. They can book accommodation and tours and have a series of informative handouts describing various aspects of Tongan life. Also available here is a leaflet describing a self-drive tourist trail around Tongatapu. A

bulletin board outside displays useful information including current tide tables.

The building itself is of some interest, having been constructed almost entirely from local materials and to local design. The interior contains about 90 sq metres of tapa depicting the royal crest, which was designed in 1862 by the grandson of King George Tupou I, while the two wooden poles in front of the office are a gift from the people of New Zealand.

Money Nuku'alofa has three banks – the Bank of Tonga, ANZ and MBF – all of which cash notes and travellers cheques and give cash advances on Visa and MasterCard. ANZ is the only bank with a 24-hour ATM (it accepts Cirrus, Visa and MasterCard). Banks open 9am to 4pm weekdays and 8.30am to noon on Saturday.

You can also change cash and travellers cheques 24 hours a day at the International Dateline Hotel. Its rates are only slightly less favourable than at the Bank of Tonga, but it charges a 10% commission on credit card advances (available to hotel guests only). The Harbour View Motel also changes foreign currency and only charges 4% on credit card advances.

The Western Union (☎ 24345) office is next to the Pacific Royale Hotel on Taufa'ahau Rd. The MoneyGram (☎ 23933) office is next to the Bank of Tonga on Railway Rd.

A currency exchange counter opens at Fua'amotu International Airport for all international flights.

The Eftpos system of paying by credit/debit card is becoming increasingly common in shops, restaurants and the more expensive accommodation in Nuku'alofa.

See Money in the Facts for the Visitor chapter for further information about changing and transferring money.

Post The main post office or GPO (☎ 21700) is on the corner of Taufa'ahau and Salote Rds and open 8.30am to 4pm on weekdays. To receive mail by poste restante (addressed to GPO, Nuku'alofa, Kingdom of Tonga), mail is collected from the window just outside the main entrance. Letters are filed alphabetically by surname or yacht name. You must ask specifically for any larger parcels you might be expecting. The Philatelic Bureau is situated upstairs (see Shopping later in this chapter).

Telephone & Fax The Tonga Communications Corporation (TCC; ☎ 26700) on Salote Rd offers international telephone and fax services. It's open 7am to midnight weekdays, 8am to midnight Saturday and 4pm to midnight Sunday. Visa and Master Card are accepted here, reverse-charge calls placed and several international calling cards can be used. You can also buy telephone cards and use them in the international cardphones in the lobby (open 24 hours a day), outside the GPO or in the Bank of Tonga on Railway Road.

Phone cards can also be bought at Friends Tours on Taufa'ahau Rd.

A local (including inter-island) telephone and fax service is available from another TCC office on 'Unga Rd. It's open 24 hours, every day. However, local calls are more easily made from the place at which you are staying, though it may cost a little more.

Email & Internet Access The fastest Internet access is available at the TCC on Salote Rd (see the preceding Telephone & Fax section). Access costs T$8 per hour, but with only two computers on offer there's often a queue.

Friends Tours (☎ 26323, e friends@kalianet.to) on Taufa'ahau Rd offers Internet access between 9am and 5pm weekdays for T$16 per hour.

Comput@ Café (☎ 26798), above the TCF supermarket on Wellington Rd, offers Internet access at T$9 per hour, but there are only two computers. It's open 9am to 7pm weekdays and 9am to 6pm on Saturday. A cybercafe is planned for the nice Suliana's cafe next door.

Travel Agents & Airline Offices Teta Tours (☎ 23690, fax 23238, e tetatours@kalianet.to), on the corner of Wellington and Railway Rds, and Taufonua Travel (☎ 23052, fax 21203), 1st floor, Tungi Arcade, are among the best travel agents in town. Also try EM Jones Travel & Tours (☎ 23422, 23423, fax 23418, e emjones@kalianet.to), on the corner of Taufa'ahau and Wellington Rds.

Airline offices in Nuku'alofa include:

Air Fiji (contact Teta Tours – see earlier)
Air New Zealand (☎ 23192, fax 23447, e mele.o@forumt.net) Tungi Arcade, Taufa'ahau Rd
Air Pacific (contact EM Jones Travel & Tours – see earlier)
Polynesian Airlines (☎ 24566, fax 24225) cnr Salote & Fatafehi Rds
Royal Tongan Airlines (☎ 23414, fax 23559, e tongasales@flyroyaltongan.com) Royco Bldg, Fatafehi Rd

Weather The Tonga Meteorological Service (☎/fax 23401, w www.kalianet.to/weather/weather.htm) on Tupoulahi Rd posts a satellite weather map outside the door every day.

Bookshops & Libraries The only bookshop of any consequence in Tonga is the Friendly Islands Bookshop (☎ 23787) on Taufa'ahau Rd. It has a good selection of newspapers and magazines, novels (including second-hand books to buy or exchange), travel-oriented titles (including Lonely Planet guidebooks) and books about Tonga and related island topics which are difficult if not impossible to find elsewhere.

The Dateline Bookshop on Wellington Rd is much more limited, but sells some cheap second-hand novels.

Tapacraft (☎ 26760) on Lavinia Rd has a free book exchange and second-hand paperbacks cost T$2. Most guesthouses have book exchanges for their guests.

With a library card (T$3 annually), you can borrow books from the library downstairs in the basilica on Taufa'ahau Rd, but it's rarely open (try between 4pm and 8pm weekdays).

Photography Fung Shing Fast Photo (☎ 24787), on Railway Rd, offers one-hour colour print processing and sells Fuji film. Foto-Fix (☎ 23466), on Taufa'ahau Rd, sells Kodak and Fuji film (including slide film), batteries and disposable cameras, does processing (not slides) and takes passport photos (T$2.10 per photo).

Laundry Virtually every hotel and guesthouse makes some arrangement for its guests' laundry needs.

The Savoy Dry Cleaner (☎ 23314), on Fatafehi Rd, will wash and dry your clothes for T$2 per kg. This is Nuku'alofa's only commercial laundry. Some travellers have complained of items going missing here, so it's a good idea to hand over a list of your clothes with your washing. Yachties with large loads of washing have reportedly been turned away from here, so sailors may require a degree of cunning when dealing with staff.

Medical Services The Nuku'alofa Pharmacy (☎ 21007, or ☎ 25496 after office hours), on Salote Rd, is open 10am to 5pm weekdays and 10am to 1pm Saturday.

The Fasi Mo e Afi Pharmacy (☎ 22955), on Salote Rd next door to the Swedish Consulate, is open similar hours.

If you want a female doctor, New Zealander Dr Glennis Mafi at the Ha'ateiho Village Mission Clinic (☎ 29052) in the village of Ha'ateiho, 5km south of Nuku-'alofa, is recommended. The consultation fee is T$20. Appointments are essential.

The German Clinic (☎ 25288, or ☎ 24625 after office hours, [e] medical@kalianet.to), on Wellington Rd, charges T$30 for consultations; Dr Betz is on call 24 hours a day. There's a pharmacy, and vaccinations and minor surgery can be done by appointment.

Vaiola Hospital (☎ 23200) is about 2km south of Nuku'alofa. No appointments are accepted and queues can be horrendous. The dispensary is open 8.30am to 11pm weekdays. Staff are well trained, but equipment is sometimes lacking. There is also a dentist here. Take the Vaiola bus from the eastern bus terminal on Vuna Rd.

Chinese medicine and acupuncture treatments are available at the Chinese Traditional Medicine Centre (☎ 25178), just west of Vaiola Hospital.

Emergency Contact the police on ☎ 922, fire station on ☎ 999 and hospital on ☎ 933 or ☎ 23200. The national emergency number is ☎ 911.

Dangers & Annoyances Nuku'alofa is a safe city, but beware of dogs loitering on the streets at night. They can be aggressive.

Royal Palace

The Royal Palace on the waterfront, a white, Victorian timber structure surrounded by large lawns and Norfolk Island pines, has become a symbol of Tonga to the world.

The royal residence was prefabricated in New Zealand in 1867, and in 1882 the upstairs verandah was added and the **Royal Chapel** was constructed behind the palace.

How to Spend Sunday in Nuku'alofa

- Go to church. The magnificent singing lifts the roof. A particular favourite with visitors is attending Centenary Chapel to worship with the king and royal family, but there are rules of social etiquette to be followed (see the boxed text 'Church on Sunday' in the Facts about Tonga chapter).
- Take a round-the-island tour and visit Tongatapu's many natural attractions, such as the Mapu'a 'a Vaca blowholes, the Ha'amonga Trilithon, the Mu'a archaeological site and the beaches.
- Hire a bicycle or moped and explore the island.
- Charter a boat/join a boat trip to the more remote outer islands.
- Take your pick of the three offshore island resorts and enjoy the stunning white-sand beaches and good snorkelling.
- Head for Ha'atafu Beach and relax with the mixed crowd of locals and visitors at the Paradise Shores Resort.
- Lounge around the pool at the International Dateline Hotel all day long for T$3.
- Sleep and eat – that's what most of the locals will be doing.

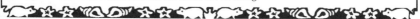

NUKU'ALOFA

PLACES TO STAY
1 Captain Cook Vacation Apartments
3 Breeze Inn
4 Seaview Restaurant & Lodge
33 International Dateline Hotel
45 Angela Motel & Guest House
62 Hotel Nuku'alofa; MBF Bank
67 Pacific Royale Hotel; One Night Stand; Wanda's
73 The Backpackers' Place
77 Toni's Guest House
78 Haufolau Apartments
80 Nerima Lodge
83 Villa McKenzie
92 Tom's Guesthouse
99 Harbour View Motel
101 Papiloa's Friendly Islander Hotel
103 The Lagoon Lodge
104 Leilani Apartments
106 Frangipani Accommodation
107 Sela's Guest House
109 Winnie's Guest House
110 Hellen's Apartments

PLACES TO EAT
2 Little Italy Pizzeria
13 Toni's Delux Food Court
15 Mr Chips; Blue Banana
23 Friends Café; Langafonua'ae Fefine Handicrafts
24 Homestyle Bakery
32 Emerald Restaurant; The Garden Bar
38 Cowley's Bread Bin
47 Taste of India
53 Suliana's; TCF Supermarket; Comput@ Café
55 Fakalato Restaurant; Snack & Milk Bar
56 John's Place
61 Sama Restaurant
63 Maseia Restaurant; Maseia Building
65 Lunarossa Restaurant; TCF Supermarket
66 The Grill Bar & Restaurant
88 Barbecue Shacks
89 The Waterfront Café
93 Pot Luck Lunches

THINGS TO SEE
6 Royal Palace
7 'Atenisi Institute
9 Queen Salote College
10 Tupou High School
11 Centenary Chapel
44 St Paul's Anglican Church
71 Centennial Church of the Free Church of Tonga
72 Royal Tombs
76 Basilica of St Anthony of Padua; Public Library; Akiko's
86 First Wesleyan Church
94 St Mary's Cathedral
113 Tongan National Centre

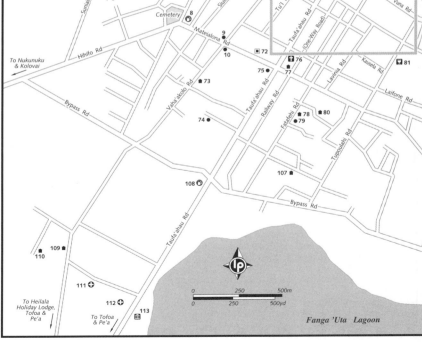

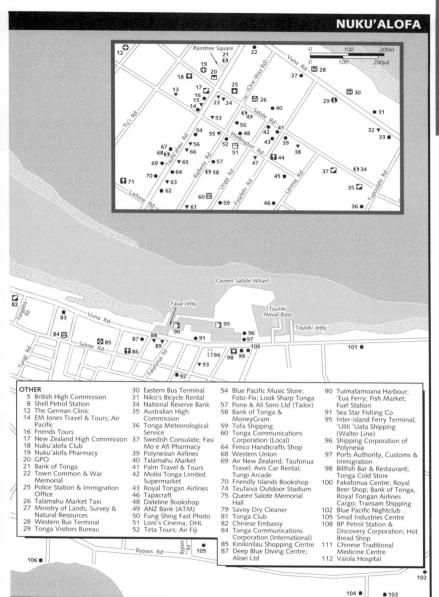

NUKU'ALOFA

OTHER
5 British High Commission
8 Shell Petrol Station
12 The German Clinic
14 EM Jones Travel & Tours; Air Pacific
16 Friends Tours
17 New Zealand High Commission
18 Nuku'alofa Club
19 Nuku'alofa Pharmacy
20 GPO
21 Bank of Tonga
22 Town Common & War Memorial
25 Police Station & Immigration Office
26 Talamahu Market Taxi
27 Ministry of Lands, Survey & Natural Resources
28 Western Bus Terminal
29 Tonga Visitors Bureau

30 Eastern Bus Terminal
31 Niko's Bicycle Rental
34 National Reserve Bank
35 Australian High Commission
36 Tonga Meteorological Service
37 Swedish Consulate; Fasi Mo e Afi Pharmacy
39 Polynesian Airlines
40 Talamahu Market
41 Palm Travel & Tours
42 Molisi Tonga Limited Supermarket
43 Royal Tongan Airlines
46 Tapacraft
48 Dateline Bookshop
49 ANZ Bank (ATM)
50 Fung Shing Fast Photo
51 Loni's Cinema; DHL
52 Teta Tours; Air Fiji

54 Blue Pacific Music Store; Foto-Fix; Look Sharp Tonga
57 Pone & Ali Sons Ltd (Tailor)
58 Bank of Tonga & MoneyGram
59 Tofa Shipping
60 Tonga Communications Corporation (Local)
64 Fimco Handicrafts Shop
68 Western Union
69 Air New Zealand; Taufonua Travel; Avis Car Rental; Tungi Arcade
70 Friendly Islands Bookshop
74 Teufaiva Outdoor Stadium
75 Queen Salote Memorial Hall
79 Savoy Dry Cleaner
81 Tonga Club
82 Chinese Embassy
84 Tonga Communications Corporation (International)
85 Kinikinilau Shopping Centre
87 Deep Blue Diving Centre; Alisei Ltd

90 Tuimatamoana Harbour; 'Eua Ferry; Fish Market; Fuel Station
91 Sea Star Fishing Co
95 Inter-island Ferry Terminal; 'Uliti 'Uata Shipping (Walter Line)
96 Shipping Corporation of Polynesia
97 Ports Authority, Customs & Immigration
98 Billfish Bar & Restaurant; Tonga Cold Store
100 Fakafonua Centre; Royal Beer Shop; Bank of Tonga, Royal Tongan Airlines Cargo; Transam Shipping
102 Blue Pacific Nightclub
105 Small Industries Centre
108 BP Petrol Station & Discovery Corporation; Hot Bread Shop
111 Chinese Traditional Medicine Centre
112 Vaiola Hospital

Sunday services used to take place in the chapel before it was damaged in a hurricane. The coronations of King George II, Queen Salote and King Taufa'ahau Tupou IV took place there in 1893, 1918 and 1967 respectively. The coronation chair in the chapel is partially constructed from the *koka* tree from Lifuka (Ha'apai) under which King George I was invested with the title Tu'i Kanokupolu. The small octagonal gazebo in the gardens is called **the Palesi** and was used as a rest house for visiting chiefs.

The palace grounds are closed to visitors but you can get a good view of the palace from the waterfront on the west side. Just beyond it, on the slopes of Mt Zion, is the **Sia Ko Veiongo**, the 'royal estate'. The fortress of Nuku'alofa once stood here and its ludicrous history of attacks and conflagrations took place. The site is now occupied by a radio tower and the **grave of Captain Croker** of the HMS *Favourite*, who was killed attacking the fortress on 24 June 1840.

Vuna Wharf

Vuna Wharf, at the end of Taufa'ahau Rd, was constructed in 1906 and once served as Tonga's main disembarkation point. It was replaced in 1966 by Queen Salote Wharf several kilometres to the east and then nearly destroyed in a serious earthquake in 1977. If you walk to the end of the wharf at low tide, you'll see two large anchors which have sunk into the muck.

Fresh fish is sometimes sold here, usually in the afternoon.

Railway (One-Way) Rd

There used to be a railway along Railway Rd which transported copra to Vuna Wharf, where it was loaded onto steamers for export. Railway Rd is the only one-way road in Nuku'alofa and it is also referred to as One-Way Rd.

Royal Tombs

The Mala'ekula, the large park-like area opposite the basilica, was named after the Katoanga Kula festival, which was held here in the days of King George Tupou I (the *mala'e* part of the name refers to a sacred

area). Since 1893 the graves of all the Tongan sovereigns as well as their husbands, wives and other close relatives have been sited here. The large green was once used as a golf course. Although it's now off-limits to the public, you still have a fairly good view from the perimeter fence.

'Atenisi Institute

The only private university in Tonga, the 'Atenisi Institute *(☎ 24819, PO Box 90 or 200)* is a unique institution that operates without subsidy from either church or state and therefore without obligation to further the views of either. Situated just west of the town centre, the institute was founded in 1967 by an extraordinary individual, 'I Futa Helu, to operate under a classic Western format in the tradition of Oxford. He writes in the university syllabus:

…concern with the classical tradition means the keeping of a traditional core of studies. This is the academic equivalent of the English attitude that a university which does not teach philosophy as a discipline is a 'Mickey Mouse' university…all South Sea island communities have created beautiful cultures, but it must be pointed out that in all these cultures criticism as an institution is discouraged, and criticism is the very heart of education.

Classes in Tongan language and culture are taught, as well as philosophy, sciences and other disciplines. Associate, bachelor's and postgraduate degree programs are offered, in conjunction with New Zealand's Auckland University. Tuition is T$270 per annum per course. Visitors spending some time in Tonga may want to check out the classes.

If you're visiting in November, try not to miss 'Atenisi's graduation ceremony. There is dancing, entertainment, royal gifting and feasting, and a unique tradition called 'presentation of the *vala*'; during this ceremony, the villages of 'Atenisi graduates present the university with gifts of elaborate fine mats and immense pieces of tapa.

British High Commissioner's Office & Residence

The epitome of Pacific colonial architecture, this beautiful waterfront building was presented to the government in 1901 in exchange for another waterfront lot and was in turn leased to the British government. On the front lawn are four cannons from the British privateer *Port-au-Prince*, which was ransacked at Lifuka (Ha'apai) in 1806.

Queen Salote College & Tupou High School

Queen Salote College *(Mateialona Rd)* was planned by King George Tupou I in 1876 as a tribute to 50 years of Christianity in Tonga. He personally donated UK£1000 to build a Wesleyan ladies college to be named after his wife. However, the project wasn't actually chartered until 1923 and it was finally positioned beside Tupou College, ostensibly a boys school (although it had accepted female students as early as 1869). In 1948 the boys college moved to the south-eastern corner of Tongatapu and Tupou High School is now beside Queen Salote College.

Langafonua Building

This gingerbread-style structure *(Taufa'ahau Rd)* was built by a British expat for his five daughters who lived in New Zealand and spent winters in Tonga. It now houses Langafonua'ae Fefine Handicrafts, a women's handicraft cooperative founded by Queen Salote in 1953.

Prime Minister's Office

The Prime Minister's Office *(Taufa'ahau Rd)*, opposite the GPO, contains numerous government offices and is said to be the source of much of the hot air blowing around Tonga. The tower was damaged in the 1977 earthquake but rebuilt shortly thereafter.

Churches

Nuku'alofa's most distinctive structure is the **Basilica of St Anthony of Padua** *(Taufa'ahau Rd)*, opposite the Royal Tombs. Much of it was built by volunteer labour between May 1977 and January 1980. The conical roof is quite something, especially during evening services when light pours through the stained glass.

The interior is quite lovely. The large ceiling beams are made of wood imported from New Zealand and the smaller cross-beams came from the Royal Estate on 'Eua. Beam joints are covered with coconut sennit mats woven locally. The altar, lectern, baptistry, pews and tables were hand-crafted and the Stations of the Cross are made of coconut wood inlaid with mother-of-pearl. At Station XI, a tiny gold coconut tree that belonged to Queen Salote Tupou III is fitted into the hair of Christ.

St Mary's Cathedral *(Vuna Rd)*, near Faua Jetty, is Nuku'alofa's other Catholic church. It looks more conventional, but is an odd mix of old and new styling and worth a look for its beautiful vaulted ceiling, stained glass and giant kava-bowl altar.

The **Centenary Chapel** *(Wellington Rd)*, behind Mt Zion, was completed in 1952 and accommodates more than 2000 people. Like the basilica, it was constructed mostly by volunteer labour. Visitors to Tonga, even non-Christians, often attend church here in order to catch a glimpse of members of the royal family (who attend services here) and to hear the magnificent, booming singing of the congregation.

A **Centennial Church of the Free Church of Tonga**, built in 1888, once stood on the present site of the Centenary Chapel, but it was moved in 1949 here to the north side of the Royal Tombs. Apparently that task was completed in one day. However, the monstrous stone construction now standing on the site was built in 1983.

The **First Wesleyan church** *(Salote Rd)* built in Nuku'alofa was once a ramshackle building. It was loaded with character and resembled a *fale* (a traditional thatched house). It has been rebuilt in recent years and is now just another church.

See the boxed text 'Church on Sunday' in the Facts about Tonga chapter for more information on visiting churches.

Parks

The **Mala'e Pangai** area of the waterfront, beside the Royal Palace, is a public ground used for royal kava ceremonies, feasts and football and cricket matches. On one corner is the (nonfunctional) dolphin fountain that was presented by the British government to commemorate the HMS *Dolphin*, the first British warship to land in Tonga. There's a line-up of big guns on the waterfront and also a flagpole that's used on ceremonial occasions.

The large lawn behind the Treasury (on the corner of Vuna and Taufa'ahau Rds) is the **town common**. There's a small bandstand and the Tongan War Memorial, honouring Tongans who served in both world wars. Across the street to the east is the quaint little parliament building, that was prefabricated in New Zealand, transported to Tonga and reconstructed in 1894.

Tongan National Centre

About 2km south of Nuku'alofa is the Tongan National Centre *(☎ 23022, Taufa'ahau Rd, Vaiola; museum: admission free; open 8.30am-4pm Mon, Wed & Fri, 7am-9.30pm Tues & Thur)*. This cultural centre's museum is a little sparse but has an interesting display of historical artefacts, including war clubs, headrests, bark cloth and kava bowls. At the time of writing, a cultural resource centre for the public was being planned.

The hour-long **cultural tours** *(T$8; 2pm Mon-Fri)* include demonstrations of cooking, basketry, tapa making, mat weaving, carving and traditional dancing.

The **Traditional Tongan Evening** *(T$20, or T$6 to see dancing only; 7.30pm Tues & Thur; book before 4.30pm)* is held in the large, high-roofed exhibition hall. The evening starts with a kava ceremony, followed by an all-you-can-eat Tongan feast and an excellent show of traditional dances.

Take the Vaiola bus from the eastern terminal on Vuna Rd (40 seniti). A taxi from town will cost about T$4. A shuttle bus (T$1) to and from town is available on the Traditional Tongan Evening.

Activities

For information on activities on offer around the Tongatapu Group – **diving**, **sailing**, **fishing**, **whale watching** – see the Activities section at the start of this chapter.

In addition, runners in Nuku'alofa can join the **Hash House Harriers** at Raintree Square at 5.15pm on Monday. For details of Thurs-

day's run, check the notice board in Molisi Tonga Limited supermarket. **Nuku'alofa Athletics Club** meets at Teufaiva Outdoor Stadium on Thursday at 5pm; admission free.

Tonga's only **golf course** (nine holes) lies opposite 'Atele Indoor Stadium on the main road at Vietongo. The not-so-challenging course is open to visitors (T$10 green fee) and clubs can be hired for T$15 per day.

Organised Tours

Island Tours An island tour is a good way to get acquainted with Tongatapu Island's most beautiful spots in a short time. Check with several operators and find out the duration of their tours, exactly what is included and when they go (most will require a minimum of four people). Prices listed below are per person.

EM Jones Travel & Tours (☎ 23422, fax 23418, e emjones@kalianet.to) Whole Island Tour T$56 (including lunch) – visits all major sites. Half Tour Western Side T$35 (including lunch) – covers mainly natural attractions. Half Tour Eastern Side T$16 (no lunch) – visits mainly historical sites.

Friends Tours (☎ 26323, fax 25730, e friends@kalianet.to) Two-hour tour of Nuku'alofa in an Asian-style tuk-tuk (available in English and German) T$15.

Kingdom Tours (☎ 25200, fax 23447, e kingdomt@forumtravel.net) A whole variety of tours on offer ranging in price from T$23 to T$53.

Palm Travel & Tours (☎ 24137, or ☎ 23505 after office hours, fax 24914, e palmtour@kalianet.to) Half-day tour T$30 – concentrates on either eastern or western Tongatapu. Whole-island tour T$50 – takes in all the main highlights.

Paradisland (☎/fax 24977, e paradisl@kalianet.to) Specialists in tailor-made holidays to Tonga, focusing on the Italian market. Island tours in Italian, English, German or Russian T$40 to T$60. Boat tours T$60.

Quick Tours (☎ 29910, fax 29410, e quick@tongatapu.net.to) All-day tours of eastern or western Tongatapu T$35. Cheaper 'Quick Tours' of the whole island, charters and tailor-made tours available. German and English spoken.

Teta Tours (☎ 23690, fax 23238, e tetatour@kalianet.to) Half-island tours T$15 – the major sights of Nuku'alofa, plus a little of eastern or western Tongatapu. Whole-island tours T$30 – includes the major sights of Nuku'alofa and Tongatapu Island.

Toni's Tours (☎ 21049, fax 22970) Full-day whole-island tours T$20 (10am to 7pm depending on clients; minimum three people; available Sunday) – these great tours are informative and the best value around (be sure to pack lunch, water, swimming gear and a torch). Tony usually winds up at Paradise Shores Resort to watch the sunset. Set-price trips to anywhere around Tongatapu are also available.

Boat Tours Boat tours can often be arranged at the place you are staying. Also try any of the game-fishing operators (see Activities earlier in the chapter).

The Royal Sunset Island Resort (again, see Activities) and Palm Travel & Tours (see the preceding Island Tours section) organise outer-island boat trips. Expect to pay T$50 per hour (minimum of four people).

Special Events
The Heilala Festival is Nuku'alofa's big festival of the year. It's a week-long celebration which features parades, workshops, fashion shows, a beauty pageant, all manner of music, arts and sports competitions, feasting and general merriment. It culminates with the King's Birthday on 4 July.

Places to Stay
If you're visiting Nuku'alofa during Heilala Week, be sure to book accommodation well in advance. All accommodation offers hot showers unless stated.

Places to Stay – Budget
Camping Camping is possible at the *Paradise Shores Resort* on Ha'atafu Beach (see Western Tongatapu later in this chapter) and at the *Tongan Beachcomber Resort* on Pangaimotu, offshore from Nuku'alofa (see North of Nuku'alofa later in this chapter).

Guesthouses & Motels *Toni's Guest House* (☎ 21049, fax 22970, Cnr Mateialona & Railway Rds) Bed in 2-bed room with fans T$10. Free airport pick-ups. Close to town, this is an old backpackers' favourite. It's a simple place with a laid-back atmosphere and Tony Matthias, a British expat knowledgeable in Tongan ways, invites his guests to share in his nightly kava circle-cum-natter session. The kitchen facilities are good and Tony's tours are highly recommended. At the time of writing, he was planning to start fishing trips.

The Backpackers' Place (☎/fax 26230, e backpack@kalianet.to, Vaha'akolo Rd) Singles/doubles/triples with ceiling fans T$15/25/40, dorm bed T$12.50. Free airport pick-ups; drop-offs T$5. A great, well-equipped hostel, set in a spacious plot 1km from the town centre, this place is geared up for backpackers. The rooms are bright and airy and there's a small library, sitting room, washing machine and good kitchen. Internet access is T$10 per hour.

Sela's Guest House (☎ 25040, fax 23755, e mettonga@kalianet.to) Singles/doubles/triples T$15/30/45, doubles with bath T$35, bed in 6-bed dorm T$10. Breakfast T$4. This is a rambling sort of place built around a pleasant wooden house and located near the lagoon, off Fatafehi Rd. Rooms are clean and the atmosphere homely and welcoming. There's a guests' kitchen.

Angela Motel & Guest House (☎ 23930, fax 22149, Cnr Wellington & Lavinia Rds) Singles T$20, doubles with bath T$30-40. The rooms are a bit stuffy in summer, and the guests' kitchen is tiny and ill equipped, but the place is conveniently located. However, at T$40, the larger double is overpriced.

Heilala Holiday Lodge (☎ 29910, fax 29410, e quick@kalianet.to) Singles/doubles T$28/38, fale with bath T$48/58-85. Breakfast included. Free airport pick-up & town tour. This is a well-run, clean, quiet and friendly place in Tofoa, 3km south of Nuku'alofa. It has a shared kitchen, swimming pool and car, scooter and bike rental. Island tours are available. A restaurant had just opened at the time of writing (mains T$10 to T$20), and is open to the public on Sunday. Catch buses to and from Nuku'alofa every few minutes from Taufa'ahau Rd, a five-minute walk away.

Breeze Inn (☎ 23947, fax 22970, Vuna Rd) Singles/doubles with bath T$30/40. Renovations were planned at the time of writing, and this quiet and comfortable place 10 minutes' walk west of the GPO, with large, clean and cool but slightly dark rooms, may go a little upmarket. The shared lounge and kitchen areas are very bright. A good choice.

Divers Lodge (☎ 23379, fax 23756, e *dee pblue@kalianet.to, Funa Rd*) Singles/doubles T$30/55. This small lodge is run by the Deep Blue Diving Centre and caters mainly for organised dive groups, but individuals are welcome. It's a light and airy building set against a backdrop of sandalwood trees on a quiet road. The rooms are clean and simple, and there's a well-equipped kitchen and a large living area. Breakfast is available on request. This place is a $2 taxi ride from Nuku'alofa town centre.

Winnie's Guest House (☎/fax 25215, e *winnies@kalianet.to, Vaha'akolo Rd*) Beds T$30 per person including breakfast, T$15 for students studying in Tonga. You'll need to book in advance for this comfortable, friendly and spacious guesthouse, formerly a family home. Sited about 2km south of central Nuku'alofa, it's popular with international medical students working at Vaiola Hospital nearby. There are five good rooms as well as a guests' kitchen, bicycles/scooters for rent (T$8/15), pool table, Internet access (T$15 per half-hour; unavailable at the time of writing but this service may be restored), large video collection and massive TV. Take the Vaiola bus from the eastern bus terminal on Vuna Rd.

Frangipani Accommodation (☎ 25936, fax 24477) Singles/doubles with bath T$26/60. Only two rooms are available in this attractive family home off Bypass Rd. It's a quiet, peaceful place with great views across the lagoon. The large double room has a fridge and tea/coffee-making facilities. Take the Halaleva bus from Nuku'alofa.

Papiloa's Friendly Islander Hotel (see Places to Stay – Mid-Range) has dorm beds with kitchen facilities for T$15 per person.

Places to Stay – Mid-Range

Tom's Guesthouse (☎ 22885, Salote Rd) Singles/doubles T$40/60, doubles with bath T$80. Prices include breakfast. This small guesthouse is spotless, well appointed and well maintained. All rooms have ceiling fans and there's a large communal area and kitchen. A good choice.

Nerima Lodge (☎ 25533, fax 25577, e *afeakin@kalianet.to, 'Amaile Rd*) Singles/doubles T$38/64.50 including breakfast. Shiny and spotless, this new place off Fatafehi Rd is well fitted out and feels comfortable, reliable and secure. It also offers authentic Japanese meals for T$15 to T$20 (the king himself gets takeaways from here) and free bike hire.

Papiloa's Friendly Islander Hotel (☎ 23810, fax 24199, e *papiloa@tongata pu.to, Vuna Rd*) Singles/doubles with bath T$50/60, 2-bed units with bath T$60-70, air-con bungalows T$65/95, dorm bed T$15. Given a general overhaul and relocation to the centre of town, this place 30 minutes' walk east of the TVB would be humming. Currently some of the apartments are slightly shabby, though the bungalows are pleasant. There's a swimming pool with pool-side bar and restaurant and those on a tight budget can often be accommodated.

Harbour View Motel (☎ 25488, fax 25490, e *harbvmtl@kalianet.to, Vuna Rd*) Singles T$40-65, doubles T$60-85, singles with air-con, TV, video & bath T$105-160, doubles T$115-170, family rooms T$123. Prices include breakfast. Opposite Queen Salote Wharf, this is a spotless, bright and modern motel with a private bar and is the pick of the upper mid-range places. All rooms have telephones and the executive suite has a jacuzzi! Cars can be rented for T$50 per day. It changes money and gives cash advances on credit cards. A little expensive, but still a choice place to stay.

Hotel Nuku'alofa (☎ 24244, fax 23154, e *sanft@kalianet.to, Taufa'ahau Rd near the basilica*) Singles/doubles with bath & fridge T$65/85. Above the MBF Bank, this single-storey hotel looks memorable from the outside but is, alas, unexceptional inside. However, the 14 air-conditioned rooms are comfortable and the restaurant and bar look OK.

Places to Stay – Top End

Villa McKenzie (☎/fax 24998, e *villamac@ kalianet.to, Vuna Rd*) Singles/doubles with bath T$100/120 including breakfast. This is one of the best top-end places to stay in

Nuku'alofa. The well-maintained old villa has only four double rooms, all with air-con. The bathrooms are a little small, but a huge sitting room and wide, shady veranda facing the waterfront make up for it. As a guest you become a member of Villa McKenzie Club, which is open 6pm to 10pm Wednesday, Thursday and Friday. The club is licensed and meals are available (T$7 to T$9). Other meals are by arrangement only.

Seaview Restaurant & Lodge (☎ 23709, e seaview@kalianet.to, Vuna Rd) Doubles with bath T$135, each extra person T$25. The hotel extension to a successful restaurant, 10 minutes' walk west of the GPO, was under construction at the time of writing. Five large rooms with balconies, and a bungalow in the garden, offer air-con, phone, Internet access, TV, video, refrigerator and tea/coffee facilities.

International Dateline Hotel (☎ 23411, fax 23410, e idh@kalianet.to, Vuna Rd) Singles/doubles/triples T$90/105/120, 'superior' rooms T$132/155/165, suites T$210. This hotel has a swimming pool (T$3 fee for nonguests), with pool-side Splash Bar (snacks are served all day), restaurant and a Tongan floor show on Wednesday and Saturday nights (T$20). All rooms have air-con, TV, telephone, refrigerator and tea/coffee facilities. The superior rooms are pleasant, although they lack the sea views of the standard rooms, but the standard rooms are a bit shabby, as are some of the communal areas – the supposedly premier hotel in Tonga shouldn't have broken or missing toilet seats and cracked sinks in its restaurant toilets. The service is shaky too. Ornithologists unable to spot the rare Tongan megapode in the wild can see a moth-eaten adult and chick in a glass cabinet just past the duty-free shop.

Pacific Royale Hotel (☎ 23344, fax 23833, e royale@kalianet.to, Taufa'ahau Rd) Economy singles/doubles T$77/99, 'superior' rooms T$99/115/125, 2-bed apartments with kitchen T$170.50. Situated in central Nuku'alofa, this was once a decent business travellers' hotel. But the '70s were a long time ago and, while some of the rooms' interiors have remained in top shape since then, you must pick carefully. And the

swimming pool could do with a clean too. The disco (the One Night Stand) and bar (Wanda's) are especially loud on Friday.

Apartments

The following are fully furnished and self-contained apartments, with kitchen, bath, sitting rooms etc. Some can be rented on a short-term basis.

Leilani Apartments (☎/fax 23910, PO Box 2137) 1/2-bed apartments T$375/425 per month. T$200 deposit. Located about 1km east of the Small Industries Centre, close to the Blue Pacific Nightclub (which can be noisy), Leilani's apartments are clean, modern and beside the lagoon. Some are a little soulless and not well furnished, but are well equipped and good value.

Hellen's Apartments (☎ 24873, office in 'Utumoengalu Bldg, One-Way Rd) 1/2-bed apartments T$40/50 per night (long-term discounts). Located off Vaha'akolo Rd, 2km south of central Nuku'alofa, these pleasant, well-appointed apartments are set in large, quiet gardens containing a small swimming pool. Take the Vaiola bus from the eastern bus terminal on Vuna Rd.

Captain Cook Vacation Apartments (☎/fax 25600, Vuna Rd, PO Box 1959) Singles/doubles/families T$65/75/85 per night (long-term discounts). In a pleasant location west of the Royal Palace, this place has six well-appointed two-bed apartments with telephones.

The Lagoon Lodge (☎ 26515, fax 24069, e lagoon.lodge@kalianet.to, PO Box 51) 1/2-bed apartments T$115-149/200 per night. Monthly from $1250. Next door to Leilani Apartments, these new, well-equipped flats (with microwave and phone) are very well fitted out. A restaurant, bar, swimming pool and conference building are planned, and boat trips. One for the expat aid worker.

Haufolau Apartments (☎ 21151) T$350 per month. This place off Fatafehi Rd, behind the Savoy Dry Cleaner, is simple, nice, but often full.

Long-Term Accommodation

Houses and flats for rent are listed at the TVB and on the bulletin board at Molisi

Tonga Limited supermarket. They can be good value if you plan to stay for a while. Prices start around T$300 per month for a simple house; elegance will set you back upwards of T$800 per month.

Places to Eat

Nuku'alofa has many good places to eat. Don't forget the restaurants farther afield at the resorts around Tongatapu and on the islands offshore, as well as the island-style buffets or feasts (see Entertainment).

Restaurants – Budget *Akiko's (☎ 25339, Taufa'ahau Rd)* Lunch T$3-4. Open 11.30am-2pm Mon-Fri. Akiko's, below the basilica, is a very popular lunch spot and is clean, cool and good value. It serves a variety of Chinese dishes, hamburgers, Tongan food and other simple fare. The fruit juices and smoothies are excellent.

Maseia Restaurant (Top flr Maseia Bldg, Taufa'ahau Rd) Lunch T$2.50-4. Open 10am-4pm Mon-Fri, 10am-12.30pm Sat. A popular restaurant (despite having as much atmosphere as a school canteen), this is clean and pleasant and serves authentic Tongan dishes and hot, filling lunches. It also closes early if the food runs out.

Pot Luck Lunches (☎ 25091) Lunch T$3-5. Open noon-2pm Tues, Wed & Fri during school terms. Good food and good service can be had at this restaurant off Salote Rd, behind St Mary's Cathedral. Food is provided by the catering and hospitality students of the 'Ahopanilolo Technical College; this is its training restaurant. They call it 'pot luck' because one set meal is prepared and you take your chances!

Sama Restaurant (Railway Rd) Lunch T$3-4. Open 11.30am-2.30pm Mon-Fri. This is a simple, clean Tongan restaurant with a limited menu – there's often only fried fish and *'ota 'ika* (raw fish) served.

Toni's Delux Food Court (Wellington Rd) Most dishes T$3-5.50. Open 10am-1am Mon-Sat. This tiny restaurant behind a small convenience store has just a few tables, but serves generous portions of well-prepared Chinese food. There's an extensive menu and a large TV to watch while you dine.

The Grill Bar & Restaurant (☎ 26874, Taufa'ahau Rd) Mains & snacks T$4-11. Open 8.30am till late Mon-Sat. The breakfasts are good here and it's a great place to relax with a drink and watch the action on the street below.

Restaurants – Mid-Range *Friends Café (☎ 22390, Taufa'ahau Rd)* Lunch T$9.50-10.50. Open 8am-4pm Mon-Fri, 8.30am-2pm Sat. This is top of the list for cappuccinos, cakes and treats. The continental lunch menu changes daily. Sophisticated, clean and deservedly popular.

Little Italy Pizzeria (☎ 25053, Vuna Rd) Pizza & pasta T$7-14. Open noon-2pm & 6.30pm-10.30pm Mon-Sat. There's great food and a pleasant atmosphere here, west of the Royal Palace, with tables inside or outside on a terrace overlooking the sea. It has a good choice of salads, delicious pasta and outstanding pizza cooked in a real pizza oven! It also does takeaways.

Taste of India (☎ 26615, Wellington Rd) Mains T$9-18. Open noon-2pm & 6.30pm-10pm Mon-Fri, 6.30pm-10pm Sat. If you're craving good, well-balanced Indian food, this is the place to visit. The menu is deliberately limited and the food is well prepared and delicious. Check out the daily specials.

Suliana's (☎ 22384, 1st flr TCF Bldg, Wellington Rd) Snacks & mains T$4-20. Open 9am-9pm Mon-Sat. Centrally located with a cool balcony, Suliana's is recommended for tasty German food (the potato and bacon omelette is excellent), pizzas, delicious pancakes and snacks. A cybercafe was planned at the time of writing.

Fakalato Restaurant (☎ 24101, Wellington Rd) Most dishes T$5-8. Open 6pm-10pm Mon-Sat. Fakalato, above the Snack & Milk Bar, is often recommended by locals as the best of Nuku'alofa's growing number of Chinese restaurants, but it can be hit-and-miss. The service is friendly and it's air-conditioned.

Emerald Restaurant (☎ 24619, Vuna Rd) Mains T$3.50-12.80. Open 11.30am-2.30pm & 5pm-10pm daily. This is a little stark as restaurants go, but it's a nice enough place that serves reasonable Chinese food and has a large menu. But the real bonus is that it's open on Sunday.

Restaurants – Top End *Seaview Hotel & Restaurant* (☎ 23709, Vuna Rd) Starters T$6-16, mains T$23-42. Open 6pm-10pm Mon-Fri. West of the Royal Palace, this is one of the most elegant (and expensive) restaurants in town. Good food and excellent service have given it a fine reputation. House specialities include steak and seafood dishes. Booking is recommended.

The Waterfront Café (☎ 21004, Vuna Rd) Mains T$12-25. Open daily till late. This is a popular and relaxed place, verging on the sophisticated, with a wooden open-plan dining area. Dishes vary in quality. If you choose wisely, meals are hearty, well cooked and nicely presented. The fish dishes are recommended.

Lunarossa Restaurant (☎ 26297, Taufa-'ahau Rd) Mains T$14-23. Open from 7pm Mon-Sat. Above the TCF supermarket, this restaurant boasts fine Italian food served with style and includes some excellent home-made pasta and a few good vegetarian options. There's also a good wine cellar. Recommended.

Fast Food *John's Place* (☎ 21246, Taufa'ahau Rd) Burgers and the like T$2-4.50. Open 7.30am-midnight Mon-Thur, 7.30am Fri-midnight Sat. John's Place concentrates on dispensing fish and chips and a variety of hamburgers (served in slightly sweet rolls). The ice-cream counter offers large and monster cones for T$1/1.50. Not bad, but no cigar.

Snack & Milk Bar (Wellington Rd) Take-aways T$3-5. Open 8am-9pm Mon-Fri, 8am-midnight Sat, 2pm-8pm Sun. This popular place with bizarre cartoons on the walls concentrates on curries, but also serves barbecue chicken and good chips.

Mr Chips (Taufa'ahau Rd) Large fish/sausage & chips T$4.50. Open 11am-11pm Mon-Thur & Sat, 11am-2am Fri. Wrapped in newspaper and delicious!

Many small *convenience stores* sell good, inexpensive ice cream and mixed barbecues of chicken, pork, sausages and cassava or taro for T$3. There are a number of good barbecue places on Vuna Rd near Tuimata-moana Harbour.

Self-Catering *Talamahu Market* (Salote Rd) is the best in the country and serves as a sort of crash course in tropical fruits and vegetables, which are the best value in town. Many prices are marked but if not, watch what the Tongans are paying.

Cowley's owns two bakeries in town, one on Taufa'ahau Rd south of town, and the other on Salote Rd, known as the *Bread Bin*. It has a variety of cakes and sweets as well as white, whole-wheat and seven-grain breads, rolls and muffins. Exceptionally sugary cakes and other baked sweets are available at the *Homestyle Bakery* (Salote Rd) and *The Hot Bread Shop* (Taufa'ahau Rd) – the latter, 1km south of town, is possibly the best bakery in town.

The *fish market* on Tuimatamoana Harbour starts around 5am (when the boats come in). If you get up too late try the *Sea Star Fishing Co* (☎ 25458) nearby or the few stalls at *Vuna Wharf* in the afternoon.

At the *'Alatini Fisheries & Meat Co* (☎ 24759, Small Industries Centre), 2km south-east of central Nuku'alofa, you can buy good-quality fish, imported meats (steak for T$14/kg), wines (T$23 for a 3L cask) and other luxury foods.

The *Tonga Cold Store* (☎ 24084, Vuna Rd), next to the Billfish Bar & Restaurant, sells mince and packaged meats.

Nuku'alofa has a number of large supermarkets. *Molisi Tonga Limited* (Salote Rd), opposite Talamahu Market, is arguably the best and has a good bottle shop. Branches of the *Tonga Cooperative Federation* (TCF; Cnr Wellington & Taufa'ahau Rds; also on Taufa'ahau Rd) have competitive prices. Ten minutes east along Salote Rd at the Kinikinilau Shopping Centre is another large *supermarket*. The *Supa-Kava Market* here has good prices on imported wines.

There's a *Royal Beer Shop* (Fakafonua Centre) near Queen Salote Wharf. *The Royal Brewery* (Small Industries Centre) is quite small but tours can be arranged. The numerous small *convenience stores* stay open all hours to sell bread, milk, alcohol and tinned foods. They're closed on Sunday, though.

Entertainment
Island Buffets & Traditional Dance
Island-style buffets and performances of traditional Tongan music and dance (all cost T$20) are presented indoors at the *Tongan National Centre* (☎ 23022) on Tuesday and Thursday nights – see earlier in this chapter – and the *International Dateline Hotel* (☎ 23411) on Wednesday and Saturday nights (featuring a rather eccentric ukulele player), and outdoors by the beach at the *Good Samaritan Inn* (☎ 41022) in Kolovai on Friday night. The one at the Good Samaritan Inn – see Western Tongatapu later in this chapter – is probably the best in terms of all-round entertainment, not least because the restaurant affords great views of the sunset.

The Good Samaritan also has entertainment on Sunday with a barbecue and live music. However, at the time of writing, the place was recovering after being hit by a freak wave during a cyclone, so inquire locally as to what's on.

Bars *Wanda's* (☎ 23344, Taufa'ahau Rd) Located beside the Pacific Royale Hotel, this small bar is decked out in a western theme, complete with saloon doors. It can get pretty lively and there's a happy hour (7.30pm to 9.30pm!) on Friday night (beer T$1.50; some spirits T$1 per shot).

The Grill Bar & Restaurant (☎ 26874, Taufa'ahau Rd) Relaxed beer consumption is possible on the balcony above the street. A nice place to start the evening and for food at any time (see Restaurants – Budget).

Nuku'alofa Club (☎ 21160, Cnr Salote & Tu'i Rds) This all-male, members-only club behind the palace is a stuffy upper-crust pub and billiards hall where you can rub elbows with expats and Tongan nobles, yuppie politicians and businessmen. Technically, you must be the guest of a 'member'.

Tonga Club (☎ 22710, Tupoulahi Rd) This dingy, historic pub situated a couple of blocks behind the International Dateline Hotel is a good place for cheap beer (Royal, of course).

Along the waterfront, heading east along Vuna Rd from the centre, are a number of open-air garden bars. Food is available at most of them.

Splash Bar (☎ 23411, Vuna Rd) This pool-side bar at the International Dateline Hotel is not bad and pretty relaxing. Non-guests can use the pool for T$3. It's especially popular at weekends and on Saturday night when everywhere else closes.

The Garden Bar (☎ 22101, Vuna Rd) Behind the Emerald Restaurant, this is slightly rough around the edges and attracts a different sort of crowd, but the beer's cheap.

The Waterfront Café (☎ 21004, Vuna Rd) Open daily. This is one of the most popular waterfront bars and a good place for socialising. It's popular with expats kicking off the evening and the food is OK (see Restaurants – Top End).

Billfish Bar & Restaurant (☎ 24084, Vuna Rd) Open noon-2am Mon-Fri, noon-11.30pm Sat. Located 300m up the road from the Waterfront Café, this is probably the most popular bar in town, with Tongans and *palangi* (Westerners) alike, though it never really gets going until 10.30pm or later. Live music of varying quality is played on Wednesday and Friday nights and karaoke is popular on the other evenings. It serves reasonable food too.

Nightclubs Friday night is the big night for going out in Tonga, and there are numerous clubs in Nuku'alofa. Discos and nightclubs get lively by around midnight and rock until dawn. Drinks are roughly the same price as at the bars in town (T$2.50 for an Ikale beer). You'll need to be reasonably dressed to get in anywhere.

On Saturday night, the partying is stifled at midnight to avoid revelling on Sunday.

Blue Pacific Nightclub (☎ 25994) Open 10pm-7am Tues-Fri. Closes midnight Sat. Admission T$4/6 for women/men. Built on what was a very fancy estate 4km southeast of central Nuku'alofa, this is the best nightclub in Tonga. It has indoor and outdoor dancing and bar areas, the former being heaving and sweaty, the latter relaxed and cool. The grounds slope down to the lagoon and it's very popular with Tongans.

Ambassador Nightclub (☎ 23338, Taufa-'ahau Rd) Open 10pm-4am Wed-Fri. Closes midnight Sat. Admission T$3/5 for women/men. This nightclub 2.5km south of central Nuku'alofa can be enjoyable, but can also be very quiet in the low season. Attached to the club is the Love Boat Restaurant, which offers food of variable quality (but does have a bar).

There's also the *One Night Stand* above Wanda's (see Bars) in the centre of town. It's more of an earthy scene (the name says it all) but not too heavy.

Cinema *Loni's Cinema* (☎ 23617, Wellington Rd) Admission T$3. Shows at 11am Fri & Sat, 8.15pm Mon-Fri, midnight Fri & Sun. Nuku'alofa's only cinema looks like it's been trashed by rioting customers inspired by the violent action movies and Jackie Chan flicks that are standard fare. Some recent releases are on offer (if the projector is working), while older films are shown with a video projector. It's a fun experience, but pick your seat carefully; wearing mosquito repellent is recommended. Popcorn (50 seniti) is sold from the video shop downstairs.

Other Venues *Queen Salote Memorial Hall* (☎ 26020, Cnr Taufa'ahau & Mateialona Rds) This hall is the venue for large-scale events. The TVB may have details on upcoming events.

'Atenisi Institute (☎ 24819) This university has a foundation for the performing arts, which gives performances four times a year at venues in Nuku'alofa.

Spectator Sports Tonga's favourite sport, rugby, is played at *Teufaiva Outdoor Stadium* off Taufa'ahau Rd, south of the city centre, from March to August. Games are played back to back all day Saturday. Entrance costs T$1 to T$3 depending on which teams are playing.

Cricket (March to July) and soccer (March to November) are played at *Mala'e*

Pangai, the lawn beside the Royal Palace, and at *Tonga College* (near the golf course). There is rarely a charge.

'Atele Indoor Stadium, opposite the golf course on the main road at Vietongo, is the venue for tennis (an international tournament is held there during Heilala Week festivities in early July), as well as volleyball, badminton, table tennis, basketball, netball and boxing. Entrance is usually T$3 to T$5.

Shopping

Talamahu Market (Salote Rd) Upstairs at this market, open from early morning to late afternoon, are a number of stalls selling some excellent Tongan art and craft, including carvings, tapa and pandanus mats. One stall sells amazing carved fishing lures (T$20). Take your time and browse around – there's a lot to choose from.

Flea market (Taufa'ahau Rd) While there is second-hand and inexpensive clothing at Talamahu Market, your best bet is the flea market, near the Ambassador Nightclub, on Saturday morning. Get there early for the best selection.

Langafonua'ae Fefine Handicrafts (☎ 21014, e lgafonua@kalinet.to, Taufa-'ahau Rd) Open 8.30am-5.30pm Mon-Fri, 8.30am-noon Sat. Founded by Queen Salote in 1953 to promote women's development and a continued interest in indigenous arts, this shop stocks a vast range of Tongan handicrafts and some paintings.

The *Friendly Islands Marketing Co-operative* (Fimco; ☎ 23155, Taufa'ahau Rd) Open 8am-6pm Mon-Fri, 8am-noon Sat. This is another handicraft shop with a wide selection.

Tapacraft (☎ 26760, Lavinia Rd) Open 10am-4pm Tues-Sat. Almost everything sold here is small, inexpensive, portable and made with travellers in mind. There are dolls and other items made of tapa, but most amazing are the original engravings from Captain Cook's voyages, printed in England in 1777 and 1784. They come with a history telling how and when they were published and are reasonably priced.

The *Philatelic Bureau* (☎ 22455, fax 24147, e gpo@kalianet.to) Collectors of stamps should check out this shop upstairs at the post office.

The **National Reserve Bank of Tonga** (☎ 24057, **e** nrbt@kalianet.to, Salote Rd) Coin and bill boxed sets are available here.

Blue Pacific Music Store (☎ 22411, Taufa'ahau Rd). This is arguably the best place in Tonga to buy music. Tapes cost T$17 and CDs T$30.

There are a host of shops down Taufa'ahau Rd. Check out **Blue Banana** (☎ 24846) which sells distinctive, bright, hand-painted T-shirts and other clothing (T$18 to T$30), and **Look Sharp Tonga** (☎ 26056) which produces very contrasting, and popular, surfer-style T-shirts (T$12 to T$18).

The only places you'll find any snorkelling gear are **EM Jones** (see Travel Agents & Airline Offices) and the **Fimco fishing store** behind the Fimco craft shop. Cheap Chinese masks cost T$25; they are – only just – better than nothing. Both shops also stock a range of fishing gear – EM Jones is better for rods and reels, while consumable items (lures, line, hooks etc) are cheaper at Fimco.

Getting There & Away

Air Tongatapu's Fua'amotu International Airport is in the south of Tongatapu Island, near Fua'amotu, a 30-minute drive from Nuku'alofa. Air Fiji, Polynesian Airlines, Royal Tongan Airlines, Air Pacific and Air New Zealand all connect Tongatapu with other Pacific destinations, while Royal Tongan Airlines has a range of services to 'Eua, Ha'apai, Vava'u and the Niuas. See Travel Agents & Airline Offices earlier in this chapter for contact details for the airlines.

See the Getting There & Away chapter for details of international flights, and the Getting Around chapter for information on flights between Tongatapu and other parts of Tonga.

Boat The MV *'Olovaha*, run by the Shipping Corporation of Polynesia (☎ 23853), and the MV *Tautahi*, run by 'Uliti 'Uata (Walter Line) Shipping (☎ 23855), connect Tongatapu with Ha'apai, Vava'u and the Niuas. Both ferry operators' offices are on

Nuku'alofa's Queen Salote Wharf, from where the boats also leave, and are open standard office hours. Other vessels provide frequent services between Tongatapu and 'Eua, leaving from Tuimatamoana Harbour.

See the Getting Around chapter for details of schedules and fares. The Getting There & Away chapter gives information on yacht travel to Tonga, and cargo ship options.

Getting Around

To/From the Airport Taxis meet all incoming domestic and international flights. The standard fare for up to four passengers between the airport and Nuku'alofa is T$15. Teta Tours (☎ 23690, **e** tetatour@kalianet .to) offers a shuttle bus service between Nuku'alofa and the airport (T$6 per person). Many hotels and guesthouses offer airport transport for guests if you let them know in advance. Many pick-ups are free; drop-offs are usually not.

Bus Nuku'alofa's two bus terminals are on Vuna Rd. 'Long-distance' buses going to outlying areas on Tongatapu depart from the western terminal (close to Vuna Wharf). The eastern terminal (opposite the TVB) serves Nuku'alofa's suburbs. Fares range from 20 seniti to T$1 one way.

The bus service starts around 6am. The last buses usually run at about 4.30pm. There's no bus service on Sunday. Don't set off for anywhere after noon unless you're planning to stay the night or are willing to take your chances hitching back.

In urban areas, bus stops are marked with a small sign reading 'Pasi'. Elsewhere, flag down a bus by waving your outstretched arm. Passengers normally pay as they get off the bus.

Car & Scooter Hire Car and scooter rental companies in Nuku'alofa include:

Alisei Ltd (☎ 24977) Vuna Rd – scooters T$20 per day
Avis (☎ 21179) Tungi Arcade, Taufa'ahau Rd; (☎ 32224) airport – cars T$70 to T$75 per day; T$8 per day excess reduction.
Budget Rent-A-Car (☎ 24059) Taufa'ahau Rd – cars from T$60 per day

Challenge Rental Cars (☎ 29707) – cars from T$45 per day

Discovery Corporation (☎ 26200) Taufa'ahau Rd – scooters T$25 for eight hours; T$50 for 24 hours

EM Jones Travel & Tours (☎ 23422) Taufa'ahau Rd – cars from T$50 per day

Harbour View Motel (☎ 25488) Vuna Rd – cars T$35 per day (guests only)

Palm Travel & Tours (☎ 24137, or ☎ 23505 after office hours) Cnr Fatafehi & Salote Rds – cars T$45 to T$55 per day

All rates include unlimited kilometres. Special rates are sometimes available for weekends or long-term rental.

Taxi Taxis are a good way to see the island quickly, but be sure to negotiate a price before setting off. All-day taxi tours of Tongatapu, including all the traditional 'tourist' sites, are T$50 to T$80 for up to four people.

Within Nuku'alofa, taxis charge T$2 to T$3 fare for up to four passengers. Fares to the outskirts of town are about T$4 to T$5.

Taxi companies are numerous, but include:

Ngele'ia Taxi (☎ 24112)
Nuku'alofa Taxi (☎ 22910)
Talamahu Market Taxi (☎ 22713)
Wellington Road Taxi (☎ 24744)

Bicycle Tongatapu is flat and perfect for cycling. A bike is convenient for getting around town and allows you to explore at leisure, though Nuku'alofa's traffic is not exactly 'bike friendly' so take care. The island's major sites can be visited in three or four days.

Niko's Bicycle Rental is run from a trailer roughly opposite the International Dateline Hotel. It's open 9am to 5pm Monday to Saturday. Bike rental is T$8 per day, with long-term rentals getting a special rate (and a tool kit). A couple of guesthouses rent bikes to guests.

Boat The three offshore island resorts all provide boat transport; see North of Nuku-'alofa later in this chapter. Ferries connect Tongatapu to 'Eua – see the earlier Getting Around chapter.

AROUND THE ISLAND

Although Tongatapu is undeniably flat, it does harbour a variety of notable natural features – caves, blowholes, a natural limestone archway and coral reefs – as well as some of the most extensive and well-excavated archaeological sites in the Pacific. The entire east coast, from the southern tip of the island right up to Niutoua, is fringed with lovely white-sand beaches. The south and west coasts are indented with some fine beaches as well.

Most of Tongatapu's interior is composed of agricultural land and rural villages, some with noteworthy churches.

Eastern Tongatapu

Captain Cook's Landing Site A memorial near Holonga village marks the site where Captain Cook landed on Tongatapu on his final Pacific voyage in 1777 and took a nap under a banyan tree before moving on to Mu'a to visit his friend Pau, the reigning Tu'i Tonga.

Kauvai Royal Estate The secluded bit of royal real estate known as Kauvai is practically surrounded by the Fanga 'Uta Lagoon. The palace sits on the shore at the end of a long, quiet road through neatly ordered royal plantations and rows of coconut trees. It's an odd landscape for Tonga, with a picturesque lagoon, some bizarre banyan trees and relatively lush vegetation. During the daytime, the access road is open to the public.

To get there without your own vehicle, take a bus to Vaini or Folaha, from where it's a 4km or 5km walk each way to Kauvai.

Mu'a & the Lapaha Archaeological Site Sometime around 1200 the 11th Tu'i Tonga, Tu'itatui, moved the royal capital from Heketa (near present-day Niutoua) to Lapaha, now known as Mu'a. The Mu'a area contains the richest concentration of archaeological remnants in Tonga.

The *langi*, or pyramidal stone tombs, constructed in ancient Tonga were traditionally used for the burial of royalty. Commoners were buried in simpler heaps of sand lined with volcanic stones, much as

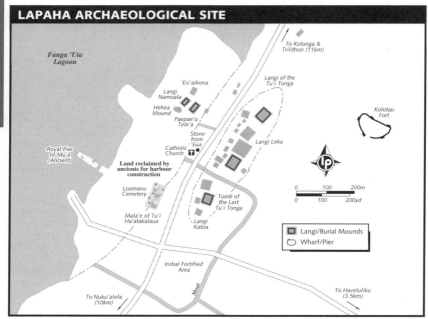

LAPAHA ARCHAEOLOGICAL SITE

Fanga 'Uta Lagoon

To Kolonga & Trilithon (11km)

'Esi'aikona

Langi of the Tu'i Tonga

Langi Namoala

Hehea Mound

Kolotau Fort

Paepae'o Tele'a

Stone from 'Eua

Catholic Church

Langi Leka

Royal Pier of Mu'a (Ancient)

Land reclaimed by ancients for harbour construction

Loamanu Cemetery

Tomb of the Last Tu'i Tonga

Mala'e of Tu'i Ha'atakalaua

Langi Katoa

0   100   200m
0   100   200yd

Langi/Burial Mounds
Wharf/Pier

Initial Fortified Area

Moat

To Nuku'alofa (10km)

To Haveluliku (3.5km)

---

they are today. Around the vicinity of Mu'a there are 28 royal stone tombs, 15 of which are monumental. Most of the others are little more than conical mounds of stone.

Just outside the site, near Mu'a's southern edge, the road crosses a shallow but prominent ditch. This is the moat which once surrounded the *kolo* (royal capital).

Paepae 'o Tele'a Tonga's most imposing ancient burial site is the Paepae 'o Tele'a (Platform of Tele'a), a monumental pyramid-like stone structure about 400m north of the moat. It was long thought to have housed the remains of Tele'a, or 'Ulukimata I, a Tu'i Tonga who reigned during the 16th century. But his body may not be inside the 'tomb' at all, since legend has it that he was drowned and his body lost. Traditional burial sites were topped by a vault *(fonualoto)*, which was dug into the sand on top of the platform and lined with stones in preparation for the body. This platform, however, contains no

such vault, which supports the theory that the Paepae 'o Tele'a is not a tomb at all but, in fact, a memorial.

With the exception of the vault, this structure contains the best and most massive examples of all the early Tongan burial tomb construction styles. The stones used are enormous. The corner stones of the bottom tier on the eastern side of the monument are L-shaped. The upper surfaces of all the stones are bevelled; their bases are firmly embedded in the earth, stabilised by the use of stone protrusions jutting out under the surface.

These and all the Lapaha construction stones are quarried limestone taken from dead coral reefs probably on Tongatapu and nearby Motutapu and Pangaimotu. They were transported using cradles slung between two seafaring canoes called *kalia*. (Some maintain that the stones were carried from the Ha'apai Group, or from Futuna or 'Uvea Island in the now French territory of Wallis & Futuna, far to the north-west.)

Oral history preserves tales of the wooden rollers, sennit ropes and incredible leverage (and, of course, slave labour) required in moving the enormous blocks to the construction sites once they'd been landed.

These days, the Paepae 'o Tele'a is suffering from age and weathering, but it remains obvious that it was built in memory of an individual who carried a lot of weight in the society that created it.

Langi Namoala While the fonualoto is missing from the Paepae 'o Tele'a, the Langi Namoala tomb, also at the Lapaha site, has a fine example of a fonualoto – but it's empty. Typical of such structures, it was covered with a stone slab first and then with *kilikili* (pumice-like volcanic gravel) collected from Kao and Tofua in the Ha'apai Group. Kilikili is still valuable as a grave decoration.

If the Namoala tomb is typical, it would have once had a shelter of tapa, coconut fronds and fine mats on top of it. This would have housed the *matapule* (talking chief), who would have lived on the langi and attended to the extensive funeral arrangements and ceremonies that followed a burial.

The Namoala langi is thought to have been the burial site of a female chief, but tradition supplies no further details. The stones used in this construction are much narrower than those in the adjacent pyramids. On the north side a stairway leads to the top.

To the north-east of the principal mounds rises the '**Esi'aikona**, an elevated platform used as a rest area by the chief and his family. Near the Namoala tomb is the **Hehea mound**, which was originally believed to be a rubbish tip created during the construction of the langi. More recently, however, it was cleared of vegetation to reveal two fonualoto amid haphazardly placed earth and rock. Unlike the other structures, the Hehea was built on artificial landfill, but it's not known who engineered this incredible reclamation project or when it was done.

The large langi that now bears a cross on top, across the road from the others in the modern cemetery, is the grave of **Laufilitonga**, the last Tu'i Tonga, who was deposed by King George Tupou I in 1826.

Mu'a & Langi Leka All the guided island tours stop briefly at Mu'a's principal archaeological sites but you could easily spend a whole day here exploring the impressive excavated **pyramid tombs** and the host of smaller pyramids scattered through the village and bush across the road in **Langi Leka**.

The large, old, stone **Catholic Church** is also of note – it looks like it was shipped directly from the UK. Inside, an impressive traditional Polynesian podium, a few statues and some lovely stained-glass work are worth checking out. With care it's possible to climb up the bell tower, but some of the stairs are rotting away and you need a head for heights.

Beside the main road outside the gate of the church there's a rather ordinary 50cm-high boulder. Tradition has it that this *makatolo* stone was hurled by the demigod Maui from the island of 'Eua at a noisy rooster that had been keeping him awake at night. Visitors to Tonga will be particularly sympathetic to his reaction to such a situation.

Getting There & Away Take the Mu'a bus (80 seniti one way) from the eastern bus terminal on Vuna Rd in Nuku'alofa. Head back to Nuku'alofa by about 3.30pm or you could be stuck.

The Fishing Pigs of Talafo'ou The village of Talafo'ou, north of the Mu'a area, is known for its smart pigs. At low tide they venture out on the tidal flat looking for shellfish!

Ha'amonga 'a Maui Trilithon Near Niutoua, at the eastern end of Tongatapu, is one of ancient Polynesia's most intriguing monuments. Its name means 'Maui's Burden' and according to legend it was carried by Maui from distant 'Uvea on a carrying yoke. But archaeologists and oral history credit its construction to the 11th Tu'i Tonga, Tu'itatui, who reigned at the turn of the 13th century.

The structure consists of three large coralline stones, each weighing about 40 tonnes, arranged into a trilithic gate, Stonehenge-style. The uprights are about 5m high and just over 4m wide at their bases. The lintel, which rests in notched grooves in the uprights, is nearly 6m long, 1.5m wide and just over 0.5m thick.

It seems that Tu'itatui was more than a little paranoid. His name means 'leader who hits the knees', indicating that 'he wielded a large stick at knee level to ward off potential assassins. Seaward of the trilithon is a large stone, 'Esi Makafakinanga, which was supposedly used by Tu'itatui as a back-rest to shield his back from surprise attack while he directed the construction work.

Some suggest that the uprights represent either the Tu'i's two competing sons or the entrance to a royal compound when Heketa, Tonga's second royal capital, was based here. Nowadays, however, it's becoming accepted that the structure functioned as a sort of Stonehenge, a structure for determining the seasons. Indeed, in the '60s King Taufa-'ahau Tupou IV theorised that an odd design on the lintel may have had something to do with determining seasons. Vegetation in line with the arms of the double-V design between the trilithon to the sea was cleared, and on 21 June 1967 – the winter solstice – the sun was observed to rise and set in perfect alignment with the clearings. It was also noted that it rose and set along the other two arms on the longest day of the year.

For the ancient Tongans, the significance of the summer solstice probably related to the beginning of the *kahokaho* (yam) harvest, which was kicked off by the biggest annual festival held in ancient Tonga, the Katoanga 'Inasi. During this celebration, the year's finest yams were donated to the royal storehouses of the Tu'i Tonga.

The Ha'amonga Trilithon is now preserved in a 23-hectare National Historic Reserve. From the entrance, a walking track winds northward past several langi (known as the Langi Heketa) and *'esi* (resting mounds), where interpretative signs make sense of the remaining mounds of stones. The track then enters the forest and continues for several hundred metres to the shore.

A number of good-quality handicrafts are sold at the trilithon site and are cheaper there than in town.

Getting There & Away Take the Niutoua bus – they're infrequent – and get off about 1km short of Niutoua (T$1); the driver can indicate the spot. Head out early and return in the early afternoon, or you may get stuck.

Muihopohoponga Reserve Near Niutoua is a 2km stretch of white-sand beach at the easternmost extreme of Tongatapu. It has been set aside as a nature reserve to protect several species of native trees and some of the natural bush land that once covered the entire island. It is accessible by walking 2km along a track leading east from Niutoua.

'Anahulu Cave & Haveluliku On the island's east coast, near Haveluliku – where you'll find more of Maui's stone projectiles – is Tonga's most famous cave. 'Anahulu Cave is full of stalactites and stalagmites and you may notice a slight musty smell caused by deposits from white-rumped swiftlets or *pekepekatae*, which build nests on the caves walls. Their screeching combines with the constant dripping of water to create an eerie atmosphere. Decades of handling and vandalising have affected the cave, but it's still a magical, otherworldly place.

At the bottom of the stairs is a freshwater pool. Swimming in the cold water is very refreshing.

Sensible walking shoes and a torch (flashlight) are essential for visiting 'Anahulu Cave. For serious exploration you'll need night diving lights.

Buses should run to Haveluliku, or at least to Fatumu just to the south, once or twice a day. Once in Haveluliku village, take the dirt road south-east down to the ocean to arrive at a parking area and a set of steps that leads to the cave and gives access to the beach. If you're already exploring Mu'a, you could walk from there; the road is now sealed.

'Oholei Beach On the shore about 4km south of Haveluliku is 'Oholei Beach, where the coastline is riddled with limestone caves and the lovely, deserted white sand seems to go on forever. Hina Cave, along the beach, is beautiful, with soft light filtering through the open roof.

Hufangalupe Five kilometres south of the village of Vaini is Hufangalupe (Pigeon's Gate), on Tongatapu's south coast. This large natural archway in the coralline limestone is flanked to the south by 30m cliffs and to the north by plantation lands. The sea pounds through the opening and tears at the walls of the bridge and adjacent pit.

By public transport, you'll have to hurry to see Hufangalupe in one day, since you'll have to walk nearly 10km. Catch a bus to Vaini, then follow the road opposite Vaini police station and walk south for almost 5km until you reach the coast. When you reach the cliffs you'll be on top of the bridge. Turn around and go back until you see a very faint track leading away to the east; follow it for a few metres and you'll soon see the archway. There's a good view into the pit from the bridge itself and it's possible to climb all the way down to the sea in the gully but it's very steep and the coral rocks are razor-sharp.

Following the dirt road eastward from the span, you'll see numerous dramatic cliffs and the turbulent sea below – quite a contrast to Tongatapu's calm, lazy north shore. This is a good place to watch sea birds, especially white-tailed tropic birds as they swoop past trailing their long, graceful tail feathers. They lay their eggs on rocky ledges and sometimes even in the arch itself. You may also see sharks and turtles in the water below the cliffs and humpback whales between July and October.

Western Tongatapu

Tongan Wildlife Centre If you've had no luck spotting a red shining parrot (also known as the 'Eua parrot or *koki*) or a Niuafo'ou megapode *(malau)* in the wild, here's your chance to see these rare birds, the star attractions at the Tongan Wildlife Centre *(☎/fax 29449, ℮ birdpark@kalianet.to, Liku Road, Veitongo; adult/child T$3/free; open 9am-5pm Mon-Fri, 9am-6pm Sat & Sun)*.

The Tongan Wildlife Centre, near the island's south coast, was established in 1990 to promote conservation awareness, collect data, carry out captive breeding and establish reserves. It is also involved in the translocation of rare and endangered indigenous

bird species, such as the Niuafo'ou megapode. A number of these birds have been moved from their volcanic home on Niuafo'ou to the similarly volcanic (and uninhabited) island of Late in the Vava'u Group. Similarly, red shining parrots have been released on Tofua in the Ha'apai Group.

Also noteworthy are the blue-crowned lorikeet *(henga)* and friendly ground dove *(tu)*, as well as the banded iguana *(fokai)*, which lives throughout Tonga but is extremely difficult to spot.

Allow 1½ hours to see the park, which is set in a tropical garden containing examples of many medicinal plants and food crops grown in Tonga.

Getting There & Away Take the Vaini or Mu'a bus to Veitongo village (50 seniti one way) and get off at the Bird Park sign. Walk south for just over 2km to Liku Rd. The Centre's entrance is just south of this intersection.

Keleti Beach The clean and lovely Keleti Beach, near the Wildlife Centre, is actually a series of coves divided by rocky outcrops. They slope gently into clear pools which are excellent for swimming at high tide and perfect for lazing in and observing the variety of life trapped there at low tide. The reef consists of a line of terraces and blowholes that shoot like Yellowstone geysers when the waves hit them at high tide. Be cautious if you are swimming here and don't get too close to the blowholes or you may be dragged under by a powerful vortex and cut to shreds.

Just above the beach is the (alas) nonfunctional Keleti Beach Resort.

Taxis from town cost T$7 each way for up to four people. Or, by bus, follow the instructions in the preceding section to get to the Wildlife Centre, then continue south for about 1km until you find a rough vehicle track that leads down to the sea.

Mapu'a 'a Vaca Blowholes The Mapu'a 'a Vaca blowholes (the name means 'Chief's Whistles') stretch for 5km along the south shore of Tongatapu, near the village of Houma. They are best viewed on a windy day with a strong swell, when water, forced up through natural vents in the coralline limestone, can shoot 30m into the air. On an especially good day, hundreds of them will be active at once (but if the tide is too high, it will wash over the terraces containing the vents and 'extinguish' the fountains). These blowholes are some of the most impressive in the South Pacific.

There's a *cafe and restaurant* not too far from the blowholes, which may also offer accommodation in the future.

For a look at the blowholes from another perspective, turn west just south of the church and school in Houma. Where this road hits the shore, there's a wonderful snorkelling beach and interesting sea-level views of the blowholes.

From Nuku'alofa catch the bus south-west to Houma (60 seniti one way) and walk 1km south to the parking area above the blowholes.

Liahona In the village of Liahona, just north-east of Nuku'alofa, is a large complex constructed by the Mormon church. Tongatapu's **Mormon temple** is here, crowned with a golden angel and surrounded by beautiful gardens. Only Mormons may enter the temple. Other buildings in the Mormon compound include a large Mormon high school. (Beulah College, which is the Seventh Day Adventist counterpart to Liahona, is near the village of Vaini.)

Immediately west of Liahona, on the north side of the road, is what is reputed to be Tonga's only **triple-headed coconut tree**! It's a very unusual sight.

Monotapu Beach Located on the north-western coast of Tongatapu, this is a beautiful beach nestling in a cove 1km wide. Just back from the sand is the ***Princess Resort*** (☎ 41400, fax 24530, e *futu@kalia net.to*). Accommodation is in motel-style units (four-person rooms from T$40 to T$60) and, down on the beach, there's a good bar and restaurant with Indian food (meals from T$6.50 to T$20). Happy hour is 6pm to 8pm Friday and Saturday. The architecture may not be exactly Polynesian, but it's great value for groups and the location is beautiful.

'Umu Tangata At the intersection of three roads, just south of the planned community of Fo'ui, is the 'Umu Tangata (Man Oven). There's no oven to see here today, but there is a legend. Long ago a cannibal chef was preparing a feast here, when he became distracted by an invasion. He left the meal unattended for so long that a tree grew out of each person. It's believed that descendants of these original trees remain to this day.

Kolovai Most of the flying foxes that lived in a sanctuary at Kolovai, just north of Fo'ui, have left, but a number of these large, noisy, fruit-eating bats still roost in the odd tree in the village.

Flying foxes have wing spans of up to 1m, are found all over the South Pacific (and hunted for the pot in most places), but in Tonga they are considered *tapu*, or sacred. Only members of the royal family are permitted to hunt them for sport.

There are plans for a cybercafe in Kolovai. The Kolovai Youth and Computer Center will be located opposite the turn-off for the Good Samaritan Inn. Internet access will cost around T$8 per hour.

Take either the Kolovai or the Hihifo bus from the eastern bus terminal on Vuna Rd in Nuku'alofa (80 seniti one way).

Places to Stay & Eat Good Samaritan Inn (☎ 41022, fax 41095, e *gsi@kalianet.to*) Single/double bungalows T$30/40, with bath T$40/60, family-size bungalows with private bath, kitchen & living area T$50/70, bed in 4-bed bungalow T$12.50, camping T$12.50 per person. Breakfast not included in dorm & camping prices. Restaurant/bar open 7am-10pm daily. Meals T$15-28. The rooms here, on Kolovai Beach, are clean and tidy and although service is patchy, the staff are friendly. Unfortunately, shortly after we visited the hotel it was devastated by Cyclone Paula, which took out much of the bar/restaurant area and some accommodation. Renovation and rebuilding began quickly and will hopefully improve some of the ageing facilities. The beach may be more rock than sand but if they reinstate the bar/restaurant overlooking the sea and continue cooking good food it will remain a great choice for spending a few days.

The highlight of the week is the Friday night all-you-can-eat Tongan buffet accompanied by a string band and a rousing performance of Tongan and Polynesian dance and song, all for T$20. On Sunday there's an all-you-can-eat family-style 'umu (traditional underground oven feast) for T$15.

Taxis from Nuku'alofa cost T$10 to T$12. The bus (80 seniti one way) to Kolovai can drop you at the turn-off, then it's a good 2km walk (or hitch). Guests get free pick-ups and daily shuttles into town.

Ha'atafu Beach Reserve Just 3km up the coast from Kolovai, the Ha'atafu Beach Reserve encompasses 8.4 hectares of shallow reef and an area of deep water just outside the breakers. The area inside the barrier reef provides reasonable snorkelling at high tide, but when the water is low, most of the reef lies just below the surface. Thanks to the reserve's location at the juncture of both reef and deep-sea habitats, more than 100 species of fish can be observed here.

Ha'atafu Beach is clean and white. Swimming is safe in the shallow areas, but beyond the barrier reef, strong currents, extensive coral beds and breaking surf make it dangerous. Apparently the best surfing on Tongatapu is found here, but it's all reef breaks suitable only for experienced surfers. Beginners will get ground onto the reef.

The Hihifo bus passes the entrances to all the resorts listed here; one-way fares from Nuku'alofa cost 80 seniti or T$1. A taxi costs T$10 to T$12.

Places to Stay & Eat Paradise Shores Resort (☎/fax 41158, [e] *parashor@kalianet.to*) Double fale T$40, with bath T$75, each extra person T$10, dorm bed T$17, camping T$15 per site. Mains T$8-12, $3 guests-only budget meals. Set in a coconut grove just above the beach, this is a good place to stay. The resort has kayaks, snorkelling gear, a jet ski, boat and an outdoor jacuzzi.

The bar and restaurant are open daily till late (and are particularly busy at weekends). There's a decent (if a little expensive) menu

with some vegetarian options. The hamburgers and pizzas are particularly famous.

Ha'atafu Beach Resort (☎ 41088, fax 22970, [e] *steve@surfingtonga.com*) Singles/doubles T$120/150, bed in 2- or 3-bed dorm T$80. Breakfast & buffet dinner included. Book direct for discounts of 25-30%. This is a beautiful set-up, laid-back and peaceful, if a little expensive. The beachfront bungalows share clean facilities. The resort specialises in all-inclusive surfing holidays. Steve Burling, the Aussie surfie proprietor, knows the local breaks and conditions, which means you can find the best surf around. Surfing safaris, boat trips and deep-sea fishing trips can all be arranged, and snorkelling gear and paddle skis are available. Airport transfers cost T$40 for up to four people.

Kanokupolu Resort Lunch & dinner T$12-18. The beachfront facade looks rather grand, but much of this resort 800m south of Ha'atafu Beach Resort remains incomplete. The restaurant is operational and the food is pretty good, but the long circular bar and shaded drinking terrace are the major drawcards.

'Otuhaka Beach Resort (☎ 41599, fax 24782, [e] *otuhaka@kalianet.to*) Double fale/bungalows T$35/45, double bungalows with bath T$65-95, luxury suite with two doubles, kitchen & bath T$125. Mains T$10-12.50. A little more low-key than the other resorts on Ha'atafu Beach, this place is quiet and peaceful. The restaurant is simple and good, the gardens are pleasant, if a little young, and 400m north along the beach is the bar of the Kanokupolu Resort. Snorkelling gear and paddle skis are available. Free pick-ups/drop-offs in Nuku'alofa.

Christianity & Abel Tasman Landing Sites

At the extreme north-west 'horn' of Tongatapu are monuments marking the landing sites where it's believed that Abel Tasman, and much later the Christian missionaries, first set foot on Tongatapu.

About 500m north of the turn-off for Kanokupolu Resort is a plaque commemorating Tonga's first Holy Communion. About 1km farther on, at the northern end of Ha'atafu village, turn right and head down to the monument commemorating the Christianity Landing Site. The monument is enclosed in a private yard so if you wish to take a photo, it's best to ask permission.

The monument marking the Abel Tasman Landing Site is almost at the tip of the point. Where the tarmac runs out north of Ha'atafu village, pass through the gate and continue straight ahead through the plantations along a dirt road for about five minutes. There's some controversy as to whether this fabulous viewpoint, looking out towards Hakaumama'o Reef and 'Atata, is actually the place where the Dutch explorer landed on 21 January 1643. Some historians think it was farther back along the coast, nearer the Christianity Landing Site.

To get there, take the Hihifo bus from Nuku'alofa's western bus terminal (80 seniti one way).

Islands North of Nuku'alofa

Diving is excellent in the shallows north of Tongatapu, and there's plenty of variety to chose from with wrecks, coral, walls and caves. There's a maze of islands ringed with white beaches and the reefs and shoals are brimming with all sorts of colourful marine life and coral. Water temperature reaches a comfortable 29°C in November and doesn't fall below 21°C in mid-winter. Underwater visibility near the main island averages 15m but closer to the barrier reefs it increases to between 30m and 50m.

Under the National Parks & Reserves Act of 1976, the government of Tonga established five marine reserves, four of which include reefs immediately north of Tongatapu. These four are: Hakaumama'o Reef Reserve; Monu'afe Island Park; the Pangaimotu Reef Reserve; and the Malinoa Island Park, which supports octopuses, groupers, damselfish, clownfish and various species of shellfish, and contains the graves of six assassins who attempted to kill Prime Minister Shirley Baker, and a nonfunctioning lighthouse. Entry to the reserves is free but

visitors are asked not to capture, collect, or destroy any form of marine life or natural aspect of the areas.

There are three resorts on the islands north of Tongatapu. Pangaimotu Island Resort caters for budget travellers and locals, while Fafá Island Resort and Royal Sunset Island Resort are more exclusive. There are also a host of beautiful deserted islands to be explored and for surfers a series of interesting-looking reef breaks between Fukave and 'Onevao.

PANGAIMOTU

Pangaimotu is the closest of the resort islands to Nuku'alofa. It's not huge (allow 30 minutes to walk around it), but there's good snorkelling in the marine reserve off the island's north-west shore and around the half-submerged wreck of *My Lady Lata II* near the landing site. Makaha'a Reef, between Pangaimotu and Makaha'a, with its very large coral heads serving as a breeding ground for an explosion of colourful fish, is an excellent place to snorkel and trips from the Tongan Beachcomber Resort cost just T$5 (plus T$5 for snorkel gear hire). A nature trail leads through the heart of the island and native and medicinal plants are labelled.

Tongan Beachcomber Resort (☎/fax 23759, ☎ 11236) Single/double fale with bath T$30/50, bed in 8-bed dorm T$15, camping T$10. Snacks & lunches $8-12.50. This resort is a popular day trip for both locals and tourists especially at weekends. It's a simple, low-key resort (cold showers only) with a relaxed atmosphere. All the accommodation was being renovated at the time of writing, and the owners intend to focus more on the budget traveller in future. Inexpensive, but pretty good, food and drinks are served in a beachfront restaurant/bar which juts out over the water. It's a great spot. Transfers cost T$12 return.

Getting There & Away

From Monday to Saturday a boat leaves for here from Tuimatamoana Harbour, Nuku'alofa, at 10am, 11am and 1pm and returns from Pangaimotu at 3pm and 5pm. On Sunday the boat leaves at 10am, 11am, noon and

1pm and returns from Pangaimotu on the hour from 3pm to 6pm. Transfers are T$12 return and take 10 minutes each way.

FAFÁ

Fafá Island is 7km from Nuku'alofa and the only development on the island is the Fafá Island Resort. A bush walk takes about 20 minutes – you'll see plenty of the ground-dwelling banded rail *(veka)* and purple swamp hen *(kalae)* and may catch a glimpse of the captive-bred red shining parrot *(koki)*. The island can be easily walked around in 30 minutes.

Fafá Island Resort (☎ 22800, fax 23592, e fafa@kalianet.to) Single/double fale T$87/99, superior fale T$175. Half/full-board T$58/70 per day. Fafá Island Resort is situated on a magnificent beach, and is more elegant and exclusive than those on Pangaimotu and 'Atata. It's one of the best places to stay in Tonga.

The 16 Tongan fale are beautifully constructed from local materials, each with electricity and private bath. The superior fale are more secluded and look onto the beach, while the standard fale are bunched together inland.

Windsurfers and Hobie Cats are available to guests (T$20 per hour), as well as snorkelling gear (free to guests; T$5 per day for day-trippers). On calm days snorkelling trips are run to Makaha'a Reef (T$6) and Malinoa Island (T$12).

Getting There & Away

Day trips, including a simple lunch and the 30-minute boat transfer, cost T$36 (plus tax). A boat leaves Tuimatamoana Harbour, Nuku'alofa, at 11am and returns at 4.30pm daily.

One-way airport transfers (including boat) cost T$21; one-way boat transfers cost T$10. For resort guests there are complimentary twice-daily trips to Nuku'alofa; transfer fees only apply when arriving and departing.

'ATATA

'Atata, 10km from the mainland, is the most remote of the three resorts. It's a much larger island than Pangaimotu or Fafá, and has some spectacular beaches and a small fishing village at its northern end, which can be visited on an organised tour.

Royal Sunset Island Resort (☎/fax 21254, e royalsun@kalianet.to, PO Box 960) Single/double bungalows on east side T$110/120, west side T$116/135, minisuites T$170. T$45 per day for all meals. There are 26 beachfront bungalows at this resort, each with fridge, tea/coffee-making equipment, ceiling fan and private bath. Bungalows on the west (sheltered) side of the island get the sunset and are more expensive. Meals and drinks are served at the restaurant/bar fale, an incredible structure supported by immense wooden beams. There's a saltwater swimming pool and a billiards table, while a Tongan buffet and floor show is held once a week. Guests are entitled to daily snorkelling trips to the reef and hire of sailing dinghies, windsurfers and paddle skis.

Sailing, diving and fishing are all possible from the resort (see Activities earlier in this chapter).

Getting There & Away

Sunday day trips, including a fabulous all-you-can-eat buffet barbecue lunch, a 30-minute snorkelling trip and boat transfers (45 minutes), cost T$30. The boat departs from Tuimatamoana Harbour, Nuku'alofa, at 10am and returns at 4pm.

Return boat transfers for guests cost T$24, or T$40 from the airport.

'Eua

area 87.44 sq km • pop 5022 (est)

Just a stone's throw south-east of Tongatapu is 'Eua, a smaller, beautifully formed island of an entirely different character. While Tongatapu is flat, well cultivated and densely populated, 'Eua is rugged, undeveloped and naturally diverse.

Bushland, rainforest and beach can all be experienced on 'Eua. Cave systems and geological anomalies are found all over the island and the sheer limestone cliffs on the east coast provide a host of stunning viewpoints. To the south-east, up on the island's highest ridge (which touches 310m), the

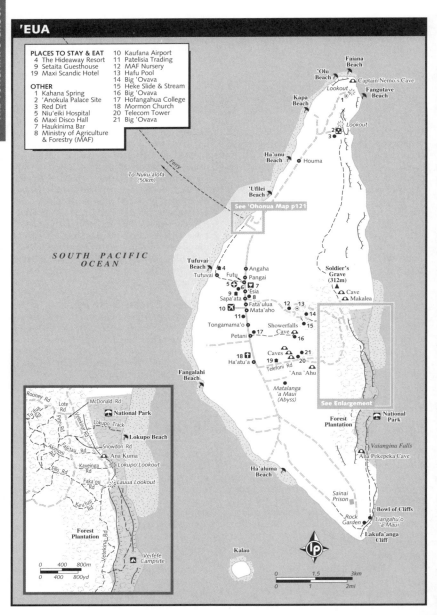

'EUA

PLACES TO STAY & EAT
4 The Hideaway Resort
9 Setaita Guesthouse
19 Maxi Scandic Hotel

OTHER
1 Kahana Spring
2 'Anokula Palace Site
3 Red Dirt
5 Niu'eiki Hospital
6 Maxi Disco Hall
7 Haukinima Bar
8 Ministry of Agriculture
  & Forestry (MAF)

10 Kaufana Airport
11 Patelisia Trading
12 MAF Nursery
13 Hafu Pool
14 Big 'Ovava
15 Heke Slide & Stream
16 Big 'Ovava
17 Hofangahua College
18 Mormon Church
20 Telecom Tower
21 Big 'Ovava

Faiana Beach
'Olu Beach
Captain Nemo's Cave
Lookout
Fangutave Beach
Kapa Beach
Lookout
2
3
Ha'unu Beach
Houma
'Ufilei Beach

See 'Ohonua Map p121

To Nuku'alofa (50km)
Ferry

SOUTH PACIFIC OCEAN

Tufuvai Beach
Tufuvai
Futu
4
Angaha
Pangai
5
7
Esia
9
Sapa'ata
8
10
Fata'ulua
Mata'aho
11
Tongamama'o
Petani
17
18
Ha'atu'a
19
Caves
21
20
Telefoni Rd
'Ana 'Ahu
Matalanga 'a Maui (Abyss)
Soldier's Grave (312m)
Cave
Makalea
12
13
14
15
Showerfalls Cave
16

See Enlargement

Fangalahi Beach

Forest Plantation

National Park
Vaiangina Falls
Ana Pekepeka Cave

Ha'aluma Beach

Sainai Prison

Rock Garden
Bowl of Cliffs
Liangahu'o 'a Maui
Lakufa'anga Cliff

Rooney Rd
Lote Rd
McDonald Rd
Tufuhia Rd
Pyke Rd
Vetekina Rd
National Park
Lokupo Track
Lokupo Beach
Akononi Rd
Faketau Rd
Snowdon Rd
Ana Kuma
Lokupo Lookout
Kaveinga Rd
Ellis Rd
Faka'osi Rd
Lauua Lookout
Kautupu Rd
Vetekina Rd

Forest Plantation

Veifefe Campsite

0   400   800m
0   400   800yd

Kalau

0   1.5   3km
0   1   2mi

cliffs overlook 'Eua National Park, a 499-hectare tract of tropical rainforest that is only just being opened up to tourists.

'Eua is Tonga's third-largest island and has great potential for bushwalking, rock climbing, whale watching and diving, but few visitors make the short trip across from Tongatapu. Those prepared to make the time and effort to explore this island will be well rewarded.

While many of 'Eua's highlights are described in this chapter as part of a bushwalking tour, due to their off-the-beaten-track nature, taxis can be used to shorten many bushwalks.

History

Abel Tasman, the first European to land on 'Eua, arrived in 1643 and named the island Middleburgh. He got on well with the Tongans he encountered and spent a few days trading. In October 1773 James Cook stopped for two days but recorded little of the visit. In 1796 several deserters from the US ship *Otter* went ashore at 'Eua and became the first European residents of the Tongan islands.

In September 1946 the island of Niuafo'ou (in the Niuas) erupted for the 10th time in 100 years. Although no-one was killed, the government of Tonga became concerned about the potential danger and decided to evacuate the island. The residents were first transferred to Tongatapu but the lack of agricultural land there necessitated another move, this time to 'Eua. The villages of central 'Eua – Angaha, Futu, 'Esia, Sapa'ata, Fata'ulua, Mata'aho, Tongamama'o and Petani – are all named after the home villages of their inhabitants on far-away Niuafo'ou. Many people have now re-settled on Niuafo'ou, but a good proportion of 'Eua's population remains composed of evacuees and their descendants.

Orientation

The western third of the island is a low coastal plain that merges into an area of forested hills, with north-south ridges forming the spine. The island's eastern edge consists of one- and two-tier cliffs sometimes up to 120m high. A road extends the length of 'Eua's western side. Most of the population lives between the villages of 'Ohonua in the north and Ha'atu'a in the south. Most of the island's basic services, including Nafanua Wharf (for the ferry) and a couple of supermarkets, are in 'Ohonua.

Basic maps of 'Eua (T$3) are available at the Friendly Islands Bookshop and from the Ministry of Agriculture and Forestry office in Sapa'ata. The latest versions should have a large-scale box covering 'Eua National Park, though track and cave locations are not very precise.

Information

In 'Ohonua, the post office is open 8.30am to 12.30pm and 1.30pm to 4.30pm weekdays. The Tonga Communications Corporation office is open 24 hours, every day, for domestic and international telephone and fax services.

The Bank of Tonga is open 9am to 12.30pm and 1.30pm to 3.30pm weekdays. It can changes all major currencies (travellers cheques or cash) and offers cash advances on credit cards. It also handles MoneyGram cash transfers.

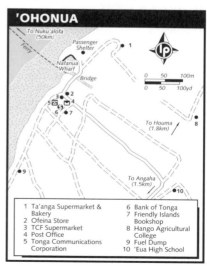

'OHONUA

To Nuku'alofa (50km)

Passenger Shelter

Nafanua Wharf

Bridge

0   50   100m
0   50   100yd

To Houma (1.8km)

To Angaha (1.5km)

1 Ta'anga Supermarket & Bakery	6 Bank of Tonga
2 Ofeina Store	7 Friendly Islands Bookshop
3 TCF Supermarket	8 Hango Agricultural College
4 Post Office	9 Fuel Dump
5 Tonga Communications Corporation	10 'Eua High School

The Friendly Islands Bookshop (☎ 50167) has a limited book selection, including a few paperbacks, and sells film and maps of 'Eua.

In Sapa'ata the Ministry of Agriculture and Forestry (MAF; ☎ 50116) is open 8.30am to 4.30pm on weekdays and is a good source of information about the 'Eua Plantation Forest, 'Eua National Park and the island's trails and attractions. There is only one official campsite on 'Eua and efforts to regulate camping are planned, so bushwalkers should discuss their routes with the staff here before setting out. It would also be worth inquiring about the planned ecological tours of 'Eua.

Royal Tonga Airlines (☎ 50188) is based at Kaufana Airport in Fata'ulua.

Niu'eiki Hospital in Pangai offers very basic facilities.

NORTHERN 'EUA
'Eua's northern half holds a variety of places of interest. Some are accessible by taxi, but many can only be reached on foot. Day bushwalks and longer circuits are possible. Wear good shoes, allow lots of time to explore and carry a compass, map and plenty of water.

North-West Coast
Unfortunately, the beautiful beaches north of 'Ohonua are not suitable for swimming. The most popular for picnics and afternoon lazing is **'Ufilei Beach**, just a 20-minute walk north of Nafanua Wharf.

The northern end of the island can be reached from 'Ohonua by walking along the coastline for five or six hours, but it requires scrambling over high rocky outcrops.

Northern End
There are some fabulous viewpoints at the northern end of 'Eua, but tracks can be difficult to find. Asks locals for directions before setting out. Also be very careful when walking off-track as the area is pockmarked with sinkholes.

From 'Ohonua, cross the bridge and continue 4.5km north to the village of **Houma**. About 2km north of the village, the track forks (the left fork leads down to **Kapa Beach**) – go right and walk up the hill until,

Why is it Cooler on 'Eua?

'Eua isn't far from Tongatapu – you can see it clearly from Tongatapu's south-west shore – and yet it's much cooler. While Tongatapu is sweltering in humid summer heat, 'Eua is perfectly pleasant. In winter, if it's chilly in Tongatapu, 'Eua can be very brisk indeed.

Why the difference? The answer lies in the combination of 'Eua's geography and the prevailing easterly trade wind. 'Eua is long north-to-south, and thin east-to-west. A high volcanic ridge stretches north-to-south along the entire east side of the island. The ridge rises 312m (1023 feet) above sea level at its highest point and is around 300m (1000 feet) high on average.

The easterly wind hits 'Eua's east side – first the cliffs rising up out of the ocean, and then the ridge. Blown upwards, the air is cooled. Then the cooled air blows down from the ridge, across to the west side of the island and the villages.

just after the sign to the Royal Estate, you should turn left down a rough 4WD track. This is as far as a taxi will want to go.

This track rambles north through scrubby bushland and forest and past a couple of marginal plantations until, after about an hour, you'll enter a broad, open pasture with magnificent **views** across lower tiers of rainforest and a 270-degree view of the sea on the east coast.

In the side of the cliff is the large limestone cave that Peace Corps volunteers have christened **Captain Nemo's Cave**. It's only one of many found in this rarely visited limestone area.

To reach **Kahana Spring**, follow the track all the way to the end, then it's a steep 150m descent north-east to the spring. Once an open pool, the spring now feeds from its source inside a cave into a white plastic pipe funnelling the water into huge, covered concrete water tanks.

From Kahana Spring you can bushwhack about 200m north to an overgrown track heading through forest. Eventually this brings you to a **viewpoint** above some dramatically high, sheer limestone cliffs. The secluded **Fangutave Beach** lies far below and it's perfectly possible (but very steep) to climb down to the beach at the northern end of the cove.

'Anokula Palace

The ruins of the half-built 'Anokula Palace sit atop windswept 120m cliffs that afford some spectacular vistas. Not much is left of the building that, if completed, would have been a royal palace. You get some beautiful views from the site, but there are better **viewpoints** to the north of the ruins (from where you'll see the island of 'Eue'iki here and part of Tongatapu) and on a rocky outcrop down to the east. Legend tells it that if you stand on this latter viewpoint at full moon and remain absolutely still you can see people swimming in the incredibly turbulent water below – lost spirits on an outing.

Little is visible of the nearby **red lake** after which 'Anokula Palace was to be named – today it looks like a red sand trap.

South of 'Anokula there are plenty of potential *campsites* among the scrub-dotted grassland, but bring your own water as no reliable supply is available.

Most taxis are happy to go as far as the palace, but no farther south. The road heading south from 'Anokula stays in good shape for 1km or so and then starts to break up, but it is possible to follow the faint 4WD track to Soldier's Grave. Inquire locally as to the condition of the route.

CENTRAL 'EUA

The eastern part of central 'Eua is covered with Tonga's greatest extent of natural forest. The 'Eua Plantation Forest covers much of the slope that rises consistently east towards the island's 300m ridge which drops dramatically into 'Eua National Park.

The western side of central 'Eua is dominated by plantations and housing. There are a number of good-looking beaches and a couple of caves to explore here.

Tufuvai Beach

This is a lovely white-sand beach. The reef here makes a natural swimming pool at high tide, though it's too shallow for swimming at low tide. There's a channel here which is suitable for strong swimmers, but only at low tide – whatever you do, don't swim in this channel when the tide is going out!

Tufuvai Beach can be reached from either Pangai or 'Ohonua with a flat, easy walk of about 2km. Either head south along the coast from 'Ohonua, or turn west into Tufuvai from the main road at Pangai. A well-used walking track leads between some houses in Tufuvai village and down to the beach.

'Eua Plantation Forest

This forest covers 'Eua's drinking water catchment area and contains exotic species grown for timber as well as small patches of protected, regenerating rainforest. It's a rather weird mix. In places the forest is dense and jungle-like, with giant tree ferns, vines and high humidity, while 200m farther on it's all straight lines of plantation pine, sandalwood, mahogany or red cedar. Underlying much of the area is eroded limestone, causing a Swiss-cheese landscape of caves and sinkholes.

Many of 'Eua's tourist highlights are found in this area and a program of signposting and tourist development is under way. Most highlights can be visited in a long day's walk or on horseback. A tractor or 4WD could get you closer to many of them. Below is an outline of one possible route through the area.

From the MAF office in Sapa'ata, on 'Eua's main tarmac road, head east along a dirt road into the 'Eua Plantation Forest and onto the **MAF Nursery** (reached in about 35 minutes). Here the road forks. To the left Rooney Rd leads up to Vetekina Rd (an overgrown 4WD track) and on to the edge of the national park in 2.6km. To the right a track leads up to **Hafu Pool**, 250m away. This pleasant and refreshing pool is formed by the damming of a small stream which trickles through a slice of rainforest.

Climb past the pool on the old 4WD track. Ignore the first right turn and after about five minutes, the 4WD track levels off and a path breaks left (north) to a huge banyan tree (the Big 'Ovava). Continue straight ahead (east) on a thin track to **Heke Stream**. *Heke* means 'slide', and this stream courses down a long, smooth rock at about a 45-degree angle, creating a natural water slide. It's beautiful in the steep-sided gully, covered in ferns and lichen, on a hot day. Farther upstream is another slide above a larger pool.

Once you've retraced your steps, the **Big 'Ovava** is just a stone's throw away. Beneath this magnificent banyan tree is an equally impressive sinkhole with a small stream running through it. It's a bit of a scramble to get down, but perfectly possible.

From the Big 'Ovava you have two choices. You can either backtrack down to the MAF Nursery and then head east up Rooney Rd (a good option in wet weather) or continue 900m up Tu'ifua Rd (a disused 4WD track) to the junction with Rooney Rd and then turn right. Either way, continue up to the end of Rooney Rd and then turn left onto Lote Rd before arriving at Vetekina Rd, roughly 50 minutes after leaving Big 'Ovava. Turn left for Makalea and Soldier's Grave, which lie in plantations to the north.

The sinkhole that is **Makalea** is reached after almost eight minutes and lies about 100m out of the forestry plantation boundary under a small banyan tree, due east (right) of the dirt road and a mango tree – you'll have to skirt through a plantation to get there. *Makalea* means 'speaking stone', and there is certainly an eerie echo in the cave, as well as some beautiful stalactites. You'll need proper climbing gear to get down.

The right turn to **Soldier's Grave** lies about 250m after the turn-off to Makalea. A stand of pandanus is about the only marker of the overgrown path that leads uphill to 'Eua's highest point (312m) and the grave of AE Yealands, about whom there is an apocryphal – or at least well-embellished – tale (see the boxed text).

From the turning to Soldier's Grave it's about a two- to three-hour walk to 'Anokula Palace at the northern end of 'Eua. Alternatively, after retracing your steps to the junction of Lote and Vetekina Rds it's only an eight-minute walk south to the beginning of

Soldier's Grave

WWII did not blight the Kingdom of Tonga as it did other Pacific Islands, though Tongans fought and died for the Allied cause. During the war a group of New Zealand signalmen were stationed on 'Eua along with a group of Tongan comrades. One day in February 1943, a 24-year-old New Zealand soldier (AE Yealands) and a Tongan got drunk and decided to play a bizarre game of hide-and-seek. They asked a friend to hide a gun for them. It was decided that the one who first found the gun was to kill the other.

Unfortunately for Yealands, the Tongan won the game. The Tongans reportedly felt so bad about the incident that they erected a monument in the soldier's honour on the island's highest point.

Lokupo Track leading down to **Lokupo Beach** (see the following 'Eua National Park section) and then a further 15 minutes south to **'Ana Kuma** or Rats' Cave. A narrow passageway leads through the rock to a small ledge and a stunning view over the rainforest to the Pacific Ocean. It's possible to scramble down an overhanging ledge to another small cave cut into the cliff face about 2m below. The cliff edge is very close when you drop down so be extremely careful, but the experience is well worth it.

South from 'Ana Kuma are two well-built viewing platforms, **Lokupo Lookout** and **Lauua Lookout**. Both are signposted and well worth visiting for views of ocean pounding onto Lokupo Beach. It's always cool and windy here and if you're lucky you'll see red shining parrots and tropic birds gliding over the rainforest below.

From Lauua Lookout retrace your steps to Vetekina Rd and then north up to the junction of Vetekina and Faka'osi Rds. Turn left (west) down Faka'osi Rd and continue down until meeting McDonald Rd, which will lead you south down to the main tarmac road.

South-west of the junction between Telefoni and McDonald Rds is **'Ana 'Ahu** (Smoking Cave), so called because of the mist that rises where a small stream plunges into the void. There is no set path; to get there head west down Telefoni Rd and where it makes a sharp right turn follow a line of pine trees to the entrance.

There are a number of other caves in this area, starting with the **sinkhole** below another **Big 'Ovava** roughly 50m north-east of the telecommunications tower on Telefoni Rd. This banyan *must* be the largest on 'Eua. The root network is truly amazing. To find this tree, continue down Telefoni Rd to the bottom of a steep slope where a dirt road on the right cuts back uphill. Follow this road to a dead end and then take the footpath on the left leading to the cave. From here it's a 30-minute walk west, downhill to 'Eua's main tarmac road.

'Eua National Park

Gazetted in 1992, 'Eua National Park protects a 449-hectare tract of tropical rainforest that was never logged.

The 800m-wide band of tropical rainforest hangs above the south-eastern coast and is bordered on the western side by the sheer cliffs that descend directly from the highest ridge on the island. The easiest access to the rainforest is down the ridge on one of two purpose-built tracks. The first is **Lokupo Track**, which leads down to Lokupo Beach from just north of the Vetekina and Snowdon Rds junction. The second is **Veifefe Track**, which leads off Veketina Rd (farther south), winding down at a more gentle angle in a north-easterly direction past *Veifefe Campsite* to the south end of Lokupo Beach. In theory, at low tide it's possible to walk along the beach between these two trails, but finding the entrance to the second trail (which is not signposted) would be difficult.

Veifefe Campsite is the only official campsite on 'Eua and although just a patch of level grass at present, it may be developed in the future (inquire at the MAF office).

Matalanga 'a Maui

The large, dank and eerie sinkhole known as Matalanga 'a Maui is reminiscent of the massive cenotes located in Mexico's Yucatán Peninsula. On bright days it appears as simply a huge hole whose walls are lined with tangled vegetation disappearing into the black void below. The story goes that it was created when the folk hero Maui buried his planting stick in the earth and shook it back and forth, rocking the entire island and leaving this deep hole.

To get there head south from Ha'atu'a onto the dirt road and take the first road on the left. Heading east pick up the third track on the right (south), which leads into a plantation. After about 20m bear right and look for a row of pine trees. Turn left just before you reach the first pine and you'll be on the edge of the abyss. Watch your step! You may not see the sinkhole until you are almost falling into it.

Take a torch for a good view down into the cool, moist underworld, but attempts to climb down into the sinkhole would be a little dicey at best. Don't try it unless you have climbing gear and are in a group.

Showerfalls Cave

This is a small cave behind a steady stream of cool, fresh water that flows through a narrow, fern-covered limestone gorge. Apparently, it's possible to walk right through this cave and come out the other end, though it gets narrow and some climbing is required. Just climbing down the waterfall (about 2m) to the cave entrance is difficult, due to slippery rocks. A soaking is guaranteed. For anything more than a cursory exploration you need ropes, waterproof torches and shoes with a good grip.

To reach Showerfalls Cave follow the rough vehicle track that heads east away from the tarmac road along the southern boundary fence of Hofangahua College in Petani. The track leads through plantations and up into the hills. A thin path crosses the track after about 20 minutes, but continue straight ahead up the increasingly overgrown track until reaching a junction. Fork left across flatter ground, then after a couple of minutes fork left again onto a vague footpath. Continue past the private property sign, down the slope and past a cave-like rock overhang before arriving at the small

The Flora & Fauna of 'Eua

Eua is probably the most accessible place in Tonga to experience the kingdom's fauna and flora. While there's been much habitat destruction, and the introduction of pigs, goats, cats and Polynesian rats has ravaged 'Eua's ecosystems, the largest tract of primary rainforest in Tonga is found here. In addition, there are considerable areas of regenerating rainforest and plantation forest, dramatic cliffs and a wonderful shoreline.

Although none of 'Eua's 13 land-bird species is unique to Tonga, the island once supported 21 species, including a large megapode that disappeared soon after the arrival of humans.

'Eua's most famous wildlife species is the large 'Eua parrot or red shining parrot (*koki* or *kaka* in Tongan). This spectacular bird was introduced to Tonga prior to European arrival and you may see (or more likely hear) them in 'Eua's forest – the forest around Liangahu'o 'a Maui is a good place to look. 'Eua has Tonga's only stable population (about 1000 birds), but deforestation and the illegal collection of live birds remain problems.

'Eua parrot

Sea-bird colonies nest on 'Eua's cliffs, and the windy east coast is a good place to see brown and black noddies (*ngongo*) and white-tailed tropic birds (*tavake*); the latter are easily recognised by long

tail streamers. Soaring great frigate birds, with their distinctive pointed wings and forked tails, are a hugely impressive sight – Lakufa'anga is a good place to see them. White-rumped swiftlets (*pekepekatae*) nest in caves here and navigate to their nests in pitch black by echo-location.

'Eua has eight endemic species of flowering plant and many medicinal and culturally important plants, which are still collected and used by many households. Much of the island is covered in plantation and grassland with small patches of coastal forest where at dusk you may see the

White-tailed tropic bird

cave-dwelling sheath-tailed bat (*pekapeka*) hunting for insects. The large flying fox, or fruit bat (*peka*), roosts in large forest or plantation trees.

In primary rainforest on the island's steep eastern slopes, the unique 'Eua gecko is found. It was only recently spotted, an indication of just how much there's left to be discovered here.

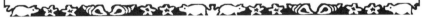

gorge a couple of minutes later. Some of 'Eua's water supply is drawn from this magical place.

SOUTHERN 'EUA
Ve'ehula Estate

Much of the southern third of the island belongs to the large Ve'ehula Estate, in the heart of which is **Sainai Prison**, Tonga's largest correctional facility. Some of the best tracts of original rainforest are found here and there are many meandering bush tracks to explore.

Ha'aluma Beach

'Eua's best beach is Ha'aluma, on the south coast, which has a lovely palm-fringed expanse of sand but is not ideal for swimming due to extensive reefs just offshore. From the beach you can plainly see the small island of **Kalau** 2km or so away and there's some good beach *camping*.

To get there, continue 4km south along the dirt track from Ha'atu'a. Where the road makes a sharp bend to the left, a track leads off more or less straight ahead and reaches the beach after roughly 1km.

Southern End

The southern tip of the island, an area known as **Lakufa'anga**, contains some of 'Eua's finest geological treasures. In dry weather an adventurous taxi driver can get take you much of the way, but you're still left with a 75-minute walk along an overgrown 4WD track.

To get there head south from Ha'atu'a, then where a 4WD track leads south to Ha'aluma Beach follow the main dirt road east. After 20 minutes of easy walking the dirt road becomes a rough 4WD track (this is where the taxi will drop you). Continue east along this 4WD track, passing a few plantations on the way, until reaching a gate in about an hour. After passing through (be sure to close the gate), follow the track out into the pasture and continue along the trail into the **Rock Garden**.

Here 'Eua's geology reads like an open book, with large slabs of eroded, grotesquely shaped coral recalling the time that this bench served as 'Eua's continental shelf. The meadow here is often full of nervous horses.

The cliff away to the south-east is Lakufa'anga Cliff (Calling Turtle Cliff). Women used to drop pandanus *leis* (garlands) from the cliff and sing to call turtles in to the shore. Unfortunately, due to overfishing, turtles are rarely seen here these days.

The beautiful **Liangahu'o 'a Maui**, a giant limestone arch, lies about 500m north of here. From the cliffs, walk northward and pick up the faint 4WD track that leads into a patch of woodland (keep an eye out for red shining parrots). Once you're a few yards inside the woods, turn left off the track and bushwhack west up the hill. After 50m or so turn right and start looking for a way (heading north) through the trees and bush – you may need to fight your way through, but the roar of the sea should guide you – to the edge of a gaping abyss. You may need to scramble around a bit to get the best view, but the natural archway is a spectacular sight.

Maui was a folk hero of epic proportions, a sort of Paul Bunyan of Polynesia, but with a reputation for having a volatile temper. This huge abyss and the natural bridge are said to have been formed when Maui angrily threw his spear across 'Eua and it lodged in the rock wall here.

This is a lovely spot. Haunting, intermittent insect choruses begin suddenly, then crescendo and disappear and the sea below roars and beats the rocks beneath the bridge.

Retrace your steps to the 4WD track then continue north (actually over Liangahu'o 'a Maui) to the **Bowl of Cliffs**, an impressive half-circle of cliffs in which the sea below churns like a flushing toilet bowl.

From here further exploration north into 'Eua National Park is possible, but to go any farther you should plan to camp overnight. The pasture near the Bowl of Cliffs would make a fine *campsite*.

Rejoin the track heading north (which keeps to the easternmost ridge), cross a fence into plantation and continue on the same track, following a white plastic water pipe once it appears. **'Ana Pekepeka** (Swallows' Cave), named after the birds flitting in and out of the darkness, is a 25-minute walk from the fence. It would be perfectly possible to *camp* on the dry floor of the cave.

Vaiangina Falls is roughly a 15-minute walk past the cave. The white pipe takes a sharp turn uphill just before Vaiangina Stream, but it's easier to walk ahead about 10m before climbing up to the tubing that leads to the stream. Vaiangina Stream emerges from between layers of limestone then disappears beneath an impassable thicket of vegetation before plunging more than 50m into the sea. The waterfall is only properly visible from the shoreline and, though the stream is hardly impressive, it's one of the only freshwater sources in the area.

In some seasons it may be possible to bash your way on to Veifefe Campsite (see 'Eua National Park earlier) and then on to 'Anokula Palace, but allow several days for such an attempt.

ACTIVITIES

As this chapter has already shown, **caving** could be a major activity on 'Eua, especially within the 'Eua Plantation Forest where there are numerous named and unnamed caves and sinkholes. However, caving isn't for amateurs, and there's a lack of essential equipment, knowledge and experience on the island. If you plan to go caving come properly equipped.

'Eua also has great **bushwalking** potential. The island is crisscrossed with a complex tangle of bush roads and tracks, accessible only by foot, horseback or 4WD vehicle. Tracks are constantly changing and disused trails quickly become overgrown. There is potential for anything from a day-walk taking in many of 'Eua's highlights to a complete loop of the island, which could take up to 10 days. Ask MAF in 'Ohonua about routes, campsites and the availability of drinking water (which can be a real problem). You'll need a tent, map, compass and plenty of water containers.

Rock climbing is certainly possible on 'Eua. The Lokupo Beach area, which is backed by steep cliffs, has good potential. Favourite anchoring spots seem to be the Lokupo and Lauua Lookouts.

Boat-based **whale watching** is not established on 'Eua, but between June and December pods of whales make their way through the channel between 'Eua and Tongatapu and can be viewed from the west coast. The Hideaway Resort (see Places to Stay) is an ideal viewpoint and will have the latest on potential whale-watching trips.

Contact the Deep Blue Diving Centre (see Activities at the start of this chapter for details) about **diving** around 'Eua. The sea caves on 'Eua are reported to be the biggest in Tonga, with the best ones found around the northern tip and down the eastern coast; one is likened to a cathedral and was only discovered in 2000. Sharks are often found here and it's claimed that visibility is 60m to 80m year-round.

PLACES TO STAY

Consult MAF (☎ 50116) about suitable *campsites* in highland and beach areas. In future there may be some restrictions. Other accommodation is limited to three choices.

Maxi Scandic Hotel (☎ 50186, Telefoni Rd) Singles/doubles/triples T$15/20/35, camping T$10 per tent. Free pick-up & delivery from Nafanua Wharf. Kitchen use

T$2 per day. Dinner T$12-15. Also known as Taina's Guest House, this is a nice, friendly place and great value. The detached rooms (a little box-like) are set in spacious grounds and there's a good communal living area and kitchen. Showers are cold. This place makes a great base for exploring 'Eua National Park and the Plantation Forest. Tours cost $12 and take in 'Anokula Palace and the prison. Bike/horse/car hire costs T$10/15/60.

Setaita Guesthouse (☎ 50124) Singles/ doubles T$25/30, camping T$10 per tent. Meals T$15. A stay in this homely (if a little musty) guesthouse, in 'Esia about 500m north of the airport, is a bit like visiting an elderly aunt. The three upstairs bedrooms share a bathroom (cold showers), a communal living area and nice verandah that provides views of the village and a cool breeze. Meals are rather average, and there's often little say in what and when to eat.

The Hideaway Resort (☎ 52055, fax 50128, e kw@kalianet.to; book through Kingfisher Enterprises, ☎/fax 23161, same email) Singles/doubles with bath (hot showers) T$50/60 including breakfast. Lunch T$3-10, dinner T$10-15. This resort in Tufuvai is not built in traditional Polynesian style, but the motel-style rooms are nice and the food is pretty good too. Its trump card, a bar and terrace built over the rocky shore – a fantastic spot for sunsets and whale watching (June to December) – was washed away during Cyclone Paula in 2001, but, at the time of writing, the owners planned to rebuild it as a fale-style bar and restaurant.

Half-day island tours cost T$20, but don't cover very many of 'Eua's natural attractions. Guided bushwalking tours in 'Eua National Park cost T$40 including lunch.

PLACES TO EAT

The only restaurants are at the aforementioned places to stay, but there are a number of places for self-caters in 'Ohonua.

Ta'anga Supermarket Open 7.30am-5pm Mon-Fri (until 10pm Thur), 7am-noon Sat. North up the hill a little from Nafanua Wharf, this is the best supermarket in town and has a wide choice of goods as well as a bakery on site.

Royal Palace, Nuku'alofa, a well-known symbol of Tonga

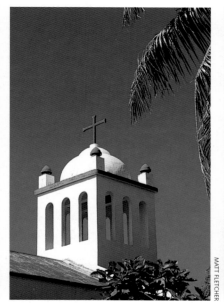
Free Church of Tonga, Ha'apai

Taufa'ahau Rd, Nuku'alofa

A bumper crop of mangoes

Music, dance, food & lapping waves; Hinakauea Beach feast

Abel Tasman landing site, Tongatapu, where Tasman set foot in 1643

The fishing pigs of Talafo'ou

Tropical hibiscus

The mysterious Ha'amonga 'a Maui trilithon, Tongatapu

Tonga Cooperative Federation (TCF) Open 8am-4.30pm Mon-Fri, 8am-noon Sat. Opposite the post office, this supermarket south of Nafanua Wharf offers a fairly limited choice, but it's closer to the centre of 'Ohonua.

Ofeina Store Open 7am-10pm Mon-Sat. This is a well-stocked and convenient general store, opposite the TCF, that sometimes has fruit, vegetables and fish.

Patelisia Trading *(Airport Rd)* Open 7am-10pm Mon-Sat. This convenience store is the nearest, and best, choice for guests of Setaita Guesthouse.

Small ***fale koloa*** (grocery kiosks) are scattered up and down the main road between Houma and Ha'atu'a. In addition there's a Saturday morning ***fruit and vegetable market*** at Nafanua Wharf.

ENTERTAINMENT

The bar at ***The Hideaway Resort*** (see Places to Stay) was, at the time of writing, being rebuilt away from the shore and was due to reopen shortly.

Haukinima Bar Open 6pm-10pm Tues & Wed, 5pm-10pm Thur, 3pm-10pm Fri, 10am-10pm Sat. Located on the main road in 'Esia, this is a fairly rough and ready sort of place, but friendly enough and not a bad place for a (cheap) beer. There's not much in the way of sophisticated spirits, but it has a couple of pool tables (which are the bar's main attractions).

Maxi Disco Hall Open 8pm-2am Fri, 8pm-11.30pm Sat. Admission T$3/2 for men/women. This red, white and blue building opposite Haukinima Bar in 'Esia is a popular dancing venue and there's occasionally a live band. No alcohol is served but it's a lively place nonetheless.

GETTING THERE & AWAY

On a calm day there is nothing to the ferry trip between 'Eua and Tongatapu. However, some people like to fly to 'Eua from Nuku'alofa and return by ferry to avoid the choppy outward ferry journey. The flight between the islands only takes 10 minutes.

See the Getting Around chapter for more information.

GETTING AROUND

'Eua has five taxis – try ☎ 50152 or ☎ 50039. Some approximate fares are: Nafanua Wharf to Pangai T$4; 'Ohonua to Ha'atu'a T$6; Pangai to 'Anokula Palace T$15; and Pangai to as far south-east as is driveable T$12. You can hire a taxi all day for around T$50 to explore the island.

You may be able to come up with other options if you ask around – most people on 'Eua who have vehicles would probably be happy to bring in a little extra cash.

Horse hire may be organised for T$10 or T$15 per day but no saddles are available.

There is no bus service but you shouldn't have any problems hitching rides with pick-up trucks up and down the main road between Houma and Ha'atu'a. Normal safety precautions apply. Elsewhere you'll probably have to walk as there's very little traffic.

Other Tongatapu Group Islands

'EUE'IKI

'Eue'iki (Little 'Eua) lies north-east of Tongatapu, just outside the barrier reef sheltering Tongatapu's lagoon. It has around 35 inhabitants (and three churches) and according to legend is the place where kava was given to Tonga (see the boxed text 'The Origin of Kava').

The island is also famous for a long tradition of shark-calling. This art has been practised on a few South Pacific islands for centuries, though in recent times the practice has been in decline. On the island of 'Eue'iki there remain a handful of shark-callers, men who can summon these fearsome fish up from the depths by reciting ancient chants while shaking a giant necklace of coconut shells over and under the water. Once the shark is drawn close to the boat a rope is looped over its head and it is killed with a war club.

The origins of, and scientific basis for, shark-calling are not easily explained. In local folklore, shark-calling stems from a centuries-old tragedy, when a young girl fell from a canoe and disappeared. But in fact the girl then turned into a shark named Hina, and since then islanders have been calling her back home. To aid in this quest the shark-caller takes on the role of Hina's mythical lover, Sinilau.

During the week of the Tongan king's birthday, Sinilau will kill all the sharks he calls up from the deep and present them to the king. Although the sharks are the embodiment of the girl lost at sea, it doesn't matter that they are killed. Hina is reborn over and over again. In 1965, according to locals, 40 sharks were called and killed for the king.

The **surfing** at 'Eue'iki (all reef breaks; not for beginners) is highly rated by some locals, who say it's fast and high. Two of the best-looking breaks are south-east of the main village on the western shore. The

The Origin of Kava

'Eue'iki is the legendary site of the origin of kava. The story goes that an 'inasi (agricultural show) was given for the Tu'i Tonga here. Unfortunately, the harvest had been poor that year, and there was a shortage of food for the king (Tongan kings have always been hearty eaters).

The family designated to provide a feast for the Tu'i Tonga had a daughter sick with leprosy. They considered her expendable, so they killed her and baked her in an 'umu. The king ate well, but he became annoyed when he was told what he'd eaten and ordered the family to bury what remained of the feast.

After a while, an odd-looking plant grew from the head of the grave. The family cared for it believing it was a gift from their daughter. Another plant soon sprouted out of her feet.

One day a rat nibbled on the first plant. It grew tipsy and staggered around until it chewed on the second plant and returned to its senses. The family then realised the properties of both plants, kava and sugar cane, and knew how to use them.

Historians believe that the story was introduced by the Tu'i Tonga when he was trying to outlaw cannibalism.

northern coast may also offer a ride or two, when the swell's big enough. The snorkelling around the island is also good.

Places to Stay & Eat
At the time of writing, **Gilligan's** (☎ *11343*, **e** *gilligans_eueiki@hotmail.com*), which will comprise a few simple fale, was being established. Check it out locally.

Getting There & Away
If you'd like to visit the island (a 90-minute trip), contact Gilligan's or ask around Tuimatamoana Harbour in Nuku'alofa for a boat going that way.

When landing on 'Eue'iki the only break in the reef is a very narrow channel directly in front of the village on the western shore. Whichever direction you're going, you'll get wet.

'ATA
In 1683 Abel Tasman sighted this volcanic island 136km south-west of Tongatapu and named it Pylstaart. 'Ata has two volcanic peaks, the higher one 382m high, but both are extinct. It has significant deposits of guano phosphates but they are rendered inaccessible by the lack of a harbour.

'Ata can only be accessed by private yacht. But finding a suitable safe anchorage would be quite difficult.

MINERVA REEF
Minerva Reef, which is awash most of the time, is at Tonga's southernmost extreme. It lies 350km south-west of Tongatapu and serves as little more than a rest point for yachts travelling from Tonga to New Zealand. Ownership of the reef is currently being disputed by Tonga and New Zealand, but it's generally accepted as Tongan territory. Australians Tom and Jan Ginder stopped there in their yacht *Seark* and described it this way:

After two days of fast sailing from Nuku'alofa we came to Minerva Reef and entered through a narrow pass in the circle of coral. Here in the Pacific, hundreds of miles from any terra firma, we dropped anchor and looking around saw breaking waves during high tide and two feet of intriguing

Blackbirders on 'Ata

In May 1863 the Tasmanian whaling ship *Grecian* landed at 'Ata after several rather unorthodox changes of crew under the command of Captain Thomas James McGrath. The details of what happened are hazy, but in 1929 two Tongans, who were 'Ata schoolchildren at the time, recalled that the ship was painted to resemble a man-of-war. The mayor of the island, Paul Vehi, went aboard and spoke with the visitors. When he returned to shore, he reported that they were interested in selling provisions and that the 'Ata people were invited to bring their wares below deck on the ship. Once their goods were accepted, they were sent into cabins, ostensibly to select items they desired in exchange. The people remaining on shore never saw them again.

John Bryan, a crew member on the *Grecian*, reported that about 130 'Ata islanders had been taken on board. (It's also likely that the *Grecian* had been responsible for the kidnapping of 30 residents of Niuafo'ou, who had willingly left that island with the promise of lucrative jobs in Fiji.) The islanders blamed the mayor for arranging the blackbirding (kidnapping and selling as slaves) but it's unlikely that he knew anything about it beforehand.

The *Grecian* was not licensed to land with slaves at Peruvian ports, where kidnapped Pacific Islanders were normally taken. It seems that the cargo (including the Tongans) was sold to the *General Prim*, a slaver which met the *Grecian* somewhere in the Cook Islands while searching for 'recruits' to carry back to Callao (Lima). When the *General Prim* arrived in South America, its captain reported that he carried 174 slaves from the island of 'Frinately' – obviously a mistranscription of Friendly.

Shortly after this incident, King George Tupou I, who was concerned with the problem of blackbirding, ordered the remaining 200 residents of 'Ata to resettle on 'Eua. 'Ata remains uninhabited to this day.

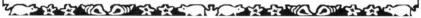

brown reef at low tide. Imagine standing in the middle of a vast ocean on a few feet of exposed coral with no land in sight. While exploring for shells we found blocks of tarred pig-iron ballast, a wonderful huge anchor, and many copper nails, all that remained of some long-forgotten tragedy.

For three days and nights we lay in quiet water, although wind whipped up the seas outside our saucer. However, the combination of full moon, spring tides and foul weather could make Minerva Reef anchorage dangerous. It was just two days to full moon so, with regret, we left.

The Ha'apai Group

area 110 sq km • pop 7757 (est)

The solitude of Ha'apai will assault your senses. This is the South Pacific of travel posters – low coral islands, colourful lagoons and reefs, kilometres of deserted white beaches fringed with coconut palms, towering volcanoes... It has all this and yet only a scattering of tourists visit each year. What you'll find is an island group more laid-back, more traditional and less influenced by Western culture than anywhere else in Tonga outside the Niuas.

The Ha'apai Group consists of 62 islands with a total land area of around 110 sq km scattered over approximately 10,000 sq km of sea. The islands, 17 of which are inhabited, range in size from less than 1 hectare up to 46.6 sq km.

The islands' people, spread across 30 villages around the Ha'apai Group, earn a living almost exclusively from agriculture and fishing. Many of Ha'apai's residents have opted for the faster pace of life offered by Tongatapu and as far afield as Australia and New Zealand, keeping the population of the island group manageably low.

History

Archaeological excavations indicate that the Ha'apai Group has been settled for at least 3000 years. Lapita pottery, carbon-dated at 3000 years old, has been excavated in the village of Hihifo, in southern Pangai.

Other sites of archaeological interest on Lifuka include the Fortress of Velata (probably built in the 15th century AD), several large burial mounds, and an ancient stone quarry at Holopeka Beach.

The first European to visit the Ha'apai Group was Dutchman Abel Tasman, who stopped at Nomuka in 1643 for fresh water. Nomuka's sweet water springs were to be the focus of many visits to the group throughout the years of European Pacific exploration.

Subsequently, Ha'apai became the scene of several notable events in Tongan history. In 1777, on Lifuka, Captain James Cook and

Highlights

- Diving the sea caves and coral arch at 'Ofolanga

- Exploring the wonderful and dramatic volcanic island of Tofua

- Staying in a traditional tapa-lined *fale* on an uninhabited island

- Walking along a palm-fringed, white-sand beach at sunset

- Dancing the night away Tongan-style at the Hula Hula nightclub

- Exploring by bicycle the flat Northern Lifuka Group

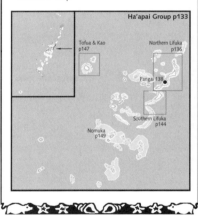

his men narrowly escaped unwittingly becoming the main course at a cannibalistic feast they had been invited to attend, a feast which resulted in Cook's christening Tonga 'The Friendly Islands' (see the boxed text in the Lifuka section later). The famous mutiny on the *Bounty* occurred in Ha'apai in 1789.

Still later, in 1806, the British privateer *Port-au-Prince* was ransacked off Lifuka's north coast; survivor Will Mariner's tale of his years spent in Tonga has become the classic account of pre-Christian life on the islands (see the following boxed text on Mariner).

Ha'apai was the first island group in the Tongan archipelago to convert to Christianity, due to the efforts of convert Taufa'ahau, who was baptised George in 1831 and became the first king of the House of Tupou. He set the stage for a united Tonga and established the royal line that remains in power to this day.

Geography

The Ha'apai Group is right at the centre of the kingdom. All the other main islands lean towards Ha'apai, thanks to the great weight of Kao and Tofua, the huge volcanoes on the north-west extreme of the archipelago.

The main body of the archipelago is composed of two groups of low-lying coral atolls and one raised barrier reef. The Nomuka Group is the island cluster farthest south. To the north-east is the line of raised reefs that forms most of Ha'apai's land area; we refer to this as the Lifuka Group. It includes the islands of Ha'ano, Nukunamo, Foa, Lifuka, Uoleva, Tatafa and 'Uiha. The Ha'apai Group's principal population centre (Pangai), its main wharf and

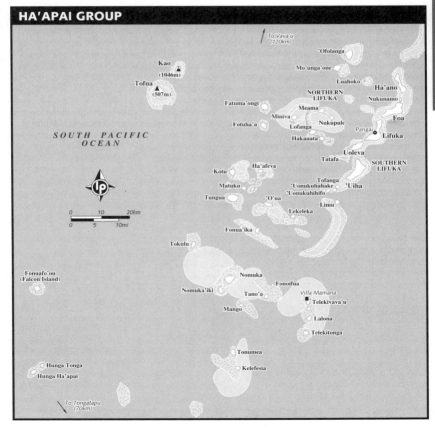

HA'APAI GROUP

William Mariner

Thanks to a series of serendipitous incidents, the world has an extensive account of the customs, language, religion and government of the Tongans before the arrival of Christianity.

In February 1805 William Charles Mariner, the well-educated 15-year-old son of an English sea captain, went to sea on the privateer *Port-au-Prince*. The voyage of plunder and pillage took the ship around the Americas and through the Pacific, finally anchoring at the northern end of Lifuka in the Ha'apai Group on 29 November 1806. The crew were immediately welcomed with yams and barbecued pork. The reception seemed friendly enough, but the following day, they became increasingly aware that some sort of plot was afoot and that appropriate caution should be exercised in dealing with the Tongans.

Captain Brown, the whaling master who had assumed command upon the death of the original skipper several months earlier, was convinced that the threat was imaginary and chose to ignore it. On 1 December the attack was launched while 300 hostile Tongans were aboard the ship. The British, sorely outnumbered, chose to destroy

BRAGG/NATIONAL LIBRARY OF AUSTRALIA

William Mariner in Tongan native dress

the ship, its crew and its attackers rather than allow it to be taken. Young Mariner had gone to procure the explosives when he met with several locals, who escorted him ashore past the fallen bodies of his shipmates.

Mariner was persecuted by the Tongans until he was summoned by Finau 'Ulukalala I the reigning chief of Ha'apai. The king assumed that Mariner was the captain's son, or at least a young chief in his own country, and ordered that his life be preserved.

Meanwhile, the *Port-au-Prince*, which hadn't been destroyed, was dragged ashore, raided and burned. The conflagration heated the cannons sufficiently to cause them to fire, creating a general panic among the Tongans. Calmly accepting his fate, Mariner pantomimed an explanation of the phenomenon and initiated a sort of rapport with the Tongans that would carry him through the following four years.

Although a few other crew members of the *Port-au-Prince* were spared, Mariner was the only one taken so completely under the wing of Finau and he was therefore privy to most of the goings-on in Tongan politics. He learned the language well and travelled about the island groups with the chief, observing and absorbing the finer points of ceremony and protocol among the people. He was given the name Toki 'Ukamea (Iron Axe). In a moment of compassion Finau appointed one of his royal wives, Mafi Hape, to be Mariner's adoptive mother, as he was sure the young man's real mother at home must have been extremely worried about him.

After the death of Finau, the king's son permitted William to leave Tonga on a passing English vessel. Anticlimactically, back in England, Will Mariner married, fathered 12 children and had an unremarkable career as a stockbroker. Were it not for a chance meeting in a London restaurant with an amateur anthropologist, Dr John Martin, his unique Tonga experiences might forever have been lost to the world. Martin, fascinated with Mariner's tale, suggested collaboration on a book and the result, *An Account of the Natives of the Tonga Islands*, is a masterpiece of Pacific literature. William Mariner drowned in a canal in southern England in 1853.

airport are all on Lifuka. Volcanic outliers to the west include Hunga Tonga, Hunga Ha'apai, Tofua, Kao and Fonuafo'ou.

Ecology & Environment
The Ha'apai Conservation Area protects the island group's lands and especially its waters, which are known for their clarity and diversity of coral and tropical fish. There are a number of interesting projects up and running. The Conservation Office (☎/fax 60289) is next to the post office in Pangai.

The water supply in Ha'apai tends to be brackish and should be used only for washing and bathing. Drinking water is collected in rainwater cisterns.

Activities
Diving & Snorkelling The reefs and shallows of the Ha'apai Group offer amazing underwater scenery. Walls, caves, channels, tunnels, drifts, drop-offs and coral gardens (with hard and soft coral and hundreds of fish species) make for a great variety of dives. Outstanding visibility (25m to 30m in summer, up to 70m in winter) and very comfortable water temperatures (23°C to 29°C) combine to create magnificent conditions for diving.

Some of the best diving in Ha'apai is found around the island of 'Ofolanga. Huge sea caves and complex underwater cave systems, as well as a truly incredible coral arch (one of only a few in the South Pacific), all await experienced divers.

The remarkable seascapes around Tofua and Kao reportedly offer Ha'apai's best diving, but getting there is next to impossible.

Diving in the Ha'apai Group is more weather-dependent than in Vava'u, as the sites are less sheltered and the best dive sites farther (sometimes a 45-minute boat ride) from the main tourist centre (Pangai). Getting out to the best snorkelling spots requires a boat, but there are a few good spots close to the shore. Pick up the leaflet *Snorkelling in Ha'apai* from the TVB. Joining dive groups as a snorkeller is possible or you can charter a local boat.

Watersports Ha'apai (☎/fax 60097, VHF Channel 16, PO Box 65) is based at the Niu-'akalo Beach Hotel north of Pangai. The most experienced dive operation in Ha'apai, Watersports Ha'apai specialises in sea-cave diving at some outer island dive sites. Two-tank dives cost T$100 including equipment, and Open Water Diver courses (in English or German) are from T$350. Snorkelling trips cost T$20 per person. Boat charters, game fishing (T$260) and extended dive trips are also available. Some readers have found diving with this organisation a little too adventurous so before setting out explain your level of experience and parameters you want to dive within.

Happy Ha'apai Divers (☎/fax 60600, e sa ndybch@kalianet.to, PO Box 61), based at Sandy Beach Resort on Foa, is a professional outfit focused around the resort's guests. Its boat is bigger but slower than the one owned by Watersports Ha'apai and diving tends to concentrate on the north Lifuka Group. It's a good option for the freshly qualified. Open from 1 April to 30 November, it offers two-tank dives for T$95 to T$105 plus T$32 for all the gear. CMAS diving instruction costs T$510, with two trial dives costing T$125. English and German are spoken.

Sea Kayaking Friendly Islands Kayak Company (☎/fax 70173, e kayaktonga@kalianet.to) operates eight-day sea-kayaking trips around Ha'apai from mid-May to early January. The cost is US$1295, but everything has to be shipped from Vava'u so prior booking is essential. See Activities in the Vava'u chapter for further details.

Watersports Ha'apai (see Diving & Snorkelling) rents sea kayaks for T$25 per day.

Whale Watching Watersports Ha'apai (see Diving & Snorkelling) runs whale-watching trips between June and November for T$60 per person. Happy Ha'apai Divers also runs whale-watching trips for T$50.

Special Events
The week-long Ha'apai Festival starts on the outer islands and concludes on Lifuka on 4 June, Emancipation Day. Visitors are heartily welcomed.

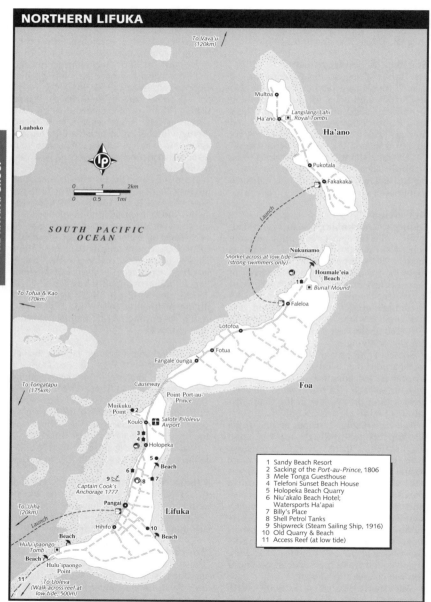

NORTHERN LIFUKA

To Vava'u
(120km)

Multoa

Langilangi Lahi
Royal Tombs

Ha'ano

Ha'ano

Luahoko

SOUTH PACIFIC
OCEAN

Pukotala

Fakakakai

Launch

Snorkel across at low tide
(strong swimmers only)

Nukunamo

Houmale'eia
Beach

Burial Mound

Faleloa

To Tofua & Kao
(70km)

Lotofoa

Fotua

Fangale'ounga

Foa

To Tongatapu
(175km)

Causeway

Point Port-au-
Prince

Muikuku
Point

Koulo

Salote Pilolevu
Airport

Holopeka

Beach

Captain Cook's
Anchorage 1777

Pangai

Lifuka

Hihifo

Beach

Beach

Hulu'ipaongo
Tomb

Beach

Hulu'ipaongo
Point

To 'Uiha
(20km)

Launch

To Uoleva (Walk across reef at
low tide, 500m)

1 Sandy Beach Resort
2 Sacking of the *Port-au-Prince*, 1806
3 Mele Tonga Guesthouse
4 Telefoni Sunset Beach House
5 Holopeka Beach Quarry
6 Niu'akalo Beach Hotel;
  Watersports Ha'apai
7 Billy's Place
8 Shell Petrol Tanks
9 Shipwreck (Steam Sailing Ship, 1916)
10 Old Quarry & Beach
11 Access Reef (at low tide)

The Lifuka Group

The string of islands along the eastern barrier reef of Ha'apai is referred to as the Lifuka Group since Lifuka, with its capital town of Pangai, is the hub of activity.

LIFUKA

Outside of the town of **Pangai**, Lifuka (population 2846) is composed almost entirely of agricultural plantations. There's little for the visitor to do on land but explore these *'api* and wander along the empty white beaches that nearly encircle the island. The western shore offers calm blue water, excellent for swimming and snorkelling, while the eastern coast is wilder and more dramatic – the prevailing wind and ocean swells come from this direction and although the island is sheltered by a barrier reef, currents are stronger on this side.

Although Pangai is the largest settlement between Tongatapu and Vava'u, it's little more than a village that you can traverse in a few minutes. All of Lifuka's basic services are found here (shopping, post office, bank etc) and several inexpensive guesthouses.

Information

Tourist Offices The Tonga Visitors Bureau (TVB; ☎ 60733), on the corner of Palace and Holopeka Rds, is open 8.30am to 12.30pm and 1.30pm to 4.30pm weekdays. It's a good source of information and offers free tide timetables and some excellent free brochures about Ha'apai. No topographical maps are available in Ha'apai.

Money The Bank of Tonga, on Holopeka Rd, exchanges foreign currencies (cash and travellers cheques), gives cash advances on Visa and MasterCard and also deals with MoneyGram cash transfers. It's open 9am to 12.30pm and 1.30pm to 3.30pm weekdays.

The Tonga Development Bank, on Holopeka Rd, open similar hours, offers Western Union money transfers.

Post & Communications The post office is open 8.30am to 3.30pm weekdays. It's in the building just off the western end of Palace Rd. Tonga Communications Corporation lies beneath the huge communications tower in the centre of Pangai. It's open 24 hours, every day, for domestic and international telephone calls. Fax services are available 8.30am to 4.30pm weekdays.

You can send/receive email at Mariners Café for T$5/1.

Airline Offices The office of Royal Tongan Airlines (☎ 60566) is next to the post office off Palace Rd.

Bookshops The Friendly Islands Bookshop (☎ 60198), on Holopeka Rd, doesn't have the wide selection of the main store in Nuku'alofa, but it's possible to order books from the larger store. It also sells film.

Medical Services The Niu'ui Hospital (☎ 60201), in Hihifo at the southern end of Pangai, is pretty basic. Appointments are necessary and the pharmacy is open 8.30am to 4.30pm.

Churches

On the lawn of the **Free Wesleyan Church** is the concrete outline of a cross commemorating a 'miracle' that occurred there in 1975. Residents report that one night they saw a flame falling from the sky to land in front of the church. In the morning they found the outline of a cross burned into the grass. Cynics in the village attribute the whole 'miracle' to mischievous teenagers with kerosene tins and cigarette lighters.

On Holopeka Rd at the southern end of Pangai is the unusual-looking **Church of Tonga**, the architect of which was clearly influenced by images of the Middle East.

Royal Palace

The Ha'apai Royal Palace is the gingerbread-style building close to the Catholic Church. When the king is in residence the street is often blocked, necessitating a detour around Lea'aetohi Sports Field.

Afa Historical Museum

Advertised as 'the World's Smallest Museum', the Afa Historical Museum is a tiny

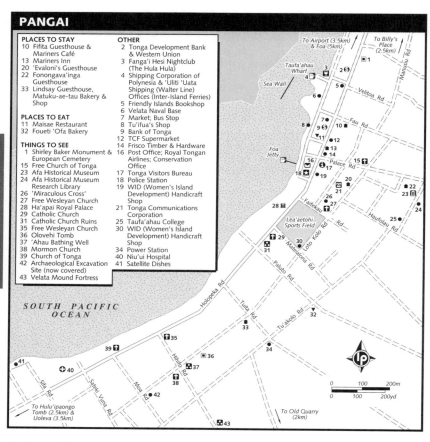

PANGAI

PLACES TO STAY
10 Fifita Guesthouse & Mariners Café
13 Mariners Inn
20 'Evaloni's Guesthouse
22 Fonongava'inga Guesthouse
33 Lindsay Guesthouse, Matuku-ae-tau Bakery & Shop

PLACES TO EAT
11 Maisae Restaurant
32 Foueti 'Ofa Bakery

THINGS TO SEE
1 Shirley Baker Monument & European Cemetery
15 Free Church of Tonga
23 Afa Historical Museum
24 Afa Historical Museum Research Library
26 'Miraculous Cross'
27 Free Wesleyan Church
28 Ha'apai Royal Palace
29 Catholic Church
31 Catholic Church Ruins
35 Free Wesleyan Church
36 Olovehi Tomb
37 'Ahau Bathing Well
38 Mormon Church
39 Church of Tonga
42 Archaeological Excavation Site (now covered)
43 Velata Mound Fortress

OTHER
2 Tonga Development Bank & Western Union
3 Fanga'i Hesi Nightclub (The Hula Hula)
4 Shipping Corporation of Polynesia & 'Uliti 'Uata Shipping (Walter Line) Offices (Inter-Island Ferries)
5 Friendly Islands Bookshop
6 Velata Naval Base
7 Market; Bus Stop
8 Tu'ifua's Shop
9 Bank of Tonga
12 TCF Supermarket
14 Frisco Timber & Hardware
16 Post Office; Royal Tongan Airlines; Conservation Office
17 Tonga Visitors Bureau
18 Police Station
19 WID (Women's Island Development) Handicraft Shop
21 Tonga Communications Corporation
25 Taufa'ahau College
30 WID (Women's Island Development) Handicraft Shop
34 Power Station
40 Niu'ui Hospital
41 Satellite Dishes

display window on the side of a shed. Among the revolving exhibits are pieces of 3000-year-old Lapita pottery, traditional head-rests, old photographs and rocks from Tofua. However, there's more to see in the museum's **research library** opposite, which contains numerous fascinating reference books about Tonga. The research library has no set hours, but is open to the public whenever the proprietor, Virginia, is there.

Olovehi Tomb

Olovehi Tomb – on Loto Kolo Rd in Hihifo, the village on the south end of Pangai – is set back from the road in a grove of ironwood. It has become somewhat overgrown and neglected, but the upright memorial stone at the south-west corner and the large beach-rock slabs that make up the tired walls echo its former splendour.

The tomb was built in the late 1700s for Nanasipau'u, eldest sister of the reigning Tu'i Tonga. It's claimed that, as part of her funeral ceremony, those selected as her attendants in the afterlife were killed and buried around the outside of this tomb. Nanasipau'u daughter, Latufuipeka, and her daughter's husband, Tuita Kahomovailahi, are also buried here.

The modern extension to the south of the tomb is the burial ground for families holding the noble title of Tuita.

'Ahau Bathing Well

On the corner of Hihifo and Loto Kolo Rds is the 'Ahau Bathing Well, which belonged to the chief Laufilitonga while he and his people were staying at the Fortress of Velata during the 1820s.

Freshwater bathing wells were owned by the highest chiefs and were *tapu* (sacred/taboo) to commoners. Unfortunately, there is little to see now and it has become a muddy pig hang-out.

A block to the south, at the corner of Moa and Loto Kolo Rds, is an **archaeological site** where 3000-year-old Lapita pottery was excavated by a team of archaeologists, but there's nothing to see nowadays.

Velata Mound Fortress

A short distance south of the 'Ahau Bathing Well is the circular Velata Mound Fortress. This type of ring ditch fortification is found throughout Tonga, Fiji and Samoa. Most of these fortifications have a single circular ditch but Velata is remarkable in having the extra protection of a double ditch. A 2.5m- to 3m-high defensive wall would have been built on the inner ring that lies between 15m and 20m inside the outer ditch.

Historians believe that Velata was first built in the 15th century. In the 1820s Laufilitonga, who later became the 39th and last Tu'i Tonga, restored the fort as a stronghold against the Taufa'ahau dynasty. In September 1826 the fortress was burned when Laufilitonga was defeated in battle by Taufa'ahau, the future King George Tupou I. Today the fortress lies on private land and the artificial ridges are virtually indistinguishable under the vegetation. A sign and concrete pillar mark the site.

Shirley Baker Monument & European Cemetery

Just north of the centre lies the grave and monument of Revd Shirley Baker, Tonga's first prime minister and adviser to King George Tupou I.

In 1890 the British 'advisers' sent to set up a protectorate and stabilise the government, which was suffering at the hands of squabbling religious factions, sent the former missionary and controversial politician into exile. However, Baker returned in 1898 with the permission of King George Tupou II and lived out his days in Hihifo, just south of Pangai, where he died on 16 April 1903.

The statue of Baker was commissioned by his daughters and is in the European Cemetery, where you can see the graves of various 19th- and early-20th-century German and English traders and missionaries. A Tongan cemetery is directly opposite.

Shipwreck

The shipwreck of an old steam sailing ship, approximately 80m long, lies just off the west coast of Lifuka. No-one knows the ship's name, but apparently it sank in 1916.

It's best reached at low tide. Go to the Shell petrol station and pick your way across the reef in the direction of Kao. The wreck is completely submerged, just beyond the edge of the reef on a sand bar.

Holopeka Beach & Old Quarries

Holopeka Beach, east of Holopeka village, is rarely visited. At low tide you can see the remnants of an old beach stone quarry and several stages of block removal. These types of quarry, common throughout Tonga from the 13th to 18th centuries, supplied the large stone blocks found in the retaining walls of chiefly tombs.

The ancient Old Quarry lies south-east of Pangai. There's a sandy beach here and the natural stone terraces in the water are similar to those along Tongatapu's south coast. At low tide the rock pools can be explored and the deep crevasses are full of coral and fish. The sea surging into the crevasses can be dangerous so only try snorkelling here at low tide on a calm day.

Southern Lifuka

On the south side of Pangai is the village of Hihifo, where the hospital sits on the coast beside two giant satellite dishes. From here,

Cook's 'Friendly Islands' Not So Friendly?

On Captain James Cook's third Pacific voyage in 1777 he spent over two months in Tonga. At Nomuka, his first landfall, chief Finau of Ha'apai told him of a wealthier island, Lifuka, where supplies would be available.

While visiting Lifuka, Cook and his men were treated to lavish feasting and entertainment. Needless to say, the foreigners were impressed. Cook dubbed the Ha'apai Group the 'Friendly Islands' after the apparent disposition of its inhabitants.

Thirty years later it was learned that the entertainment had been part of a Tongan conspiracy to raid the ships *Resolution* and *Discovery* for their plainly visible wealth. The plan was to gather the Englishmen into a convenient place, so that they could be quickly killed and their ships looted. There was, however, a dispute between Finau and his nobles over whether the attack would occur by day or under cover of night. Having previously agreed to follow the chief's plan to take action during the afternoon, the nobles failed to do so at the appointed time. Finau was so incensed at such a defiance of his orders that the operation was abandoned altogether and the Englishmen never learned how narrowly they had escaped.

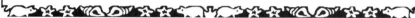

you can continue south along the dirt road all the way to **Hulu'ipaonga Point**, where there's a fine beach, but you need to be careful of strong currents.

About 200m short of the beach, on the west of the road is the **Hulu'ipaongo Tomb**. As described by Captain Cook, this is the highest burial mound in Lifuka and the Mata'uvave line of chiefs is buried here. The first Mata'uvave was sent to Ha'apai in the 15th century to establish political control over northern Ha'apai for Tu'i Tonga Kau'ulufonuafekai. His success resulted in his appointment as governor and Tu'i Ha'apai.

It's possible to walk between the southern tip of Lifuka and the northern tip of Uoleva at low tide, but an incoming tide can make this dangerous (see Uoleva later in this chapter).

Activities

For details of **diving**, **snorkelling**, **sea kayaking** and **whale watching** options around the Ha'apai islands, see Activities at the start of this chapter.

Tennis can be played at the Taufa'ahau & Pilolevu Tennis Club (☎ 60179; contact Taufu'i) or the Navea Tennis Club (☎ 60059; contact Moimoi Fakahua). It costs T$2 per day for nonmembers. 'Evaloni's Guesthouse (☎ 60029), on Loto Kolo Rd, offers

Lifuka tours for T$10 per person (minimum four people).

Places to Stay

Most accommodation on Lifuka can make arrangements for boat trips, bicycle and horse hire and many offer free pick-up from the airport or Taufa'ahau Wharf. All showers are cold unless stated otherwise.

Camping on beaches or undesignated areas is illegal throughout the Ha'apai Group unless you are on a guided trip.

Pangai *Fonongava'inga Guesthouse* (☎ 60038, e vimahi@kalianet.to, Palace Rd) Singles T$10-20, doubles T$20-30. This large establishment, also known as Langilangi Guesthouse, is nice and homely, with a guests' kitchen, large communal area and wide veranda. Given enough warning, breakfast (T$6) and dinner (T$12) can be arranged. Sunday lunch is cooked in the 'umu (underground oven); you're welcome to join in and see how it's done.

'Evaloni's Guesthouse (☎ 60029, Loto Kolo Rd) Singles/doubles T$10/20, doubles with bath T$25, singles/doubles with bath, tea/coffee-making facilities & fridge T$40/50. This is a welcoming, ramshackle place representing pretty good value. Rooms have fans and the suites are OK, though the decor is hardly South Seas. There's a communal

kitchen and meals can be ordered in advance (breakfast T$5 to T$10, dinner T$7 to T$15). Bike rental is T$10 per day (guests only). The Lifuka Tours that the owners run cost T$10 per person (minimum of four people).

Lindsay Guesthouse *(☎/fax 60107, Cnr Loto Kolo & Tuita Rds)* Singles/doubles T$15/25, with bath T$40/50. This clean and friendly place has hot showers, a comfortable shared sitting room, dining room and kitchen. Consequently it's often full. There is a small grocery shop and bakery on the premises and guests can hire bikes for T$5 per day. Meals can be ordered in advance (breakfast or lunch costs T$6, dinner T$15 to T$20).

Fifita Guesthouse *(☎ 60213, Fau Rd)* Singles/doubles T$15/30. Well placed above Mariners Café in the centre of Pangai, this nice little guesthouse is simple, clean and cheap. Rooms are pleasant and there's a small kitchen and communal area. The upstairs veranda is well shaded and gets a good breeze.

Mariners Inn *(☎/fax 60504,* e *mariners @kalianet.to, Holopeka Rd)* Doubles T$85. Under construction at the time of writing, this new enterprise by the owner of Mariners Café will consist of two self-contained units with air-con, with a bar and restaurant out the back.

Around the Island All beachside accommodation is located outside Pangai. The east coast has big waves, while the west coast is sheltered and offers magnificent sunsets and views of Kao.

Billy's Place *(☎ 60336)* Singles/doubles with shared bath T$45/55-65 (minimum two nights). Prices include a good breakfast, bike hire & airport transfers. No children under 12. Situated 1.5km north-east of Pangai, on the east (windward) coast of Lifuka, this is one of the best places to stay in Ha'apai. The well-presented bungalow-style rooms are spread over a large, well-tended plot and there's a good communal terrace as well as shelters down on the beach (which is very private and has some reasonable snorkelling). Occasionally pizza

is cooked in the evening. Billy's Place is a 10-minute bike ride from Pangai.

Niu'akalo Beach Hotel *(☎ 60028)* Singles T$20-30, doubles T$25-37. Breakfast T$8, dinner T$15. At the time of writing, this hotel, 1km north of Pangai, was run-down and its future undecided. The useable standard rooms are a little cramped but adequate, though the shared facilities could bring on a bout of depression. The superior rooms are pleasant and airy, but pick your room with care. The payoff is a lovely beach just metres away, and the presence of Watersports Ha'apai (see Activities) which operates from a bungalow on site. The hotel offers lifts to town for T$2; minibus charters to Houmale'eia Beach on Foa are T$30.

Telefoni Sunset Beach House *(☎ 60270)* Singles/doubles T$15/28. This place in Holopeka, 3km north of Pangai, was being renovated at the time of writing, but the owners also let the slightly shabby three-bedroom Angleika House, just across the road, for T$400 per month.

Mele Tonga Guesthouse *(☎ 60042)* Singles/doubles T$15/20. Breakfast & lunch T$5, dinner T$8. Cooking gas T$5 per day. Situated just eight minutes south-west of the airport and 3km north of Pangai, this simple place in Holopeka is a bit of a beachfront find for bargain hunters. Eight simple, small and clean rooms are available in two quiet and secluded bungalows just back from the western shore. There's a separate kitchen fale. About 100m south of the guesthouse a channel leads out from the beach and through the reef to a reasonable snorkelling spot.

From the airport turn left onto the main road then after five minutes turn right down a 4WD track just before a Mormon church. If no-one is about continue down the main road towards Pangai and call in at the first house on the left, about 50m on from the Mormon church.

Places to Eat
Eating out in Pangai is limited. There are just two restaurants.

Mariners Café *(☎ 60374, VHF Channel 16, Fau Rd)* Meals & snacks T$3-14. Open

THE HA'APAI GROUP

8am-8pm Mon-Sat, 6pm-8pm Sun. This cosy, friendly little place below Fifita Guesthouse is Ha'apai's only real restaurant option in the evening. Its breakfasts, snack foods (burgers and sandwiches mostly) and straightforward main meals are good quality and prices are reasonable. It's a real tourist/palangi hang-out and the knowledgeable staff can help book tours and dispense advice. Bikes can be hired for T$8 per day and you can send/receive email for T$5/1. It also sells film.

Maisae Restaurant Mains & barbecues T$3. Open 8.30am-2pm Mon-Fri. This clean and friendly locals' restaurant, off Holopeka Rd opposite the TCF, basically just serves great-value barbecue meals and fried-fish dishes to eat in or take away.

Several guesthouses will accept nonguests for dinner if you book in advance. *'Evaloni's Guesthouse* and *Fonongava'inga Guesthouse* are both good places to eat. For prices see Places to Stay.

Pangai's *produce market* is held on the steps of the decaying building on the corner of Fau and Holopeka Rds. Saturday mornings are busiest, but pickings are often slim.

The *Tonga Cooperative Federation (TCF; Holopeka Rd)* is Ha'apai's only supermarket, and choice is fairly limited. You may have more luck at a *fale koloa* (small grocery kiosk), particularly the cluster near the Friendly Islands Bookshop at the junction of Holopeka and Velitoa Rds. Most fale koloa sell some fruit and vegetables and stay open until 9pm.

Pangai has two bakeries: the *Matuku-ae-tau Bakery (Lindsay Guesthouse, Cnr Loto Kolo & Tuita Rds)* and the *Foueti 'Ofa Bakery (Cnr Paluto & Tu'akolo Rds)*, open the usual hours on weekdays and Saturday. On Sunday they open between 6pm and 8pm.

The small *kiosk* next to the Maisae Restaurant sells fish. Demand is high so get here early. Also try *Tu'ifua's Shop* on the waterfront.

On Foa, snacks (sandwiches, burgers, pizza, T$5 to T$17) are available for nonguests at the upmarket *Sandy Beach Resort* between 10am and 4pm. Dinner is available for guests only.

Entertainment

Fanga'i Hesi Open 8pm till late Thur, Fri & Sat. Admission T$3/2 for men/women. Also known as Hula Hula, this is Ha'apai's one nightclub. Behind Taufa'ahau Wharf, it can be a pretty loose affair, with random drunkenness and a little fighting here and there. Westerners will be the source of much interest and female travellers will constantly be asked to dance (whether or not they're in a couple). Not the safest place for women going solo, but good times can be had if you're with the right Tongan crowd.

On Friday nights, *kava clubs* meet in several halls around Pangai. Ask someone to point you in the right direction – these are largely male affairs, though.

Church entertainment takes place at various times; *dances* and other activities are sometimes held in church halls.

If you've got the hang of Tongan numbers you could go to *bingo*, which is held in the Holopeka village hall some Friday nights. Whole families come to play for prizes of food. A game costs 20 seniti, but you should contribute food to the prize pot.

Shopping

Women's Island Development Handicraft Shops (☎ 60478, Holopeka Rd & also Loto Kolo Rd) These two craft shops sell tapa, cards and various woven items made from pandanus leaves.

Coconut oil scented with candlenut or sandalwood can be purchased from several *fale koloa*.

Getting There & Away

Air The main Lifuka-Foa road bisects Ha-'apai's Salote Pilolevu Airport, 3km north of Pangai. Royal Tongan Airlines flies daily (except Sunday) between Ha'apai and Tongatapu and three times a week between Ha-'apai and Vava'u. See the Getting Around chapter for details.

Boat The MV *'Olovaha* and the MV *Tautahi* stop twice weekly at Pangai, once heading north, once heading south. The offices of the Shipping Corporation of Polynesia (☎ 60699) – for the *'Olovaha* – and the *'Uliti*

'Uata Shipping (Walter Line; ☎ 60855) – for the *Tautahi* – are beside the passenger shelter at Taufa'ahau Wharf and only open on days when the ferries arrive. See the earlier Getting Around chapter for ferry schedules and fares.

If you're arriving in Ha'apai by yacht, it's strongly recommended that you check in with the customs officer upon arrival. The customs office is inside the passenger shelter on Taufa'ahau Wharf. Although the entrance to the harbour looks tricky on the sea chart the marker buoys are perfectly aligned.

There are marginally protected anchorages along the lee shores of the islands of Lifuka, Foa, Ha'ano, Uoleva, Ha'afeva, Nomuka and Nomuka'iki. Fuel will have to be transported in jerry cans from the depot 1km north of Pangai, but gas is available at Frisco Timber & Hardware (☎ 60384) on Holopeka Rd. Yachties should be aware that getting sufficient supplies is sometimes difficult in Ha'apai.

Getting Around
To/From the Airport Some places to stay offer free airport transfers. Taxis charge T$3 to T$5 between the airport and Pangai. The bus between Pangai and the airport turn-off costs 40 to 50 seniti.

Bus Two buses operate between Hihifo, south of Pangai, and Faleloa, the northernmost village on Foa. There's no fixed schedule; buses run roughly between 8am and 4pm weekdays and 8am and noon Saturday. The trip from Pangai to Faleloa costs 60/80 seniti for the small/large bus.

Bicycle Lifuka and neighbouring Foa, connected by a causeway, are both fairly flat, and ideal for exploring by bicycle.

Bicycles can be rented from Billy's Place and Mariners Café. Some guesthouses rent out bicycles to guests. Expect to pay T$5 to T$10 per day.

Car & Horse The TVB can arrange car rental (T$60 per day) and horse rental (T$20 per day). Many of the guesthouses can also arrange these.

Taxi There are several taxis operating in Pangai. Try phoning Siaosi (☎ 60072), Paita (☎ 60155) or Asui (☎ 60169).

FOA
Foa (population 1393) lies directly north of Lifuka and the two islands are connected by a causeway. The wonderful Houmale'eia Beach is at the extreme northern end of Foa and there's some reasonable snorkelling on the western side (the best reef is opposite the Sandy Beach Resort). There's an ancient burial mound just east of the road about 500m south of Houmale'eia Beach. There's a good deal of bushland along the middle west coast north and west of Lotofoa, where the coast is pockmarked with some interesting caves and sculpted rock formations.

Places to Stay & Eat
Sandy Beach Resort (☎/fax 60600, e *sandy bch@kalianet.to)* Doubles with bath T$160. Breakfast/dinner T$12/39. No children under 12. This upmarket resort is situated on the magnificent white-sand beach at the northern end of Foa, 1.5km north of Faleloa (a 15-minute walk from the village). Houmale'eia Beach is a five-minute walk north of the resort. The nice, modern beachfront bungalows, set out in a row, may be a little unimaginative but have fans, tea/coffee-making facilities and verandas. Airport transfers and hire of bicycles, snorkelling gear and paddle skis are included in the price. Other (paid) activities include diving, game fishing, horse riding and day trips to other islands. The food (for guests only) is excellent and you'll be well looked after.

Nonguests are welcome to use the bar.

Getting There & Away
Two buses run between Pangai and Faleloa, Foa's northernmost village, between about 8am and 4pm weekdays and 8am and noon Saturday (60/80 seniti one way for the small/large bus).

If you choose to cycle to the resort, it's 15km north of Pangai. The terrain is quite flat and the road is reasonable – it takes about an hour. A taxi from Pangai to Houmale'eia Beach costs about T$8 to T$10.

THE HA'APAI GROUP

NUKUNAMO

A shining white beach covered with beautiful shells surrounds the small uninhabited island of Nukunamo, immediately north of Foa. The mound here, which looks like an ancient burial mound, was built as a platform, used by members of the royal family for hunting pigeons.

At low tide, Nukunamo is accessible on foot or by snorkelling from the north end of Foa, but the currents through the pass are quite powerful so only strong swimmers should attempt it. You'll also need to be in tune with the tide tables or risk being stuck on a deserted island for 12 hours longer than anticipated!

HA'ANO

The strikingly clean and well-tended island of Ha'ano encompasses 6.6 sq km and is home to 580 people. The population is proud of its churches and four pleasant villages, which are, from north to south, Muitoa, Ha'ano, Pukotala and Fakakakai. Ha'ano also has lovely beaches.

To get to Ha'ano, take the bus to Faleloa on Foa and catch one of the water taxis that leave from Faleloa jetty early morning and mid-afternoon. One-way fares between the islands cost T$2 per person.

Horse and cart day trips around Ha'ano can be arranged through the TVB or call ☎ 60374. However, they were not happening at the time of writing.

UOLEVA

Uoleva lies 1.5km south of Lifuka and if you're looking for paradise on a budget this is the place to come. A few people cross over from Lifuka to tend their livestock, but the island is basically uninhabited and has some of the finest, most peaceful white-sand beaches imaginable. There's little to do other than swim, snorkel and fish. The reefs at the western end of Uoleva and the broad bays on the island's sheltered northern shore offer good snorkelling through the channels in the fractured reef and the Community Clam Circle here is well worth seeing. The 16th-century **burial mounds** at the centre are difficult to find without a guide.

Places to Stay & Eat

Daiana Resort (☎ *60292 or book through the TVB*) Singles/doubles T$18/25. Dinner/breakfast T$12/4. Set in a coconut plantation, close to the Captain Cook Resort, are four very traditional fale (traditional thatched Tongan huts) whose cool interiors are lined with tapa and pandanus mats. The Daiana Resort is a great place to stay. It's simple and hospitable and Kalafi (the owner) can suggest some good snorkelling spots – ask him to show you the Community Clam Circle. Bathroom facilities are basic and so is the kitchen, and meals must be arranged

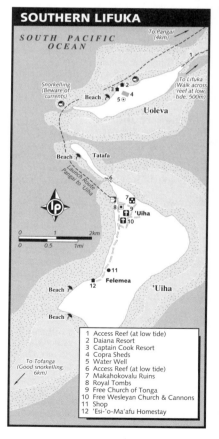

SOUTHERN LIFUKA

1 Access Reef (at low tide)
2 Daiana Resort
3 Captain Cook Resort
4 Copra Sheds
5 Water Well
6 Access Reef (at low tide)
7 Makahokovalu Ruins
8 Royal Tombs
9 Free Church of Tonga
10 Free Wesleyan Church & Cannons
11 Shop
12 'Esi-'o-Ma'afu Homestay

when you book. Boat transfers are T$10 per person one way.

Captain Cook Resort *(☎ 60014 or book through the TVB)* Singles/doubles T$15/20. Breakfast/dinner T$4/8. Cooking gas T$2 per day. Situated right on a beautiful, broad, 4km white-sand beach on the north-west coast, this place is all about location. There's a good bungalow on the beach (the others are slightly shabby and not very private) and bathroom facilities are very basic. Meals are tasty and very good value, but must be arranged when you book. Boat transfers are T$10 per person one way. Hire of a single sea kayak is T$15 for four hours, and snorkelling gear is $2 per day.

In the past Lonely Planet has received a number of complaints from readers in connection with the Captain Cook Resort, mostly advising single women to steer clear of the place. However, in recent years there have been no major complaints and locals maintain that the previous problems have been resolved.

Getting There & Away

Captain Cook Resort and Daiana Resort both offer transfers for guests from Foa Jetty in Pangai. Alternatively, catch a ride on a 'Uiha-bound boat and ask to be dropped at Uoleva (around T$5) – boats leave from Foa Jetty and passages can be arranged at Tu'ifua's Shop (☎ 60605) on the waterfront in Pangai.

Another option is to charter a boat for the day. This can also be arranged through Tu'ifua's Shop, the TVB, the resorts themselves or numerous guest houses in Pangai. Prices start at around T$50 per boat.

It is possible to walk/wade (there is one deep channel to cross) to Uoleva, but this can be dangerous (locals have drowned crossing here). Make sure you get local advice and only cross at low tide, or an hour or two either side of low tide. Do not cross on a windy day, if the sea is high or the current too strong as there is the danger of being swept away.

The walk from Lifuka takes at least 30 minutes and it's another hour and a half to reach either of Uoleva's resorts.

'UIHA

The clean, friendly island of 'Uiha (population 867) has two villages: 'Uiha with the main wharf, and Felemea, about 1.5km south, where there's a fine place to stay.

Royal Tombs

In the centre of 'Uiha village is a large elevated burial ground which contains royal tombs. Late in 1988 the tombs of three relatively obscure members of the royal family were shifted here, two from Pangai and one from Tongatapu, accompanied by much pomp and ceremony. Ostensibly the project was to consolidate the tombs of the royal family, but there were rumours of treasure in the cemetery compound that prompted the king to look for an excuse to excavate the otherwise *tapu* (sacred/taboo) area. Nothing of importance was unearthed during the excavation.

Church

Walking beyond the royal tombs, you can't miss 'Uiha's odd-looking **Free Wesleyan Church** – it resembles something out of a fairy tale. As evidence of the sinking of the *Margarita*, the 'Uihans display **two cannons**, one planted in the ground outside the church in 'Uiha village and the other in front of the altar inside – the latter is used as a baptismal font!

Makahokovalu Ruins

At the northern end of 'Uiha, about a 10-minute walk from the village, are the Makahokovalu Ruins. The name means 'Eight Joined Stones', but there are actually nine standing on end in an L-shape. A few similar stones are found lying about the site, reportedly scattered by a cyclone. There hasn't been much theorising as to the purpose or origin of the complex, but it's a pleasant walk out there.

In 1988, while the royal tombs were being relocated, the king's daughter Princess Pilolevu decided to visit the site. In one day a new road was cut to the ruins and the stones were cleared of years of overgrowth. The road was cleared again for another royal visit in the early 1990s. Since then,

THE HA'APAI GROUP

The Margarita

On 26 January 1863 the Peruvian blackbirder (slave ship) *Margarita* left Callao (Lima) and was never seen again. According to a preacher on 'Uiha at the time, a ship called in and lured several islanders aboard. When their families on shore realised what had happened, they banged iron pots, hoping to deceive the slavers into returning to shore to pick up more people who'd decided to go along.

The ploy worked, the ship was seized, the Tongans were released and then the ship, which was probably the *Margarita*, was subsequently destroyed.

sometimes it's cleared, and sometimes it gets overgrown.

Places to Stay & Eat

'Esi-'o-Ma'afu Homestay (☎ 60128 – the village phone, VHF Channel 16, or book through the TVB) Single/double fale T$20/25. Breakfast/dinner T$6/10-18. This wonderful place to stay is right on the beach at Felemea and staying here you'll get a good introduction to village life (and will probably be woken in the early hours by enthusiastic singing and church bells). There's one room in the house and four fale with coconut thatch roofs and tapa and pandanus mats inside. You can cook in the small kitchen or with notice the owners will prepare delicious Tongan food. There's a family 'umu most Sundays.

Boat trips to other islands for picnics, swimming, snorkelling and fishing can be arranged for about T$20 per person. Other activities include horse riding, tennis and volleyball at the village sports ground, or learning about village handicrafts.

Getting There & Away

Boats to 'Uiha from Pangai can be arranged by the TVB or by Tu'ifua's Shop (☎ 60605) on the waterfront in Pangai. It costs around T$10 per person one way and boats leave from Foa Jetty. 'Esi-'o-Ma'afu Homestay provides transfers for T$25 for one person or T$15 per person for two or more, one way.

TATAFA

Uninhabited Tatafa is surrounded by a lovely beach and is a short low-tide walk across the reef from northern 'Uiha. There's a rainwater cistern on the island but it's still wise to carry some water or to ask permission (on 'Uiha or Lifuka) to drink coconuts. Tatafa has good snorkelling and a large colony of flying foxes.

Other Ha'apai Group Islands

TOFUA & KAO

Volcanic Tofua, the site of the mutiny on the *Bounty*, would be one of Tonga's major tourist highlights if access was easier. Its sister island, Kao, is Tonga's highest mountain.

The Ha'apai Conservation Area Office (☎/fax 60289) in Pangai is a good source of advice and information on the islands. It's essential to carry plenty of food and water with you. The Ministry of Lands, Survey & Natural Resources (☎ 23611) in Nuku'alofa sells a black-and-white dyeline print covering Kao and Tofua (T$14), but unfortunately the scale is 1:50000.

Tofua

The island of Tofua has the most active of Tonga's volcanoes (it's constantly steaming, belching and rumbling) and in 1874 the king evacuated the island due to excessive volcanic activity. Later, people returned to live here again but the population seems to have drifted away – in 1996 only five people were reported living on the island. At present a few people seem to be living (at least part of the time) at Manaka on the east of Tofua, but Hokala on the north coast seems deserted, though people may stay in the old school occasionally. The tending and harvest of kava brings people to Tofua and much of the island's outer slopes are dedicated to the crop. Tofua also produces tamanu trees for canoes and *toa* (ironwood) in small noncommercial quantities.

The island is 55 sq km in area, and much of the inner slopes of the crater are covered in tropical rainforest. At the bottom of the circular crater is a beautiful, crystal-clear 250m-deep lake, 38m above sea level and covering 7 sq km. The active volcano, known as Lofia, smokes and spews away near the crater's 507m-high northern rim. Plans are afoot to convert at least some of the island to a national park.

There's a reasonable *campsite* just above the landing site at Hokala on the northern shore. For fresh water go to the old school roughly 450m away, where there's a rain-water tank. Follow the overgrown track which leads south from the campsite; after about five minutes the track crosses a small dip and then continues west up a little gully. After a couple of minutes the track leads right (north) out of the gully beside an ironwood tree. Follow the track south-west and through a mango and coconut plantation to reach the old school a couple of minutes later.

Mutiny on the Bounty Beach On Tofua's south-western beach, on 28 April 1789, Captain Bligh of HMS *Bounty* and 18 loy-als landed after the famous mutiny. Is-landers clubbed quartermaster John Norton

to death. Bligh and the rest of the men es-caped and embarked on a 6500km journey to Timor in an open boat, with minimal rations and short of water, having not dis-covered Tofua's large freshwater lake.

Visiting Tofua's Crater Climbing to the edge of Tofua's crater rim can be easily managed in a day and affords spectacular views of nearby Kao, Tofua's crater lake and the smouldering Lofia Volcano. Be sure to carry plenty of water and wear decent walk-ing boots with good traction and support. If you plan to climb down to the lake or to Lofia it's worth taking your time and camp-ing on the old crater rim – it's mosquito-free but there's very little shade and no water.

The crater rim is a tough one-hour climb from the old school at **Hokala**. To find the track, head 50m due south from the old school towards the ridge. The overgrown track is about 20m south-west of a small corrugated-iron enclosure. Once you've found the track, it's fairly easy to follow and heads south to south-east up the ridge, the vegetation gradually getting shorter as you climb; look out for the beautiful orchids.

At the crater rim, a series of small cairns pick out a trail heading north-west. After about 30 minutes (just before the vegetation finishes and the ash fields begin) a route leads down to **Lofia Volcano** and the **Crater Lake**. The difficult scramble down from the old crater rim, across the barren ash fields and up to the rim of Lofia Volcano takes about an hour, and unless you can find a better route you may need to cross a deep gorge. Keep an eye on the wind direction and stay out of the volcano's noxious fumes. From Lofia Crater rim to the lake, it takes about 45 minutes and there's no trail through the virgin rainforest that encircles the lake.

Kao

On clear days, the immense and frighten-ingly beautiful volcanic cone of Kao (no longer active) is visible from Lifuka and the other main islands. Kao's 1046m summit is frequently shrouded in cloud. Rainforest skirts the bottom third of the mountain and the upper slopes are covered with dense

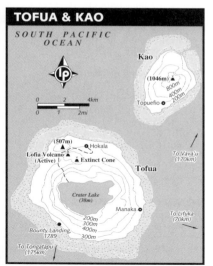

TOFUA & KAO

SOUTH PACIFIC OCEAN

Kao
(1046m)
Topuefio
800m
400m
200m

(507m) Hokala
Lofia Volcano
(Active) Extinct Cone Tofua
To Vava'u
(170km)

Crater Lake
(38m)
Manaka
To Lifuka
(70km)

200m
300m
400m
Bounty Landing,
1789
300m

To Tongatapu
(175km)

0   2   4km
0   1   2mi

THE HA'APAI GROUP

ferns. Only a handful of people live here to farm kava and there's talk of turning the whole island into a national park.

The very tough four-hour climb to the summit, usually following one of the southern ridges, is not recommended without a guide as there is no marked trail, and the vegetation is very dense in places. The people who live on the island may be willing guides; a gift of food would be an appropriate thank-you. Freshwater sources are unreliable and weather conditions rapidly change for the worse on the summit. When the cloud blows in, visibility can drop below 50m in a few minutes. Plenty of water, a compass and warm, waterproof clothing are essential. Good walking boots and trousers will make the trek much more enjoyable.

Strong swimmers will enjoy the dramatic snorkelling off **Topuefio**, Kao's southern landing site. There are plenty of large fish and a few coral heads cling to the volcanic rock, which, about 20m offshore, suddenly drops off into the deep blue.

Getting There & Away

Reaching Tofua or Kao is not easy. Few boats are prepared to make the journey and if they are it will be expensive. If you can get a large group together in Lifuka you may be able to charter the Ministry of Education's launch MV *Pako* (T$1600 with crew for five days) which is a suitable boat for the trip.

Locals from Lifuka with kava plantations on Kao or Tofua occasionally head out to tend their crop, but once you've persuaded someone to take you out, you'll probably be there for weeks.

Forest-covered red and black lava cliffs rise directly out of the surf and make landing at either island difficult, especially in a strong swell. You'll need a small dinghy to reach the shore and be careful of the slippery rocks when landing. On Tofua there's a landing site below the disused village of Hokala. The landing site on Kao is at Topuefio, which is marked by a couple of fale.

If it's any consolation, Tongans believe that the shark god, Tu'i Tofua, protects the

passengers of any boat in the vicinity of Tofua. Should a boat sink, the vessel and its passengers will be carried to shore by benevolent sharks!

Game fishing and diving around Kao and Tofua are supposed to be excellent and you may be able to persuade Watersports Ha'apai on Lifuka to take you. Charters can also be organised through the Royal Sunset Island Resort in the Tongatapu Group, or MV *Hakula* in Vava'u. See the relevant chapters for further details.

LUAHOKO

About 10km or 15km north-west of Pangai, the island of Luahoko is known for the many sea birds and sea turtles which call it home. The island has protected status to conserve the birds and turtles, but some Tongans still occasionally come here to (illegally) collect eggs.

HA'AFEVA

About 40km south-west of Lifuka, the small island of Ha'afeva has a land area of only 1.8 sq km but a population of about 300 people, making it a crowded place. Plantations occupy all uninhabited land outside the village and although Ha'afeva has a friendly nature, it's generally rather unkempt and lacks good beaches. On a reef northwest of the island, the sunken fishing boat *Eki'aki* makes for good diving.

Getting There & Away

Ha'afeva is accessed most easily on the MV *'Olovaha*, which calls in here weekly on its trips between Tongatapu and Lifuka. See the Getting Around chapter for schedules. Small local boats go from Ha'afeva to the tiny outer islands of Matuku, Kotu and Tungua, all of which offer excellent snorkelling. It may also be possible to charter a boat from Ha'afeva to Kao or Tofua.

NOMUKA & NOMUKA'IKI

Only 7 sq km in area and with a population of fewer than 550, Nomuka was historically important because of its freshwater springs. The first European to arrive on the island was the Dutchman Abel Tasman, who named it Rotterdam while picking up water there. Subsequent well-known visitors included Captain James Cook, Captain William Bligh and William Mariner.

Nomuka has no tourist accommodation but you may be able to sleep in a hall close to the landing site. A large, brackish lake dominates much of Nomuka's hilly interior and the island is surrounded by raised coral formations of up to 45m high. There are two smaller lakes near the island's northern end. During drier periods of the year, one of these lakes appears reddish-orange from the air, due to algae that is concentrated as the lake dries out.

Nomuka's companion island, Nomuka-'iki, is used as a prison where indentured convict labourers serve their sentences on the plantations.

Getting There & Away
Access is normally by small boat coming from either Lifuka or Ha'afeva. However,

Life on Nomuka, 1797

the Free Church of Tonga operates a boat that travels between Tongatapu, Nomuka and Lifuka. Sometimes it runs weekly, sometimes monthly.

Though it's not on their schedule, the inter-island ferries may occasionally stop here.

TELEKIVAVA'U
Probably the most exclusive and beautiful accommodation in Tonga has been built on this tiny island. *Villa Mamana (☎ 872 761 616028 – no area codes apply, fax 872 761 616029, e mamana@les-raisting.de)* asks US$480 per double and only accommodates one party of four adults at a time (children under 12 are free). Boat transfers are from Tongatapu. One for celebrities.

FONUAFO'OU
From 1781 to 1865 there were repeated reports of a shoal 60km west of Nomuka. In 1877 smoke was seen rising from that spot and by 1885 a cinder, scoria and pumice island 50m high and 2km long had risen from the sea, spewed up in a violent submarine eruption.

In recognition of its birth, Tonga planted its flag on the island and claimed it for the king. It was named Fonuafo'ou – meaning 'New Land' (or Falcon Island as it was referred to by Europeans).

Then in 1894 Fonuafo'ou went missing. Less than two years later there appeared an island 320m high, which subsequently also disappeared. In 1927 it emerged again and by 1930 had risen in a series of fiery eruptions to 130m in height and 2.5km in length.

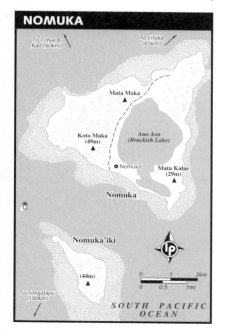

NOMUKA

To Tofua & Kao (60km)

To Lifuka (65km)

Mata Maka ▲

Koto Maka (49m)

Ano Ava (Brackish Lake)

● Nomuka

Mata Kalae (29m) ▲

Nomuka

Nomuka'iki

(44m) ▲

To Tongatapu (100km)

SOUTH PACIFIC OCEAN

0   1   2km
0   0.5   1mi

THE HA'APAI GROUP

J WEBBER/NATIONAL LIBRARY OF NEW ZEALAND

By 1949 there was again no trace of Fonuafo'ou, which had once more been eroded by the sea.

Unless you're on a private yacht, the only way to catch a glimpse of Fonuafo'ou (if it's around when you're there!) is to ride one of the ferries returning to Tongatapu from Niuafo'ou, which normally pass within a few kilometres of it.

HUNGA TONGA & HUNGA HA'APAI

These twin volcanic islands in the far southwestern corner of the Ha'apai Group contain large guano deposits, but the lack of an anchorage makes exploitation of them impractical. Hunga Tonga reaches a height of 161m and Hunga Ha'apai 131m. Both volcanoes have been dormant since European discovery.

The Vava'u Group

area 119 sq km • pop 15,905 (est)

Vava'u Island's Port of Refuge, a long, narrow channel between limestone islands, is one of the South Pacific's best, most protected harbours. This, plus the fact that the Vava'u Group boasts uniquely picturesque islands fringed with vibrant coral reefs, myriad jumbled channels, deep waterways and lovely secluded anchorages, makes it one of the world's great sailing locations.

But there's much more to Vava'u than great sailing. The group stands in contrast to other Tongan island groups, not only geographically (no other group is so hilly), but because of the range of activities offered here. Thanks to exquisite and diverse coral reefs teeming with fish, hidden caves and fabulous underwater landscapes, the diving and snorkelling are world-class. Between June and December scores of humpback whales arrive and Vava'u is one of the few places you're permitted to swim with these giant mammals. Sea kayaking, mountain biking, game fishing and bushwalking are all possible here. The group has some splendid beaches, often sheltered in secluded coves. Although getting to them usually requires a little effort, it's certainly worth it.

This tranquil group of islands has a population of around 16,000. Neiafu, on Vava'u Island, is home to a third of these people, while the rest are scattered across 50-odd thickly wooded, islands. The pace of life is slow and Neiafu the only place with any sort of bustle. Many people visiting Vava'u partake in as many activities as possible, but those on a tighter budget should take heed that among the emerald hills and islands lie quiet villages, hidden caves and windswept cliffs that can be enjoyed at minimal cost.

The peak tourist season is from May to November, with another flurry from mid-December to late January.

History

Vava'u is believed to have been settled for around 2000 years.

Highlights

- Diving above stunning coral gardens and geological marvels
- Swimming underwater into the wondrous Mariner's Cave
- Sailing between countless beautiful islands, beaches and coves
- Admiring the wild coast and cliffs from 'Utula'aina Point
- Swimming, snorkelling or kayaking with humpback whales
- Whooping it up at the Port of Refuge Yacht Club Friday yacht race

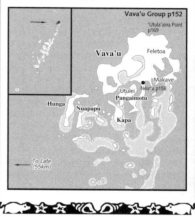

The first European to visit was Don Francisco Antonio Mourelle of Spain, en route from the Philippines to Spanish America. Mourelle's ship, the *Princesa*, had run short of supplies and after a fruitless visit to the volcanic island Fonualei (which they named Amargura, meaning 'bitterness') they sighted Vava'u Island on 4 March 1781. It was Mourelle who named the harbour at Neiafu Puerto de Refugio or 'Port of Refuge'. Tongans knew it as Lolo 'a Halaevalu, or 'Oil of the Princess Halaevalu', because of the

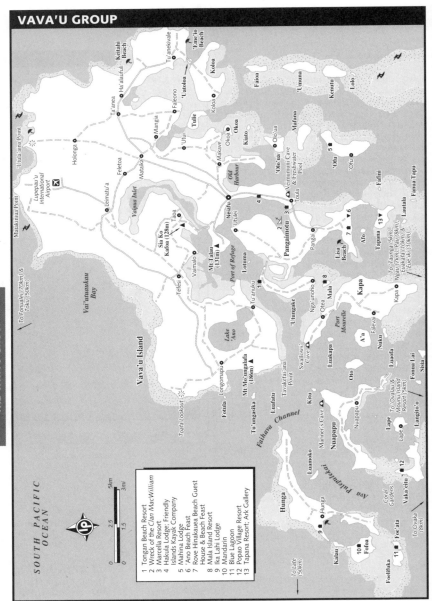

VAVA'U GROUP

1 Tongan Beach Resort
2 Wreck of the *Clan MacWilliam*
3 Marcella Resort
4 Hakula Lodge; Friendly Islands Kayak Company
5 Mahina Lodge
6 'Ano Beach Feast
7 Rove Hinakauea Beach Guest House & Beach Feast
8 Mala Island Resort
9 Ika Lahi Lodge
10 Mandarin
11 Blue Lagoon
12 Popao Village Resort
13 Tapana Resort; Ark Gallery

smooth, natural sheen that appears on the water's surface on calm days. Mourelle claimed the new-found paradise for Spain and named it Islas de Don Martin de Mayorga after the viceroy of Mexico. The islanders welcomed the Spaniards and stocked their ship before they departed.

In 1793, Spain sent Captain Alessandro Malaspina to Vava'u to survey the new territory and inform the inhabitants of the Spanish claim – somewhere in Vava'u a decree of Spanish sovereignty is buried, but the captain didn't stay on Vava'u for long.

William Mariner also spent a great deal of time here (see the boxed text 'William Mariner' in the Ha'apai Group chapter). Indeed, Mariner was involved in Finau 'Ulukalala I's conquest of Vava'u. When the English brig *Favourite* landed on Vava'u Island in November 1810, the king of Vava'u, Finau 'Ulukalala II – the son of 'Ulukalala I – permitted Mariner to return home with it.

But when he saw the marvels on board the ship, the Tongan king begged to be permitted to accompany Mariner. He said he was willing to forsake his princely life in the islands for even a lowly station in England. He wanted to learn to read, write and operate mechanical wonders.

Captain Fisk of the *Favourite* refused young Finau's entreaties, whereupon the Tongan made Mariner swear that he would some day return and carry the king back to England. Unfortunately, Mariner never returned to Tonga.

'Ulukalala II's tomb can be seen in the village of Feletoa, on Vava'u Island. His son was converted to Christianity by King George Tupou I of Ha'apai. When 'Ulukalala III died, George was entrusted to look after the throne of Vava'u for the boy king 'Ulukalala IV. But George seized the opportunity to add the group to his own realm and in 1845 he formed a united Tonga.

Geography

The main body of the Vava'u Group – which lies 275km north of Tongatapu – consists of a single landmass, a block of limestone tilted toward Ha'apai. At the extreme northern end high cliffs plunge straight into the

Captain Cook's Fateful Turn

MW

On Captain James Cook's third Pacific voyage he spent over two months (April to July 1777) in Tonga. At Nomuka he met chief Finau of Ha'apai.

When Finau announced he was setting out to visit Vava'u to the north and Cook expressed interest in accompanying him, the chief assured him that the islands contained no suitable anchorage or landing place for large ships such as Cook's and that such a trip would be foolhardy. Instead of opting for adventure, the Englishman sailed southward through the convoluted reefs and shoals of the southern Ha'apai Group. Upon landing at Tongatapu, Cook learned that he had been deceived: Vava'u contains the finest anchorages in the entire kingdom.

surf and there's little coral offshore. The southern part of the group is a submerged zone of numerous small islands, often surrounded by short cliffs (which rarely exceed 50m). Most of the islands are wholly or partially surrounded by coral reefs, which often drop away dramatically to the ocean floor.

The tallest, and often the most thickly forested, of the islands are the volcanic outliers of the group, including Toku and Fonualei (195m) to the north, as well as Late (519m) and Late'iki (Metis Shoal) to the west. A line of coral reefs runs from the south-eastern corner of Vava'u Island down to Maninita, the southernmost island in the group.

Climate

With almost 2200mm of precipitation annually, Vava'u has Tonga's wettest climate. Most rain falls between late November and April, which is also the cyclone season, and in fact most of this rain is produced by occasional, heavy tropical storms. March is the wettest month, but gentle warm rains and occasional downpours occur at any time of year.

Vava'u is warmer than Tongatapu and can be particularly hot and sticky during the cyclone season. That said, there are fine days at this time of year and, if you can stand the humidity, it's not a bad time to visit.

Prevailing easterly and south-easterly trade winds blow at an average of 15 knots, but between November and April, northerly and north-westerly winds can occur. These winds are usually accompanied by more unsettled seas, which can impact on activities on the western side of the group, such as sailing, diving and fishing.

See Climate in the Facts about Tonga chapter for more information.

Activities

Vava'u has excellent diving, snorkelling, sailing, whale watching, fishing and kayaking, and mountain biking and other activities are also available. While many of them are possible elsewhere in Tonga, in Vava'u much is geared towards activity-based tourism, and everything is close at hand and convenient. See the Activities special section for more information.

Diving Vava'u offers some world-class diving in a diverse range of environments. Dive sites of all kinds are found here, from hard and soft coral gardens to wrecks (see the boxed text on the *Clan MacWilliam*), vast sea caves and other geological marvels. You'll need to contact Vava'u's two dive operators for full details.

Beluga Diving (☎/fax 70327, e beluga@ kalianet.to, VHF Channel 16, PO Box 70) is located at Fangafoa Marina in Neiafu and operates three dive boats. Two-tank dives (at two different sites) cost T$95/85 in high/ low season. PADI Open Water Diver courses

---

Wreck of the *Clan MacWilliam*

The wreck of the copra steamer *Clan Mac-William* lies in 37m of water in the southern arm of the Port of Refuge. Built in 1918, this 127m (423-foot), 6000-ton Clan Shipping Line freighter steamed into Neiafu Harbour in December 1927 with a smouldering fire in the No 3 copra hold. The forward holds collapsed, cracking open the steamer's plates. One story has it that the captain and first engineer refused to abandon ship and went down with it; another relates that the captain locked the first engineer into the engine room to prevent him from abandoning the effort to save the ship!

Teeming with marine life, the wreck is now a popular dive site.

---

are T$300, while Dive Master courses cost T$850. Good-quality dive gear is available for hire (mask, snorkel and fins are T$10 per day). This well-run company has a good reputation with newly qualified and experienced divers alike.

Dolphin Pacific Diving (☎/fax 70292, e divedpd@kalianet.to, VHF Channel 71, PO Box 131) is located on Fatafehi Rd opposite The Moorings, with a dive shop beside Sailing Safaris. It has an equally fine reputation and is a PADI Gold Palm Resort and instructor development centre. A two-tank boat dive is T$90. PADI Open Water Diver courses are T$350 and numerous advanced courses are available. You can book through its New Zealand office (☎ 64-7-862 8959, fax 862 7444, e a.d.i@xtra.co.nz, PO Box 103, Paeroa).

Fishing Almost all fishing is concentrated in the area west of Vava'u where the ocean is over 1000m deep and a number of Fish Attracting Devices (FADs) are located. Most marlin are caught between June to November (August and September are the peak months), though marlin are caught year-round. It's possible to rent fishing gear at Ikapuna Store (see Neiafu's Shopping section later in this chapter). While most boats concentrate on trawling for the big game fish, bottom fishing and saltwater fly fishing can be catered for. All equipment is usually provided, but fly fishermen should bring their own tackle. For Tongan-style fishing trips (with hand lines) ask around at Neiafu wharf or where you're staying.

Most of the boats listed below can be contacted on VHF Channel 71.

Dora Malia (☎ 70698, ☎ 70416, fax 70174, PO Box 106) is a 10.5m (35-foot) boat skippered by Paul Mead, who specialises in tuna and marlin fishing. Both light and heavy tackle are available. Charters are T$300/400 per day for two/four fishers. Paul can be contacted at Ikapuna Store on Fatafehi Rd in Neiafu.

MV *Hakula* (☎ 70872, fax 70875, e fish vavau@kalianet.to, PO Box 23) is a 10.2m (34-foot), purpose-built, fully equipped game-fishing boat catering for up to six anglers. Charters cost A$600 per day, with reductions in the low season (January to April). Half-day charters are available and the boat occasionally ventures south to Tofua and Koa in the Ha'apai Group in search of exciting fishing grounds.

Kiwi Magic (☎/fax 70441, e kiwifish@kalianet.to, PO Box 153) offers deep-sea fishing charters aboard its custom-built 10.2m (34-foot) sport-fishing boat. Trips run from 10am to 4pm and cost T$150 per person, including lunch (minimum two people).

Target One (☎/fax 70647, e target1@kalianet.to, PO Box 3) is a fast, 8.1m (27-foot) sport-fishing boat. Game fishing charters cost T$360 per day (maximum of three people), though 'Island Fishing Cruises' – mostly bottom fishing – cost T$90 per person (minimum two people, maximum five). Half-day and split charters are available.

On the island of Hunga, Ika Lahi Lodge (e ikalahi@kalianet.to, PO Box 24) operates three 10.8m (36-foot) game-fishing boats, catering for six anglers on each. Charters are about T$750 per day. The lodge can also be contacted via Neiafu's Bounty Bar.

Mounu Island Resort (☎ 70747, fax 70493, e mounu@kalianet.to, VHF Channel 77), on Mounu Island, also runs a game-fishing boat catering for a maximum of four anglers. Day charters cost T$500.

Sailing The Moorings (☎ 70016, fax 70428, VHF Channel 72, PO Box 119), the world's largest yacht charter company, has a fleet of 12 yachts and two catamarans. Yachts range from 12m (38-foot) to 15m (50-foot), with accommodation for two to 10 passengers. Prices range from US$390 to US$745 per day, depending on the size of yacht, season and discounts. Bareboat charters are available as well as full or partial provisioning, skippers (T$100 per day) and cooks (T$80 per day). It is preferred that bookings are made through The Moorings' agents across the world. Check out its Web site (w www .moorings.com) for details.

Sunsail (☎/fax 70646, e sunsail@kalianet .to, VHF Channel 68) is also a multinational operation and runs eight yachts and three catamarans ranging between 9.9m (33-foot) and 15.3m (51-foot). Prices for bareboat charters are between NZ$475 and NZ$990 per night in low season (January to March), rising to between NZ$595 and NZ$1125 in high season (May to mid-December). Provisioning, a skipper and cook are available as extras. Bookings can be made at Sunsail's agents across the world. Check out its Web site (w www.sunsail.co.nz) for details.

Sailing Safaris (☎/fax 70650, e info@sail ingsafaris.com, VHF Channel 68, PO Box 153) runs a smaller-scale, more affordable operation. Three yachts (5.4m, 7.8m and 10.8m, or 18-foot, 26-foot and 36-foot, respectively) are available and cost between T$100 and T$400 per day (minimum three nights). Add T$90 per day for a skipper (one female skipper is available) and T$70 per day for a cook. Bareboat day sails (10am to 5pm) start at T$80. Charters for over a week are cheaper. Its office is next to 'Ana's Café.

Melinda Sea Adventures (☎ 70861, e mel inda@sailtonga.com, VHF Channel 16) operates the sailing yacht *Melinda*, a comfortable, 13m (44-foot), traditionally rigged gaff ketch. Fully crewed charters (minimum of three days) cost US$150 per person per day (minimum of two people, maximum of four) – all food included. Off-season (February to April), an all-inclusive three-day trip for two people costs US$225. *Melinda* is a heavy, smooth-sailing craft, itineraries are flexible and you can do as much or as little sailing as you like. Day trips and whale watching are also available. Contact the operators at their office on the corner of Fatafehi and Falaleu Rds, below the convent, or in the USA (☎ 415-332 8591); visit W www .sailtonga.com on the Web.

Maps A condensed version of the sea chart covering Vava'u (and showing all decent anchorages) is available from Sailing Safaris for T$15. The Moorings and Sunsail yacht charter companies have sea charts available for their customers. Alternatively, pick up your sea charts from the Hydrographic Unit at Touliki Naval Base in Nuku'alofa (☎ 24696; see Maps in the Facts for the Visitor chapter). Yachties should be aware that these charts are not accurate enough for GPS navigation.

Sea Kayaking Friendly Islands Kayak Company (☎/fax 70173, e kayaktonga@ kalianet.to, VHF Channel 71, PO Box 10) operates from mid-May to early January. This environmentally conscious company has a decade's experience running camping and paddling expeditions around Vava'u (and Ha'apai). Six/eight-day guided tours for US$1070/1295 are offered. No experience is required, but all trips require a minimum of four people (maximum of 10). Tents/camping mats/snorkelling equipment are hired separately for T$5/4/5 per day. All routes are flexible, but strongly influenced by weather and tide patterns.

Guided day trips are also possible (T$60 per person including lunch). The usual practice is to paddle out to a good snorkelling spot, but between July and November paddling among humpback whales is possible.

Kayak rental alone is T$20, but you must stay within the harbour area.

Beluga Diving (see Diving) also rents out double kayaks with dry bags at T$25 per day.

Snorkelling Almost all the fishing boats and dive operators will take people out on snorkelling trips on an ad hoc basis. Prices range from T$25 to T$40 per person, though with the fishing boats you may need to char-

ter the whole vessel, so get a group together. Joining a diving trip as a snorkeller is usually no problem, though some sites lie at reasonably deep depths (5m or more).

Most boat tours and some whale-watching trips invariably include a little snorkelling (see Boat Tours later in this chapter).

Sailing Safaris (see Sailing) runs more regular snorkelling trips visiting coral gardens and sea caves around Vava'u. They cost T$25 per person (minimum of five people). The Tongan Beach Resort (☎/fax 70380, VHF Channel 71), on 'Utungake, also offers full-day snorkelling trips for T$30 per person (minimum of four people) and will pick up from Neiafu.

Whale Watching The main season for whale watching is between July and November and is increasingly popular; for some licence holders (dive and fishing operators, for instance) it supplements existing business.

Whales Alive (☎ 70303) is a nongovernmental organisation devoted to protection of the whales and has an information booth (and whale-watching trip booking agency) next to the Vava'u Guest House.

Whale Watch Vava'u (☎ 70747, e mounu @kalianet.to, VHF Channel 77) operates daily trips for T$65 per person (minimum of six people; lunch an extra T$10) aboard a purpose-built vessel. Trips leave from the wharf below the Bounty Bar, where bookings can be made.

Sailing Safaris (see Sailing) also conducts full-day whale-watching trips daily for T$60 per person (lunch an extra T$10). *Whale Song*, its whale-watching boat, is equipped with hydrophones and snorkel gear. Yachties get a discount.

Dolphin Pacific Diving (see Diving) offers whale-watching trips at T$50 or T$60 per person. Trips are fitted around the dive operation (divers will often be treated to a spot of whale watching between dives), but whale-watching charters are possible.

Kiwi Magic (see Fishing) offers whale-watching trips for T$65 per person. Trips run from 10am to 5pm.

Melinda Sea Adventures (see Sailing) also runs whale-watching trips aboard the vessel

Melinda. Sailing, snorkelling and whale watching are often combined in day trips (T$65 per person, including lunch; minimum two people). Discounts apply in low season.

Friendly Islands Kayak Company (see Sea Kayaking) has a new 14-person whale-watching boat under construction, and is likely to charge T$65 per person.

Other Activities Many of the operators listed earlier also offer other activities away from their main business. See the preceding sections for full contact details.

Beluga Diving (see Diving) rents out **windsurfers** for T$28/48 a half/full day and will soon offer **paragliding** (T$48 per 30-minute flight).

Information on **surfing** is very speculative but some good waves break along the reef stretching south from Kenutu and between Luatafito and Maninita Islands. Matakiniua Point, north of Vava'u, may have potential.

Adventure Backpackers (see Places to Stay) can put together deserted island camping trips. It also hires out mountain bikes for T$15 a day. The Friendly Islands Kayak Company (see Sea Kayaking) runs guided **mountain biking** trips (T$22/35 for a half/full day, lunch not included), and an **Adventure Week** (US$995 including food and accommodation) between May and February. This includes sea kayaking, whale watching, mountain biking and sailing or diving.

Few people **rock climb** in Vava'u, but the short (around 50m) sea cliffs of Tu'ungasika and Luafatu (among others) look promising. Logistics could be tricky.

Sailing Safaris (see Sailing) hires out small **power boats** for T$50 per day, including fuel, VHF radio and life jackets.

Water-skiing is available for guests at the Tongan Beach Resort (see Places to Stay).

At the time of writing, the operators of Whale Watch Vava'u (see Whale Watching) were planning to start **bird-watching** tours of Vava'u Island and outer islands such as Maninita in the south-east.

Special Events
The Vava'u Festival, the biggest festival of the year, takes place during the week leading up to 4 May, the crown prince's birthday. This week-long party includes a variety of events, from processions to weaving and dance classes to sports matches, drinking bashes and feasts.

Vava'u Island

area 90 sq km • pop 12,418 (est)
Vava'u Island is the main island in the Vava'u Group. The island is sometimes known as Vava'u lahi and also referred to as Vava'u – as is the group – which can be confusing. Islands linked to Vava'u Island by causeways are referred to by their island names.

NEIAFU
pop 5908 (est)
Neiafu is the administrative capital of the Vava'u Group. The police headquarters, hospital, telecommunications office and most of Vava'u's tourist facilities are here.

The centre of Neiafu nestles between several low hills. To the north-west lies flat-topped Mt Talau (131m). Over the hill to the north is Vaipua (Two Waters) Inlet. Eastward is Neiafu Tahi (the 'Old Harbour') and heading south is a ridge of land leading to Pangaimotu.

History
Prior to European contact, Neiafu was a sacred burial ground of the indigenous people and political unrest and tribal skirmishes were forbidden. Every person entering the village was required to wear a *ta'ovala*, or waist mat, as a symbol of esteem for the chiefs entombed there.

The waterfront area around Halaevalu Wharf is called Matangimalie (Pleasant Winds). Formerly it was the site of a palace built by Finau 'Ulukalala II. In 1808 Finau built a fortification on slightly higher ground at Pou'ono. The fort was called Vaha'akeli (Between Trenches), a reference to the moats surrounding it.

Information
Tourist Offices The Tonga Visitors Bureau (TVB; ☎ 70115, fax 70666, VHF Channel 16)

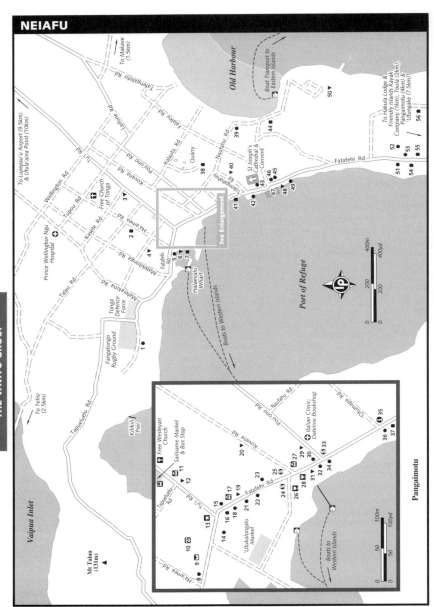

NEIAFU

PLACES TO STAY
2	Port Wine Guest House
16	Adventure Backpackers; Royal Tongan Airlines
37	Puataukanave Motel & Nightclub; SF Paea & Sons; Samoa Air
38	Hill Top Hotel; Sunset Restaurant & Pizzeria
41	Le Alvina Lodge
44	Garden Bay Village Resort
54	Paradise International Hotel
55	Vava'u Guest House; Kiwi Magic; Whales Alive
56	Twin Views Motel; Pasikala Scenic Tours

PLACES TO EAT
3	Mangele Bakery
4	Siaosi Fainga'a Bakery (George's Bakery)
6	Lt Maria Restaurant; Shipping Corporation of Polynesia & 'Uliti 'Uata Shipping (Walter Line) Offices
12	Lopaukamea Specialities; Sia Leka's 24-Hour Takeaway
19	Kalia II Takeaway
20	Tangitau & Sons Bakery

29	Cake Shop
31	Royal Beer Shop
40	Lighthouse Café
48	'Ana's Café; The Moorings
50	Ocean Breeze Restaurant

OTHER
1	Fangatongo Primary School
5	Olga's Clothing
7	Customs Department
8	Vava'u Library
9	Post Office
10	Tonga Communications Corporation; Vava'u Handicrafts
11	Lopaukamea Taxi
13	Police Station; Immigration Office; Fire Stations
14	'Alatini Fisheries
15	EM Jones
17	JV Taxis
18	Ikapuna Store
21	Vava'u Trading Centre Supermarket
22	Pacific Timber & Hardware
23	TCF Supermarket
24	ANZ Bank (ATM); Western Union
25	MBF Bank

26	Ifo Ifo Bar; One Way Taxi
27	Liviela Taxi
28	Bounty Bar; Teta Tours; Whale Watch Vava'u
30	Angela Handicrafts
32	Friendly Islands Bookshop; DMGS Gift Shop
33	Bank of Tonga
34	Kalia Room
35	Tonga Visitors Bureau; Langafonua Handicrafts Shop; Leiola Duty Free Shop
36	Fimco Handicrafts
39	Vava'u Ice Products (VIP)
42	Nazareth House Nasaleti
43	Melinda Sea Adventures
45	Vava'u Laundry; Dolphin Pacific Diving
46	Leiola Duty Free Shop
47	Sailing Safaris; Dolphin Pacific Diving; SS Marine Centre
49	Fangafoa Marina; Beluga Diving; Sunsail; Coral Island Cruises
51	Faka'anaua Ki Houmelei
52	Puanani Nightclub
53	Fa Sea Jewellery

on Fatafehi Rd is open 8.30am to 4.30pm weekdays and 8.30am to 12.30pm Saturday. The staff are informed, helpful and have heaps of brochures on offer as well as a good free tourist map of Neiafu and Vava'u. Accommodation reservations cost 50 seniti if it's local, T$1 for elsewhere in Tonga.

Money Cash or travellers cheques can be exchanged at the Bank of Tonga and ANZ or MBF banks on Fatafehi Rd. The Bank of Tonga and MBF bank open 9am to 3.30pm weekdays and 8.30am to 11.30am Saturday. The ANZ is open to 4pm weekdays and has an ATM inside, while the Bank of Tonga offers MoneyGram money transfer services – both these banks provide cash advances on Visa and MasterCard credit cards.

Western Union (☎ 70888) has an office next to ANZ, open standard banking hours.

Post & Communications The post office is on Fatafehi Rd above Halaevalu Wharf,

open 8.30am to 4pm. Poste restante mail (c/o Return or Delivery, Post Office, Neiafu, Vava'u) is held for you for six months.

Tonga Communications Corporation, behind the post office, offers domestic and international telephone services 24 hours every day. Fax services are available 8.30am to 4.30pm weekdays.

There are no cybercafes in Vava'u, but Sailing Safaris and the Bounty Bar offer an email service (T$5 to send, T$1 to receive).

Many businesses in Vava'u communicate by VHF radio and a yachties' information net is held on VHF Channel 6 at 8.30am weekdays.

Vava'u has one radio station (FM1 at 89.3FM) and Channel 9 TV station, which broadcasts mainly religious programs and '70s reruns.

Bookshops & Libraries There's a branch of the Friendly Islands Bookshop (☎ 70505) on Fatafehi Rd, but choice is very limited.

The Dateline Bookshop (☎ 70213) next to the Italian Clinic has a similar, small selection.

The tiny Vava'u Library, opposite the post office, is open from noon to 5pm Tuesday to Friday. There are plans to add a small museum section devoted to local history. Annual membership costs T$2.

Beluga Diving sells waterproof copies of *Reef Fish In-A-Pocket – Indo-Pacific* (T$15), while Sailing Safaris offers *The Snorkeller's Guide to the Coral Reef – A User's Manual* (T$26).

Most places to stay have reading libraries and/or book exchanges for guests.

Photography Film is sold at several shops around Neiafu, though the best retailer is, oddly, Pacific Timber & Hardware (☎ 70500) on Fatafehi Rd. It sells slide, black-and-white and colour print film, as well as waterproof disposable cameras.

Laundry Vava'u Laundry, opposite The Moorings, has modern machines and will wash, dry and fold your sweaty garments for T$5 per load.

Most places to stay offer laundry service for guests or washing facilities.

Medical Services For health problems see Dr Alfredo Carafa at the Italian Clinic and Pharmacy (☎/fax 70607, e itali.clinic@kalianet.to) on Pou'ono Rd, who is available 9am to 1pm weekdays or by appointment. Consultations are T$30; dive health certification is T$15. The clinic at Prince Wellington Ngu Hospital (☎ 70202, 70204) charges T$20 for consultations; just turn up and wait. The pharmacy opens 8.30am to 4.30pm weekdays.

Emergency The police (☎ 922, ☎ 70233, ☎ 70236) and fire (☎ 933, ☎ 70233) stations are on Tu'i Rd, in the centre of town. For medical emergencies call ☎ 933.

Free Wesleyan Church

Built in 1970, this church has some interesting stained-glass work, including depictions of John and Susan Wesley, Queen Salote Tupou III and Jesus Christ. It's built on the site of the old Wesleyan church destroyed by a devastating cyclone in March 1961. All that remains of the old church is a hall, which is used as a Siu'ilikutapu College classroom by day and a kava club by night.

Hala Tafengatoto

The name means 'the Road where Blood Flows'. Tradition has it that this sunken trail, the route to the village of Feletoa, ran with the blood of warriors killed during the conquest of Vava'u by Finau 'Ulukalala II.

This trail is one of a network of sunken clay pathways found around the main island of Vava'u. It meets the Old Harbour in Neiafu's eastern environs.

Pou'ono & Pou'ono Cemetery

Pou'ono means 'Six Posts' and refers to the traditional six posts of a meeting *fale*. This green was the site of the Vava'u courthouse until a new one was built in the 1990s.

Ta'emoemimi, the daughter of Tu'ipulotu'ilangi Tu'oteau, the 35th Tu'i Tonga, is buried in an ancient *langi* tomb in the cemetery opposite the green. The cemetery also contains the graves of two early-19th-century Wesleyan missionaries, Reverend Francis Wilson and David Cargill.

Old Harbour (Neiafu Tahi)

Neiafu's Old Harbour is much shallower than the Port of Refuge but it served as Vava'u's main landing site until the arrival of relatively large European ships. Around 1808, Finau 'Ulukalala II, in the midst of the conquest of Vava'u, bound several resisting chiefs into decomposing canoes and left them adrift in Neiafu Tahi to drown.

Near the entrance to Hala Tafengatoto are several freshwater springs bubbling into the Neiafu Tahi. The most reliable is Matalave, which lies around the harbour to the east. Nearby is the rocky outcrop that is said to have been the primary Vava'u landing site of the *kalia*, the double-hulled canoes used in ancient times.

St Joseph's Cathedral

Attempts to establish a Catholic mission in Vava'u began in 1837, but it wasn't until

Women in pandanus *ta'ovala*

Traditional Tongan dancer

Pandanus is woven into a multitude of items, from mats to hats.

Beach shelter constructed from local materials

Applying decoration to *tapa*

Ferry calling at Halaevalu Wharf, Neiafu

Tricky landing at anchorage-less Niuafo'ou

Calm waters at Taufa'ahau Wharf, Pangai

Choose a room with a view on one of the Friendly Islands' picturesque coastlines.

over a century later that construction of the wonderful cathedral began; it was to take nine years. The white and red facade survived the strong cyclone in 1961 and is a classic example of Catholic colonial architecture. The interior is also impressive – a large sculpture of Christ on the cross hangs above the altar. Standing high above the Port of Refuge, close to The Moorings on Fatafehi Rd, the cathedral is a beacon for arriving yachties.

Hala Lupe

Hala Lupe, the 'Way of Doves', is the name given to the stretch of road along the waterfront between St Joseph's Cathedral and The Moorings office. The road was constructed by female prisoners convicted of adultery by the church. Their mournful singing was likened to the sound of cooing doves.

Kilikili Pier

'Kilikili' is the name for the black volcanic slag pebbles used to decorate grave mounds throughout Tonga. Those used today come mostly from Kao and Tofua in the Ha'apai Group. The Kilikili Pier, at the far western end of Neiafu, once served as a British coal station. It was so named because the coal loaded there by the foreigners resembled, to the Tongans, those familiar little pebbles.

Mt Talau National Park

Established in 1995, the park protects Mo-'unga Talau, the 131m flat-topped mountain dominating the Port of Refuge, which can be climbed in an hour – either get a taxi to the trailhead, or walk from town, in which case allow around 2½ hours. To get there, head west past the rugby field along Tapue-luelu Rd and up through a residential area, until the road narrows into a bush track. When it begins to descend, a side track turns off to the right and leads steeply up over slippery rock surfaces to the summit.

The marked trail through the park links four viewpoints that encompasses views of Neiafu, the Port of Refuge, the Vaipua causeway and the 128m-high Sia Ko Kafoa across Vaipua Inlet. The truncated mountain in the distance (no-one knows where the top of this one wound up) is 186m-high

---

Mt Talau Loses its Peak

There's a popular Tongan legend that explains how Mt Talau came to lose its peak. It seems that a mischievous Samoan *tevolo*, or devil spirit, decided to filch the attractive peak and carry it away to his homeland. There is some disagreement as to what happened next; some maintain that a patriotic Tongan tevolo caught the offender and forced him to drop the peak by convincing him of the imminent arrival of daylight, the time for all devils to be back under cover. Another source claims that the mountain simply became too heavy and the thief dropped it. Whatever the case, the mountain top splash-landed in the middle of the Port of Refuge. It is now called Lotuma and is used as the Vava'u naval base of the Tongan Defence Forces.

Mo'ungalafa, rising above the freshwater Lake 'Ano at the west end of Vava'u Island.

Walking here you may see the rare *fokai* (banded lizard) and *hengehenga* (Tongan whistler), a rare and distinctive bird – males have bright yellow chests. Many of Vava'u's 17 other bird species can be seen here along with numerous tree and plant species. Some have been labelled, though some signs have been vandalised. A map and guide to the park is available free from the TVB. See the boxed text 'Mt Talau Loses its Peak' for the legend about the mountain.

Organised Tours

Island Tours Tour companies come and go, so contact the TVB for further information. Taxi firms are happy to provide tours, but rates vary. Expect to pay T$40/80 for a half/full day. Be aware that after heavy rain some roads become impassable to anything but 4WD vehicles.

Full-day tours offered by Pasikala Scenic Tours (☎ 70597, or ☎ 70510 after office hours), based at the Twin Views Motel, cost T$25 per person (minimum of three people).

Teta Tours (☎/fax 70488), Fatafehi Rd, offers full-day island tours for T$15 per person (minimum of four people), but we've heard mixed reports.

Natural Mystic Adventures (☎ 70599, e nmystic@kalianet.to, PO Box 30) runs a host of land tours around Vava'u. In the low season, you'll need to inquire whether anything is operating.

Boat Tours Several Neiafu operators run day boat excursions that typically include Swallows' and Mariner's Caves, picnicking on an uninhabited island and snorkelling at an offshore reef, but they'll also cater to individual whims. The presence of humpback whales (July to November) is a special bonus.

Verne, a popular local character, operates day trips on his 11.4m (38-foot) trimaran *Orion*. Contact him on VHF Channel 16, at 'Ana's Café or through the TVB. Trips cost T$60 per person (minimum of three), including a simple lunch and use of snorkelling gear. The flexible schedule takes in some of the islands' highlights and allows time for snorkelling and stopping on an outer island.

Day tours are also offered by Sailing Safaris, Kiwi Magic and Melinda Sea Adventures. See the Sailing and Fishing sections at the start of the chapter.

Coral Island Cruises (☎ 70975, fax 70976, e cicruise@kalianet.to, PO Box 40) offers the most luxurious way to see the Vava'u Group. The MV *Oleanda*, an 18-cabin cruise ship, departs most weeks on a four-night cruise. The trips are very much about exploring Tonga's ecosystems, above and below the waves, and the boat is fully equipped with diving and snorkelling equipment. Prices start at T$725 per person in a four-berth cabin, rising to T$2250 for single occupancy of the Royal Suite. (There's also a cruise between Tongatapu and Vava'u every second month – see the Getting Around chapter.)

Places to Stay

There are plenty of places to stay, both in and near Neiafu and on some of the other islands in Vava'u. Booking is advisable between April and December.

Unless stated, all showers use cold water.

Places to Stay – Budget

Vava'u Guest House & Restaurant (☎ 70300, fax 70441, e kiwifish@kalianet .to, Fatafehi Rd)* Singles/doubles with shared bath T$10/15, bungalows with bath T$22/27. Rightly popular with budget travellers (the bungalows are a good deal), this is a relaxed, comfortable place with basic cooking facilities and a reasonable bar/restaurant (open on Sunday). It's also handy for informal, mixed-sex soccer games that take place on the adjacent area of grass. Located 1.2km south of the town centre, it's just across the road from the bar and pool of the Paradise International Hotel.

Port Wine Guest House (☎ 70479, Ha-'amea Rd) Singles/doubles with shared bath T$10/20. This is a friendly, homely place, if a little basic. The main six-room guesthouse offers the best accommodation, and the nicest kitchen, but it's often rented on a long-term basis. Another smaller building is available, but it's a little shabby and the shared kitchen is basic. Guests are welcome to use the *'umu* (underground oven) on Sunday.

Adventure Backpackers (☎/fax 70955, e backpackers@kalianet.to, Fatafehi Rd) Bed in bunk room T$15, bed in 6/4-bed dorm T$18/20, singles/doubles T$40/50, double with bath T$60. This fresh Western-style hostel next to Royal Tongan Airlines has bright, clean, secure rooms (with ceiling fans) plus an excellent shared kitchen and communal area, as well as hot showers in winter. It's centrally located and although more expensive than other budget places, represents good value. Bike hire is T$15 per day, and snorkel gear is T$8 per day. Airport pick-up costs T$10 for one or two people. The staff are helpful and can organise all manner of tours and trips. Book ahead.

Garden Bay Village Resort (☎ 70137, fax 70025, Old Harbour) Singles/doubles with bath T$20/35. Though 1.5km east of Neiafu centre, this place is in a good location, but the bungalows, set in pleasant spacious gardens, are showing their age and slightly dingy. Eating here is not recommended, but if you must, order meals a few hours in advance (mains cost T$6 to T$8). Use of the kitchen is free. Occasionally there's a noisy nightclub here on Friday and Saturday.

Puataukanave Motel (☎ 70644, fax 70080, Fatafehi Rd) Singles/doubles with bath T$37/48. Below SF Paea & Sons department store are six modern rooms, with fridges and kettles. Reasonably well maintained and representing good value, the rooms have balconies but, alas, they overlook the Puataukanave Nightclub, which rages until the small hours on Thursday, Friday and Saturday nights.

Places to Stay – Mid-Range

Le Alvina Lodge (☎ 70509, fax 70873, Fatafehi Rd) Singles T$38-45, doubles T$55-65, including breakfast. A pleasant terrace, where a good breakfast is served, overlooks the Port of Refuge, while aficionados of 1980s decor will enjoy the interiors. There's no hot water but there's a kitchen and room has fans. A warm, welcoming and comfortable place.

Twin Views Motel (☎ 70597, fax 70666) Singles/doubles with bath T$55/75, deluxe rooms with bath T$75/100. T$25 per extra person. This row of spacious, well-equipped units off Fatafehi Rd is set on the hill just behind Vava'u Guest House, 1.25km from town. This position affords great views of both the Port of Refuge and the Old Harbour. All units include a good kitchen, large sitting room and two double bedrooms. A good place, if a little isolated.

Hill Top Hotel (☎ 70209, e sunset@ kalianet.to, Holopeka Hill) Doubles with bath T$65-80. Breakfast T$7-10. Split between two houses sitting atop Holopeka Hill (the name means 'Place of Gathering Bats'), this place was approaching completion at the time of writing. The styling is Italian and the more expensive rooms have verandas offering 180-degree views over the Port of Refuge, the Old Harbour and neighbouring islands. The adjacent Sunset Restaurant is excellent (see Places to Eat later in this chapter) and boat tours will be offered when the hotel opens. It's bound to be popular.

Places to Stay – Top End

Hakula Lodge (☎ 70872, fax 70875, e fish vavau@kalianet.to) Singles/doubles with bath A$125/145. Substantial discounts during low season; special high-season 'standby' rate. Situated about 2.25km south of Neiafu, this is a really fine place to stay.

Each of the two units has a well-equipped kitchen area, bathroom, phone, fan and air-conditioning. Rooms are spacious and lead out to a raised veranda overlooking the Port of Refuge. A path leads down through a pleasant garden to a jetty from where you can swim. The owners operate the MV *Hakula* (see Fishing earlier in this chapter). Free airport transfers and island tours are offered to guests.

Paradise International Hotel (☎ 70211, fax 70184, e paradise@kalia.to, Fatafehi Rd) Doubles with bath T$89-169. T$20 per extra person. All rooms have private verandas, air-con, fridge and tea/coffee-making facilities. The nicer, more expensive rooms overlook the Port of Refuge. The grounds are pleasant and there's a large restaurant/ bar area beside a large (clean) pool – T$2 per person per day for nonguests. Free airport transfers are supplied. It doesn't set the world on fire, but, hey, this is the best large-scale hotel in Tonga, and as such represents pretty good value.

Places to Stay – Out of Town

Marcella Resort (☎/fax 70687) Singles/ doubles with bath T$40/60. This resort of multiple bungalows in Toula, a T$3 taxi drive south from Neiafu, is hardly in a prime location, but it's a decent enough place. There's a pleasant view of the Port of Refuge, plus a tennis court and free use of bicycles for guests. The food's OK and the resort has a relaxed, friendly atmosphere. Some of the bungalows look hastily constructed, but there's a beach 15 minutes away (see Toula & Veimumuni Cave later in this chapter) and you can swim off the wharf, below the resort.

Tongan Beach Resort (☎/fax 70380, e holidays@thetongan.com, VHF Channel 71) Singles & doubles with bath T$130, 2-bed bungalows with bath T$250. The row of bright, clean motel-style units (with sea views and fridges) is on 'Utungake, a few steps from Hikutamole Beach. Two bungalows are built over the sea. It's a great spot, and there's a lovely outdoor fale bar and a restaurant (which is more stylish than the rather standard rooms) specialising in seafood and 'Pacific Rim' cuisine – the meal plan costs T$60 per day. Snorkelling trips can also be organised (see Snorkelling in the earlier Activities section), and sea kayaking and water-skiing are possible for guests. The daily water taxi to Neiafu costs T$4 to T$6 each way.

Hinakauea Rove Beach Guest House (*VHF Channel 16*) Singles/doubles with bath T$20/40. Tucked away on the beautiful Hinakauea Beach on Pangaimotu's southern end are two basic concrete bungalows. There's no electricity, but it's an ideal place for those seeking a little beachside isolation – Pangai, the nearest village, is 2km away along a rough dirt track. A gas stove is available for self-caterers or you can eat with a local family (breakfast/lunch/dinner T$8/10/15). Book through the TVB or Adventure Backpackers. There's a fine Tongan feast here on Thursday evening (T$20) and the lively restaurant of ***Tapana Resort*** is just over the bay on Tapana (small boats can be hired for T$20 per day). A taxi to town costs T$7.

Places to Eat

Unless you self-cater or are content to feed on barbecues and fried takeaway food, it's not easy to eat cheaply in Vava'u. There are a couple of local, budget, lunch-time restaurants, but in the evening you're looking at T$3 fish and chips or around T$10 for a main course in a good, tourist-oriented restaurant.

Restaurants ***Lopaukamea Specialities*** (*Tu'i Rd*) Mains T$3. Open noon-3pm Mon-Fri. Tucked behind a general store next to the lamentable Sia Leka's 24-Hour Takeaway, this is a good-value fried and raw fish restaurant.

Lt Maria Restaurant (*☎ 70324, Near Halaevalu Wharf*) Mains T$3. Open 8am-5pm Mon-Fri, 8am-noon Sat. This pleasant, simple restaurant serves just fried and raw fish.

Ifo Ifo Bar (*☎ 70285, One-Way Rd*) Mains T$5. Open 9am till late. Simple, local food is served throughout the day, while the bar can stay open into the early hours of the morning.

Bounty Bar (*☎ 70576, VHF Channel 16, Fatafehi Rd*) Snacks & mains T$5-12. Open 8.30am till late Mon-Sat. The food is not as

good as at 'Ana's Café, but the airy balcony overlooking the Port of Refuge is ideal for beer drinking or supping on good, fresh fruit juices.

'Ana's Café (*☎ 70664, VHF Channel 72*) Snacks & mains T$4-12. Open 8am-11pm Mon-Fri, 8am-3pm Sat. Not exactly cheap, but deservedly popular, with good food and drink, friendly staff and a good atmosphere next to the water. Off Fatafehi Rd, it's the home of the Port of Refuge Yacht Club and focus of the local sailing scene – the Friday night yacht race is run from here (see Yacht Races in the Entertainment section). Happy hour is 5pm to 6pm weekdays, there's darts on Tuesday, and Wednesday is quiz night.

Sunset Restaurant & Pizzeria (*☎ 70838, VHF Channel 16, Holopeka Hill*) Mains T$13-28, pizza T$7-15. Open 8am-10am & 6pm-10pm daily. Next to the Hill Top Hotel, this is a great Italian restaurant with authentic pizza and pasta, good house wine and fabulous views over the Port of Refuge and the Old Harbour. A fine place to indulge, and it's open for breakfast.

Mermaid Restaurant (*☎ 70730, VHF Channel 16*) Mains T$10-20. Open 10am-11.30pm Mon-Sat high season, 3pm-11.30pm low season. This is one of the best restaurants in town, but at the time of writing, the owner was about to move his whole operation (and change the name) to a site below SF Paea & Sons department store. May the great food (from an ever-changing and varied menu), relaxed atmosphere and live music long continue.

Paradise International Hotel (*☎ 70211, Fatafehi Rd*) Mains T$15.50-28.50, breakfast T$3.50-11.50. Open 7.30am-11pm daily. Offering an international menu, the food here ranges from good to disappointing. Handy on Sunday night.

Vava'u Guest House Restaurant (*☎ 70300, Fatafehi Rd*) Mains T$8.50-11.50. Open 7.30am-9am & 7pm-9pm Mon-Sat. This simple restaurant serves chicken and fish dishes, mostly in an Oriental vein. The seasoning can be a bit heavy-handed, but the gumbo is excellent. Demand permitting, there's a T$12 Sunday lunch-time barbecue – book in advance.

Ocean Breeze Restaurant *(☎ 70582, VHF Channel 74, Old Harbour)* Mains T$11.50-31.50. Open noon-2pm & 6pm-10pm Mon-Sat. On the waterfront overlooking the Old Harbour, Ocean Breeze offers a varied menu showing influences from India and South-East Asia. The food is good but not excellent. It has tables both indoors and outdoors on several terraces. If you're coming by boat, you can pull right up to its jetty.

Marcella Resort *(☎ 70687)* Mains T$14.50-18.50. Open noon-2pm & 6pm-10pm daily. The restaurant at this resort in Toula offers average, but overpriced, European-style food in a very pleasant setting overlooking the Port of Refuge.

Tongan Feasts If you're craving a Tongan feast, three options are listed below. Those at Hinakauea and 'Ano Beaches feature weaving demonstrations and crafts to buy, while all include traditional Tongan music and dance, plus ample buffets of Tongan specialities cooked in an 'umu (a pit oven).

Hinakauea Rove Beach Guest House *(VHF Channel 16)* T$20 including transport. 5.30pm Thur. On Pangaimotu's Hinakauea Beach, Sione Tongia runs an excellent feast (the food is authentic and delicious), with dancing by village children. Book through the TVB or through your accommodation.

'Ano Beach T$20 including transport. 5pm Sat. Another good feast on Pangaimotu, this unfortunately only operates in the high season or for large groups. Book through Teta Tours.

Tongan Beach Resort *(☎ 70380)* T$25. 7pm Wed. A weekly Tongan feast – but not always with a roasted piglet – and Sunday evening beach barbecue are held at this resort on 'Utungake.

Fast Food There are several options on Tu'i and Fatafehi Rds, but it's often the case that if you order a meal outside dining hours it won't be freshly cooked or you'll have to wait. Order in advance to be on the safe side.

Kalia II Takeaway *(Fatafehi Rd)* T$3. Open 11am till late Mon-Sat. From a small yellow and green shack, tasty take-outs of fried fish, chicken and chips are produced.

Occasionally you can get curries and burgers as well. Order in advance.

Royal Beer Shop *(Fatafehi Rd)* T$3.50-6. Open 8am-11pm Mon-Sat. Not only a fine booze emporium that's open late, this is also a takeaway. It serves burgers, fish, chicken, sausage and the occasional barbecue. Excellent on its good days.

Sia Leka's 24-Hour Takeaway *(Tu'i Rd)* T$1.50-4. Open midnight Sun to midnight Sat. A fall-back option when everywhere else is closed, this serves barbecues, curries and fried fish.

Self-Catering ***Tonga Cooperative Federation*** *(TCF)* and ***Vava'u Trading Centre*** *(Fatafehi Rd)* Open 8.30am-4pm Mon-Fri, 8.30am-noon Sat. Both supermarkets stock a good range of imported grocery products and staples.

Other smaller shops around Fatafehi and Tu'i Rds stay open until around 11pm Monday to Saturday.

Royal Beer Shop *(Fatafehi Rd)* This kiosk holds a small stock of groceries, but a large amount of booze. One bottle of Ikale beer costs T$1.50. (See Fast Food.)

'Utukalongalu Market, close to Halaevalu Wharf, is the best place in Vava'u to get fruit and vegetables. This covered market is very busy on Friday and on Saturday morning (sometimes it stays open over Friday night).

The freshest fish can be found in the early morning at the jetty on the Old Harbour or at Halaevalu Wharf. But for quality and Western-style convenience, head to ***'Alatini Fisheries*** *(☎ 70939)* opposite 'Utukalongalu Market. It's expensive, but choice cuts of fish and frozen imported meats are available, as well as a good selection of cheese, yogurt and wine.

Lighthouse Café *(VHF Channel 16)* Open from 7.30am Mon-Sat. Excellent European-style breads, Danish pastries, cakes, snacks, fruit smoothies and the like are available from this cafe/bakery close to the Catholic Cathedral.

Siaosi Fainga'a Bakery (or 'George's Bakery'), opposite the Church of Tonga on Tapueluelu Rd, offers basic white bread and rolls, as do ***Tangitau & Sons Bakery*** on

Kovina Rd and **Mangele Bakery** on Tu'i Rd; all these places open after 5pm on Sunday. A nameless little **fale kaloa** (small shop) on Pou'ono Rd, opposite the Italian Clinic, sells excellent cinnamon buns plus chocolate and banana muffins.

The **Vava'u Ice Products** (VIP; ☎ 70222) factory at the Old Harbour makes ice cream, ice blocks and choco dips.

Entertainment

Bars The Ifo Ifo Bar, Bounty Bar and 'Ana's Café (see Restaurants) are the main town-centre drinking establishments.

Yachties tend to congregate at **'Ana's Café**, especially on Friday when happy hour starts at 5pm and finishes when the last boat in Friday's yacht race crosses the line.

The **Bounty Bar** is a fun place in the evening and can get quite lively. The weekday happy hour is 5pm to 6pm. On Thursday it's extended until 7pm and on Friday there's live music.

Ifo Ifo Bar is a place with a more local feel and cheap Ikale and Tongan food. It too can get up a head of steam in the evening, especially on Friday night.

It's a little way out of town but the bar at the **Vava'u Guest House** (see Places to Stay) attracts a wide, and interesting, mix of folks, especially on Friday and Saturday nights. Its popularity is helped by the cheap beer (T$2 for an Ikale) and the fact it's open on Sunday.

The bar at the **Paradise International Hotel** (see Places to Stay) is a little sterile and barn-like, but it's not a bad place to meet tourists. And it's open late (until 2am on Thursday and Friday) and on Sunday. There's musical entertainment on Saturday night.

Kava Clubs The **Nazareth House Nasaleti** kava club, near St Joseph's Cathedral, offers socialising, chatting, card playing and kava drinking. Participants pay a flat fee of T$3 per person for all the kava they can slosh down. This is a men's club; the presence of unaccompanied women would probably be misinterpreted.

For information about other **kava clubs** in Neiafu, ask any local man to steer you in the right direction.

Nightclubs **Puataukanave Nightclub** (Fatafehi Rd) Admission T$3/2 for men/women. Open 8pm-2am Thur, 8pm-4am Fri, 8pm-11.45pm Sat. Below SF Paea & Sons building, this is Neiafu's most popular disco, and a place guaranteed to go on till dawn on Friday, as anyone trying to sleep in the vicinity will testify. The open-sided dance floor doesn't get too sweaty and you'll see most of Vava'u's bright young things here.

Puanani Nightclub (Fatafehi Rd) Admission T$3/2 for men/women. This place 1km south of Neiafu is a little rough around the edges and female travellers not willing to dance with every man in the place should stay away.

Garden Bay Village Resort Admission T$3/2 for men/women, free for resort guests. On the Old Harbour, this is an occasionally run disco on Friday and Saturday night.

Yacht Races The **Port of Refuge Yacht Club** is based at 'Ana's Café. The only requirements for membership are arrival in Tonga on a yacht or launch (the 'Olovaha doesn't count!). Between May and December, at around 5pm every Friday a relaxed yacht race starts outside 'Ana's Café. If you want to crew, turn up at 4pm when the skippers meet. Every racer wins some kind of prize.

Spectator Sports Rugby and football games are held more or less year-round at church school pitches and Fangatongo Rugby Field (on Saturday, games are held all day – entry is T$1 to T$2 depending on who's playing). Ask locals for details. Football is often free to watch.

Shopping

Numerous craft shops lie along Fatafehi Rd. For weaving, tapa and wood carving try **Langafonua Handicrafts Shop**, **Fimco Handicrafts** (☎ 70164), **Angela Handicrafts** and **Vava'u Handicrafts** (☎ 70718). **The Kalia Room** (☎ 70283) has T-shirts, jewellery and wood carvings and **DMGS Gift Shop** (☎ 70715) sells original hand-painted T-shirts and jewellery.

Fa Sea Jewellery (☎ 70853, Fatafehi Rd), just north of the Paradise International

Hotel, has carvings and jewellery in bone, black coral, shells and wood. Commissions are possible. You'll also find crafts at 'Utukalongalu Market.

Leonati Fakatava produces quality, original carvings in wood and bone as well as tapa pictures. He sells his work through The Moorings, but is happy to take commissions at his home (☎ *70179*) on the inland side of Fatafehi Rd 250m south of the Paradise International Hotel.

For tailor-made clothing try *Olga's Clothing* (☎ *70064*), near the harbour, and *Faka'anaua Ki Houmelei* (☎ *70803*), 150m north of the Paradise International Hotel.

There's a Saturday morning flea market at *Sailoame Market* on Tu'i Rd.

For fishing supplies, and some snorkelling equipment, head to the *Ikapuna Store* (☎/fax *70174, Fatafehi Rd*). A wide range of tackle and lures is available as well as basic trawling rods and reels. Rods can be hired for T$10 per day.

Leiola Duty Free Shop, beside the TVB and opposite The Moorings, sells alcohol, jewellery and perfume.

Getting There & Away

The information below is a rough guide only. The Getting There & Away chapter has further details on international transport to and from Vava'u. See the Getting Around chapter for information on transport between Vava'u and other parts of Tonga.

Air Lupepau'u Airport is on the northern side of Vava'u Island, about a 15-minute drive from Neiafu. Royal Tongan Airlines (☎ 70149, fax 70253), Fatafehi Rd, operates twice-daily flights between Vava'u and Tongatapu (thrice-daily on Friday and Saturday), three flights per week between Vava'u and Ha'apai, and weekly flights (on separate days) to Niuatoputapu and Niuafo'ou (the Niuas).

There are also weekly international flights via Vava'u between Tongatapu and Niue. Samoa Air flies from Pago Pago (American Samoa) to Vava'u and back once a week. The agent for Samoa Air (☎ 70644, fax 70080) is the SF Paea & Sons department store, opposite the Tonga Visitors Bureau. At the time of writing, Air Fiji was planning a weekly service between Nadi (Fiji) and Vava'u.

Boat Two ferries travel each week between Tongatapu and Vava'u. Both operators' offices are at Neiafu's main wharf and open the day before the ferry arrives and the day of the ferry. MV *Tautahi* belongs to 'Uliti 'Uata (Walter Line) Shipping (☎ 70490), based in the green and white sentry box. MV *'Olovaha* is owned by the Shipping Corporation of Polynesia (☎ 70128), based in a red container.

Arriving by yacht in Vava'u is reasonably straightforward, if a little time-consuming. There are moorings around the 'Ana's Café and Fangafoa Marina area, and many more south towards the Paradise International Hotel. The only chandlers is the SS Marine Centre (☎ 70650, [e] info@sailingsafaris .com, VHF Channel 68). It's situated beside the Sailing Safaris office. Though still under construction at the time of writing, it plans to offer poste restante, fax and email services. Eighteen moorings (T$10 per night) will be available as well as fuel (diesel, petrol, propane etc), engineering services, water, ice, laundry facilities and yacht slipway for boats up to 15m (50 feet) and 20 tonnes. Sunsail (☎/fax 70646, [e] sunsail@kal ianet.to, VHF Channel 68) also has a slipway.

The Getting There & Away chapter has details on opportunities for cargo ship passage to and from Vava'u.

Getting Around

To/From the Airport The Paradise International Hotel bus meets all incoming flights and provides free transport for hotel guests, or T$4 per person for everyone else. Several other places to stay will provide airport transport if you let them know you're coming. Taxis charge T$8 for the airport-Neiafu trip.

Bus Buses leave from the Sailoame Market terminal in Neiafu for most parts of Vava'u. There are buses to Pangaimotu, Tu'anekivale, Holonga and Leimatu'a. They do not run to any strict schedule but leave when they accumulate enough passengers. These

THE VAVA'U GROUP

buses often come from the villages to town in the early morning and go back in the afternoon, making it difficult for travellers staying in town to use the buses for day trips to the villages. Fares should be under T$2.

Car & Scooter Sailing Safaris (☎ 70650) rents scooters for T$30 per day including one tank of fuel, and a Pajero 4WD for T$100 per day. Some taxi firms claim to offer car hire, but this is often for a car plus driver for a day (expect to pay around T$80).

Taxi Taxi companies in Neiafu include:

JV Taxis (☎ 70136) Open 24 hours
Liviela (☎ 70240, or ☎ 70216 Sunday) Open 7am to midnight
Lopaukamea (☎ 70153) Open 24 hours
One Way Taxi (☎ 70684)

The maximum rate is T$2 for trips around Neiafu. Rough costs from Neiafu are T$7 to 'Ano and Hinakauea Beaches, T$8 to the airport and T$10 to Keitahi Beach and to 'Utula'aina Point.

Bicycle Vava'u is hilly, but fairly manageable by bicycle. Several guesthouses hire bicycles to guests and the Friendly Islands Kayak Company runs mountain-bike tours. Adventure Backpackers had the best bikes at the time of writing (T$15 per day).

Horse The tourist office or your accommodation can probably put you in touch with someone with a horse. Expect to pay about T$10 per day, but be warned: there are no saddles available and most of the horses are barely tamed.

Boat Hitching to outer islands by yacht is possible, but some yachties have commented that yachts cruising short distances around Vava'u are unlikely to need a spare pair of hands. If you're looking to crew, check out the bulletin boards at the Bounty Bar, 'Ana's Café and Adventure Backpackers.

Sailing Safaris (☎ 70650) hires out small power boats for T$50 per day, including fuel, VHF radio and life jackets, but for passenger transport to outer islands, ask around close to 'Utukalongalu Market and at the jetty on the Old Harbour. You'll probably be able to strike a bargain with someone who's going your way. All offshore island resorts provide boat transport, for a fee.

Tide timetables are available from EM Jones (☎ 70422), Fatafehi Rd, while daily weather reports are posted at 'Ana's Café.

AROUND THE ISLAND

Vava'u is a different world once you're outside Neiafu. Not that Neiafu is bustling, but the rest of the island is just a tranquil jumble of small villages, plantations and bush. Arguably, the people become more friendly the further from Neiafu you travel.

Vava'u Island is full of beautiful and interesting features, most of them quite different from those of the outer islands of the Vava'u Group. The easiest way to get around is by taxi, scooter or guided tour but, with a bit of effort, individuals can get a fairly good idea of what there is to see by bicycle, public transport or on foot.

If you're travelling around the island it might prove helpful to divide your journey into two parts, east and west, because the road system lends itself to this and because a full day is required to 'do' each half.

The TVB has put together a series of self-guided tourism trails that cover all the island's highlights. Each place of interest is marked by a numbered concrete post. A map explaining these trails is available from the TVB.

Western Vava'u Island

Sia Ko Kafoa Vava'u Island is nearly bisected by the **Vaipua Inlet**, which separates the Neiafu area from western Vava'u. The inlet was used by ancient Polynesian canoes en route to the fort complex at the village of Feletoa, which means 'Many Brave Warriors'.

The two sides of the island are connected by a causeway. On the western shore are the twin hills of Lei'ulu and Sia Ko Kafoa. Historically, this area has served as a **burial ground**, an *'esi* or resting site, a lookout and a fortification. It can be comfortably visited from Neiafu in a morning or afternoon or as part of a road tour of the western end of Vava'u Island.

From Neiafu, follow the road north, cross the causeway spanning Vaipua Inlet then follow the road right as it climbs up to **Taoa** (meaning 'Spear'). The name was given by the 14th Tu'i Kanokupolu, the cruel Tuku-'aho, in the late 1700s. Tuku'aho sought refuge in Taoa from a murder conspiracy plotted by Finau 'Ulukalala II. In 1799 he returned to Tongatapu, where he was executed by Vava'u assassins.

Lei'ulu, the hill behind Taoa, is used as a burial ground. Walk downhill along the coral road behind Lei'ulu hill; when the road begins to angle right on an uphill slope, about 10 minutes from the village, you'll see the track to **Sia Ko Kafoa** (128m) turning uphill to the left.

On the summit is an 'esi, a mound used as a rest area by chiefs and nobles and a place where young virgins were presented to amorous chiefs.

Lake 'Ano This freshwater lake at the extreme western end of the island is an eerie sort of place. It's accessible only by a steep, muddy climb down from **Longomapu**. If approaching it via the main road from the north, turn left at the intersection in the village and follow that road for several hundred metres. Look carefully for a track turning off to the right and leading downhill – this road is difficult after heavy rain. You can fish for edible *lapila* in the lake.

Mt Mo'ungalafa With a little effort you can climb Mt Mo'ungalafa (186m), the highest point on Vava'u Island, via a track just south of Longomapu. The spectacular view from the top takes in all of Vava'u and is well worth the effort.

Toafa Lookout On a clear day, the Toafa Lookout cliff, to the north-west of Longomapu, affords a view all the way to the volcanic island of Late, providing a contrast to the more sea-level vistas on the island's south coast.

'Utula'aina Point 'Utula'aina Point provides perhaps the most spectacular view on Vava'u Island and should not be missed. There are also a couple of other beaches that can be visited. To get to the trailhead for all

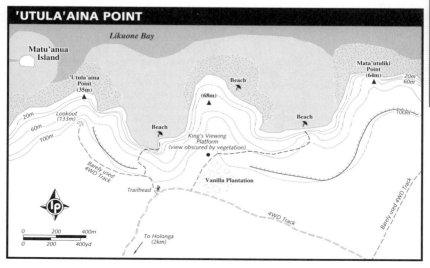

'UTULA'AINA POINT

Likuone Bay

Matu'anua Island

'Utula'aina Point (35m)

Mata'utuliki Point (64m)

20m
60m

Beach

(68m)

Lookout (133m)

20m
60m
100m

Beach

Beach

100m

King's Viewing Platform (view obscured by vegetation)

Barely used 4WD Track

Trailhead

Vanilla Plantation

0   200   400m
0   200   400yd

To Holonga (2km)

4WD Track

Barely used 4WD Track

three destinations, head north from Holonga village to a shady parking spot beneath a mango tree, just before the main vehicle track makes a sharp right turn. There's a TVB tourism trail post here.

To get to 'Utula'aina Point, walk straight ahead (north) and follow the rough (and shaded) 4WD track for 10 minutes to a wonderful **lookout**, surrounded by steep cliffs above a turbulent sea. On exceptionally clear days the volcanic outliers of Toku and Fonualei are visible. Look out for whales between July and November.

Fifty metres before arriving back at the trailhead, as the track bends right, a narrow path on the left leads off (almost north at first) down to a beautiful secluded **beach**. It's a steep climb, but you're likely to have the place to yourself (you should still watch your belongings, though; there have been thefts here). A shallow coral shelf restricts swimming, but you can do a little snorkelling at high tide.

To get to the second beach walk east from the trailhead along the 4WD track and then turn left at the first T-junction. Head straight through the vanilla plantation (north) and follow the narrowing path to a copse and earth mound (it's either a burial mound or a viewing platform for ancient Tongan kings, depending on whom you talk to). From the mound a path leads (in about 10 minutes) north-east down through forest and kava plantations to a **beach**. It's just as beautiful as the one close to the point and just as dramatic, guarded on each side by towering sentinels of rock.

Be sure to carry plenty of water for all these walks – none is available on the coast.

Feletoa The small village of Feletoa between Neiafu and Holonga is the site of a **fortification** constructed in 1808 to resist the conquest of Vava'u by Finau 'Ulukalala II. At the time, Feletoa was the centre of government for Vava'u, thanks to easy canoe access up Vaipua Inlet. The fortification is surrounded by clearly visible trenches or moats, which twice cross the main road. It is thought that the mound with the large water tank was a lookout.

Between Feletoa and the nearby village of Mataika, on the south side of the road, is a **burial site** containing the langi tomb of the ubiquitous Finau 'Ulukalala II. Finau died of what appears to have been internal haemorrhaging after an animated wrestling contest in Neiafu. This was in spite of the sacrifice of a young Neiafu child in an attempt to appease the greater powers of the day.

Matakiniua Point Thanks to the high grasses and mud, the beautiful area of high cliffs north of the airport is best accessed on foot in dry weather, although under optimum conditions it could be negotiated in a sturdy 4WD vehicle. The loop trip from **Leimatu'a** to the coast, westward along the cliffs and back to Leimatu'a would require at least half a day on foot.

Eastern Vava'u Island

Makave Most tours of eastern Vava'u Island involve beach-hopping, and this beach is one of the most interesting. From the Old Harbour, walk past the entrance to Hala Tafengatoto (see the Neiafu section earlier in this chapter) and follow the shore east towards Makave village, the legendary home of a mysterious dark, giant people.

An hour from Neiafu, on the beach below Makave village, you'll find an ancient **canoe mooring** beside an obtrusive rock and cave. Farther east are the refreshing **freshwater springs** of Matalave.

The name Makave (Take a Stone) refers to the ancient custom of piling a stone on **Kilikilitefua Wall** upon the birth of a child. To visit this wall, follow the faint track leading back to the road from the end of the beach. Turn south here and continue along the peninsula until you reach a small rise. At this point the remains of the stone wall, now less than 1m high, can be seen stretching nearly 100m across the peninsula. It once reached a height of 1.5m, but bits of it were removed for use in concrete cisterns.

Toula & Veimumuni Cave Three kilometres south of Neiafu is the village of Toula. East of the village, carved into the rock beside the eastern shore, is Veimumuni Cave, a freshwater spring and swimming hole. Upon arriving at the village from Neiafu, turn left (east) just past the Mormon church. Continue east through the village and up the hill until you reach a cemetery. As the dirt road bends left, follow the path straight ahead, under a gnarled tree and down to the cave above the seashore.

Several legends are associated with this cave, all of which have as their main character a beautiful spirit maiden who appeared on the rock before the cave and teased mortal men with her beauty. But the teasing didn't stop there; she also tempted every passing soul with the contents of the mysterious cave.

One version has her finally being outwitted by a *tea* (albino) woman, who became the first mortal to taste the water inside the cave before being tickled into submission by a pair of *tevolo* (devil spirits). In reference to this story, the wells around Toula are called *vai 'ene* (tickling water). Another version of the tale has her being tricked into the clutches of an amorous young gardener.

From the cave, walk north along the shore to a series of further **caves**, once used by Toula villagers to bury enemies from other villages. At low tide an variety of interesting marine life can be found in the rock pools.

Other Beaches At the easternmost end of the island, near the village of **Tu'anekivale**, are a couple of pleasant beaches, better for strolling or sunbathing than for swimming or snorkelling.

The nicest is **Keitahi Beach**, about 2km east of the road between Ha'alaufuli and Tu'anekivale. Currents are rather dangerous at high tide, but strong snorkellers will find some interest in the large tide pools about 100m offshore. At low tide, anyone with proper footwear can wander out across the reef. The owners of the beach now charge T$5 for entry.

'Eme'io Beach is reached by taking the left fork from Tu'anekivale and continuing about 2km to the shore. It's a peaceful and scenic area to explore on foot but it's not good for swimming.

Farther south across the causeways to 'Uataloa and Koloa Islands are a few scattered beaches, but of greater interest are the **mangroves** in the waterways around this swampy area.

Other Vava'u Group Islands

PANGAIMOTU
area 8.86 sq km • pop 1336 (est)
Just across the scenic causeway from Toula village is Pangai (Royal Island), so called because it belongs to the royal estate. The main village of Pangai was the home of the chief Vuna, whom Will Mariner discusses in some detail in his book. Vuna was one of the infamous 'handsome men' of Tonga, whose insatiable lust for young virgins and irresistibility to women led to some serious social disruption.

Beaches
'Ano and **Hinakauea Beaches**, near the south end of Pangaimotu, are actually two different parts of the same beautiful beach, with sheltered turquoise water, emerald vegetation, good snorkelling and a safe anchorage. Hinakauea Rove Beach Guest House offers a place to stay and feast (see Places to Stay – Out of Town), or you can catch a dinghy across to the island of Tapana for T$5 per person.

Tavalau Beach is a five-minute scenic walk north from the eastern end of the 'Utungake causeway.

'Utulei
The village of **'Utulei** lies across the Port of Refuge from Neiafu's Kilikili Pier. It was here that writer and long-time resident Patricia Ledyard Matheson set her autobiographical accounts of island life (see the following boxed text). You can kayak or catch a boat across the harbour from Neiafu, or drive round, park at the top of the hill and walk down to the village.

Near the turn off to 'Utulei, a quarry has left a massive gash in the hillside. There is a beautiful view across the Port of Refuge from the top of this hill.

THE VAVA'U GROUP

Patricia Ledyard Matheson – Local Legend

One of Tonga's most famous *palangi* (foreign) authors, Patricia Ledyard Matheson lived at 'Utulei for 51 years until her death in October 2000. During that time she wrote three books: *Friendly Isles: A Tale of Tonga; 'Utulei, My Tongan Home;* and *The Tongan Past*, revolving around her life in Tonga, its people and traditions.

She was born in San Francisco in 1913 and served in the Pacific during WWII, during which she volunteered for front-line duty. Feeling drawn to Tonga, Pat arrived in Vava'u during 1949 to take up a position as principal of Siu'ilikutapu College. She soon married and set up home at the entrance to the Port of Refuge. Known for her hospitality, sharp wit and sharper sense of humour, she established a fine academic library. Pat was still crossing the harbour to Neiafu in a small boat with a dodgy outboard motor weeks before she died. She is buried in the village cemetery on 'Utulei.

TAPANA

There are a few beaches on this island, which is popular with yachties. In front of *Tapana Resort* are a number of moorings and the Spanish restaurant here is very popular and lively – one reader reported that his evening here was the most memorable while in Vava'u. Check with the TVB for further details. The *Ark Gallery*, located on a house boat, sells local art works including paintings, carvings and printed T-shirts.

'UTUNGAKE & MALA

'Utungake is a long, thin island connected by a causeway to Pangaimotu. Its main attraction is the Tongan Beach Resort (see Places to Stay – Out Of Town). Another pleasant beach is near the southern tip of 'Utungake.

The small island of Mala, just south of 'Utungake, has a good swimming and snorkelling beach but a strong current flows between these two islands and **Kapa** farther south. Mala's recently opened *Mala Island Resort* (☎ 70852, ⓔ mala@kalianet.to) has a nice, big restaurant (open to nonguests), but at US$200 a night the tapa-lined, aircon bungalows don't cut it. There are a number of moorings and yachties are welcome, but beware of a legendary cannibal god who reputedly lives on Mala and is said to capture and devour passing boaters.

SOUTHERN VAVA'U ISLANDS
Hunga & Fofoa

At the centre of the westernmost cluster of islands of the Vava'u Group is a large, placid **lagoon**, formed by Hunga and the neighbouring islands of Kalau and Fofoa. It looks like a volcanic crater lake, with three small openings to the sea. Consequently it offers superb anchorage, although entering can be tricky.

Ika Lahi Lodge (ⓔ ikalahi@kalianet.to, PO Box 24) Doubles with fans & air-con T$200. Meals T$50 per day per person. This is a new lodge on the Hunga shore of the beautiful sheltered lagoon. Close to the deep ocean, the resort places an emphasis on fishing, but yachties are most welcome (there are 10 moorings). Small catamarans, laser sailing dinghies, snorkelling gear and sea kayaks are available to guests. The lodge can also be contacted via Neiafu's Bounty Bar.

Up on the cliffs behind the resort is a **lookout** from where humpback whales can be seen from July to November.

Mandarin (VHF Channel 6, Private Bag, Hans Schmeiser, Fofoa Island) T$100 per day. This is a simple, one-room, two-bed house on the north side of Fofoa overlooking the lagoon. It has a kitchen and veranda with barbecue, while a small power boat (with driver) is included in the daily rent. No short lets are possible – a week is the minimum.

Foe'ata & Foelifuka

The island of Foe'ata, immediately south of Hunga, offers glorious white **beaches** and good **snorkelling** in a secluded atmosphere. At low tide it's a simple walk across a sand bar to Foelifuka. *Blue Lagoon* (☎/fax 70247, ⓔ bluelagoon@kalianet.to, VHF Channel

16) Fale sleeping up to 4 T$160. Meals T$60 per person per day. This lodge and restaurant has six large fale beside a truly idyllic beach on Foe'ata. Constructed from local materials, each fale is unique and built around its immediate environment. Part eco-lodge, part eccentric dream resort (some of the bathrooms are particularly wacky), it offers reputedly the best food in Vava'u. It's already popular with yachties and boat trippers (lunch costs between T$14 and T$28). Transfers cost T$100.

Nuapapu

Nuapapu is best known for the hidden cave at its northern end, one of Vava'u's most renowned tourist attractions. It's now named **Mariner's Cave** after Will Mariner, who was apparently the first European to see it.

Inside the cave you'll experience a strange atmospheric phenomenon. Pacific swells surging through the entrance compress trapped air and when the sea recedes every few seconds, the moisture condenses into a heavy fog, the result of water vapour cooling as it expands. As soon as another wave enters the opening, the fog instantly vanishes. To enter the cave, snorkelling gear is recommended. You need to be a confident swimmer to try this and don't go in if the swell is strong. Enter the cave when the swell pulls you towards it, exit when the swell pushes you out, and be sure to look up before surfacing. The main entrance is a couple of metres below the surface and the tunnel is about 4m long. For scuba and skin divers there is a second exit at 15m depth.

Between the southern end of Nuapapu and the adjoining island of Vaka'eitu are the **Coral Gardens**, which once offered some of the best snorkelling in Vava'u. Badly damaged by a cyclone in 1990, they are wonderful once again.

Vaka'eitu

Vaka'eitu was once owned by the Wolfgramm family, some of Vava'u's earliest German settlers. More recently, the land has been divided into individual *'api* (plantations), while the ***Popao Village Resort*** *(☎ 70308,* ✉ *popao@kalianet.to)* has been constructed. Though once a great place for

---

Mariner's Cave

Will Mariner was shown this hidden cave by Finau 'Ulukalala II. Puzzled that several chiefs he'd seen dive into the water had failed to return to the surface, he was instructed to follow their example and was guided into the dim cathedral-like cavern. After returning to the canoe for a torch, he observed that the cave was about 14m high and 14m wide, with narrow channels branching off into darkness all around. As they drank kava on a rock platform inside, one of the chiefs related this story:

A tyrannical governor of Vava'u learned of a conspiracy against him and ordered the primary conspirator drowned and all his family killed. The conspirator's beautiful daughter, betrothed to a young chief, was rescued by another chief, who also had amorous intentions. To prevent her imminent demise, he spirited her away into a secret cavern and visited her daily, bringing gifts of food, clothing, coconuts and oils for her skin. His ministrations were so sincere that, eventually, he won her heart as well as her gratitude.

Realising that he couldn't just bring her out of the cavern, he formulated an elaborate plan, which involved a secret voyage to Fiji with some underling chiefs and their wives. When they inquired why he would attempt such a trip without a Tongan wife, he replied that he would probably find one along the way. True to his word, he stopped the canoes before the bare rock above the cave entrance, dived into the water and emerged a few minutes later with the girl, whom his companions surmised to be a goddess until they recognised her as the daughter of the condemned conspirator. They all went off to Fiji, only returning to Vava'u two years later after hearing of the death of the tyrant governor.

And they all lived happily ever after.

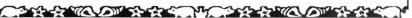

backpackers, it seems that the future of the resort is uncertain. Check with the TVB.

Kapa

The main attraction of Kapa Island is the beautiful **Swallows' Cave** ('Anapekepeka), which cuts into a cliff on the west side of its northern end. The cave is, in fact, inhabited not by swallows but by hundreds of white-rumped swiftlets *(Collocalia spodiopygia)* that flit about in the dim light and nest in the darkness.

The floor of the cave is about 18m below the water surface and the only access is by boat. The best time to visit is in late afternoon when the slanting sunlight lights up the water. On entering the cave, you'll see **Bell Rock** hanging down on your left. When it's struck with a solid object, the rock emits melodic vibrations. Deeper in the cave, you'll see a shaft of light shining through a hole in the ceiling; from there, you can follow a rocky trail into the adjoining dry cave.

If you're on a tour, stipulate in advance that you wish to snorkel in the cave or you may just get a quick trip through. When swimming into the cave, be aware of the current that sweeps past the entrance and may cause problems for weak swimmers.

Port Mourelle, on the protected western bay of Kapa Island, was the original landing site of the Spaniard Don Francisco Antonio Mourelle, the first European to visit Vava'u. It was here that he took on water from the **springs** of the swamp near Falevai (House of Water). A track from Port Mourelle leads north and south along the spine of the island. If you'd like to camp, ask permission in any of the island's three villages, Kapa, 'Otea and Falevai.

Nuku

The tiny, uninhabited island of Nuku, off Kapa, is a favoured spot for numerous official functions, celebrations and private parties. The lovely white beach is the main attraction as the snorkelling is unexceptional – and there's a bit of a current at the western tip of the island. Locals often paddle over from Kapa to collect T$1 from anyone who stops here. It isn't much to pay

to enjoy such a beautiful place and they don't collect on Sunday!

Taunga, Ngau & Pau

To enjoy an idyllic beach on a sporadically inhabited island, try the inviting islands of Ngau and Taunga, just south of Kapa.

These islands offer fine snorkelling, idyllic beaches and four good anchorages. At low tide, Ngau and Taunga are connected by a fine sandy beach. Ngau is in turn connected to the uninhabited island of Pau by a slender ribbon of sand. There's a superb anchorage in the bight of Ngau on the eastern shore.

'Eue'iki

The uninhabited raised island of 'Eue'iki has easy boat access to the stunning white beach and several good camping sites, and there's no coral near the shore, making it ideal for swimming. There's a coral garden off the southern shore. This was the island where the Australian reality-TV series *Treasure Island* was filmed. Ask around and you'll hear lots of behind-the-scenes stories about the show's production, parties and other misdemeanours. The story of the pig killing is particularly gruesome.

'Euakafa

On the summit (100m) of this relatively small island is the overgrown tomb of Talafaiva, a queen of Tonga (see the following boxed text). Hiking, swimming and snorkelling are all possible here – there's a coral garden south of the island.

Mounu, 'Ovalau & 'Ovaka

Just a short distance south-east of Vaka'eitu are the islands of Mounu and 'Ovalau, two more of those idyllic sunning, snorkelling, swimming and lazing-on-the-beach sort of places that travellers dream of finding. You can walk completely around Mounu in a few minutes and there's good snorkelling.

Mounu Island Resort (☎ 70747, fax 70493, ⓔ mounu@kalianet.to, VHF Channel 77) Fale with private bath T$200 per night (T$175 low season). Meals T$65 per day. This beachfront resort has a minimum stay of three nights unless agreed in advance;

'The Fo'ui Did It'

Back in the mists of time, a Tongan chief called Tele'a came to live on 'Euakafa because he considered Vava'u the most beautiful part of the kingdom. He took a lovely girl, Talafaiva, as his third wife and accepted her dowry, which consisted of 100 other attractive girls. The whole family set up house on the plateau of little 'Euakafa.

Outside the royal residence grew a *fo'ui* tree, which Talafaiva wanted chopped down. But Tele'a refused to do so. One day, while Tele'a was out fishing, Lepuha, one of Tonga's irresistible 'handsome men', arrived to 'conquer' the king's bride. By climbing the fo'ui tree, he was able to avoid the royal guard and enter the castle in order to seduce the queen. All would have been well had he not tattooed his signature mark on her belly.

When Tele'a saw the mark he was outraged, but all the queen could do was blame the tree that she'd wanted to destroy in the first place. 'The fo'ui did it,' she said, and the fo'ui has served as a Tongan scapegoat ever since.

Tele'a ordered his wife beaten for her indiscretion, but in doing so his servant inadvertently killed her. The chief built her a tomb on the summit of 'Euakafa, which can still be visited, although a body has never been found. Some claim that it was stolen by Lepuha. The fo'ui, by the way, has gone as well.

---

children under 12 are not accepted. Nearby, the larger island 'Ovaka is also pleasant, but it doesn't hold a candle to its neighbours.

Maninita

The tiny wooded island of Maninita in the extreme south of the Vava'u Group is about as secluded as it's possible to get. The terraced coral reef on the approach forms lovely tide pools and there's some good snorkelling. The forests in the island's centre are pristine, peaceful and home to many species.

The anchorage is situated on the western side of the island.

EASTERN VAVA'U ISLANDS

Transport to the eastern islands is much shorter and easier if you start from Neiafu's Old Harbour rather than the Port of Refuge.

'Ofu

The waters surrounding this friendly place, south-east of the Old Harbour, form Vava'u's primary habitat of the prized *'ofu* shell. However, these shells are endangered, so please resist the temptation to buy the numerous specimens you'll no doubt be offered here. There's quite a trade in tourist items in the village, which is a nice place to visit. In fact, exploring the whole island is worth a day.

Mahina Lodge *(VHF Channel 16)* Singles/doubles T$40/50, fale T$20. This place provides the only accommodation on the island, but an air of shabbiness is creeping in here and there. The main house is lovely and the fale are cheap, but inquire locally about the condition of the place before booking and beware of hidden costs.

Kenutu, Lolo & 'Umuna

The small island of Kenutu, just east of 'Ofu, has superb beaches and the coral patches south of the island offer magnificent snorkelling and diving. The land itself is heavily wooded but there's a well-defined trail across it to steep cliffs on the eastern coast.

The reef between Kenutu and Lolo, immediately south, is very dramatic and should not be missed. On the eastern side the waves crash and boil, while the crystalline waters on the western shore are calm.

In the centre of 'Umuna, the uninhabited island just north of Kenutu, is a large cave containing a freshwater pool. Both Lolo and 'Umuna are accessible from Kenutu by crossing the reef on foot at low tide.

OUTLYING VOLCANIC ISLANDS
Late

Late, west of the main group, is dominated by a 555m-high volcanic crater, dormant

THE VAVA'U GROUP

since 1854. On clear days, its distinctive silhouette is visible from the mainland. Late was evacuated by King George I when he realised that some of the outer areas of his kingdom were being ravaged by black-birders (South American slave traders) The people of this island were resettled in Hunga beside the lagoon and Late remains uninhabited.

In the 1990s, Late became the site of another resettlement project, but this time in the opposite direction. The Tongan Wildlife Centre on Tongatapu is attempting to transfer breeding pairs of the endangered Niuafo'ou megapode to Late (which covers 15 sq km and is heavily forested) from its native Niuafo'ou, where habitat loss and hunting have pushed the megapode to the verge of extinction. For further information, see the boxed text 'The Niuafo'ou Megapode' in the Niuas chapter.

Late'iki

Late'iki first emerged in 1858 but was gone by 1898, breaking the surface between Late and the immense cone of Kao (Ha'apai) far to the south. The island was next seen on 12 December 1967, when it made a 'pulsing glow on the horizon' during a particularly violent eruption. Within a week it had reached an altitude of 18m, but subsequently went down again. In May 1979 the island

locals nicknamed Metis Shoal began spewing and erupting.

On 7 July 1979 the king decided to take action. He sailed to the site and looked on as his son planted the Tongan flag on the new land and christened it Late'iki, which means 'Little Late'. Who knows how long it will stick around this time!

Fonualei

Fonualei, 64km north-west of the main island of Vava'u, can be seen from the northern cliffs of that island on a clear day. In 1846 the island erupted, covering parts of the main island with volcanic ash. This is the island Mourelle named Amargura (Bitterness) when he discovered it was barren and wouldn't provide him and his crew with much-needed and long-awaited supplies.

The best way to have a look at Fonualei is to sail between Neiafu and the Niuas. The ferries pass within a couple of kilometres of its eastern coast.

Toku

The old, worn volcanic island of Toku, near Fonualei, was evacuated during the blackbirding scare of the 1860s. Its inhabitants resettled in 'Utulei village on Pangaimotu and Toku remains uninhabited. It is possible, but difficult, to climb, as there are no tracks. There's a freshwater lake near the summit.

The Niuas

The remote Niuas (meaning 'Rich in Coconuts') consist of three small volcanic islands in the extreme northern reaches of Tonga, occupying a total land area of only about 70 sq km.

Tongan tradition remains very much alive in the Niuas. Many of the inhabitants still live in thatched Tongan *fale*, and Niuatoputapu and Niuafo'ou are where the highest quality white mats in Tonga are made.

As in the Ha'apai Group, the solitude of their environment has given the people a decidedly mellow attitude towards their world and visitors. It's highly unlikely that anyone who goes to the trouble of visiting the Niuas will feel that the effort went unrewarded.

NIUATOPUTAPU

area 18 sq km • pop 1400 (est)

The island of Niuatoputapu (Very Sacred Coconut), 240km north of Vava'u, is shaped like a shoe with the toe pointed north-east. Topographically, it resembles a squashed sombrero, with a steep, narrow, 130m-high ridge in the centre surrounded by a coastal plain, much of which is plantation land.

The north coast is bound by a series of reefs, but there is a passage through to Falehau Wharf. Yachts anchor just north-west of the wharf.

Niuatoputapu is ideal for walking; most of its interesting sights can be covered in just two days. All three villages – Falehau, Vaipoa and the administrative capital, Hihifo – lie in a 5.5km line along the northern coast. They are all sleepy little places, and the arrival of visitors is an exciting event, especially during the months when there are no yachts at anchor. Wherever you wander on this island you'll be greeted with a smile, and every child you meet will demand to know your name, exhausting the capacity of their English vocabulary in the process. (However charming, this does get a bit tedious after a while.)

Niuatoputapu has 14 churches, with Wesleyan and Catholic the two major denomina-

Highlights

- Exploring Niuafo'ou's lava fields, freshwater lakes and walking trails
- Cooling off in the fresh waters of Niutoua Spring
- Scouring the shore of Vai Lahi for a glimpse of the endangered Niuafo'ou megapode
- Watching the drama of the precarious loading and unloading of the MV 'Olovaha at Niuafo'ou
- Walking the ridges that lie at the heart of Niuatoputapu
- Combing the beaches and water channels of western Niuatoputapu

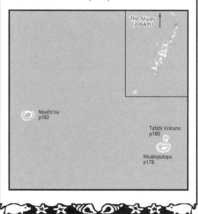

tions. Far from cosmopolitan Nuku'alofa, this is a very traditional place and dress and behaviour are conservative. It's particularly important to dress modestly in the Niuas, despite it being hotter here than elsewhere in Tonga. No-one should wear 'short shorts' – long, baggy ones are probably OK – and women would do best to wear skirts below the knee. Even when swimming you should wear at least a T-shirt and long shorts.

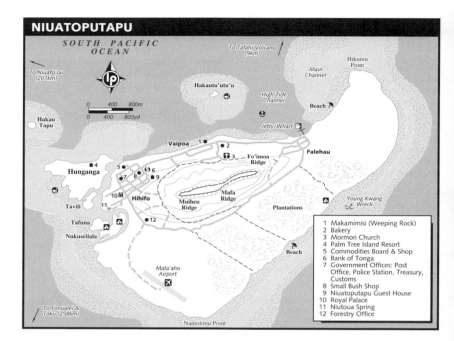

NIUATOPUTAPU

1 Makamimisi (Weeping Rock)
2 Bakery
3 Mormon Church
4 Palm Tree Island Resort
5 Commodities Board & Shop
6 Bank of Tonga
7 Government Offices: Post Office, Police Station, Treasury, Customs
8 Small Bush Shop
9 Niuatoputapu Guest House
10 Royal Palace
11 Niutoua Spring
12 Forestry Office

There's good diving outside the reef, and plenty of lobster, but no diving equipment is available on the island.

To learn more about Niuatoputapu, especially its history and archaeology, look for the book *Niuatoputapu: The Prehistory of a Polynesian Chiefdom* by Patrick Kirch. The island has many archaeological sites, but most are overgrown and hard to find.

Information

The 'capital' of the Niuas, the sleepy village of Hihifo on the north-west corner of Niuatoputapu, boasts the police station, the post office and a small cooperative store.

Money can be changed at the Treasury. Telephone services to Niuatoputapu commenced in 1998.

Niutoua Spring

The cool, sparkling pool of Niutoua Spring flows through a crack in the rock just west of Hihifo. It's full of friendly fish. A swim here will take the bite out of a typically sticky day in the Niuas. The legend of the spring is equally charming, whichever version you hear – and there are at least four!

One relates that the son of a former chief, Ma'atu, married a princess from Tongatapu but the marriage fell on the rocks and the princess began having dalliances. Polite society of the day, however, did not permit such indiscretions and the girl was sentenced to execution. Defiant to the end, she spat on the ground as she was being carried away, thereby forming the spring. Apparently worried that the water would be cursed, chief Ma'atu placed a ban on fishing in the spring.

Bathing at Niutoua isn't banned, but bear in mind that the spectacle of *palangi* (Westerners) swimming will quickly draw an audience. This show must be pretty good value for Tongans: kids ditch school and adults abandon their work in order to attend the free entertainment.

Beaches

Niuatoputapu is surrounded by magnificent white beaches of remarkable diversity. You could walk around the island on the 11km stretch of beach in about seven to eight hours.

The most beautiful beaches are on the north-west side of the main island and on Hunganga, the offshore islet. The beaches north-east of the wharf are tranquil and ideal for cool early-morning walks before the sun begins to beat down.

Along the 'sole' of the island you can walk for hours on sandy, deserted beaches. The reef is close, making swimming difficult, and the shallows are full of marine life, including thousands of sea cucumbers. Makamimisi (Weeping Rock), right on the coast, is the outlet to the sea for a spring that's a little way inland; when it's dry, you can pound on this rock with another rock and it will bring up fresh water.

Near the eastern end of the island is the wreck of the Korean fishing boat *Young Kwang*, which ran aground in the mid-1980s. There isn't much left of it, only metal scraps.

Western Waterways

Near Hihifo, a maze of shallow waterways winds between the intermittent islets of Nukuseilala, Tafuna, Tavili and Hunganga. At low tide, they form vast expanses of sand and leaning palms, and you can walk anywhere in the area by wading through a few centimetres of water. At high tide the passages (especially between Niuatoputapu and Hunganga) are excellent for swimming.

Ridge Walk

The central ridge, which comprises three smaller ridges, affords a grand view of the coastal plain and the multicoloured reefs of the lagoon. Reaching it will take a bit of effort. It's not a difficult climb, just heavily vegetated and, in places, nearly vertical.

The best way to go, it seems, is from the village of Vaipoa. Pass the bakery and the Mormon church and continue upwards through the maze of trails until you reach a very steep taro plantation. Scramble up as best you can. Once you're about 20m above the highest taro plant, you're on the ridge.

You can follow the ridge in either direction. The eastern route entails a near-vertical rock climb of about 10m but it's easy to do, with clear footholds.

Places to Stay & Eat

There are lots of excellent *campsites* west of Hihifo and on the beach along the island's south coast. It's best to ask permission before setting out. Details of the following two places to stay should be confirmed by inquiring locally.

Palm Tree Island Resort (☎/fax 85090) Single/double fale with bath T$90/120. This small, new resort on the islet of Hunganga is far and away the best place to stay in the Niuas. It's very peaceful here, and the four fale have hot water and electricity, making it a perfect retreat with no loss of comfort. There's a dinghy shuttle to Hihifo or you can walk across at low tide. Snorkelling, fishing and walking trips can be arranged.

Niuatoputapu Guest House (☎ 85021) Singles/doubles T$18/22. Breakfast/lunch/dinner T$4/5/10. Also known as Kalolaine's Guest House, this is the only other place to stay. It's pretty basic, but remains friendly, clean and homely and can be found at the south-east end of Hihifo – there's no sign, but everyone knows where it is. Meals must be booked in advance.

It's a good idea to bring your own food when you come to the island – remember this is a remote place with little available food. Limited groceries may be purchased at the several small shops. Bread is available at the bakeries in Hihifo and Vaipoa after about noon every day including Sunday.

Getting There & Away

Air Christian holidays and the start/end of school terms can make getting to/from Niuatoputapu very difficult – book well in advance. At other times the weekly flights are often far from weekly and seem to be pretty low on Royal Tongan Airline's priority list. It has also been reported that seats on 'fully booked' flights can miraculously become available just prior to departure. It's best to get a confirmed seat, but any trip to the Niuas should be handled with flexibility. In addition, there is no direct flight from Tonga-tapu to Niuafo'ou – all go via Vava'u. Mata'aho Airport is 2km south of Hihifo.

See the Getting Around chapter for more information.

Boat Getting to Niuatoputapu by boat may be tricky but it's not impossible. The MV *'Olovaha* arrives from Vava'u roughly once a month. It continues to Niuafo'ou, return-ing a couple of days later on the long (2½-day) return journey to Tongatapu. Always check the *'Olovaha*'s schedule in Nuku'alo-fa before you make any plans to visit the Niuas by sea. See the Getting Around chap-ter for more information.

Most visitors to Niuatoputapu arrive on private yachts between June and September – Niuatoputapu is a port of entry, so many yachts stop here en route from the Samoas to the Vava'u Group. During this season you may be able to crew on a yacht leaving 'Apia (Samoa) or Pago Pago (American Samoa) for Niuatoputapu.

A note of caution for arriving at the port: there is only one marker and two range sites (which are inaccurate by about 5m). If you get the range sites to line up you'll run aground! Again, see the Getting Around chapter for more information.

TAFAHI
area 3.4 sq km • pop 190
From the north coast of Niuatoputapu, the perfect cone of Tafahi dominates the view. If there were a search for an island fitting the description of the mythical Bali Hai, Tafahi would be a contender. One can't help gazing out across the water to Tafahi and wondering what it's like over there.

Tafahi, 9km north of Niuatoputapu, is an extinct volcanic cone 656m high, with a base area of 3.42 sq km. Vanilla and kava are grown in small quantities and the island sup-ports a permanent population of 150. Some of Tonga's best kava comes from this island.

If you get a very early start, you can climb to the crater and down in a day. An inter-mittent trail connecting the two landing sites, on the west and south sides of the island, leads up the relatively gradual north-

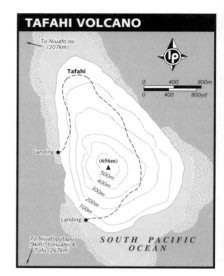

ern slope to within striking distance of the summit. At the crater on a clear day you can see the peak of Savaii's Mt Silisili (Samoa), which is 1850m high and over 200km dis-tant. Carry food and plenty of water.

Getting There & Away
The northern landing is the one that is used, but it's difficult – you can only come in on a wave, and only at high tide; the same for leaving. If the tide is with you, you can go over from Niuatoputapu in the morning and come back in the afternoon. The journey takes an hour, but you should arrange a price before departure – as much as T$80 has been demanded for a return trip.

Tafahi has only a primary school, so some families bring secondary school students from Tafahi over to Niuatoputapu on Mon-day and back to Tafahi again on Friday. You might catch a ride more cheaply if you can arrange to go with one of these boats.

NIUAFO'OU
area 50.3 sq km • pop 735
Niuafo'ou, also known as Tin Can Island, is the most remote island in Tonga, lying 640km north and slightly west of Tongatapu. The

name Tin Can Island was coined by a pre-WWII palangi resident, CS Ramsey, in honour of the island's unusual postal service. Since there was no anchorage or landing site on the island, mail and supplies for residents were sealed up in a biscuit tin and tossed overboard from a passing supply ship. Strong swimmers would retrieve the parcels. Outbound mail was tied to the end of metre-long sticks, and swimmers would carry them, balanced overhead, out to the waiting ship.

To most Tongans, Niuafo'ou is an enigma. They may have a vague idea of where it is but psychologically it is unimaginably far, like a Timbuktu or a Shangri-la. Such distant countries as Britain and Canada are more familiar to most Tongans than this remote corner of their home country. Perhaps for this reason, Niuafo'ou's inhabitants are credited with fortitude and often regarded with reverence by other Tongans. In 1852 Walter Lawry, an early missionary, wrote of the people of Niuafo'ou:

…they prefer a land vitrified and comparatively sterile, without water and having no harbour or landing-place and where the sea is generally very turbulent, because, they say, their fathers lived there before them and there they are buried.

Although it isn't as bleak as all that these days, a full third of the island consists of barren and impassable lava flows. Most of the island's water is contained in its large crater lakes and in a sulphur spring.

Very little English is spoken on Niuafo'ou, except for the island's government

The Niuafo'ou Megapode

A line in a popular song written by a lamenting Niuafo'ou exile goes: 'Megapodes, speak your mind while you're near to your burrows, else turn away without looking back...', referring to the Niuafo'ou megapode *(Megapodius pritchardii)*, locally known as *malau*, which is native only to this island.

This fascinating brown and grey bird subsists on seeds, insects, worms, fruit and even small geckos. Although it spends the days on the forest floor, at night it roosts in the treetops.

Pairs of megapodes usually inhabit a territory of about 2 hectares somewhere along the shores of Niuafo'ou's crater lakes, keeping track of each other with a sort of mating duet. When it's time to lay an egg, a megapode hen digs a burrow 1m to 2m deep in the loose volcanic soil near active steam vents (usually in the same place where she herself hatched).

In the burrow, she deposits a disproportionately large egg and covers it with earth, leaving it to incubate unattended in the naturally heated volcanic environment. A hen may lay up to 10 eggs, normally at intervals of about two weeks.

After around four weeks, the chicks hatch, and are then forced to make their own way to the surface. This gruelling job can take a couple of days. On the way to daylight, they are at risk from the long-legged ants which prey on newly hatched chicks by going for their eyes. When they finally emerge, they already bear a full coat of feathers and are able to fly and fend for themselves.

Owls and domestic cats prey on adult megapodes, but the greatest threat is from humans. People and their animals not only destroy the megapode's habitat, but locally megapode eggs and flesh are preferred to chicken. As a consequence, this incredible bird is threatened with extinction. At present, the Tongan Wildlife Centre (☎/fax 29449, e birdpark@kalianet.to) on Tongatapu is experimenting with transplanting chicks to the uninhabited volcanic island of Late in the Vava'u Group. If you would like further information, contact the centre or drop in (see Western Tongatapu in the Tongatapu Group chapter for details).

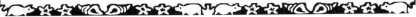

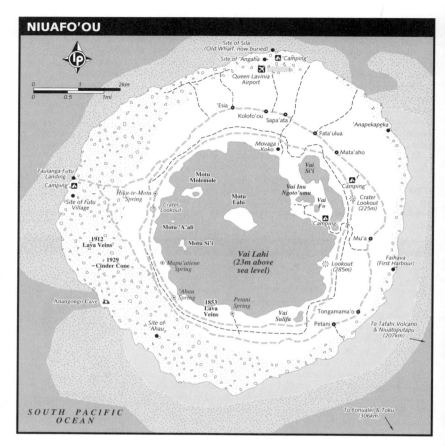

NIUAFO'OU

Site of Sila
(Old Wharf, now buried)
Site of 'Angaha
'Camping'
Queen Lavinia
Airport
'Esia
Kolofo'ou
Sapa'ata
'Anapekapeka
Fata'ulua
Movaga
Koko
Mata'aho
Taulanga Futu
Landing
'Camping'
Site of Futu
Village
Hiku-te-Motu
Spring
Motu
Molemole
Motu
Lahi
Vai
Si'i
Vai Inu
Ngoto'umu
Vai
Fo
'Camping'
Crater
Lookout
(225m)
Crater
Lookout
Motu 'A'ali
Motu Si'i
'Camping'
Mu'a
1912
Lava Veins
1929
Cinder Cone
Mapu'atiene
Spring
Vai Lahi
(23m above
sea level)
Lookout
(285m)
Faihava
(First Harbour)
Anangongo Cave
'Ahau
Spring
1853
Lava
Veins
Petani
Spring
Vai
Sulifa
Tongamama'o
To Tafahi Volcano
& Niuatoputapu
(207km)
Site of
'Ahau
Petani
SOUTH PACIFIC
OCEAN
To Fonualei & Toku
(306km)

workers and a couple of US Peace Corps volunteers stationed here. Niuafo'ou is the only island in Tonga that has a distinct dialect, one that's more akin to Samoan than to Tongan.

History

During the past 150 years, Niuafo'ou has experienced 10 major volcanic eruptions, causing the destruction of three villages. In the eruption of 1853 the village of 'Ahau on the south-west corner of the island was flattened by a lava flow, leaving this area the most wild and desolate part of the island. In the devastating eruption of 1929 the village of Futu on the western end of the island was buried beneath sea-bound lava. This area has been colonised again by a few hardy souls and serves as a very marginal landing site. In 1943 a particularly violent eruption destroyed plantations and decimated natural vegetation, causing a general famine.

The most significant eruption, however, certainly wasn't the worst. In September 1946, earthquakes and lava flows on the northern slope buried the erstwhile wharf and capital village of 'Angaha. There were no injuries due to the quick evacuation of the area, but the village of 'Angaha was destroyed and homes were levelled.

The government then debated whether 'Angaha, the seat of government, should be rebuilt or whether the entire island should be abandoned. Assuming community life could not continue without local government and that future eruptions could render the place uninhabitable anyway, Queen Salote decided evacuation was the answer. Beginning in late October, the reluctant islanders were shuttled by boat to Tongatapu and thence resettled on 'Eua.

The few recalcitrant inhabitants, 22 in number, who refused to leave during the general evacuation were forcefully collected in October 1947, and the island was then left uninhabited.

In 1958, after numerous petitions by homesick islanders, the government relented and allowed resettlement of Niuafo'ou, but refused government aid to anyone who returned. Two years later the island had a population of 345, which has grown steadily to reach over 700.

Visitors will find the Niuafo'ou people fiercely proud of their lonely island. In the words of one who was taken to 'Eua against his will and returned 14 years later: 'Here we intend to stay. If Niuafo'ou blows up again, however great the fire and danger, I shall never leave the island. I prefer to stay here and die.'

Geography
Geologically, the doughnut-shaped island is a collapsed volcanic cone. The island's land area consists of a caldera 5km in diameter encircled by new lava flows.

The crater is occupied almost completely by Vai Lahi (Big Lake, an appropriate name), a freshwater lake which contains four major islands: Motu Lahi (Big Island), Motu Si'i (Small Island) and Motu Molemole (Smooth Island), which has its own crater lake; the fourth island, Motu 'A'ali, appears above the surface only when the water level is low.

Three smaller lakes, Vai Si'i (Small Lake, also known as Vai Mata'aho after the nearby village), Vai Inu and Vai Fo, lie in the north-east corner of the crater separated from the big lake by sand hills covered in casuarina. One other significant lake, Vai Sulifa, also called Vai Kona (Poison Water), is a bubbling sulphur spring, found at the southern extreme. There are no significant water sources outside the crater.

It is thought that the volcano once reached an altitude of 1300m, but these days the highest point is only about 285m above sea level. Although there's been no obvious volcanic activity since 1946, the volcano is still classified as active.

The island is surrounded by open ocean – there is no coral reef around it, and no sandy beaches. People do not swim in the sea here; they swim in the lake, if at all.

Flora & Fauna
Niuafo'ou's most unusual inhabitant is the Niuafo'ou megapode (see the preceding boxed text). Apart from the beautiful barn owl *(lulu)*, the only other wildlife of note is the *lapila* fish (in English, the telapia fish) of the crater lakes. Like the megapode, the lapila is a staple of the local diet, but as yet there's no sign that it is endangered.

Information
Telephone service to Niuafo'ou commenced in 1998. Mail usually comes via aeroplane – one stops in once every three weeks – but if the plane is full, the mail will be left behind. Money can be changed at the Treasury.

Things to See & Do
Anyone fortunate enough to reach Niuafo'ou will undoubtedly just want to explore. There's a track leading right around the doughnut, which may be walked in about six hours at a leisurely pace. Even so, Niuafo'ou is worth more time. It's the sort of place you'd like to settle into for a month or two (if you miss the boat or plane, you may have to!) and try to grasp the remote appeal of this island.

One Niuafo'ou sight which must be seen is the splendid lake, **Vai Lahi**, which nearly fills the island's large and mysterious crater.

Along the southern and western shores is a vast, barren moonscape of **lava flows**. In the late 19th and early 20th centuries they oozed over the villages of 'Ahau and Futu, burying them completely.

Near the airport on the north shore, there is a variety of interesting features – mounds of volcanic slag, lava tubes, vents and craters – readily accessible from the main road. Beneath this flow is the village of 'Angaha, a sort of Tongan Pompeii.

Between Mu'a and Mata'aho, a trail leads up to a magnificent **viewpoint** looking out over Vai Si'i, Vai Lahi and the islands. Between Futu and 'Esia, another trail affords a view of the entire expanse of Vai Lahi. From Mu'a, a rough road crosses the sandy isthmus between the two major lakes and leads down to the shore of Vai Lahi.

All around the crater, small trails lead to interesting sites, including a bubbling sulphur spring and lava vents. The sulphur lake, **Vai Sulifa** (also called Vai Kona), is best reached from Petani village.

Places to Stay & Eat

There are numerous excellent *campsites* on the crater and beside the various lakes. Boil all lake water before drinking. In other areas, locals are normally happy to let you fill your water bottles from their rainwater tanks. Bear in mind, though, that camping is not the ordinary custom here and it will draw a lot of attention and curiosity. Many local people would be more than happy to take you in for a night, though a gift of corned beef or the like – even such staples as flour – would be greatly appreciated, as deliveries are rare and stocks run low.

Travellers have reported that Niuafo'ou's Catholic priest is happy to take in guests. Indeed, the *mission* sounds like a most pleasant place to stay and you can arrange meals and get a shower. A contribution to church funds would obviously be appropriate.

Several small *shops* are scattered through the villages, but they rarely have anything of interest, or anything at all, unless the boat has recently come in. Ordinarily, only local food is available, and there's not much variety. It's wise to bring all your food with you, if you can.

Getting There & Away

Due to its volcanic nature, Niuafo'ou lacks a decent anchorage or landing site, leaving access at the mercy of the wind and waves. Until the 1990s, Niuafo'ou was regarded as one of the least accessible inhabited islands in the world.

Air In theory, Royal Tongan Airlines flies into Niuafo'ou's Queen Lavinia Airport once a week. However, like air services to Niuatoputapu, it's a little unreliable and the same problems apply (see Getting There & Away in the Niuatoputapu section).

Landing at Niuafo'ou

Niuafo'ou has no anchorage and no wharf, and the entire island is exposed to the full wrath of the sea. Ships stop about 150m offshore and the crew drops two lines into the water, which are retrieved by swimmers and carried to the cement platform that serves as the landing site. Passengers, luggage and cargo are literally dropped or thrown into a wooden dory at an opportune moment and ferried ashore, where hulking Tongans wait to pluck them out of the rolling and pitching craft and deposit them on a platform.

Returning craft are filled nearly to the gunwales with copra. Oil drums and pens of squealing pigs are thrown (again, literally) on top of the sacks, and taro, yams, bananas and assorted produce are tucked in wherever there's space. Finally, passengers are heaped and balanced on top of all this paraphernalia! When only a few centimetres of freeboard remain and water is pouring into the boat – and the centre of gravity of the whole mess hovers at least 1m above the gunwales – the boats are shoved off through the surf. Passengers must constantly lean in one direction or another to prevent what would appear to be the imminent capsize of the vessel. On arrival at the ship, all passengers, pigs and other cargo are rolled, herded and pitched aboard.

There is no flight between Niuafo'ou and Niuatoputapu. See the Getting Around chapter for more information.

Boat Getting to Niuafo'ou by boat is a fraught business – not only because of the gruelling boat ride up here, but also the landing (see the boxed text). And if the weather isn't at its best, the boat must turn around and leave without stopping.

See Getting There & Away in the Niuatoputapu section and the Getting Around chapter for further information about the monthly boat service to the island.

Language

Tongan belongs to the Austronesian family of languages which includes other Polynesian languages such as Samoan, Hawaiian, Maori and Tahitian, as well as Malay, Malagasy and Melanesian languages. This connection forms the most solid basis for the accepted theory that the Polynesian peoples originated in South-East Asia.

The same Tongan language is spoken on all the islands in Tonga, with one exception: on Niuafo'ou, the most north-westerly island, a dialect which is closer to Samoan is spoken.

Since their language is spoken only in Tonga, the Tongans are both pleased and surprised when foreigners make an attempt to speak it at all.

Pronunciation

The Tongan alphabet has only 16 letters, with five vowels and 11 consonants.

It's worth listening to the way native speakers pronounce vowels because vowel length can affect the meaning of some words. You may see vowels written with a macron or *toloi* (eg, ā), which indicates that they are long. The long sound is simply an extended and accented (stressed) version of the short vowel. Stress is placed on the next to last syllable in most Tongan words, unless there's a long vowel, in which case that syllable receives the stress.

Another important element of Tongan language is the glottal stop, represented by an apostrophe ('). It signals a momentary halt in the flow of air through the vocal cords, similar to the non-voice between the syllables of 'uh-oh'.

Diphthongs, or combinations of vowels, are pronounced by enunciating each of the component sounds individually. When a glottal stop is inserted between two vowels, a stop must be made in the pronunciation. This, too, is a significant element of Tongan language that changes not only the pronunciation but also the meaning of words: for

example, *tae* means 'cough', but *ta'e* means 'faeces'! *Hau* means 'earring', but *ha'u* means 'come here'.

Even if you do mistake the pronunciation of glottal stops, and long and short vowels, Tongan people are usually helpful about it and they'll still try to understand what you're saying.

The letters used in the Tongan alphabet are pronounced more or less as follows:

Vowels

a   as in 'far' or as in 'ball'
e   as in 'end'
i   as in 'Fifi'
o   as in 'go'
u   as in 'tune'

Consonants

f   as in 'far'
h   as in 'here'
k   as the 'c' in 'curd'
l   as in 'love', with a slap of the tongue
m   as in 'me'
n   as in 'no'
ng as in 'singer', not as in 'finger'
p   midway between the 'p' in 'park' and the 'b' in 'bark'
s   as in 'sand'
t   midway between the 't' in 'tip' and the 'd' in 'dip'
v   as in 'very'

Pronouns

I/mine	*koau/'a'aku*
you/yours	*ko koe/'a'au*
he, she, it	*ia*
we/ours	*'oku mau/mautolou*
you/yours (plural)	*ko moutolu/ko moua*
they	*'oku nau/nautolu*

Basics

Hello.	*Malo e lelei.*
Goodbye.	*'Alu a.* (to someone leaving)
	Nofo a. (response to someone staying)

Good morning. *Malo e lelei ki he pongipongini.*
Good evening. *Malo e lelei ki he efiafini.*
Welcome. *Talitali fiefia.*
Yes. *'Io.*
No. *'Ikai.*
Maybe. *Mahalo pe.*
Please. *Faka molemole.*
Thank you *Malo ('aupito).*
(very much).
You're welcome. *'Io malo.*
How are you? *Fefe hake?*
Fine, thank you. *Sai pe, malo.*
Excuse me. *Kataki.*
I'm sorry *Faka molemole'iau.*
(forgive me).

Language Difficulties
I understand. *'Oku mahino kiate 'au.*
I don't understand. *'Oku ikai ke mahino kiate 'au.*
Do you speak *'Oku ke lava 'o lea*
English? *faka palangi?*
Does anyone speak *'Oku 'iai ha taha'oku*
English? *lea faka palangi?*

Small Talk
What's your name? *Ko hai ho hingoa?*
My name is ... *Ko hoku hingoa ko ...*
Where are you *Ko ho'o ha'u mei fe*
from? *fonua?*
I'm from ... *Ko 'eku ha'u mei ...*
How old are you? *Koe ha ho ta'u motua?*
I'm ... years old. *'Oku 'ou ta'u ... ta'u motua.*
Are you married? *Kuo ke'osi mali?*

I'm a ... *Ko 'eku ha'u ...*
  tourist *eve'eva*
  student *taha ako*

Do you like ...? *'Oku ke sai'ia 'ihe ...?*
I like it very much. *'Oku 'ou sai'ia 'aupito.*
I don't like ... *'Oku ikai teu sai'ia ...*
Just a minute. *Tali si'i.*
May I? *Faka molemole kau?*
It's all right/ *'Io 'oku sai/sai pe ia.*
  no problem.

How do you say ...? *Koe ha ho lea ...?*
What is this called? *Ko 'e ha hono hingoa 'o 'e me'a ko 'eni?*
Miss/Mrs/Mr *ta'ahine/fine'eiki/ tangata'eiki*
man *tangata*
woman *fefine*
boy *tamasi'i*
girl *ta'ahine*

Getting Around
I want to go to ... *'Oku ou fie 'alu ki ...*
I want to book a *'Oku 'ou fiemau hoku*
  seat for ... *nofo anga ki he ...*
How long does *Koe ha 'ae loloa o e*
  the trip take? *folau?*
Where is the ... to *Ko fe'ia ... ki*
  (Vava'u)? *(Vava'u)?*

What time does *Koe ha taime'oe ... 'e*
the ... leave/arrive? *'alu ai/foki mai?*
Where does the ... *Ko fe feitu'a ... 'oku*
leave from? *'alu mei ai?*
  aeroplane *vakapuna*
  boat *vaka*
  bus *koe pasi*
  canoe *koe papao*
  ferry *vaka foko tu'u*

one-way (ticket) *'alu pe* or *ha'u pe (tikite)*
return (ticket) *'alu moe ha'u (tikite)*
ticket *tikite*
ticket office *loki faka tau tikite*
timetable *taimi tepile*

I'd like to hire a ... *'Oku o'u fiema'u ho'o ...*
  bicycle *pasikala*
  car *ka*
  guide *faka 'eve'eva'i*
  horse *hoosi*
  motorcycle *paiki*

Directions
Where is ...? *Ko fe'ia a'e ...?*
How do I get to ...? *Teu 'alu fefe ki ...?*
Is it near/far? *'Oku 'ofi/mama'o?*
Where is the toilet? *Ko fe 'a e fale malolo?*
How far is it to ...? *Ko 'e ha hono mama'o 'o ... mei heni?*

Signs

Teu hu i fe (**Hu'anga**)	**Entrance**
Hu'anga ki tu'a	**Exit**
Fakamatala	**Information**
'Oku ava	**Open**
'Oku tapuni	**Closed**
Tapu	**Prohibited**
Polisi	**Police**
Fale Polisi	**Police Station**
Fale malolo	**Toilets**
Tangata	**Men**
Fefine	**Women**

Stop/Go.	*Tu'u/'Alu.*
(Go) straight ahead.	*('Alu) hangatonu ai pe.*
Turn left.	*Afe to'ohema.*
Turn right.	*Afe to'omata'u.*

at the ... corner	*'i he ... tafa'aki*
next	*hoko*
second	*fika ua*
third	*fika tolu*

behind	*'i mui*
opposite	*fehangahangai*
up	*'olunga*
down	*lalo*
here	*heni*
there	*he*
everywhere	*fetu'u kotoa pe*
north	*tokelau*
south	*tonga*
east	*hahake*
west	*hihifo*

street/road	*hala*
suburb	*lotokolo*
village	*kolo si'i si'i*

Around Town

bank	*pangike*
bridge	*hala kavakava*
church	*fale lotu*
city centre	*i loto kolo*
currency exchange	*'ofisi vete pa'anga*
embassy	*'api 'oe 'amipasitoa*
hospital	*fale mahaki*
market	*maketi*
palace	*palasi*
post office	*positi 'ofisi*
restaurant	*fale kai*
telephone office	*fale telefoni*
tourist office	*'ofisi taki mamata*

When do you open/ close?	*Temou ava/tapuni he fiha?*
I want to make a telephone call.	*'Oku 'ou fie ma'u keu telefoni.*
I'd like to change some money/ travellers cheques.	*'Oku 'ou fiema'u kefetongi 'eku silini/ sieke.*

beach	*matatahi*
island	*motu*
lake	*ano vai*
ocean (deep)	*moana*
rain	*'uha*
ruins	*maumau*
sea	*tahi*
sun	*la'a*
tower	*taua*
wind	*matangi*

Accommodation

guesthouse	*fale nofo totongi*
hotel	*hotele*
shower	*saoa*

Where can I find a place to stay?	*Ko e fe ha feitu'u lava 'o nofo ai?*

Do you have a ... available?	*'Oku 'iai ha'o ... 'ata'ata'a?*
bed	*mohe'anga*
cheap room	*loki ma'ama'a*
single room	*mohenga toko taha*
double room	*mohenga toko ua*

for one night	*po e taha*
for two nights	*po e ua*

How much is it per (night/person)?	*'Oku fiha 'ae (po e taha/ki he toko taha)?*
Is breakfast included?	*'Oku kau ai e kai pongopongi?*
Can I see the room?	*Teu lava'o sio?*

Do you have hot water?	*'Oku 'iai ha'o vai mafana?*
Do you have a clean sheet?	*'Oku 'iai ha'o kafu ma'a?*
I'm/We're leaving now.	*Teu/Te mau 'alu he taimi ni.*

Shopping

I'm looking for ...	*Ko 'eku kumi ...*
the chemist	*fale talatalavai*
clothing	*vala*
souvenirs	*mea'ofa*

Where can I buy ...?	*Teu fakatau mei fe ha ...?*
How much does it cost?	*Fiha hono totongi?*
I'd like to buy it.	*'Oku ou fie fakatau ia.*
It's too expensive for me.	*Fu'u mamafa kiate au.*
Can I look at it?	*Teu sio ki ai?*
I'm just looking.	*'Oku ou siosio pe.*
Do you take travellers cheques?	*'Oku ke tali 'ae sieki?*
Do you have another colour/ size?	*'Oku i'ai hao toe lanu/fika?*
How much?	*'Oku fiha?*
How many?	*Ko e me'a 'e fiha?*

big/bigger	*lahi/lahi ange*
small/smaller	*si'i si'i/si'i si'i ange*
more	*lahi*
less	*si'i*
expensive	*mamafa*
cheap/cheaper	*ma'ama'a/ma'a ma'a ange*
good	*lelei*
bad	*kovi*
pretty	*faka 'ofa 'ofa*

Food

| I'm hungry/thirsty. | *'Oku o'u fiekaia/ fieinua.* |

breakfast	*kai pongipongi*
lunch	*kai ho'ata*
dinner	*kai efiafi*
set menu	*koe ha ho'o mou u me'a kai*

food stall	*kai tepile*
grocery store	*fale koloa*
market	*maketi*
restaurant	*fale kai*
supermarket	*supamaketi*
bread	*ma*
chicken	*moa*
eggs	*fo'ai moa*
fish	*'ika*
food	*me'akai*
fruit	*fo'i 'akau*
meat	*kakano'i manu*
pepper	*polo*
pork	*puaka*
salt	*masima*
soup	*supo*
sugar	*suka*
vegetables	*vesitapolo*

beer	*pia*
coffee	*kofi*
milk	*hu'akau*
mineral water	*hina vai (sota)*
tea	*ti*
wine	*uaine*

hot	*vela*
cold	*momoko*
with	*teu 'aimoe*
without	*he'ikai teu 'ai*

Time & Dates

| What time is it? | *Koe ha e taimi ko 'eni?* |

It's ... (o'clock).	*Koe hoko e ...*
1.15	*taha tahanima*
1.30	*taha tolu noa*
1.45	*taha fa nima*

When? (past)	*'Anefe?*
When? (future)	*'Afe?*
today	*'ahoni*
tonight	*'apo*
tomorrow	*'apongipongi*
day after tomorrow	*'aho 'osi 'apongipongi*
yesterday	*'ane'afi*
all day	*'aho kotoa*
every day	*'aho kotoape*
in the morning	*taimi pongipongi*
in the evening	*taimi 'efi'afi*

Monday	*Monite*
Tuesday	*Tusite*
Wednesday	*Pulelulu*
Thursday	*Tuapulelulu*
Friday	*Falaite*
Saturday	*Tokanaki*
Sunday	*Sapate*

January	*Sanuali*
February	*Fepueli*
March	*Ma'asi*
April	*'Epeleli*
May	*Me*
June	*Sune*
July	*Siulai*
August	*'Akosi*
September	*Sepitema*
October	*'Okatopa*
November	*Novema*
December	*Tisema*

Health

I'm ...	*Koau 'oku o'u ...*
asthmatic	*mahaki hela*
diabetic	*suka*
epileptic	*mahaki moa*
Don't give me penicillin/ antibiotics.	*'Oua e 'omai ae penisilini/antibiotics kia au.*
antiseptic	*faito'o tamate siemu*
aspirin	*'asipilini*
condoms	*konitomu*
contraceptive	*mea ta 'ofi fanau*
diarrhoea	*fakalele*
medicine	*foi akau*
nausea	*tokakovi*
sunblock cream	*kilimi la'a*
tampons	*hafe*

Numbers

1	*taha*
2	*ua*
3	*tolu*
4	*fa*
5	*nima*
6	*ono*
7	*fitu*
8	*valu*
9	*hiva*
10	*hongofulu*

Emergencies

Help!	*Tokoni!*
Call a doctor!	*Ui ha toketa!*
Call the police!	*Ui ha polisi!*
Go away!	*'Alu mama'o!*

11	*taha taha* (or *hongofulu ma taha*)
12	*taha ua* (or *hongofulu ma ua*)
13	*taha tolu* (or *hongofulu ma tolu*)
14	*taha fa* (or *hongofulu ma fa*)
15	*taha nima* (or *hongofulu ma nima*)
16	*taha ono* (or *hongofulu ma ono*)
17	*taha fitu* (or *hongofulu ma fitu*)
18	*taha valu* (or *hongofulu ma valu*)
19	*taha hiva* (or *hongofulu ma hiva*)
20	*uanoa* (or *uafulu*)
21	*uanoa taha* (or *uafulu ma taha*)
30	*tolunoa* (or *tolungofulu*)
40	*fanoa* (or *fangofulu*)
50	*nimanoa* (or *nimangofulu*)
60	*ononoa* (or *'onongofulu*)
70	*fitunoa* (or *fitungofulu*)
80	*valunoa* (or *valungofulu*)
90	*hivanoa* (or *hivangofulu*)
100	*teau*
101	*teau taha*
110	*teau hongofulu*
200	*uangeau*
300	*tolungeau*
1000	*tahaafe*
1001	*tahaafe taha*
10,000	*tahamano*
11,000	*tahamano tahaafe*
12,000	*tahamano uaafe*
20,000	*uamano*
100,000	*tahakilu*
200,000	*uakilu*
one million	*tahamiliona*

Glossary

ahi – sandalwood
'alo – son or daughter
'api – plantation of 3.34 hectares
ATM – automated teller machine

'esi – resting site or mound

fa'e – mother
faikakai – breadfruit pudding
faka Tonga – the 'Tongan way'
fakaleiti – men who dress and behave as women
fakapale – custom of rewarding Tongan dancer with money; literally 'to award a prize'
fale – a traditional thatched house
fale koloa – small grocery kiosks
falekai – restaurant
feke – octopus
feta'aki – single piece of tapa cloth
fihu – valuable, silk-like pandanus mat
fingota – shellfish

heilala – Tonga's national flower

'ika – fish
'inasi – traditional Tongan agricultural fair or festival

kailao – war dance
kalia – large seafaring canoes
kava – intoxicating drink made from the root of the pepper shrub
kava kalapu – kava club
kiekie – decorative waist band with dangling strands of pandanus, seeds or cloth
kilikili – pumice-like volcanic gravel
koloa – wealth
kumala – sweet potato
kupesi – relief of tapa pattern

lafo – Tongan game played with pieces called *pa'anga*
lakalaka – a traditional dance
langanga – strips of tapa
langi – pyramidal stone tomb

mala'e – sacred area/field

malau – local name for the Niuafo'ou megapode, a bird native only to Niuafo'ou
mali – spouse
matapule – 'talking chief' involved in ceremonies and burial rituals of the nobility
Maui – demigod who, according to one myth, fished Tonga out of the sea
ma'ulu'ulu – dance performed at feasts and on public holidays
motu – coral islet

ngatu – decorated/finished *tapa* product

pa'anga – Tongan unit of currency (T$)
palangi – foreigner (originally *papalangi*)
peka – flying fox (or fruit bat)
pekepekatae – white-rumped swiftlets
popao – outrigger canoe

RTA – Royal Tongan Airlines

seniti – currency unit; 100 seniti equals T$1
sipi – mutton

tamai – father
ta'ovala – pandanus mat tied around the waist; worn on formal occasions
tapa – mulberry bark cloth
tapu – sacred
tau'olunga – graceful traditional dance performed by a solo woman at ceremonies
TCC – Tonga Communications Corporation
TCF – Tonga Cooperative Federation (supermarket)
tevolo – devil spirit
tiki – wooden statue representing old Polynesian god
toa – ironwood tree
tokoua – brother or sister, often used broadly to include cousins
Tu'i Tonga – royal title
tuitui – candlenut
tupenu – men's wraparound skirt which extends below the knees
TVB – Tongan Visitors Bureau

'umu – traditional underground oven

LONELY PLANET

ON THE ROAD

Travel Guides explore cities, regions and countries, and supply information on transport, restaurants and accommodation, covering all budgets. They come with reliable, easy-to-use maps, practical advice, cultural and historical facts and a rundown on attractions both on and off the beaten track. There are over 200 titles in this classic series, covering nearly every country in the world.

 Lonely Planet Upgrades extend the shelf life of existing travel guides by detailing any changes that may affect travel in a region since a book has been published. Upgrades can be downloaded for free from **www.lonelyplanet.com/upgrades**

For travellers with more time than money, **Shoestring** guides offer dependable, first-hand information with hundreds of detailed maps, plus insider tips for stretching money as far as possible. Covering entire continents in most cases, the six-volume shoestring guides are known around the world as 'backpackers bibles'.

For the discerning short-term visitor, **Condensed** guides highlight the best a destination has to offer in a full-colour, pocket-sized format designed for quick access. They include everything from top sights and walking tours to opinionated reviews of where to eat, stay, shop and have fun.

CitySync lets travellers use their Palm™ or Visor™ hand-held computers to guide them through a city with handy tips on transport, history, cultural life, major sights, and shopping and entertainment options. It can also quickly search and sort hundreds of reviews of hotels, restaurants and attractions, and pinpoint their location on scrollable street maps. CitySync can be downloaded from **www.citysync.com**

MAPS & ATLASES

Lonely Planet's **City Maps** feature downtown and metropolitan maps, as well as transit routes and walking tours. The maps come complete with an index of streets, a listing of sights and a plastic coat for extra durability.

Road Atlases are an essential navigation tool for serious travellers. Cross-referenced with the guidebooks, they also feature distance and climate charts and a complete site index.

LONELY PLANET

ESSENTIALS

Read This First books help new travellers to hit the road with confidence. These invaluable predeparture guides give step-by-step advice on preparing for a trip, budgeting, arranging a visa, planning an itinerary and staying safe while still getting off the beaten track.

Healthy Travel pocket guides offer a regional rundown on disease hot spots and practical advice on predeparture health measures, staying well on the road and what to do in emergencies. The guides come with a user-friendly design and helpful diagrams and tables.

Lonely Planet's **Phrasebooks** cover the essential words and phrases travellers need when they're strangers in a strange land. They come in a pocket-sized format with colour tabs for quick reference, extensive vocabulary lists, easy-to-follow pronunciation keys and two-way dictionaries.

Miffed by blurry photos of the Taj Mahal? Tired of the classic 'top of the head cut off' shot? **Travel Photography: A Guide to Taking Better Pictures** will help you turn ordinary holiday snaps into striking images and give you the know-how to capture every scene, from frenetic festivals to peaceful beach sunrises.

Lonely Planet's **Travel Journal** is a lightweight but sturdy travel diary for jotting down all those on-the-road observations and significant travel moments. It comes with a handy time-zone wheel, a world map and useful travel information.

Lonely Planet's eKno is an all-in-one communication service developed especially for travellers. It offers low-cost international calls and free email and voicemail so that you can keep in touch while on the road. Check it out on **www.ekno.lonelyplanet.com**

FOOD & RESTAURANT GUIDES

Lonely Planet's **Out to Eat** guides recommend the brightest and best places to eat and drink in top international cities. These gourmet companions are arranged by neighbourhood, packed with dependable maps, garnished with scene-setting photos and served with quirky features.

For people who live to eat, drink and travel, **World Food** guides explore the culinary culture of each country. Entertaining and adventurous, each guide is packed with detail on staples and specialities, regional cuisine and local markets, as well as sumptuous recipes, comprehensive culinary dictionaries and lavish photos good enough to eat.

OUTDOOR GUIDES

For those who believe the best way to see the world is on foot, Lonely Planet's **Walking Guides** detail everything from family strolls to difficult treks, with 'when to go and how to do it' advice supplemented by reliable maps and essential travel information.

Cycling Guides map a destination's best bike tours, long and short, in day-by-day detail. They contain all the information a cyclist needs, including advice on bike maintenance, places to eat and stay, innovative maps with detailed cues to the rides, and elevation charts.

The **Watching Wildlife** series is perfect for travellers who want authoritative information but don't want to tote a heavy field guide. Packed with advice on where, when and how to view a region's wildlife, each title features photos of over 300 species and contains engaging comments on the local flora and fauna.

With underwater colour photos throughout, **Pisces Books** explore the world's best diving and snorkelling areas. Each book contains listings of diving services and dive resorts, detailed information on depth, visibility and difficulty of dives, and a roundup of the marine life you're likely to see through your mask.

OFF THE ROAD

Journeys, the travel literature series written by renowned travel authors, capture the spirit of a place or illuminate a culture with a journalist's attention to detail and a novelist's flair for words. These are tales to soak up while you're actually on the road or dip into as an at-home armchair indulgence.

The range of lavishly illustrated **Pictorial** books is just the ticket for both travellers and dreamers. Off-beat tales and vivid photographs bring the adventure of travel to your doorstep long before the journey begins and long after it is over.

Lonely Planet **Videos** encourage the same independent, tough-minded approach as the guidebooks. Currently airing throughout the world, this award-winning series features innovative footage and an original soundtrack.

Yes, we know, work is tough, so do a little bit of deskside dreaming with the spiral-bound Lonely Planet **Diary** or a Lonely Planet **Wall Calendar**, filled with great photos from around the world.

TRAVELLERS NETWORK

Lonely Planet Online. Lonely Planet's award-winning Web site has insider information on hundreds of destinations, from Amsterdam to Zimbabwe, complete with interactive maps and relevant links. The site also offers the latest travel news, recent reports from travellers on the road, guidebook upgrades, a travel links site, an online book-buying option and a lively travellers bulletin board. It can be viewed at **www.lonelyplanet.com** or AOL keyword: lp.

Planet Talk is a quarterly print newsletter, full of gossip, advice, anecdotes and author articles. It provides an antidote to the being-at-home blues and lets you plan and dream for the next trip. Contact the nearest Lonely Planet office for your free copy.

Comet, the free Lonely Planet newsletter, comes via email once a month. It's loaded with travel news, advice, dispatches from authors, travel competitions and letters from readers. To subscribe, click on the Comet subscription link on the front page of the Web site.

Lonely Planet Guides by Region

L onely Planet is known worldwide for publishing practical, reliable and no-nonsense travel information in our guides and on our Web site. The Lonely Planet list covers just about every accessible part of the world. Currently there are 16 series: Travel guides, Shoestring guides, Condensed guides, Phrasebooks, Read This First, Healthy Travel, Walking guides, Cycling guides, Watching Wildlife guides, Pisces Diving & Snorkeling guides, City Maps, Road Atlases, Out to Eat, World Food, Journeys travel literature and Pictorials.

AFRICA Africa on a shoestring • Botswana • Cairo • Cairo City Map • Cape Town • Cape Town City Map • East Africa • Egypt • Egyptian Arabic phrasebook • Ethiopia, Eritrea & Djibouti • Ethiopian Amharic phrasebook • The Gambia & Senegal • Healthy Travel Africa • Kenya • Malawi • Morocco • Moroccan Arabic phrasebook • Mozambique • Namibia • Read This First: Africa • South Africa, Lesotho & Swaziland • Southern Africa • Southern Africa Road Atlas • Swahili phrasebook • Tanzania, Zanzibar & Pemba • Trekking in East Africa • Tunisia • Watching Wildlife East Africa • Watching Wildlife Southern Africa • West Africa • World Food Morocco • Zambia • Zimbabwe, Botswana & Namibia
Travel Literature: Mali Blues: Traveling to an African Beat • The Rainbird: A Central African Journey • Songs to an African Sunset: A Zimbabwean Story

AUSTRALIA & THE PACIFIC Aboriginal Australia & the Torres Strait Islands •Auckland • Australia • Australian phrasebook • Australia Road Atlas • Cycling Australia • Cycling New Zealand • Fiji • Fijian phrasebook • Healthy Travel Australia, NZ & the Pacific • Islands of Australia's Great Barrier Reef • Melbourne • Melbourne City Map • Micronesia • New Caledonia • New South Wales • New Zealand • Northern Territory • Outback Australia • Out to Eat – Melbourne • Out to Eat – Sydney • Papua New Guinea • Pidgin phrasebook • Queensland • Rarotonga & the Cook Islands • Samoa • Solomon Islands • South Australia • South Pacific • South Pacific phrasebook • Sydney • Sydney City Map • Sydney Condensed • Tahiti & French Polynesia • Tasmania • Tonga • Tramping in New Zealand • Vanuatu • Victoria • Walking in Australia • Watching Wildlife Australia • Western Australia
Travel Literature: Islands in the Clouds: Travels in the Highlands of New Guinea • Kiwi Tracks: A New Zealand Journey • Sean & David's Long Drive

CENTRAL AMERICA & THE CARIBBEAN Bahamas, Turks & Caicos • Baja California • Belize, Guatemala & Yucatán • Bermuda • Central America on a shoestring • Costa Rica • Costa Rica Spanish phrasebook • Cuba • Cycling Cuba • Dominican Republic & Haiti • Eastern Caribbean • Guatemala • Havana • Healthy Travel Central & South America • Jamaica • Mexico • Mexico City • Panama • Puerto Rico • Read This First: Central & South America • Virgin Islands • World Food Caribbean • World Food Mexico • Yucatán
Travel Literature: Green Dreams: Travels in Central America

EUROPE Amsterdam • Amsterdam City Map • Amsterdam Condensed • Andalucía • Athens • Austria • Baltic States phrasebook • Barcelona • Barcelona City Map • Belgium & Luxembourg • Berlin • Berlin City Map • Britain • British phrasebook • Brussels, Bruges & Antwerp • Brussels City Map • Budapest • Budapest City Map • Canary Islands • Catalunya & the Costa Brava • Central Europe • Central Europe phrasebook • Copenhagen • Corfu & the Ionians • Corsica • Crete • Crete Condensed • Croatia • Cycling Britain • Cycling France • Cyprus • Czech & Slovak Republics • Czech phrasebook • Denmark • Dublin • Dublin City Map • Dublin Condensed • Eastern Europe • Eastern Europe phrasebook • Edinburgh • Edinburgh City Map • England • Estonia, Latvia & Lithuania • Europe on a shoestring • Europe phrasebook • Finland • Florence • Florence City Map • France • Frankfurt City Map • Frankfurt Condensed • French phrasebook • Georgia, Armenia & Azerbaijan • Germany • German phrasebook • Greece • Greek Islands • Greek phrasebook • Hungary • Iceland, Greenland & the Faroe Islands • Ireland • Italian phrasebook • Italy • Kraków • Lisbon • The Loire • London • London City Map • London Condensed • Madrid • Madrid City Map • Malta • Mediterranean Europe • Milan, Turin & Genoa • Moscow • Munich • Netherlands • Normandy • Norway • Out to Eat – London • Out to Eat – Paris • Paris • Paris City Map • Paris Condensed • Poland • Polish phrasebook • Portugal • Portuguese phrasebook • Prague • Prague City Map • Provence & the Côte d'Azur • Read This First: Europe • Rhodes & the Dodecanese • Romania & Moldova • Rome • Rome City Map • Rome Condensed • Russia, Ukraine & Belarus • Russian phrasebook • Scandinavian & Baltic Europe • Scandinavian phrasebook • Scotland • Sicily • Slovenia • South-West France • Spain • Spanish phrasebook • Stockholm • St Petersburg • St Petersburg City Map • Sweden • Switzerland • Tuscany • Ukrainian phrasebook • Venice • Vienna • Wales • Walking in Britain • Walking in France • Walking in Ireland • Walking in Italy • Walking in Scotland • Walking in Spain • Walking in Switzerland • Western Europe • World Food France • World Food Greece • World Food Ireland • World Food Italy • World Food Spain **Travel Literature:** After Yugoslavia • Love and War in the Apennines • The Olive Grove: Travels in Greece • On the Shores of the Mediterranean • Round Ireland in Low Gear • A Small Place in Italy

Lonely Planet Mail Order

Lonely Planet products are distributed worldwide. They are also available by mail order from Lonely Planet, so if you have difficulty finding a title please write to us. North and South American residents should write to 150 Linden St, Oakland, CA 94607, USA; European and African residents should write to 10a Spring Place, London NW5 3BH, UK; and residents of other countries to Locked Bag 1, Footscray, Victoria 3011, Australia.

INDIAN SUBCONTINENT & THE INDIAN OCEAN Bangladesh • Bengali phrasebook • Bhutan • Delhi • Goa • Healthy Travel Asia & India • Hindi & Urdu phrasebook • India • India & Bangladesh City Map • Indian Himalaya • Karakoram Highway • Kathmandu City Map • Kerala • Madagascar • Maldives • Mauritius, Réunion & Seychelles • Mumbai (Bombay) • Nepal • Nepali phrasebook • North India • Pakistan • Rajasthan • Read This First: Asia & India • South India • Sri Lanka • Sri Lanka phrasebook • Tibet • Tibetan phrasebook • Trekking in the Indian Himalaya • Trekking in the Karakoram & Hindukush • Trekking in the Nepal Himalaya • World Food India **Travel Literature:** The Age of Kali: Indian Travels and Encounters • Hello Goodnight: A Life of Goa • In Rajasthan • Maverick in Madagascar • A Season in Heaven: True Tales from the Road to Kathmandu • Shopping for Buddhas • A Short Walk in the Hindu Kush • Slowly Down the Ganges

MIDDLE EAST & CENTRAL ASIA Bahrain, Kuwait & Qatar • Central Asia • Central Asia phrasebook • Dubai • Farsi (Persian) phrasebook • Hebrew phrasebook • Iran • Israel & the Palestinian Territories • Istanbul • Istanbul City Map • Istanbul to Cairo • Istanbul to Kathmandu • Jerusalem • Jerusalem City Map • Jordan • Lebanon • Middle East • Oman & the United Arab Emirates • Syria • Turkey • Turkish phrasebook • World Food Turkey • Yemen **Travel Literature:** Black on Black: Iran Revisited • Breaking Ranks: Turbulent Travels in the Promised Land • The Gates of Damascus • Kingdom of the Film Stars: Journey into Jordan

NORTH AMERICA Alaska • Boston • Boston City Map • Boston Condensed • British Columbia • California & Nevada • California Condensed • Canada • Chicago • Chicago City Map • Chicago Condensed • Florida • Georgia & the Carolinas • Great Lakes • Hawaii • Hiking in Alaska • Hiking in the USA • Honolulu & Oahu City Map • Las Vegas • Los Angeles • Los Angeles City Map • Louisiana & the Deep South • Miami • Miami City Map • Montreal • New England • New Orleans • New Orleans City Map • New York City • New York City City Map • New York City Condensed • New York, New Jersey & Pennsylvania • Oahu • Out to Eat – San Francisco • Pacific Northwest • Rocky Mountains • San Diego & Tijuana • San Francisco • San Francisco City Map • Seattle • Seattle City Map • Southwest • Texas • Toronto • USA • USA phrasebook • Vancouver • Vancouver City Map • Virginia & the Capital Region • Washington, DC • Washington, DC City Map • World Food New Orleans **Travel Literature:** Caught Inside: A Surfer's Year on the California Coast • Drive Thru America

NORTH-EAST ASIA Beijing • Beijing City Map • Cantonese phrasebook • China • Hiking in Japan • Hong Kong & Macau • Hong Kong City Map • Hong Kong Condensed • Japan • Japanese phrasebook • Korea • Korean phrasebook • Kyoto • Mandarin phrasebook • Mongolia • Mongolian phrasebook • Seoul • Shanghai • South-West China • Taiwan • Tokyo • Tokyo Condensed • World Food Hong Kong • World Food Japan **Travel Literature:** In Xanadu: A Quest • Lost Japan

SOUTH AMERICA Argentina, Uruguay & Paraguay • Bolivia • Brazil • Brazilian phrasebook • Buenos Aires • Buenos Aires City Map • Chile & Easter Island • Colombia • Ecuador & the Galapagos Islands • Healthy Travel Central & South America • Latin American Spanish phrasebook • Peru • Quechua phrasebook • Read This First: Central & South America • Rio de Janeiro • Rio de Janeiro City Map • Santiago de Chile • South America on a shoestring • Trekking in the Patagonian Andes • Venezuela **Travel Literature:** Full Circle: A South American Journey

SOUTH-EAST ASIA Bali & Lombok • Bangkok • Bangkok City Map • Burmese phrasebook • Cambodia • Cycling Vietnam, Laos & Cambodia • East Timor phrasebook • Hanoi • Healthy Travel Asia & India • Hill Tribes phrasebook • Ho Chi Minh City (Saigon) • Indonesia • Indonesian phrasebook • Indonesia's Eastern Islands • Java • Lao phrasebook • Laos • Malay phrasebook • Malaysia, Singapore & Brunei • Myanmar (Burma) • Philippines • Pilipino (Tagalog) phrasebook • Read This First: Asia & India • Singapore • Singapore City Map • South-East Asia on a shoestring • South-East Asia phrasebook • Thailand • Thailand's Islands & Beaches • Thailand, Vietnam, Laos & Cambodia Road Atlas • Thai phrasebook • Vietnam • Vietnamese phrasebook • World Food Indonesia • World Food Thailand • World Food Vietnam

ALSO AVAILABLE: Antarctica • The Arctic • The Blue Man: Tales of Travel, Love and Coffee • Brief Encounters: Stories of Love, Sex & Travel • Buddhist Stupas in Asia: The Shape of Perfection • Chasing Rickshaws • The Last Grain Race • Lonely Planet ... On the Edge: Adventurous Escapades from Around the World • Lonely Planet Unpacked • Lonely Planet Unpacked Again • Not the Only Planet: Science Fiction Travel Stories • Ports of Call: A Journey by Sea • Sacred India • Travel Photography: A Guide to Taking Better Pictures • Travel with Children • Tuvalu: Portrait of an Island Nation

LONELY PLANET

You already know that Lonely Planet produces more than this one guidebook, but you might not be aware of the other products we have on this region. Here is a selection of titles that you may want to check out as well:

**Time & Tide -
The Islands of Tuvalu**
ISBN 1 86450 342 4
US$19.99 • UK£12.99

**Healthy Travel Australia,
NZ & the Pacific**
ISBN 1 86450 052 2
US$5.95 • UK£3.99

Tahiti & French Polynesia
ISBN 0 86442 725 5
US$17.99 • UK£11.99

South Pacific
ISBN 0 86442 717 4
US$24.95 • UK£15.99

South Pacific phrasebook
ISBN 0 86442 595 3
US$6.95 • UK£4.99

Fiji
ISBN 0 86442 679 8
US$15.99 • UK£9.99

New Zealand
ISBN 1 86450 122 7
US$21.99 • UK£13.99

Samoa
ISBN 0 86442 555 4
US$14.95 • UK£8.99

Diving & Snorkeling Fiji
ISBN 0 86442 771 9
US$16.99 • UK£10.99

**Diving & Snorkeling
Tahiti & French Polynesia**
ISBN 1 86450 071 9
US$16.99 • UK£10.99

**Available wherever books
are sold**

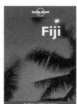

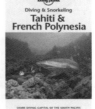

Index

Text

Bold indicates maps.

Boxed Text

MAP LEGEND

CITY ROUTES

Freeway .... Freeway	= = = = ... Unsealed Road
Highway ... Primary Road	.... One Way Street
Road ... Secondary Road	.... Pedestrian Street
Street .... Street	⊏⊐⊏⊐⊐ ... Stepped Street
Lane .... Lane	⇒= = ... Tunnel
.... On/Off Ramp	.... Footbridge

REGIONAL ROUTES

= = = = ... 4WD Track
.... Primary Road
.... Secondary Road
.... Minor Road

BOUNDARIES

▬·▬·▬·· .... International
▬··▬··▬·· .... State
— — — .... Disputed
◂▬▬▬ .... Fortified Wall

HYDROGRAPHY

.... River, Creek
.... Lagoon
.... Lake
.... Marine Reserve
⊙ .... Spring; Rapids
⊣⊢⧫ .... Waterfalls

TRANSPORT ROUTES & STATIONS

⊢—○— .... Train
⊢ + + + ⊢ ... Underground Train
▬●▬ .... Metro
▬ ▬ ▬ .... Tramway
⊩—⊪—⊪ ... Cable Car, Chairlift

----▣ .... Ferry
- - - - - ... Walking Trail
· · · · · · · · · ... Walking Tour
.... Path
▬▬▬ .... Pier or Jetty

AREA FEATURES

.... Building
⊕ .... Park, Gardens
.... Market
.... Reef
.... Beach
.... Cemetery
.... Cliff
200m
100m .... Contours

POPULATION SYMBOLS

✪ **CAPITAL** .... National Capital	● **CITY** .... City	◉ Village .... Village
⊙ **CAPITAL** .... State Capital	● Town .... Town	.... Urban Area

MAP SYMBOLS

■ .... Place to Stay   ▼ .... Place to Eat   ● .... Point of Interest

✠ ☒ ..... Airfield, Airport	⌂ .... Cave	☀ .... Lighthouse	⊡ ⊟ ... Post Office, Internet
⊕ .... Anchorage	⬒ .... Chalet or Hut	☼ .... Lookout	⊻ ⚘ ... Shipwreck, Trailhead
▣ .. Archaeological Site	ⅱ ⊞ .... Church	▲ .... Monument	⊠ .... Shopping Centre
⊖ .... Bank	⊠ ⊡ Dive Site, Snorkelling	▲ ▲ .. Mountain, Volcano	⊠ .... Swimming Pool
⊟ ⊡ ... Bus Stop/Terminal	⊡ .... Embassy	⊞ .... Museum	⊠ ⊟ ..... Taxi, Transport
⬕ ..... Camping Ground	⊕ .... Golf Course	⊙ .... Petrol Station	⊠ ⊙ .. Telephone, Toilet
⚏ .... Caravan Park	⊕ .... Hospital	⊞ .... Police Station	❶ .. Tourist Information

Note: not all symbols displayed above appear in this book

LONELY PLANET OFFICES

Australia
Locked Bag 1, Footscray, Victoria 3011
☎ 03 8379 8000 fax 03 8379 8111
email: talk2us@lonelyplanet.com.au

USA
150 Linden St, Oakland, CA 94607
☎ 510 893 8555 TOLL FREE: 800 275 8555
fax 510 893 8572
email: info@lonelyplanet.com

UK
10a Spring Place, London NW5 3BH
☎ 020 7428 4800 fax 020 7428 4828
email: go@lonelyplanet.co.uk

France
1 rue du Dahomey, 75011 Paris
☎ 01 55 25 33 00 fax 01 55 25 33 01
email: bip@lonelyplanet.fr
www.lonelyplanet.fr

World Wide Web: www.lonelyplanet.com *or* AOL keyword: lp
Lonely Planet Images: lpi@lonelyplanet.com.au